British Clandestine Activities in Romania during the Second World War

British Clandestine Activities in Romania during the Second World War

Dennis Deletant

Visiting 'Ion Raţiu' Professor of Romanian Studies, Georgetown University, USA

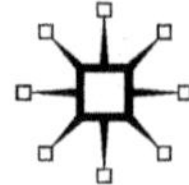

First published 2016 by
PALGRAVE MACMILLAN

Palgrave Macmillan in the UK is an imprint of Macmillan Publishers Limited, registered in England, company number 785998, of Houndmills, Basingstoke, Hampshire RG21 6XS.

Palgrave Macmillan in the US is a division of St Martin's Press LLC, 175 Fifth Avenue, New York, NY 10010.

Palgrave Macmillan is the global academic imprint of the above companies and has companies and representatives throughout the world.

Palgrave® and Macmillan® are registered trademarks in the United States, the United Kingdom, Europe and other countries.

ISBN 978–1–137–57451–0

This book is printed on paper suitable for recycling and made from fully managed and sustained forest sources. Logging, pulping and manufacturing processes are expected to conform to the environmental regulations of the country of origin.

A catalogue record for this book is available from the British Library.

Library of Congress Cataloging-in-Publication Data
Deletant, Dennis, 1946–
British Clandestine Activities in Romania during the Second World War/Dennis Deletant (Georgetown University, USA).
pages cm
Summary: "British Clandestine Activities in Romania during the Second World War is the first monograph to examine the activity throughout the entire war of SOE and MI6. It was generally believed in Britain's War Office, after Hitler's occupation of Austria in March 1938, that Germany would seek to impose its will on South-East Europe before turning its attention towards Western Europe. Given Romania's geographical position, there was little Britain could offer her. The brutal fact of British-Romanian relations was that Germany was inconveniently in the way: opportunity, proximity of manufacture and the logistics of supply all told in favour of the Third Reich. This held, of course, for military as well as economic matters. In these circumstances the British concluded that their only weapon against German ambitions in countries which fell into Hitler's orbit were military subversive operations and a concomitant attempt to draw Romania out of her alliance with Germany"—From publisher's website.
Includes bibliographical references and index.
ISBN 978–1–137–57451–0 (hardback)
1. World War, 1939–1945—Secret service—Great Britain. 2. World War, 1939–1945—Underground movements—Romania. 3. Subversive activities—Romania—History—20th century. 4. Espionage, British—Romania—History—20th century. 5. Great Britain. Special Operations Executive—History. 6. Great Britain. MI6—History—20th century. 7. Great Britain—Relations—Romania. 8. Romania—Relations—Great Britain. I. Title.
D810.S7D45 2016
940.54'864109498—dc23 2015026443

Contents

Map of Romania

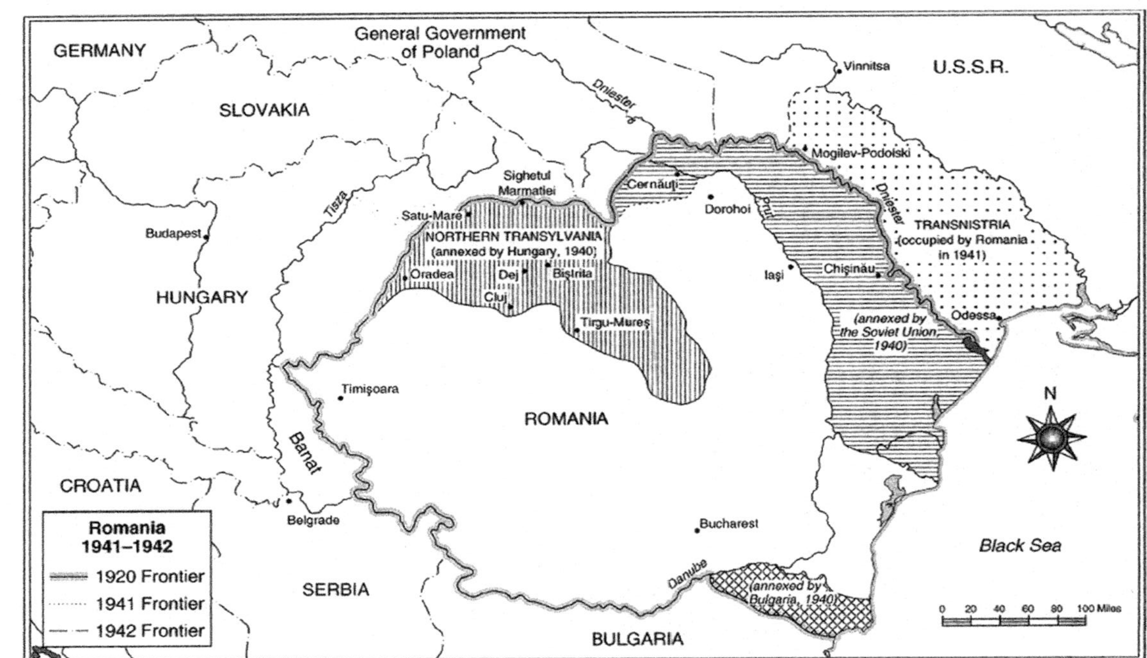

Map of Romania 1941–1942, showing national border changes from 1920
(compiled by the author)

Acknowledgements

Without the support of numerous friends and several institutions this study would not have been completed. Among the latter I wish to thank The British Academy for a Small Research Grant from the Elisabeth Barker Fund. This enabled me to pursue research on this topic between 2006 and 2008 in Britain and Romania. The School of Slavonic and East European Studies of University College, London, where I taught between 1969 and 2011, the University of Amsterdam, to which I was seconded for several semesters between 2003 and 2010, and my present academic home, Georgetown University, where since August 2011 I have the honour of being the *Ion Raţiu Visiting Professor of Romanian Studies*, provided me with travel grants to conduct research in Romania for this study. I owe a particular debt to Georgetown University and Nicolae and Pamela Raţiu of the Raţiu Foundation for their encouragement in my academic endeavour.

Amongst my many friends in Romania I wish to thank first and foremost George Cipăianu and his brother Enea. They are my invaluable anchor in Cluj-Napoca, extending a warm welcome in their home and providing me with countless opportunities to review the progress of my study with them and their colleagues at the Babeş-Bolyai University, Ioan Piso, Liviu Ţîrău, Ioan Ciupea, Marius Bucur, Gheorghe Mândrescu and Ştefan Matei. Special mention is deserved for Ottmar Traşca of the Romanian Academy 'Gheorghe Bariţiu' Institute of History in Cluj-Napoca who shared with me his research into German-Romanian relations during the Second World War, while Virgiliu Ţârău and Claudiu Secaşiu of the National Council for the Study of the *Securitate* Archives (CNSAS) in Bucharest facilitated access to the files of Romania's wartime security services. All three have demonstrated a generosity of spirit which transcends the bounds of formal contact and I extend to them my warm thanks.

In Bucharest, family friends Mihaela, Sandu and Ana Hodoş deserve particular mention. Without their warm hospitality and stimulating conversation on all matters Romanian I would not have gained those insights which are necessary for a sensitive understanding of the country's past.

Şerban Papacostea, Ioan Chiper, Viorel Achim and Cristian Vasile of the 'Nicolae Iorga' Institute of History, and Andrei Muraru and Ştefan Bosomitu at the Institute for Investigation of the Crimes of Communism, helped me to identify and access secondary Romanian literature and relevant journal publications. I have drawn enormous benefit from the discussion of my research with Dr Papacostea and Andrei Pippidi, both of whom I am honoured to count as close personal friends. In the recent past Armand Goşu and

Dragoş Petrescu, head of the collegium of CNSAS, have offered perceptive appreciations of my research.

In London, the late Ivor Porter was a constant reference point while Alan Ogden generously discussed his research on the 'Ranji' mission with me. Dan Brett, Irina Marin, Trevor Thomas, Martyn Rady, Radu Cinpoeş and Alex Boican provided invaluable intellectual stimulation. In Washington DC I was fortunate to receive precious insights into Romania of the 1940s from my friends Ernest Latham, Mircea Răceanu, Radu Ioanid, Vladimir Tismăneanu and the late Andrei Brezianu. Ruth Sulynn Taylor in Charles Town, West Virginia, has been a generous and affectionate host to my wife and to me down the years. Angela Stent, the Director of the Center for Eurasian, Russian and East European Studies at Georgetown University, Ben Loring, her deputy, and Christina Watts, the Center's administrative officer, have leavened the invaluable support which they have given to my academic endeavours with charm and good humour. In the National Archives and Records Administration in College Park, Maryland, Ashby Crowder and Andrea Zemp were expert pilots in helping me to navigate the archives.

An enormous debt is owed to Maurice Pearton. Maurice read the manuscript of the book and helped to give it its final shape. His knowledge and understanding of 20th-century economic and political history saved me from a number of critical errors. I record here my gratitude for his unstinting assistance and respect for his invaluable guidance in my research over the last thirty years.

For my wife Andrea I reserve my most profound thanks for her understanding and forbearance during frequent periods of self-imposed isolation in my study whilst writing this book.

Biographies of Key Figures

Ion Antonescu (born 15 June 1882, Piteşti; died 1 June 1946, Jilava prison, Bucharest). After the First World War, Antonescu served as military attaché in Paris and in London and, in 1934, as chief of the Romanian general staff. Named minister of defense in 1937 by King Carol II, he was dismissed in the following year. Antonescu was appointed prime minister with absolute powers on 5 September 1940, after Romania had one third of its territory partitioned amongst the Soviet Union, Hungary and Bulgaria (June–September 1940). He established a military dictatorship and aligned himself with the Axis powers. He won widespread popular support for his decision to join Hitler in his attack on the Soviet Union in June 1941 in pursuit of recovering Bessarabia and Northern Bukovina. As losses mounted on the Russian front his regime lost popular backing and he was removed by a coup d'état on 23 August 1944 led by King Michael. Antonescu was sentenced to death by a Romanian communist people's court and was executed as a war criminal by firing squad in June 1946.

Mihai Antonescu (born 18 November 1904, Dâmboviţa county; died 1 June 1946, Jilava prison, Bucharest), a very distant relative of Ion Antonescu; deputy prime minister and minister of foreign affairs from 29 June 1941 to 23 August 1944. He was tried alongside Ion Antonescu as a war criminal, found guilty and executed.

Traian Borcescu (born 22 November 1899, Cireşanu, Prahova county; died 1997 (?), Bucharest) was head of counter-intelligence from 1942 until the 23 August coup of 1944. He was arrested on 26 March 1945 at the home of Emil Bodnăraş, a GRU agent who after 23 August 1944 effectively became head of the Romanian security service. Bodnăraş had invited him to lunch there. After turning down a proposal from the latter that he work with the Soviets, represented at the meal by Colonel Timofteiv, the NKVD advisor in Bucharest, he was given blacked-out glasses and taken by car to an airfield and flown to Moscow where he was interrogated about his wartime activity by Viktor Abamukov, Beria's deputy. After two weeks he was returned to Bucharest and taken into custody on Bodnăraş' orders and held, first in Jilava prison, and then in Malmaison, where he was interrogated on several occasions by Bodnăraş. He was released on 23 December 1945 but re-arrested on 26 May 1949, tried for his role under the Antonescu regime, and sentenced to hard labour for life. In January 1963 his sentence was reduced to 25 years and he was amnestied on 13 April 1964 (author's interview with Traian Borcescu, 8 March 1995). I am also grateful to Ioan Ciupea of the

Museum of National History in Cluj who allowed me to consult his own research on Borcescu.

Edwin George Boxshall (born 4 February 1897, Bucharest; died 26 January 1984, London). Boxshall was born in Bucharest where his father William ran a small business importing tractors. His mother, Marie Meyer, was of German background. Following the occupation of Bucharest by German forces in 1916, he moved with the British Military Mission under Captain Thomas Laycock to the temporary northern capital of Iaşi with the rank of second lieutenant. Tasked with gathering intelligence on events in Bessarabia and southern Russia, he was detained by Bolshevik forces and held at Hotin on the Dniester River. Released by allied forces, he returned to Iaşi in autumn 1918 and together with other members of the Military Mission was evacuated by train via Murmansk to Britain. Richard Davenport-Hines, 'Boxshall, Edwin George (1897–1984)', *Oxford Dictionary of National Biography* (Oxford: Oxford University Press, 2004), online edn., January 2008, http://www.oxforddnb.com/view/article/45718 (accessed 6 August 2014).

In 1919 he returned to Bucharest as representative of Vickers and Nobel Industries (later ICI) and was instrumental in selling submarine equipment to the Romanian Navy (CNSAS, Fond I, 937812, Vol. 2, f.14). His marriage on 25 April 1920 in Bucharest to Elise 'Madie', the third daughter of Prince Barbu Stirbey (1872–1936), administrator of the royal domains, lover of Queen Marie, and prime minister for a month in June 1927, gave him unique access to the seats of power in Romania and he was to use these to assist him in his commercial activities. Although in some sources it is stated that he was station chief of MI6 in Bucharest for most of the interwar period this is not the case. In 1940 he came back to London to work in the Romania section of SOE under George Taylor. When his father-in-law came to Cairo in March 1944 to discuss armistice terms with the allies, Boxshall went to meet him. Boxshall and his wife divorced in November 1947 and he remarried. Boxshall remained in Britain where in 1959 he became adviser to the Foreign and Commonwealth Office, with responsibility for the SOE archives. He retired in 1982.

Constantin (Dinu) Brătianu (born 13 January 1866, Bucharest; died 23 August 1953 (?), Sighet prison). Second son of Ion C. Brătianu (1821–1891), appointed leader of the National Liberal Party in 1934. Constantin (Dinu) Brătianu was arrested by the Communist authorities during the night of 5–6 May 1950, and imprisoned at Sighet without trial. The date of his death is unclear, one source giving 20 August 1950, another 23 August 1953 (see Florian Tănăsescu and Nicolae Tănăsescu (2005), *Constantin (Bebe) I. C. Brătianu – Istoria P.N.L. la interogatoriu* (Bucharest: Editura Paralela 45), p. 179).

Alexandru Creţianu (1895–1979) was the nephew of Prince Barbu Ştirbey. After studying law at the University of Iaşi, he entered the Romanian diplomatic service in September 1918 and held posts in London (1918–22), Rome (1923–6) and Berne (1926–9). He served as head of the League of Nations section of the Foreign Ministry (1929–32), as head of the political department (1933–8), and as secretary-general (December 1938–October 1941) but resigned in protest at Marshal Antonescu's policies. In September 1943 he was appointed minister in Turkey at the suggestion of Maniu and with the acquiescence of Mihai Antonescu with instructions to contact the Allies about armistice conditions. In March 1945 he refused to accept the authority of the Groza government and remained in Turkey until June 1946 when he left for Switzerland. He was tried and sentenced to life imprisonment *in absentia* in the trial of Iuliu Maniu and other National Peasant Party officials in autumn 1947. He settled later in the United States and became a US citizen in 1954. He died in Florida.

Alfred George Gardyne de Chastelain (born 28 February 1906, London; died Calgary, 1974) studied engineering at London University. On 4 November 1927 he joined Unirea (Phoenix Oil and Transport Company) in Bucharest with a salary of £80 per month (Arhiva Consiliului Naţional pentru Studierea Arhivelor Securităţii, henceforth CNSAS, Fond I, 937873, f.1). His expertise led to his recruitment by MI(R) in operations to sabotage the oil wells in Ploieşti but attacks by the Iron Guard on the British engineers involved in these plans forced him to leave Romania in October 1940. In 1941 he took over from Colonel Bill Bailey as head of SOE in Istanbul (his code symbol was DH/13 and designation 'Field Commander Turkey'; see The National Archives, hereafter TNA, HS 8/971). Parachuted into Romania in December 1943 as head of the *Autonomous* mission (see Chapter 7), he was captured and interned in Bucharest until 23 August 1944. On the following day he flew to Istanbul. Refused permission by the Foreign Office to return to Romania, he settled ultimately in Canada where he died in 1974.

Valeriu (Rică) Constantin Simion Georgescu (SOE code name 'Jockey') (born 3 February 1904, Brăila; died 31 October 1993, Switzerland). He studied engineering at Birmingham University and worked for the Unirea Company – where he met de Chastelain – before joining the Româno-Americană (Standard Oil) company. He married Ligia Bocu, daughter of Sever Bocu, the head of the National Peasant Party in the Banat; his 'godfather' at the wedding was Iuliu Maniu. He was a member of a group of National Peasant Party activists in Banat who, in January 1938, were besieged by the police in their local party headquarters in Timişoara after violent clashes with the Iron Guard. The siege was lifted at the intervention of Maniu. After the Vienna Award of August 1940, Georgescu helped to establish the association 'Pro Transylvania' and with the support of SOE and Maniu set up a radio link with London in spring 1941. Arrested with his associates on 15 August by the Germans and handed over to the Romanian authorities, he was treated leniently in prison and released on 23 August 1944 after the King's coup against Antonescu.

He served as Under-Secretary of State at the Ministry of Industry, Trade and Mines from 1 September until 4 November 1944 and was Director-General of Româno-Americană between September 1944 and 1946. In 1947 he and his wife left Romania without their two sons to visit the United States and did not return. They became US citizens in 1952. Efforts to persuade the Romanian authorities to allow their children to join them proved unsuccessful until the direct intervention of President Eisenhower. In 1954 Eisenhower wrote to Gheorghe Gheorghiu-Dej asking him to investigate the case and, in order to remove one cause of friction between the two countries, 'expedite a satisfactory solution' (Eisenhower to Gheorghiu-Dej, 25 February 1954, AWF/D. Eisenhower, Dwight D. to Valeriu C. Georgescu, 23 July 1953. In *The Papers of Dwight David Eisenhower*, ed. L. Galambos and D. van Ee, doc. 339, World Wide Web facsimile by The Dwight D. Eisenhower Memorial Commission of the print edition (Baltimore, MD: The Johns Hopkins University Press, 1996), http://www.eisenhowermemorial.org/presidential-papers/first-term/documents/339.cfm). The Romanian leader agreed to the release, 'considering that the elimination of any misunderstanding cannot but be useful' (Gheorghiu-Dej to Eisenhower, March 12 1954, *ibid.*) The family was reunited in New York City on April 13 1954 (*New York Times*, April 14 1954). Georgescu later moved to Switzerland where he died on 31 October 1993.

Julius Hanau (born April 1885, South Africa; died May 1943, Cairo). He held a British commission in the First World War and after fighting on the Salonika front he remained in Belgrade where he became a successful businessman. He was recruited into MI6 and played a role in organizing resistance in Yugoslavia following the outbreak of war. He was withdrawn from the Balkans to London in June 1940 prior to the German invasion of Yugoslavia, when his activities had become so well-known to the Germans that it was feared that he would be murdered. In London, Hanau was put in charge of SOE's West African mission, where he was responsible for operation 'Postmaster', the cutting out of ships from Santa Isabel in Fernando Po, and the acquisition of the ship 'Gascon' and its cargo, both notable coups at a time when SOE was not enjoying much success. Hanau was crucial in planning the occupation of Madagascar and overcoming elements of Vichy French resistance there. In October 1942 Hanau was sent (after a period of sick leave having contracted malaria in West Africa) to Cairo to plan actions in the Balkans, but he died of a heart attack in May 1943 (TNA, HS 9/653/2; Nick van der Bijl (2013), *Sharing the Secret: The History of the Intelligence Corps, 1940–2010* (Barnsley: Pen and Sword), p. 74 and http://www.nationalarchives.gov.uk/releases/2003/may12/selectedagents.htm (accessed 30 March 2015)).

William Harris-Burland (1902–1985). After qualifying as a chartered accountant, Harris-Burland worked in Poland, Romania and Germany in the interwar years. In 1939 he returned to Britain and offered his services to the War Office which recruited him into MI(R) and sent him to Poland with a small party under the command of Colin Gubbins. Following the fall of Poland the party escaped to Romania where Harris-Burland was placed in charge of the Anglo-Danubian Shipping Company in Bucharest and given responsibility for chartering barges on the Danube to prevent them falling into German hands. He continued this activity as General Manager of the Goeland Transport and Trading Company, created specifically for this purpose in February 1940.

After the entry of German troops into Romania Harris-Burland paid off the Goeland staff and in February 1941 joined SOE's Belgrade office. He was captured with other members of the mission, including Tom Masterson, George Taylor (who was Mediterranean section head of MI6) and Hugh Seton-Watson, by Italian forces while withdrawing to the Adriatic coast. Held at Ciancino in the Apennines, the group was exchanged for some Italian prisoners and returned to England via Spain in June 1941. Harris-Burland was then posted to Istanbul as head of the SOE office with responsibility for chartering Turkish shipping, partly to keep it out of German hands, and partly to divert materials useful to the Germans such as chrome ore. In September 1944 he was appointed to the British Military Mission to Romania in charge of transport. He held the rank of Lieutenant-Colonel. He was recalled to London in March 1946 to work on the reorganization of the German iron and steel industry and posted to Germany where he remained until 1953 when he returned to England and became Director of Accounts and Statistics in the British Transport Commission.

Iuliu Maniu (born 8 January 1873, Şimleu Silvaniei, Transylvania, Hungary [now in Romania]; died 5 February 1953, Sighet prison, Romania). Maniu attended elementary school in Blaj and secondary school in Zalău, and went on to study in Vienna and Budapest where he took a degree in law. On his return to Transylvania he became a professor of law at the Greek-Catholic seminary in Blaj and legal advisor to the metropolitan bishop. He joined the Romanian National Party of Transylvania whose programme focused on the establishment of Transylvanian autonomy and the assertion of Romanian rights commensurate with the Romanians demographic majority in the province. In 1909 he was elected a deputy in the Hungarian parliament where he was a powerful advocate of Romanian aspirations. After being called up into the Austro-Hungarian army in 1915 he emerged from military academy with the rank of second lieutenant and was despatched, first to the Russian front, and then to Italy.

As a member of the National Committee of the Romanian National Party he was one of the principal figures that organized the Grand National Assembly of 1 December 1918 which proclaimed the union of Transylvania with Romania. Maniu was elected President of the Directory Council which administered Transylvania from 2 December 1918 until 4 April 1920 when the government of the province was handed over to Bucharest. On 9 August 1919 Maniu was elected President of the National Party – as it was known after the Union – and in October 1926, on its merger with the Peasant Party, he became President of the National Peasant Party. In November 1928 he led the party to victory in the general election and served as prime minister until June 1930 when Prince Carol returned to Romania. Maniu had supported the return of the prince on condition that he renounced his mistress Elena Lupescu, but Carol's unwillingness to do so prompted him to resign on 7 June. His place was taken by George Mironescu who annulled the act excluding Carol from the throne and then resigned himself. After a period of confusion Maniu was recalled on 13 June after Carol gave an undertaking to be crowned with his wife Helen in September.

On learning of Lupescu's return to Romania Maniu submitted his resignation once more on 6 October 1930. In October 1932 Carol turned to Maniu at the height of a grave economic crisis to head the National Peasant Party government following the resignation of Alexandru Vaida-Voievod. Maniu once again set the conditions of June 1930 for his acceptance, namely Carol's re-marriage to Queen Helen. He also demanded that the King rule in the spirit of the 1923 constitution and dismiss his influential clique of advisers, the 'camarilla'. Although Carol agreed to the conditions it soon became clear that he had no intention of abiding by them. The result was that Maniu broke off personal relations with the King and resigned in January 1933. At the same time, he stood down as President of the National Peasant Party and ostensibly withdrew from politics. However, the increasingly dictatorial stance of the King led the NPP to call upon Maniu in November 1937 as the champion of constitutional government and he returned to lead the party. His desire to thwart Carol's moves to install a royal dictatorship led him to sign an electoral pact with Corneliu Codreanu, head of the Iron Guard, in the same month, which had the desired effect of defeating the Tătărescu government. However, Carol dissolved the newly elected parliament and instituted a government of his own choice under Octavian Goga. With Carol's suspension of the constitution in February 1938 Maniu's fear of the institution of a royal dictatorship was confirmed. On 30 March, a decree dissolving all political parties was issued and a strict regime of political censorship applied.

Maniu's protests to Carol went unheeded and he thus began what was to be a six-year period as head of the democratic opposition in Romania. His attempts to reconcile his pro-Allied sympathies with his contempt for totalitarian rule and mistrust of the Soviet Union gave the British, with whom he was in contact throughout the war, the impression of vacillation and indecision. The arrest of senior figures in the National Peasant Party while trying to flee the country on 14 July 1947 provided the Communist-led government with a pretext for arresting Maniu and his deputy Ion Mihalache on 25 July on the grounds of plotting to overthrow the state. They and several other prominent members of the National Peasant Party were tried, found guilty and given life sentences on 11 November. After four years in Galaţi prison (14 November 1947–14 August 1951) Maniu was transferred to Sighet jail where he died on 5 February 1953 (Andrea Dobeş (2006), *Ilie Lazăr* (Cluj-Napoca: Argonaut), p. 176).

Thomas Samuel Masterson (born 21 July 1881, London; died 4 August 1944, London) grew up in Romania with his family. He studied as an oil engineer and assisted Colonel Norton Griffiths in the sabotage of the Ploieşti oilfields in November 1916. After the First World War he became Director-General of the Unirea Oil Company. Attached to the Ministry of Economic Warfare, he supervised plans drawn up in 1939 for the sabotage of the Romanian oilfields in concert with the French. In November 1940 he was despatched to Belgrade as First Secretary at the British legation and head of SO(2) operations in Yugoslavia and Albania. Captured by the Italians after the evacuation of Belgrade with others including George Taylor and Hugh Seton-Watson, he was held at Cianciano in the Apennines by Italian forces while withdrawing to the Adriatic coast. The group was exchanged for some Italian prisoners and Masterson made his way back to London via Spain in June 1941. He was then transferred to Cairo and placed in charge of the Balkan section of the political subversion department of SO(2). In spring 1942 he was posted to Washington to advise Colonel William Donovan on Balkan and Middle Eastern matters. He returned to Cairo in November 1942 and then to London. On 24 January 1943 Masterson gave the first in a series of fifty broadcasts in Romanian on the BBC urging Romania to break with Germany and join the Allies. In February 1944 he was posted again to Cairo with the local rank of Colonel attached to the SOE mission to advise on the Romanian armistice negotiations. He returned to London on 28 April, was taken ill shortly afterwards, and died on 4 August 1944 (for some of these details see Bickham Sweet-Escott (1965), *Baker Street Irregular* (London: Methuen), pp. 62–4 and 97).

Michael I, King of Romania (born 25 October 1921, Foişor Castle, Sinaia, Romania, the son of Carol II of Romania (then Crown Prince of Romania) and Princess Elena of Greece). When Carol eloped with his mistress Elena 'Magda' Lupescu and renounced 'temporarily' his rights to the throne in December 1925, Michael succeeded to the throne upon King Ferdinand's death in July 1927. Michael was King of Romania from 20 July 1927 to 8 June 1930 and again from 6 September 1940 to 30 December 1947. He carried out the coup of 23 August 1944 against Romania's pro-German leader, Marshal

Ion Antonescu. He was forced to abdicate in 1947 by the government controlled by the Communist Party of Romania. As a great-great-grandson of Queen Victoria of the United Kingdom through both of his parents, he is a third cousin of: Queen Margrethe II of Denmark; King Harald V of Norway; King Juan Carlos I of Spain; King Carl XVI Gustav of Sweden; and Queen Elizabeth II of the United Kingdom.

Titel Petrescu (born 5 February 1888, Craiova; died 2 September 1957, Bucharest). Leader of the Social Democratic Party, Petrescu's fate was emblematic of that of opposition leaders. He was arrested on 6 May 1948, held in the security police headquarters in Bucharest, sent to Jilava prison, and finally tried in camera in January 1952 for crimes against the state. He was sentenced to life imprisonment and served three years in Sighet jail before being transferred to the Calea Rahovei headquarters of the *Securitate* in Bucharest in December 1954, where he was told by the Minister of the Interior, Alexandru Drăghici, that a number of his colleagues in the former SDP would be released from prison if he signed a letter giving his support to the regime for publication in the Party daily *Scînteia*. He refused and was sent in August 1955 to Râmnicu Sărat jail where he learned from fellow prisoners of the death in prison of numerous Socialists. He agreed to sign a text on 13 September on condition that all leading SDP members were released and he himself was freed but kept under virtual house arrest. The letter appeared in *Scînteia* on 18 December 1955 but only a small number of SDP colleagues were released (see *Cartea Albă a Securității* (Bucharest: SRI, 1994), Vol. 2, doc. 237, pp. 527–9). Petrescu complained to Petru Groza, the President of the Grand National Assembly, after which further releases were announced.

Ivor Forsyth Porter (born 12 November 1913, Barrow in Furness; died 29 May 2012, London). Ivor attended Barrow-in-Furness Grammar School and Leeds University where he followed a passion for literature. He was appointed British Council lecturer in English at Bucharest University in March 1939 and then secretary at the British legation in 1940. He left Romania on 12 February 1941 with other legation staff, and in Cairo was recruited on 1 March into SOE. Porter was transferred to the British legation in Bucharest in May 1946 to give him firmer diplomatic immunity. He left Romania at the end of 1947 and went on to serve in the Foreign Office in Washington, Paris, Nicosia, India, and between 1971 and 1974 to Senegal, Mali, Guinea and Mauretania. Although an extremely private person, he showed great warmth towards his friends, and affection for the countries and peoples to which he was posted. He retained a particular interest in Romania and in the fate of its monarch and in defenders of democracy. His sympathy for King Michael was translated into a biography (*Michael of Romania*, 2005 (London: Sutton Publishing)), which was the first to draw upon the king's private papers and captured the sadness of Michael's more than forty years' exile.

Thomas Charles David Augustan Russell (born 28 August 1915, South Mimms, Hertfordshire; died 4 September 1943, Vârciorova, Romania). Educated at Eton where he was a member of the Officers Training Corps, Russell went up to Trinity College, Cambridge where he read Agriculture and Estate Management. He continued his studies at the Royal Agricultural College, Cirencester and then started a career in farming based at Broke Hall at Nacton near Ipswich. According to SOE papers he was later at Heidelberg and Bonn universities and spoke fluent German. On the outbreak of war, Russell was introduced to the Scots Guards by Lt. Gen. Sir William Pulteney. Commissioned from Sandhurst on 25 May 1940, Russell joined the Scots Guards Training Battalion on 5 October (Alan Ogden (2010), *Through Hitler's Back Door: SOE Operations in Hungary, Slovakia, Romania and Bulgaria, 1939–1945* (Barnsley: Pen and Sword), p. 242). He took part in September 1942 in the raid on Tobruk and, dressed as a German officer, was later responsible for arranging the escape of two officers and eight other ranks for which he was awarded the Military Cross. Russell was parachuted into Yugoslavia on 15 June with instructions to endeavour to cross into Romania and to establish himself in the Godeanu mountains where he was to arrange a reception area for further British Liaison Officers' (TNA, HS 5/798). Russell was killed in mysterious circumstances, found shot in the back of the head, less than a week after his 28th birthday (Alan Ogden (2007), 'Romanian Riddle: The Unsolved Murder of Capt. David Russell MC, Scots Guards', *The Scots Guards Magazine*: 124–9).

George Hugh Nicholas Seton-Watson, son of Robert William (born 15 February 1916, London; died 19 December 1984, Washington DC), Professor of Russian History in the School of Slavonic and East European Studies, University of London from 1951 to 1983. Hugh served in SOE between 1940 and 1945 (his SOE symbol was DH/72).

Robert William Seton-Watson (born 20 August 1879, London; died 25 July 1951, Isle of Skye). After graduation from Oxford University in 1901, Seton-Watson travelled in Central Europe, focusing his attention upon Hungary which he visited in 1906. His experience there made him a forceful critic of Hungary's policies towards its subject peoples, the Romanians, Slovaks and the Serbs. After writing a number of articles in this vein for *The Spectator* he published in 1908 his first major work, *Racial Problems in Hungary*. His close interest in Central Europe brought him into firm friendship with the Vienna correspondent of *The Times*, Henry Wickham Steed, and with the Czech politician Tomás Masaryk. After the outbreak of the First World War Seton-Watson sought to put into practice what he had preached. He served as honorary secretary from 1914 of the Serbian Relief Fund and after Masaryk fled to England to escape arrest, Seton-Watson supported him and found him employment. Together in 1916 they founded *The New Europe*, a weekly periodical which promoted the cause of the Czechs, Romanians and South Slavs and which Seton-Watson published from his own pocket. In 1917 and 1918 he worked in the Enemy Propaganda Department of the Intelligence Bureau of the War Cabinet where he assisted in the preparation of British propaganda to the peoples of Austria-Hungary.

Defending the status quo was a prime aim of Seton-Watson during the interwar period and therefore, as a firm advocate of the territorial integrity of Greater Romania, and of Czechoslovakia, it was no surprise that he became a harsh critic of British Prime Minister Neville Chamberlain's policy of appeasement. In his *Britain and the Dictators: A Survey of Post-War British Policy* (1938), he made one of the most outspoken attacks on this policy. After Chamberlain's resignation in 1940, Seton-Watson was given a position in the Foreign Research and Press Service (1939–40) and Political Intelligence Bureau of the Foreign Office (1940–2), based in Balliol College, Oxford. He remained a vocal spokesperson for Romania and such was the appreciation of his activity that he received regular stipends from the Romanian government, even after Antonescu's advent to power in September 1940. Mihai Sturdza, the Legionary Foreign Minister, recommended that payments to Seton-Watson be curtailed on the grounds that he was a 'democrat' and was working for British intelligence. Antonescu disagreed and gave instructions for the stipend to be continued. To this effect in December, 'Seton-Watson has been a good friend of Romania. He always supported us in the matter of Transylvania. His democratic activities do not interest me' (Holly Case (2009), *Between States: The Transylvanian Question and the European Idea during World War II* (Stanford, CA: Stanford University Press), p. 65 and note 272 to Chapter 1, p. 247 citing ANIC, Fond Preşedenţia Consiliului de Miniştri Cabinetul Militar Ion Antonescu, Dosar 194/1940, Factura de subvenţii pentru Seton-Watson, ff.100, 102, 102v (Case expresses her gratitude to Vladimir Solonari for sharing this document with her)). Romania's entry into the Second World War on the side of Nazi Germany in June 1941 effectively torpedoed any pro-Romanian influence Seton-Watson sought to bear on British policy. With his hopes of the emergence of a liberal democratic Romania from the Second World War shattered by the imposition of Communism, he retired to the family home on the Isle of Skye in Scotland where he died on 25 July 1951.

Arthur Albert Tester (born 23 August 1895, Stuttgart; died 24 August 1944, Romania (?)). Son of Fred Tester, an English subject, and his wife, maiden name Kaufelin. Oberleutnant Rudolf Pander, who worked in the *Abwehr* office in Bucharest, claimed under interrogation by US counter-intelligence officers in December 1945 that 'German penetration of the British Intelligence Service was achieved through the use of an English banker called Tester' (NARA, Rudolf Pander – interrogation report 7 December 1945, Military Intelligence Center USFET, CI—IIR/35, RG 165, Entry (P) 179C, Box 738 (Location: 390: 35/15/01), p. 7). The Berlin police replied on 10 June 1939 in an inquiry from Scotland Yard about Tester that 'he is known here as a dangerous international swindler' (TNA, KV 2/617/351).

A résumé of documents found in the German Foreign Ministry and microfilmed on 3 August 1946 by the FO/State Documents Field Team listed Tester's activities as follows: 1939 (? September) To Roumania via Greece; 1940 (October) Remained in Roumania when German army entered; Prior to April 1941 Working for *Abwehr* in Roumania, Bulgaria and Greece on counter-espionage work; 1941 (15–21 June) Berlin to discuss working for Foreign Ministry (Press Section); 1941 (22 June–31 July) Athens; (1–16 August) Belgrade and Sofia – on missions for OKW; (16 August) Back in Bucharest;1942 (10–17 June) Berlin – to discuss doing propaganda there; 1944 (15 May) Left Bucharest (? for an Interrogation at Pressburg) (TNA, KV 2/2266).

Brigadier E. R. Greer, Deputy-Head of the British Military Mission in Bucharest, reported on 17 September 1945 to MI5 that the general assumption was that Tester was dead and 'it is likely that no-one took much trouble in marking the graves correctly at Arad during the *coup d'état* of 24 [*sic*] August 1944'. Greer is referring to the exhumation of a body from a grave in the *Pomenirea* cemetery in Arad marked as being that of Tester. In the same report he wrote: 'After comparing the evidence of the dentists with the report of the exhumation, we have arrived at the assumption that the exhumed body was not Tester's. We have, indeed, carefully followed up any rumours that he was still living and found nothing whatever to substantiate them' (TNA, KV 2/618). A review of the evidence regarding Tester's death was compiled by an FO official, G. E Wakefield, on 3 November 1947. He stated that on 26 September 1944 the *Daily Express* quoted a British United report from Bucharest that Tester had been 'killed in Transylvania by a Rumanian frontier-guard when he tried to escape into Hungary'. On 6 October 1944 it published a report by its correspondent Cedric Salter in Bucharest that Tester had 'faked his death' at a Transylvanian frontier post, after the anti-German coup on 23 August, when he was escaping to Hungary: 'A guard fired on his car and he was slightly wounded in the leg... He arranged that an unrecognizable body of about his own build, wearing the remnants of his clothes and with his wrist watch and cigarette case, should be found near his burned car'. He then reached his farm near Hunedoara in Transylvania, and from there went on to Budapest.

As a result of the rumours that the death was a fake, the Romanian authorities twice exhumed a body from what was presumed to be Tester's grave in the *Pomenirea* cemetery in Arad. When these exhumations took place is not known, but it was before 8 February 1945 when a third exhumation took place in the presence of a member of the British Consular Advisor's staff. It was not known whether the grave from which this body was exhumed was undoubtedly the one in which Tester was buried since there was nothing on the tall wooden cross which marked the grave to suggest that it was Tester's. Wakefield concluded: 'It would seem almost certain, therefore, that the body exhumed is not that of Tester, and further – assuming that the right grave was opened (as to which we have no evidence), that the *Daily Express* story of a fake death and burial is true' (TNA, KV 2/2266). On the other hand, no evidence that Tester survived his attempt to cross the Romanian-Hungarian frontier when challenged by Romanian frontier-guards has ever surfaced (my thanks go to Dr Ottmar Traşcă of the George Bariţiu Institute of History in Cluj-Napoca for assistance in compiling this note).

Nicolae Titulescu (born 4 March 1882, Craiova; died 17 March 1941, Cannes). Titulescu practised law in Bucharest after graduating in Paris in 1904 and was elected a deputy to the Romanian assembly in 1912 where he shone as a brilliant debater. He served as Minister of Finance in the Romanian government based in Iaşi in 1918. After the Peace of Bucharest (May 1918) he left the country and settled in Paris where he argued the Romanian case to leading French and British politicians. He participated in the peace negotiations with the Allies and was a signatory for Romania of the Trianon Treaty. He returned to Romania and became Minister of Finance in the Averescu government of 1920–1. When the Liberals came to power under Ion Brătianu in January 1922 he was offered the post of Minister to London. For five years, until July 1927, Titulescu's wit and skill at handling people and affairs won him many friends and admirers among British public figures. In April 1924 he skilfully defended Romania's refusal to consider claims of Romanian bond holders before the Committee of the London Stock Exchange and later in the year, at the International Conference on War Reparations, paved the way for Romania to recover part of her claims.

He extended his circle of admirers at the League of Nations with his forensic skill in his rejection of the claims of Hungarian landowners against Romania in respect of expropriation following the 1921 land reform. Titulescu believed fervently in the League, regarding it as a guardian of the status quo implicit in the Versailles peace and the guarantor of international security. Romania's own security was dependent on the maintenance of international order and this Titulescu, on becoming Foreign Minister in October 1932, sought to consolidate through the system of alliances between states that opposed revision of the peace treaties of 1919–20. During 1933 and 1934 it became increasingly clear that it was Germany which threatened European peace and therefore Titulescu advocated the creation of a system of collective security based on France and the Soviet Union. It was he who played a central role in bringing about the mutual assistance pact between

Moscow and Paris in 1935. Titulescu hoped that the Soviet-French agreement would form the nucleus of a large coalition of anti-revisionist states and to this end he took Romania down the road to alliance with the Soviet Union.

The first result of his efforts had been the London Convention of July 1933 by which the Soviet Union recognized Romania's sovereignty over Bessarabia. In June 1934 an exchange of letters between Titulescu and Maxim Litvinov marked the resumption of diplomatic relations between the two countries and paved the way for Titulescu to seek a defensive alliance with the Soviet Union. Consequently, in September 1935, Titulescu began discussions with Litvinov over the conclusion of a Soviet-Romanian Treaty of Mutual Assistance. Before Titulescu could proceed further, he was dismissed by King Carol as a result of internal and external manoeuvres coordinated by Prime Minister Tătărescu against his person and his policy. Although elected as a National Peasant Party deputy in December 1937, Titulescu did not remain long in Romania after King Carol imposed his dictatorship in February 1938, and settled in France. He never returned to his native land.

Abbreviations

ACC	Allied Control Commission
AMAN	Arhiva Ministerului Apărării Naţionale (Archive of the Ministry of National Defence, Piteşti)
ANIC	Arhivele Naţionale Istorice Centrale (The Central Historical National Archives (formerly the State Archives) Bucharest)
ASRI	Archive of the Romanian Information Service (the Romanian Security Service)
CNSAS	Consiliul National pentru Studierea Arhivelor fostei Securităţi (National Council for the Study of the Archives of the former *Securitate*)
DGFP	*Documents on German Foreign Policy*, Series D: 1937–45, 14 Vols. (Washington DC, London, and Arlington VA, 1949–76)
FO	Foreign Office
GRU	Main Intelligence Directorate of the General Staff of the Armed Forces of the Russian Federation
GS(R)	General Staff (Research)
LANC	League of National Christian Defence
MAE	Arhiva Ministerului Afacerilor Externe (Archive of the Ministry of Foreign Affairs, Bucharest)
MI9	Military Intelligence Section 9
MI(R)	Military Intelligence (Research)
MWT	Ministry of War Transport
NDB	National Democratic Bloc
NDF	National Democratic Front
NKGB	People's Commissariat of State Security, 1943–6
NKVD	People's Commissariat for Internal Affairs, 1934–43
OER	Officers' Emergency Reserve
OPC	Office of Policy Coordination
OSS	Office of Strategic Services
PWE	Political Warfare Executive
RCP	Romanian Communist Party
RSHA	Reich Main Security Office
SD	*Sicherheitsdienst*
SDP	Social Democratic Party
SIME	Security Intelligence Middle East
SIS	Secret Intelligence Service
SO(2)	Special Operations 2

SOE	Special Operations Executive
SRI	Serviciul Român de Informaţii
SSEES	School of Slavonic and East European Studies
SSI	Serviciul Special de Informaţii (Romanian Intelligence Service)
TNA	The National Archives, Kew, London
USAAF	United States Army Air Force
W/T	Wireless transmitter

Introduction

An overview of British-Romanian relations after 1918 suggests that Britain and Romania were never able to regard each other squarely until December 1989. Until that date, from the British point of view, Romania was part of something broader – French policies in South-East Europe, German domination of the area in the late 1930s and during the Second World War, and then the Soviet Union's postwar hegemony. Romania had an uncomfortable neighbour – Russia, against whom she sought a guarantor. France played that role after the First World War, to be replaced by Germany after the *Anschluss* with Austria of March 1938. As Maurice Pearton has pointed out, 'Anglo-Romanian relations resolved themselves into successive attempts to establish a working rapprochment between two distinct sets of perceptions and aspirations which were slightly out of focus with each other'.[1]

For the British Romania was not a primary concern. To the proverbial man in the street it meant in the 1930s, Madame Lupescu and oil. Romania was a three-day journey by train from the Gare de l'Est, the departure point for the Orient Express – not Victoria Station – thus few Britons ventured there. Romanians tried to counter British disinterest by arguing that their country was 'the strategic crossroads' to the Near East and would consolidate Britain's position there, but they failed to appreciate that in terms of British strategic thinking, Romania was not a 'crossroads' but a cul de sac.[2]

That thinking changed when Romania became of vital importance to Hitler's war machine. Between 1929 and 1937 the level of Romania's foreign trade with Germany had not changed significantly, but the *Anschluss* opened up the possibility of increased German dominance of Romania's economy, particularly with regard to oil (discussed more fully in Chapter 2).

Any economic, manufacturing or trade links that Romania might have wished to develop with Britain were difficult considering her isolated geographical position and the proximity of Hitler's Third Reich, and direct military aid was out of the question. From the British point of view the only alternative seemed to be clandestine military operations to help thwart German influence and control over the country and the region.

This book examines those operations. It is partly inspired by a letter, reproduced in the Conclusion, which was written in February 1945 by Alfred George Gardyne de Chastelain, the head of the Special Operations Executive (SOE) in Istanbul from 1941, to a close Romanian friend. De Chastelain expressed his regret that during the previous four years SOE had received so many promises of action in one form or another from Iuliu Maniu, the head of the Romanian opposition to the pro-German dictator Marshal Ion Antonescu, none of which came to anything, that there was a gradual reduction in interest on the part of London until Maniu finally reached a point where he was almost disregarded as a political factor. It was with the greatest of effort that a few of de Chastelain's colleagues 'managed to maintain interest in Roumanian affairs'.

I was drawn to these affairs in the mid-1960s, and in particular to the subject of British clandestine activities in Romania during the Second World War, by Eric Tappe, my tutor at the School of Slavonic and East European Studies (SSEES), now part of University College, London.

Eric Tappe was born in London on 8 July 1910, the son of a banker of German extraction. In 1928 he won an Open Scholarship in Classics at Oriel College, Oxford and upon graduation in 1932 was appointed Sixth Form Classics master at Brighton College. Four years later he moved to a similar post at King Edward VII School in Sheffield. In October 1940 he was called up to the Royal Signals and commissioned, serving in 59 Division in Northern Ireland before being posted in April 1942 to Oxford to organize the Signals Unit of the University Senior Training Corps.

Two years of signals work in wartime Oxford prompted him to look for a more adventurous role and in March 1944 he answered a call for volunteers to learn Romanian. This decision was to have a profound implication for his post-war academic career. While following a Romanian course at SSEES he received orders to undergo parachute training for a drop into Romania, where he later learned that he was expected to link up with the anti-German resistance.

The Romanian volte-face produced by King Michael's coup against Marshal Antonescu on 23 August 1944 pre-empted this mission and he was assigned instead – after arriving more conventionally by plane in Bucharest from Bari – to the British Military Mission which was sent in early September as a component of the Allied Control Commission. The ACC had been set up by the Soviet Union, the United States and Britain to supervise the implementation of the armistice agreement between the Allies and Romania signed in Moscow on 12 September. Tappe served with the mission chiefly as Staff Officer, but with occasional duties as interpreter to its Head, Air Vice-Marshal Donald Stevenson.

This period of service in Romania, from October 1944 until February 1946, was the most eventful period of Tappe's life. He witnessed the imposition of Communist rule in Romania and the heavy-handed behaviour of the Soviet authorities towards the Romanians, among whom he made several friends. Whenever he could he used his official position to protect them; an example of this was his habit on off-duty periods of pinning Union Jacks to Romanian-owned cars to prevent their being commandeered by Soviet officers. He himself experienced an example of the lawlessness of the Soviet authorities in Bucharest when one night, as the senior officer on duty at the HQ of the British Mission, he foiled an attempt in May 1945 by Soviet troops to kidnap General Nicolae Rădescu, the former Romanian Prime Minister, who had taken refuge there to escape arrest, by giving the order to British guards for warning shots to be fired over the heads of the advancing soldiers.

In February 1946 Tappe was recalled to Britain and demobilized. He resumed his position at King Edward VII School until his appointment to a Lecturership in Romanian language and literature at the SSEES at the University of London in April 1948. Tappe's distaste for the ruthless methods employed by the Communist authorities to subjugate Romania made him a keen supporter, academically and financially, of émigré scholarly journals.

He never forgot the friends he left behind in Romania. Despite his being banned from the country by its government until 1963 (and when he did return he was placed under overt surveillance), he maintained discreet links with some of his friends and worked to obtain the release from prison of those who had been jailed. In 1962 he received word of a former Romanian employee of the British Military Mission in Bucharest, Maria Golescu, who had been arrested in 1949 for working with the British. The lady's release from prison could be secured, he was told, by payment of a 'ransom' of $4,200 (a considerable sum at the time) to the Romanian government.

Since Maria had no family in Romania capable of raising such an amount, Tappe took it upon himself to raise the bulk of the monies after unsuccessfully seeking a contribution from the British government, and upon payment of the ransom Maria was allowed to travel to Britain with her aged mother. She was granted a small pension by the British government which was regularly supplemented by monies given by Tappe, and both she and her mother lived out the rest of their lives in Eastbourne. Maria Golescu died in November 1987.

Tappe often punctuated his seminars on Romanian literature with digressions into his experiences in Romania as a young officer on the British Military Mission. Several of the mission members, unlike Tappe, had been members of SOE and had been involved in establishing and maintaining wireless and courier contact with figures in the anti-Axis opposition in Romania, and Tappe learned much about their activity at first hand.

Details of that activity were passed on by Tappe to his students and thus my curiosity was aroused, even though my postgraduate study was focused upon the history of the Romanian language and its earliest manifestations in written form. A research scholarship, awarded by The British Council in 1969 under the terms of the British-Romanian cultural agreement, enabled me to spend nine months in Bucharest, during which, as one of my aims, I tried to track down some of the Romanians with whom the British had worked during the war. It soon became clear to me that in doing so I attracted the attention of the security police, the *Securitate*, not only towards myself but also towards such persons who were compromised in the eyes of the Communist authorities by their association with SOE. I therefore shelved this particular ambition.[3]

Publication in Romania in the period of Communist rule of material on British-Romanian contacts during the war was limited to a handful of creative novels that dramatized events but which, by their very nature, lacked the rigour of an academic framework. This approach, in the absence of scholarly presentation and analysis, had the effect of distorting events and contributed to the regime's efforts to forge its own version of history by manipulating accounts of the distant and not-so-distant past.

My interest in British clandestine activities in Romania was revived in the spring of 1983, when Hugh Seton-Watson[4] suggested that I might like to consult the papers of Archibald Gibson, *The Times* correspondent in Romania from 1928 to 1940. Gibson's name and association with Romania were previously unknown to me. His name seldom appeared in British accounts of Romania of this period although he is mentioned as *The Times* correspondent in Bucharest by fellow journalists David Walker[5] and Patrick Maitland.[6] Romanian secondary sources said virtually nothing about him save giving him the (incorrect) attribute of working for SOE; he was, in fact, head of the MI6 station in Bucharest.[7]

Nevertheless, the affection with the country which Gibson and I shared induced me to discover what I could about the man, his career and experience. To this end Hugh recommended a meeting with Maitland, a colleague of Gibson's who had served as Special Correspondent (Balkans and Danubian) for *The Times* between 1939 and 1941. Maitland invited me to tea at the House of Lords and divulged that Gibson's position as *The Times* correspondent in Romania had been a cover for his activity as an officer of MI6 in that country and requested that I use Gibson's papers with discretion. He also informed me that Archibald had been recruited into MI6 by his brother Harold, who had a distinguished career in the service of the Crown.

Archibald Gibson's papers had been preserved by his widow Kyra with whom Maitland put me in touch. Kyra graciously received me in her flat and after a lengthy conversation about my interest in Romania, led me to a study in which there was a large wooden trunk. Inside were crammed folders with drafts of her husband's articles for *The Times*, cuttings of the published versions, photographic albums and several curricula vitae, compiled by Archibald between 1945 and 1965. The trunk also contained a number of medals awarded to Harold Gibson as well his own curriculum vitae, typed up in October 1958, six months after the date of his retirement from the Foreign Office.

Kyra told me that I was welcome to select the material that was of interest to me and take it away, but on condition that I would return it once I had no further need of it. Fortunately, I had driven to see Kyra and therefore was able to bundle the papers into the boot of my car. I remained in touch with Kyra and several months later telephoned her to say that I was ready to give back the papers. She told me that I could keep the cuttings and a number of photographs, and on that basis I returned the remainder.

It was from these papers that I was able to chart the careers of both Harold and Archibald. Harold Charles Lehr Gibson, eldest son of Charles J. Gibson, was born in 1897 in Moscow where he attended primary school. He completed his education at Tonbridge School and in March 1917 was recruited into MI6 for his knowledge of Russian, being attached to the British Consulate General in Moscow as a clerk. In October he was transferred to the Military Permit Office of the British Embassy in Petrograd and in March 1918 returned to the Consulate General in Moscow.

He left Russia in October 1918 for London with the remnants of the British and French Missions. Between December 1918 and February 1919 he was on 'special duties for the War Office in Greece, Turkey and Romania'.[8] One month later he was despatched to the British Military Mission in Odessa as interpreter. In May 1919 he joined the mission of Sir Halford Mackinder to South Russia, to report on the state of the anti-Bolshevik forces led by General Denikin and in July was appointed secretary to a Foreign Office fact-finding commission in Bessarabia. In October 1919 he was sent to the MI6 station in Constantinople under cover of working at the General Headquarters of the Allied Forces of Occupation, to report 'mainly on matters relating to Russian security and refugees'.[9] His next posting was to Bucharest, in December 1922, as head of station where he worked until March 1931 when he was transferred to Riga.

From there Harold moved on to Prague in February 1934 as Chief Passport Control Officer (First Secretary from 1938), in which capacity he ran the MI6 station in the Czech capital and liaised with Colonel František Dastich[10] and Colonel František Moravec,[11] consecutive heads of Czech Military Intelligence. Moravec ran two German agents, A-52 (Major Salm) and A-54 (Major Paul Thümmel), who provided detailed information of German military plans which Harold passed on to London. On the eve of the German occupation of Czechoslovakia in March 1939, Harold arranged for the transfer of the Czech military intelligence service's files and the escape of Moravec and his principal officers to London.[12]

In February 1941 Harold was sent to Istanbul as head of station. Here he had responsibility not only for Turkey but also had to coordinate the work of the displaced Athens, Belgrade, Bucharest, Budapest and Sofia stations.

Among those who reported to him were his brother Archie, Kenneth Jones, Christopher Jowitt, Arthur Ellerington, Edward Smith-Ross, Bernard O'Leary and Roman Sulakov.[13] At the same time Harold contributed to the Inter-Service Balkan Intelligence Centre (a cover name for MI6) which had been set up in Ankara in December 1939 under the direction of the military attaché, Brigadier Allan Arnold. He also worked with the Czech military intelligence representative in Istanbul, Lt. Col. Heliodor Pika, in running agent A-54 until Pika's transfer to Moscow in spring 1941, since Istanbul was considered the most convenient neutral territory where Thümmel could meet them.

Harold remained in Istanbul as head of station until September 1944, when he joined the British Military Mission to Bulgaria. At the end of the month the British mission was expelled from Bulgaria by the Russians, probably because they were aware of Harold Gibson's senior position in MI6 and his knowledge of Russian, but the mission was allowed to return in the following month, without him. In August 1945 Harold went back as head of station to Prague where he was listed as First Secretary at the British Embassy. He established contact with Czech anti-Communist groups and, after his departure in September 1948, was accused by the Czech authorities of involvement in a plot to undermine the state. At the same time, his friend in Czech military intelligence from his Istanbul days, Heliodor Pika, was placed on trial for espionage against the Soviet Union and Czechoslovakia on behalf of Britain. He was found guilty and hanged in Prague on 21 June 1949.

Harold was posted to Berlin in January 1949 as head of station, being attached to the staff of the Political Adviser's Branch of the Control Commission to Germany (British Section). After serving two years there, he returned to London where he remained until August 1955, the year in which he was sent to Rome as station head. He retired in 1958 but stayed on in the Italian capital to be with his second wife, Ekaterina Alfimova (whom he married in 1948), who ran a ballet school.[14] On 24 August 1960 he was found shot dead in his home. An MI5 enquiry established that there was no evidence to suggest foul play.[15]

Archibald McEvoy Gibson (Archie to his family and friends) was born in Moscow on 3 March 1904 of Anglo-American parentage. His mother, Dagmar Gibson, née Lehrs, was an American by birth; his father, Charles John Gibson Junior, was assistant manager of the Nevsky Stearin soap and candle warehouse in Moscow. The Gibson family's commercial association with Russia had been established by Archie's great-grandfather James who, as an exporter of herrings and coal from Britain to Sweden, extended this trade to Russia in the middle of the nineteenth century. Out of the profits James founded a number of enterprises in Russia, among them the Kalinkin Beer and Mead Company (*Kalinkinskoe Pivo-Medovarennoe Tovarishchestvo*) in St Petersburg, and the Nevsky Stearin Company (*Nevskoe Stearinovoe*

Tovarishchestvo), which had a soap and candle factory in St Petersburg and a depot in Moscow.

James' third son, Charles John Gibson Senior, became, after a spell at the Nevsky St Petersburg factory, the manager of the depot in Moscow, and later appointed his own son Charles, Archie's father, as assistant manager. The Moscow company offices were in the *Rossiya* society building on the *Bolshaya Lubyanka* Square but I have been unable to trace the location of the depot, in the grounds of which both Charles senior and junior lived in separate houses. It was here that Archie and his two brothers, Harold and James, grew up with their parents.

Their house was one of the first in Moscow to have electric light and a telephone, and was endowed with a large garden and tennis court which absorbed the energy of the three boys. Archie's elder brother Harold was his senior by almost seven years and attended school in Moscow from 1909 to 1913 when he was sent by his parents to Tonbridge School in Kent. Archie did not see him for two years until his return to Moscow to complete his education, interrupted in England by the outbreak of war, at the technical faculty of Moscow University. Archie's own schooling was provided at home by a competent and exacting Russian lady who taught him, in Archie's own words, 'the Russian equivalent of the "Three Rs" '[16] and by an Englishman who spoke his native language with a strong Russian accent.

When he left Russia at the age of fourteen, Archie spoke and read Russian fluently, an ability which, on his own admission, became his greatest asset in life by enabling him to earn a living. The revolution in Russia forced the Gibsons to leave the country. They settled in London. After the benefits and comfort of their privileged position in Moscow, the family had to adjust to comparatively cramped housing and the eccentricities of life in an England that they hardly knew. Archie and his younger brother James (nicknamed Alick) ended their long break from tuition in May 1919 when they began lessons with a local vicar in Surbiton, the Revd. W. Braybrooke. Although he learned his first Latin from the vicar, Archie thrilled more to the pillion rides that the Revd. Braybrooke's nephew, who was not yet demobilized from the Royal Flying Corps, gave him and his brother on his 2.75 horsepower Douglas motorcycle.

A year with another 'crammer' called Ash (autumn 1919 to autumn 1920) was followed by Archie's enrolment in a matriculation class at King's College London in October 1920 but shortage of money forced him to abandon it in the following August. Obliged to seek employment, he was eventually taken on at the beginning of 1922 as a clerk in the accounts department of the American Express Company in Haymarket at a weekly wage of thirty shillings. He remained there for two years before his elder brother Harold arranged a far more attractive opening in the service of the Crown with an invitation to join him in Bucharest. On 29 March 1924 Archibald was on his way to Romania with the cover of a correspondent for *The Times*.

Archibald left Romania with several members of the British legation on 22 October 1940 and was assigned to the MI6 station in Istanbul. He returned to Bucharest as a Special Correspondent of Kemsley Newspapers after King Michael's coup of 23 August 1944 against Antonescu on 1 September 1944. He finally left Romania in June 1945. From Istanbul he cabled a number of articles on the situation in Romania which appeared over a month later in *The Sunday Times* on 15 and 22 July 1945. As it was not then the policy of Kemsley's to publish anything controversial about the Soviet Union, Gibson was asked to rewrite these articles, 'putting', as he says, 'much water in my wine'.[17] *The Sunday Times* diluted them still further by suppressing what Gibson considered to be the more vigorous passages.

On 29 June he set out from Istanbul for Britain to enjoy a period of leave and to discuss his next assignment. His familiarity with the Balkans persuaded his employers to send him back to Turkey in September as Balkans and Middle East correspondent and in this capacity he travelled to Palestine, Iran and Greece. His coverage of the Greek elections of 31 March 1946 dissatisfied Kemsley's who, as Archibald complained, expected him to be as quick off the mark as the agencies without allowing him to engage local help. Unable to meet the London deadline, he was finally given three months' notice.

After his dismissal he deputized from July to October for the *Reuters* staff correspondent in Athens but on the latter's return found himself without employment. He returned to Britain in November and began to draft a book about Romania between 1930 and 1945, based partly on his despatches for *The Times*. He completed the first draft in 1948, by which time he had brought his account up to the abdication on 30 December 1947 of King Michael.

Numerous attempts to find a publisher proved unsuccessful. Most replies rejected his manuscript either on the grounds of paper economy, or of the subject matter which was deemed 'too narrow'. In the early 1950s Archibald finally abandoned his efforts. At the same time he had embarked on a fresh career as a translator, first for a small chemical company established by a wartime colleague, then in the service of the Crown, and finally for *Reuters*. It was in this final post that he retired in September 1965. Archie Gibson died in London on 6 October 1982.

According to a friend of Archie he was 'a great favourite with the Romanians. He mixed freely with them, was extrovert, good humoured and polite. Harold was completely the opposite and looked as though he bore the weight of the world on his shoulders.'[18] Unlike Harold's CV, Archibald's version did not permit a deduction that he was in the service of MI6, and his other papers contained few details of the service's operational activities in Romania between 1936 and 1945. My curiosity over these had nevertheless been aroused and I attempted to discover more about them through official channels in London but in vain.[19] Extending my search to the files of the SSI,[20] the pre-Communist Romanian Intelligence Service, in Ceauşescu's Romania was out of the question. I therefore contented myself with a commentary on a lengthy typescript based by Archibald on his experience of Romania, in particular of Bucharest.[21]

Archie's papers afforded me a glimpse into the activities of both MI6 and SOE in Romania and acted as a prompt for me to visit the Public Record Office – now the National Archives in Kew – to study the relevant Foreign Office files and to approach a handful of officers from both agencies for their memories and appraisals of actions. Their names are cited in the book with their permission.

It was only after the fall of Ceauşescu in December 1989 that in Romania the counter-intelligence archive was opened, in parts, to scholars, both Romanian and otherwise. Among the persons who offered to help me with my research was Traian Borcescu, Antonescu's head of counter-intelligence between 1942 and 1944.[22] It was in one of two interviews that Borcescu gave to me in March 1995 that I first heard the name of Alexander Eck and of the network he ran in Romania in the service of MI6 between 1940 and 1944.[23] Eck's file only became available in 2009 for consultation in the Archive of the National Council for the Study of the Archive of the *Securitate* (CNSAS), thus allowing me that to pursue the leads given by Borcescu.[24] Although the code name of the network is given in Keith Jeffrey's official history of MI6, namely *Nannygoat*, neither Eck nor his collaborators were identified by name.[25]

In contrast, significant research has been published on SOE's work in Romania. Ivor Porter, an intrepid SOE officer who was parachuted into Romania in December 1943, gives a personal account of his experience in the country after being appointed a lecturer in English in Bucharest in March 1939 and his subsequent recruitment by SOE in his *Operation Autonomous: With SOE in Wartime Romania* (London, 1989), while Alan Ogden, in *Through Hitler's Back Door: SOE Operations in Hungary, Slovakia, Romania and Bulgaria, 1939–1945* (Barnsley, 2010) focuses upon the *Ranji* mission of summer 1943. I am particularly grateful to Alan for allowing me to quote extensively from his study of the mission.

This book offers the first comprehensive study of SOE and MI6 operations in Romania between 1940 and 1945. Drawing largely upon archival sources in Britain, Romania, Germany and the United States, it is divided into ten chapters.[26] The first is dedicated to the most extraordinary event to occur in Romania during the Second World War, namely the coup orchestrated by the young (22-year-old) King Michael on 23 August 1944, and the events leading up to it. Antonescu's removal as a result of the coup satisfied a major objective of SOE, as this study will show.

Chapters 2, 3 and 4 provide context by discussing Romania's problems of internal cohesion after its enlargement as a consequence of the Paris Peace Settlement in 1919–20, the country's drift into Germany's orbit after 1938, and the image of Britain in Romania at this time. The *Anschluss* of March 1938 marks the point at which Hitler's designs for Europe became clearer to Britain and greater prominence was given to considerations about Romania.

The conclusion drawn was that Britain's only weapon against German ambitions in countries which fell into Hitler's orbit were military subversive operations and Chapters 5 and 6 examine these in the period 1939–43. Revival of wireless contact with Iuliu Maniu, head of the National Peasant Party, persuading through him, Marshal Ion Antonescu, to abandon the Axis, and the provision of a channel of communication of armistice terms by the allies, represented the aims of the *Autonomous* mission of December 1943. The consequences of the mission are presented in Chapter 7.

MI6 used its principal network in Romania for the gathering and transmission of intelligence about Axis military activity between the rivers Dniester and Bug in Southern Ukraine, an area that was administered by Romania between 1941 and the early part of 1944, as well as a conduit for aspects of its intelligence work in Hungary. Chapter 8 offers an account of the network's operation based on a detailed declaration written by its head, Alexander Eck, for the Romanian authorities after his arrest in June 1944.

Chapter 9 describes the eradication of opposition to the imposition of Communist rule while the final chapter describes the fate of SOE Romanian activists after 1945.

To assist readers unfamiliar with several of the personalities mentioned in the book I have placed biographies of key figures, both British and Romanian, in the front section of this book (see pp. x–xxii).

1
Mission Accomplished: The Coup of 23 August 1944

The most extraordinary event to occur in Romania during the Second World War was the coup orchestrated by the young (22-year-old) King Michael on 23 August 1944, and the events leading up to it. The coup overthrew the wartime leader, Marshal Ion Antonescu, who had taken Romania into the war as an ally of Germany and stubbornly remained loyal to Hitler even as the tide of war was turning against them. Antonescu, aware of the fragility of Romania's territorial integrity in the face of the Soviet advance in summer 1944, continued to hold out for armistice terms with the Allies which would guarantee Romania's independence of Soviet authority.

Yet the more he delayed, the closer the Red Army moved to Bucharest and the greater the threat of occupation. Only King Michael and his advisers seemed to grasp the fact that Stalin would be tempted to withhold his assent to armistice conditions if he manoeuvred himself into a position to impose them through military might. Antonescu's refusal to accept what he considered to be unsatisfactory terms from the Allies, together with his reluctance as a military man to desert his German ally who was now on the defensive, prompted King Michael to order his arrest.

As the military situation steadily deteriorated after the Soviet victory at Stalingrad in January 1943, Marshal Antonescu's mind began to turn to consideration of an understanding with the Allies.[1] His thoughts were shared by Mihai Antonescu, Vice-President of the Council of Ministers, who took the lead in taking soundings of the Italians.[2] The Marshal tolerated the sending out of such peace feelers, both from within his own government and from the opposition leader Iuliu Maniu. Mihai Antonescu gave some indication of his own change of heart in January 1943 to Bova-Scoppa, the Italian minister in Bucharest. Bova-Scoppa went to Rome to present a report of his conversation with Antonescu to Galeazzo Ciano, the Italian Foreign Minister, who had already anticipated the new mood of the Romanian leaders. In his diary entry for 10 January Ciano noted:

> I think the Germans would do well to watch the Romanians. I see an about-face in the attitude and words of Mihai Antonescu. The sudden will

> for conciliation with Hungary is suspicious to me. If the Russian offensive had not been so successful I doubt that all this would have taken place.[3]

Mihai Antonescu's proposal elicited some sympathy from Ciano who recorded on 19 January:

> Bova-Scoppa has made a report on his long conference with young Antonescu who has returned from German headquarters. The latter was very explicit about the tragic condition of Germany and foresees the need for Romania and Italy to contact the Allies in order to establish a defence against the bolshevization of Europe. I shall take the report to the Duce and shall make it the subject of a conversation which I have been planning for some time. Let us not bandage our heads before they are broken, but let us look at the situation realistically and remember that charity begins at home.[4]

Mussolini, however, was not swayed by Ciano's argument:

> Taking my cue from Bova's report I told the Duce what I thought. The Duce began by replying that 'he was sure that the Germans would hold tenaciously'. Then he listened to me attentively. He naturally refused Antonescu's offer, saying that 'the Danube is not the way we must follow'. But he did not react when at a certain point I said openly that we too should try to make some direct contact.[5]

The Duce reiterated his view on the following day, 21 January:

> As I anticipated Mussolini wanted to reread the Bova report. He described Antonescu's language as over-subtle and he reaffirmed in terms much stronger than those of yesterday his decision to march with Germany to the end.[6]

This rebuff prompted Mihai Antonescu to attempt direct contact with the diplomatic representatives of the Allies in neutral countries with a view to concluding a separate peace. He himself raised the matter with Andrea Cassulo, the Papal Nuncio in Bucharest, while the Romanian minister in Berne was instructed to make contact with the Papal Nuncio there. In March the Romanian minister in Madrid asked his Portuguese and Argentinian counterparts to let the American ambassador Carlton Hayes know of Romania's desire to conclude a peace with the Allies.

Similarly, Victor Cadere, the Romanian Minister in Lisbon, took soundings in October of President Salazar and of the British Ambassador. In December the Romanian chargé in Stockholm, George Duca, contacted the British and American ministers in the name of Maniu and Brătianu. All these efforts foundered on the Anglo-American insistence upon 'unconditional surrender', proposed by Roosevelt and accepted by Churchill at the Casablanca Conference in January 1943, which could not be reconciled with Antonescu's desire to guarantee Romania's post-war independence from the Soviet Union.

When questioned by the writer Alexandru Brătescu-Voineşti, in an interview published on 5 March 1943 in the pro-regime *Poruncа Vremii* (*The Command of the Times*), as to why, having sided with the Axis, he did not maintain links with the Allies in case they emerged victorious, Marshal Antonescu retorted, 'how, in the first instance, could such a stance be hidden from our own allies? And then, our major virtue, admired without reservation by our own great allies, is, alongside the bravery of our army, our loyalty, sincerity and lack of duplicity. This loyalty will represent one of the most precious possessions when peace is concluded.'[7]

These peace feelers were not unknown to Hitler. At their meeting at Klessheim Castle in Salzburg on 12 April 1943 the Führer confronted Antonescu with the information he had about them from German intelligence regarding the approaches made in Madrid and asked him to 'analyse them' from the point of view of their impact on the international community. 'He did not expect an immediate answer from Antonescu' to this unexpected problem. 'He would fully understand, even if Antonescu did not give him a reply.'

Antonescu replied on the spot: 'He could assure Hitler that the entire Romanian nation supported him now, more than ever, and that he would not allow anyone to carry out a policy other than that which he (Antonescu) considered the best one, in the interests of Romania and of Europe.' He promised the Führer that Romania would continue alongside Germany until the end of the war: 'The policy of the opposition, especially Maniu, did not count... However, he (Antonescu) could not touch Maniu, since he (Antonescu) knew his people and did not want, through measures taken against Maniu, to make a martyr of this man who was advanced in years and who had negative ideas, thereby granting him what he had long wished to obtain.'

Antonescu told Hitler that he would never take an initiative without informing him and undertook to investigate the action of the Romanian minister in Madrid. At the same time he defended Mihai Antonescu: 'It was inconceivable that Mihai would have tried to conclude peace or to request assistance from the Americans or other states, since he (the Marshal) would not have anyone alongside him who would be disloyal to Germany.' Hitler accepted this declaration of loyalty.[8]

Nevertheless, Hitler returned to the subject the next day. He was concerned that the approaches made in March by the Romanian minister in Madrid gave the impression to the foreign (Portuguese and Argentinian) diplomats that Romania and Germany were ready to conclude a peace with the Allies. The Führer stated that 'the important problem was that the main enemies of the Axis had formed a completely erroneous impression about the position of Germany and Italy and that was due solely to the action of Mihai Antonescu'. He asked the Marshal to ensure that such a thing never happened in future. The latter replied that he was grateful that they had discussed this problem, 'but the truth was totally the reverse of what Germany knew'.[9]

Antonescu was less than honest with the Führer in this matter. He was aware of the approaches made by his Foreign Minister and did nothing to stop further soundings of all three Allies made by Mihai Antonescu and Maniu through different channels over the following twelve months. In their turn, the Western Allies, led by the British, sought to maintain regular contact with King Michael. In autumn 1943 a British intelligence officer, using the cover of a journalist, met the King and Queen Helen at the palace in Bucharest in order to gain a first-hand account of the political situation in Romania and Michael's own position. A note of the interview, made by Henry Spitzmuller, a French diplomat who remained in Romania after the fall of France to serve the Allied interest,[10] offers a rare contemporary first-hand account of Michael's predicament and his relations with Antonescu, which shows them to have been severely strained. The King told the officer, a Mr House,[11]

> not to forget to explain that consideration for my country's future does not blind me to the fact that the Allies' policy is based on cooperation between the three Powers and I therefore understand that Russia and Romania must come to some kind of agreement.
>
> Mr House then remarked that the Allies had repeated most recently that unconditional surrender remained the essential condition of any armistice. 'I know', the King replied, 'but it is not because of this formula that I would refuse to negotiate if the occasion arose. Without underestimating its importance, I consider and hope that even the framework of this formula would permit interpretations which would allow me to accept it.'
>
> The conversation then concentrated on the possibility of a *putsch* linked to an approach by the King to the Allies. The King and all those present explained to Mr House that such a move would result in the complete and immediate occupation of the country by the Germans, who would then have all the resources of Romania at their disposal. The King and his counsellors again explained to Mr House that the situation in Romania at that moment was unique in the sense that Marshal Antonescu's government represented only a tiny minority which, having taken power and maintained it with the support of the Germans, had imposed and continued to impose on the country a policy which was contrary to its wishes and its interests. A new government which would truly represent

> the people's wishes could only come to power through a *putsch*, which was impossible at the present moment without close cooperation with the Allies.
>
> 'If the Allies made a landing in the Balkans', the King said, 'everything would be simpler. The peninsula is practically undefended, but if Romania were to be occupied by the Germans the situation would immediately become less favourable.'[12]

The acceptance of unconditional surrender by the Romanians, whether from Iuliu Maniu, the leader of the opposition National Peasant Party or from Antonescu, was the stumbling block in all subsequent negotiations held between Maniu's representatives and the Allies in Cairo in the spring of 1944.[13] Yet approaches made in December 1943 by Soviet officials to Romanian diplomats in Stockholm suggested that their government wished to set up independent contacts with Antonescu and Maniu and was prepared to accept less than unconditional surrender.

A curious situation thus emerged in which both the Romanian government and opposition were seeking to obtain the best possible terms for an armistice in parallel negotiations, one in Cairo with the Allies collectively, and the other in Stockholm with the Russians separately. Not surprisingly, both Antonescu and Maniu believed that they were in a position to bargain over unconditional surrender, hence the misunderstanding that arose between the Allies and Maniu, and the increasing British irritation with the latter. Maniu wanted some assurance as to what conditions he could get before making any plans to overthrow Antonescu and was particularly anxious to prevent Soviet occupation of Romania. The Russians, on the other hand, doubtless took the pragmatic view that it was more realistic to treat with Antonescu since he controlled the army and an about-turn by the latter against the Germans would preclude the need for a coup by the opposition which the Communists did not control.

Antonescu's own position on the desirability of an armistice is evident from a memorandum of what appears to have been a meeting between the Marshal and Maniu dated 21 January 1944.[14] Antonescu argued that it was very difficult for Romania to withdraw from the war, given the importance of Romania's oil to Germany. Maniu said that 'realistic solutions should be found to change our military and diplomatic position'. The memorandum continued:

> What are these solutions? Marshal Antonescu asked that they should be put to him in practical terms, but you [Maniu] were unable to do this. Mr Maniu thinks, however, that Marshal Antonescu has a mission and that he can take the country out of the war immediately. What would this mission be? Mr Maniu must be explicit. Over the last three years he has been floating the same theoretical ideas, which seem deceptive.

> But Mr Maniu avoids and hestitates to ask himself, and in particular, to show how Romania's withdrawal from the war could carried out in practical terms – a withdrawal which is the wish of the Marshal and of the entire population – [and] whether the allies and the Germans would guarantee our borders and future. Yet neither side is giving us these guarantees, nor will they, or – what is more to the point – can they give them, guarantees which we have been seeking for three years.
>
> In these circumstances, who can attempt capitulation or a laying down of arms especially when – in either case – Romania will be forced, like Italy, to tolerate fighting on its own territory by both sides.[15]

Hitler was made aware of the continuing Romanian overtures to the Allies and ordered plans to be drawn up for the occupation of the country. Similar plans had already been prepared for the occupation in March 1944 of Hungary, whose reliability as an ally had long been shown to be wanting. Before taking action against the Marshal, however, the Führer decided to give him one last chance. The two leaders met at Klessheim on 23–4 March 1944 where Hitler railed against the duplicity of the Hungarians, declaring to Antonescu that he had irrefutable evidence of their intention to withdraw from the war.[16]

Unaware that his future hung in the balance Antonescu pledged continued loyalty to Hitler. Not for the first time, Hitler was impressed by Antonescu's sincerity and decided not to remove his friend.[17] His faith in his Romanian ally was borne out by Antonescu's obstinate refusal to turn against Germany by accepting armistice conditions laid down by the Allies.

We can only speculate on the consequences of a decision by Hitler to occupy Romania; there is no doubt that King Michael would have had the support of most of his generals in ordering his army – half of which was held in reserve in Romania to defend the country – to take up arms against the Germans, and that the ensuing hostilities, by crippling German resistance, would have accelerated the Soviet advance westwards in Moldavia. Of one thing, however, we can be certain; German occupation would have had the same monstrous impact on Romania's surviving Jews of Moldavia and Wallachia, as it did on the Jews of Hungary. After the German occupation of that country on 19 March 1944, Jews were rounded up in ghettos with the collaboration of the Hungarian gendarmerie and sent to Auschwitz.

Antonescu, aware of the fragility of Romania's territorial integrity in the face of the Soviet advance, continued to hold out for armistice terms which would guarantee the country's independence from Soviet authority. However, as he delayed the Red Army was advancing ever closer and on 29 March Cernăuţi in Northern Bukovina was taken. Odessa, the Crimea's main port, fell on 10 April, effectively putting to an end Romania's occupation of Transnistria, while the evacuation of the Crimea was completed on 13 May.

Antonescu remained adamant about not abandoning his German ally, now very much on the defensive. At a Council of Ministers' meeting on 6 May 1944, the Marshal made his position clear in this regard:

> So, gentlemen, [we should have] a perfectly correct attitude in our relations with the Germans: in 1940 we bent down before them, are we now to hit them when they are beaten and faced with destruction? We cannot do that, gentlemen. I was not a Germanophile and will never be. I told Hitler so. You cannot ask the Romanian people to love the German people. When we lost all [those] territories as a result of the political and military actions of the Germans, you cannot ask the Romanian people to love you. The Romanian people marches alongside the German people out of self-interest, and when you are in a position to help it [the Romanian people] win its rights, it will show its gratitude to you. We must behave correctly towards the Germans.[18]

Antonescu gave these same reasons for remaining loyal to his German ally at his trial in May 1946. When questioned about his meeting with Hitler on 6 August [it took place, in fact, on 5 August], Antonescu replied:

> Before 6 August I wanted to go to Germany on my own initiative – I had never been before on my own initiative, but now in 1944 I wanted to – to raise the matter of the Romanian army's withdrawal from the war. As a soldier, I have been throughout my life a man of honour and loyal, and I did not want to break with Germany, because Germany was and can be a great power, and Romania, being a small power, must think of that. And so, I wanted to break with Germany in a decent way and to warn her: you did not keep your word to guarantee Romania's frontiers, there are not sufficient forces to meet a concerted Russian attack, and so Romania runs the risk of being totally overrun and destroyed, therefore I am withdrawing from the war. I was advised not to do this by everyone; they were all terrified of what would happen in Romania if I told Hitler and gave him advance warning. Think of it, a war between us and the Germans on our territory, which would cause the damage that it did, and besides that, I was not a partisan, I could not and would not, even if I lived a million years, stab a comrade who had been alongside me in an action in the back.[19]

This stubbornness of Antonescu determined the King, in concert with the opposition leaders, to plot his overthrow.[20]

Following the disaster that befell Romanian troops at Stalingrad, King Michael, in his 1943 New Year broadcast to his people, called for peace and for Romania to discontinue the war alongside Hitler. Marshal Antonescu was furious, as was the German Minister in Bucharest who protested violently.

Irritated by what he considered to be the indecisiveness of the opposition led by Maniu and Constantin (Dinu) Brătianu, leader of the National Liberal Party, the young King declared later that he had been ready to take Romania out of the war against the Allies in February 1944 but that 'whenever plans appeared to be maturing he was prevented from taking action by objections raised by the opposition'.[21]

The King's impatience was doubtless a sign of his youth (he was only twenty-two), and the elderly Maniu advised more prudently against a coup at that time on the grounds that there were too many German troops in the country. Nevertheless, the King could turn to the wise counsels of his mother and Queen Helen, of General Sănătescu, the head of the military household, and of Grigore Niculescu-Buzeşti, the head of the cypher and communication section of the Foreign Ministry.

At this time Maniu was in regular radio contact with the British through Nicolae Ţurcanu (code-named 'Reginald') who had been sent into Romania in June 1943 as a member of the Special Operations Executive *Ranji* mission. At the end of October 1943, Maniu had expressed a desire to leave Romania in order to contact the Russians with British assistance. In response the Foreign Office told Maniu that any approaches from Romania, be they from individuals or from the government, should be addressed to all three Allies and that they should take the form of an offer by a duly authorized emissary to sign an unconditional surrender to the three principal Allies.[22]

The Foreign Office told the Soviet government about Maniu's request. At the end of December 1943 the Romanian Counsellor in Stockholm, George Duca, contacted the British and American Ministers in the name of Maniu about peace terms, unaware that his own Minister, Frederick Nanu, had been approached on 26 December by what Nanu took to be an NKVD officer, with an offer to deal with the Romanian government.[23] Clandestine contact was maintained for several months. Nanu was told that the Russians would keep the Western Allies informed and that strict secrecy should be maintained.

On 13 April 1944 armistice terms agreed by the representatives of the American, British and Soviet governments in Cairo were transmitted to the Marshal and to Maniu. They called for a Romanian volte-face against the Germans, the payment of reparations to the Russians, the confirmation of Bessarabia and Northern Bukovina as Soviet territory, the restoration of Northern Transylvania to Romania, and the granting to Soviet troops of unrestricted movement, although not occupation, throughout Romania during the period of the armistice.[24]

The receipt of the terms seems to have caused a breach to open up between the Marshal and Maniu. In a letter he wrote in mid-April, Maniu stated that Antonescu 'wished to continue the war at the side of the Germans', while Maniu accepted the terms and said that once he was certain that Antonescu could not be moved, he would act in conjunction with the King.[25] An appeal to Antonescu to cease hostilities against the Allies was submitted under the signature of sixty-nine university teachers in April. Overtly pro-Soviet in sentiment, it reflected political reality as regards the key role that the Soviet Union would play in determining Romania's fate, accepting at face value the promises of the Kremlin:

> At this crucial time for the existence of the Romanian people, the Soviet Government, in agreement with the governments of Great Britain and the United States, states before the whole world that it does not intend to destroy the Romanian state, nor to annex territories beyond the frontiers of 1941, nor to change the existing social system of the country...
>
> The Romanian people, exhausted by a war too long for its resources, cannot fight any longer. Step out into the streets and ask the passers-by, go into the villages and towns, listen to the voice of the people. Everywhere you will see despair in their eyes and [hear] the same reply: NO.
>
> Why should we continue to fight? The vital interests of the state and of our people require the immediate cessation of war, however difficult this step might be. The sacrifices which Romania should make will be incomparably smaller and less painful than the continuation of the war.[26]

On 5 May 1944 Eden saw the Soviet ambassador to London, Feodor Gusev, and 'casually' mentioned the possibility of some sort of understanding on the problems of Greece and Romania, as Eden put it later, 'agreeing between ourselves as a practical matter that Rumanian affairs would be in the main the concern of the Soviet government while Greek affairs would be in the main our concern, each government giving the other help in the respective countries'.[27]

The suspicion that the Western Allies, and in particular Britain, had abandoned Romania to the Russians, troubled Maniu who used the Romanian emissary to Cairo, Constantin Vişoianu, to voice these concerns to Christopher Steel, the British representative, at the end of May. This provoked Antony Eden, the Foreign Secretary, to instruct Steel to tell Vişoianu that there was no use in his trying to obtain assurances about British policy 'as distinct from that of the Soviet government'.[28] But there was no rebuke from Eden when Steel, in answer to a further question from Vişoianu as to whether Maniu should form 'a democratic coalition embracing the Romanian Communist Party, replied that in his own view a broad national union of this kind would be "warmly welcomed" by Allied public opinion'.[29]

This cautious advice probably confirmed Maniu's view that it would be good politics to bring the Communists into a coalition and when Vişoianu asked Daniel Semionovici Selod, the assistant to Nikolai Novikov, the Soviet representative in Cairo, to suggest a name to contact, Selod replied 'Lucreţiu Pătrăşcanu'.[30] Although held under house arrest throughout 1943 and early 1944 at a mountain village called Poiana Ţapului near Sinaia, the

King's summer residence, Pătrăşcanu was kept informed of plans to take Romania out of the war by his brother-in-law, Colonel Octav Ulea, Master of Ceremonies at the Palace.[31]

In April 1944 Pătrăşcanu negotiated an agreement with Titel Petrescu, the leader of the Social Democrats, to set up a United Workers' Front, thus giving the Communist Party greater authority. Both men took part in the secret preparations for the coup under the King's chairmanship. Pătrăşcanu was brought into meetings of a sub-committee under Colonel Dumitru Dămăceanu which prepared plans for the defence of Bucharest, and at the beginning of June he suggested that the Communist Party's military representative, Emil Bodnăraş (code-named 'engineer Ceauşu'), should attend since he could organize small bands of armed workers who could assist in a volte-face.

Bodnăraş was no ordinary official of the Communist Party: he was also an NKVD officer whose role in the preparations for the coup remains shadowy and has consequently fomented speculation, including the suggestion that he was used by Marshal Antonescu as a clandestine conduit to the Soviet authorities.[32] After the Axis defeat at Stalingrad it was clear to Antonescu that it would be prudent to establish closer links with the Russians and Bodnăraş was an obvious channel.

Unlike his colleagues Dej, Apostol, Chişinevski and Georgescu, he had been exempted from internment at the Târgu-Jiu prison camp, after being released from Caransebeş prison in December 1942, on the grounds of having been an officer in the Romanian army. Bodnăraş made his first appearance at one of the meetings to prepare the coup at a house on Calea Moşilor on the night of 13 June.[33] Even members of the King's circle were impressed by Bodnăraş' dedication and the latter, in his turn, was sufficiently convinced by the thoroughness of the plans to be able to satisfy his Communist colleagues that the Romanian Communist Party only stood to enhance its position by joining the National Peasant, National Liberal, and Social Democratic parties in the formation of the National Democratic Bloc (NDB) on 20 June 1944.[34]

More detail about the NDB was provided by the business magnate Max Auşnit, who had fled Romania on 17 June 1944 in a Heinkel 111 bomber taken by Prince Matei Ghica-Cantacuzino, an air-ace, from Ianca airfield near the Danube port of Brăila. Auşnit was accompanied by Alexandru Racotta, an executive for the oil company Astra Română, and Radu Hurmuzescu.[35] Auşnit had been asked by Maniu to give Prince Barbu Ştirbey, the emissary sent to the Allies in Cairo in March with the agreement of Marshal Antonescu, a progress report on Maniu's plan to overthrow the Antonescu regime and at a meeting in Cairo on 20 June attended by the Foreign Office representative Christopher Steel, the State Department counsellor Mr Shannon, the Soviet Representative Daniel Semionovici Selod, Lt. Col. Edward Masterson of SOE, Ştirbey and Constantin Vişoianu,[36] a second emissary sent by Maniu in April, he reported that an agreement amongst the four opposition parties to form a bloc had been signed 'some ten days ago'.[37]

A week later, the Allied representatives in Cairo received the plan drawn up by the King and the NDB for the coup. To be successful, Maniu argued, the coup had to be accompanied by three Allied actions. First, there should be a major Soviet offensive on the Romanian front within twenty-four hours of the volte-face; second, three airborne brigades, either Anglo-American or Soviet, with an additional 2,000 parachute troops should be dropped at the time of the coup; third, there should be a heavy bombardment of communications with Hungary and Bulgaria. The plan met a favourable response from both the British and American representatives, yet when the American suggested a tripartite meeting to discuss it, the Soviet representative Nikolai Novikov said that this would be premature.

Novikov waited in vain for instructions from Moscow. The Russians had nothing to lose by pinning their hopes on a bilateral deal with Marshal Antonescu; this had the double advantage for them of dealing directly with Romania's military leader, thereby obviating the need to negotiate with Maniu, and of giving them time, in view of the Marshal's hesitancy, to prepare for their military occupation of Romania. Indeed, at the beginning of June, Madame Alexandra Kollontay, a veteran revolutionary and the Soviet minister in Stockholm, had offered improved armistice conditions to Nanu which, in addition to an unconditional promise to return Transylvania, pledged to allow 'free areas' where the Romanian government would be sovereign and where no foreign troops would be allowed to enter, to show leniency over reparations, and to allow 15 days between the signing of an armistice and a Romanian declaration of war on Germany.[38]

At the Marshal's request Hitler received him at his headquarters at Rastenburg in East Prussia on 5 August. The Führer, according to a Romanian officer present, used the meeting, lasting some six hours, to deliver a rant against all who had betrayed him, especially the German people, who had showed no gratitude for the heights to which he had raised them.[39] To Antonescu's complete surprise, Hitler posed the leading question as to whether Romania intended to fight on; the Marshal temporized by saying that this depended upon Germany's commitment to assist Romania in stemming the Russian advance, and upon the attitude of Hungary and Bulgaria.[40] He returned to Bucharest in deep depression and did nothing about the Soviet terms.

In the meantime, Maniu was desperately seeking a reply from Cairo to the coup plan sent on 27 June. On 7 July the King and his advisors, including the opposition leaders, fixed 15 August as the date for action, hoping to synchronize their action with a Soviet offensive. The longer the coup was delayed, the greater the chance that the Red Army would push forward, occupying more Romanian territory and giving Moscow a reason for preferring a straightforward military conquest of the country without any help from the King and the opposition. Moreover, the increasingly frequent Anglo-American air raids on the oilfields around Ploieşti and on Bucharest were a reminder to the Romanians of the cost of the alliance with Germany. Still Maniu heard nothing from Cairo, and the coup was postponed. Finally, on 20 August the long-awaited Soviet offensive came, prompting Maniu to inform Cairo that the King and his group had decided to take action.

On that date the Soviet generals Malinovsky and Tolbukhin successfully launched a massive assault entrusted to two armies of almost one million troops and 1,500 tanks against the combined German and Romanian forces straddling the River Prut. The northern offensive, aimed at Focşani, Bucharest and Turnu Severin, breached the front south of Iaşi and the King rushed from Sinaia to Bucharest to consult with his advisors.[41] The representatives of the political parties could not be located. The King asked Colonel Dămăceanu how long he needed to get his part of the plan ready, namely to seize the telephone exchange and the radio station, and was told 'five days'.

The coup was therefore fixed for 26 August at 1 pm. The Marshal and Mihai Antonescu would be invited to lunch, after which there would be an audience to discuss the course to be adopted. If the Marshal refused negotiation with the Allies, the King would dismiss him and appoint a new government to be drawn from the opposition parties. This government would invite the Germans to evacuate Romania and empower its emissaries in Cairo, Barbu Ştirbey and Constantin Vişoianu, to sign an armistice.

On the following evening, 21 August, the plans agreed by the King and his advisors the day before were approved by the members of the NDB at their last full meeting before the coup. It was attended by the King, Maniu, Brătianu, Pătrăşcanu, Titel Petrescu, Grigore Niculescu-Buzeşti (head of Foreign Ministry communications), Ion Mocsony-Styrcea (Marshal of the King's Household),[42] General Constantin Sănătescu, and Mircea Ionniţiu (the King's private secretary).[43] Pătrăşcanu came with a draft proclamation for the King's approval and argued, with Petrescu's backing, for a government of national unity led by Maniu. Maniu refused and pressed for a government of technicians, headed by a soldier, to handle the armistice conditions and the presence of the Red Army. The matter was left in the hands of Maniu and Pătrăşcanu who were to draw up a list of ministers by 23 August. It was agreed that the politicians should disperse until the projected day of action, 26 August.

Yet once again, unforeseen circumstances intervened in the timing of the coup. Antonescu, dismayed by the rapid advance of the Soviet forces, was moving back and forth between the front in Southern Moldavia and Bucharest and decided to return to the front on 23 August. This meant that he would be absent from the capital on the day fixed for the coup. The news, which had been picked up fortuitously by Styrcea whilst he was at the Marshal's villa in Snagov,[44] was quickly transmitted to the King who was able to get word to Maniu that the coup should be brought forward to 23 August.

Mihai Antonescu, the Prime Minister, was unnerved by the deteriorating military situation and decided, on his own initiative, to negotiate an armistice with the Allies. He told the Marshal on the evening of 22 August and the latter raised no objections.

That same evening the Marshal told the German minister Clodius that he would make one last effort to halt the Russians, and that in the event of failure, he reserved the right to act as he saw fit. After the meeting with Clodius, Mihai Antonescu sent a courier to Stockholm instructing Nanu to tell Madame Kollontay of the Romanian government's willingness to conclude an armistice. In the event the courier arrived on 24 August, the day after the coup.[45]

Early in the morning of 23 August, Mihai Antonescu and Madame Antonescu tried to persuade the Marshal to see the King and agree to an armistice. Although the Marshal refused to commit himself, Mihai telephoned the King's office and spoke to Ionniţiu who woke the King. Michael agreed to see them both at 3 pm. In a last-ditch effort to get the Marshal to conclude an armistice, Maniu and Constantin Brătianu asked the historian Gheorghe Brătianu, the Liberal leader's nephew, to use the respect he enjoyed with the Romanian leader to persuade him to see the King that afternoon. The Marshal listened to Brătianu's arguments and apparently agreed to go to the Palace, but on condition that Maniu and Gheorghe Brătianu sent him a letter by 3 pm confirming that they stood behind him in signing an armistice.[46]

The King now convened his advisors and decided that the showdown with the Marshal should take place at his audience that afternoon. Niculescu-Buzeşti and Styrcea left the palace to warn Maniu and Pătrăşcanu respectively but Maniu was not at home and Pătrăşcanu's contact said that Pătrăşcanu and Titel Petrescu would come to the palace, but only after nightfall. Similarly, Gheorghe Brătianu could find neither his uncle nor Maniu and was therefore unable to meet the Marshal's condition that he should bring a letter from both by 3 pm. When Gheorghe Brătianu turned up to see the Marshal empty-handed the latter was furious and said that Mihai Antonescu could go to the palace alone and pass on the Marshal's apologies to the King.[47]

Mihai Antonescu arrived for his audience at the appointed time and was received by the King and General Sănătescu. He offered Marshal Antonescu's apologies, at which point Sănătescu left the room and telephoned the Marshal, saying that there was no point in snubbing the King at this critical time. The Marshal relented and agreed to come. He was escorted into the drawing room to meet the King who was with Mihai Antonescu and Sănătescu. The Marshal proceeded to give a detailed account of the situation at the front and said that he would only conclude an armistice after warning Hitler.

The King replied that the military situation would brook no further delay; since Soviet troops were already in occupation of part of the country an armistice should be signed immediately. Asked by the King whether he would stand aside for someone who would contact the Allies the Marshal replied, 'Never'. After withdrawing briefly to his study to inform his advisors – Styrcea, Buzeşti, Ionniţiu and General Aurel Aldea – that the moment had now come for the Marshal's arrest, the King returned to the drawing room and told the Marshal that, in concordance with the wishes of the Romanian people as expressed through the four democratic parties, he was taking the country out of the war to save it from disaster. If the Marshal refused to implement the King's wish that an armistice be concluded, then he should consider himself dismissed.[48]

When the Marshal retorted that he took orders from no one the King replied that, in that case, he was dismissed and he left the room. As he did so he signalled to his aide, Colonel Emilian Ionescu, to arrest the Marshal and Mihai Antonescu. Ionescu summoned the four-man guard that had been prepared for such an eventuality and amid the protests of the Marshal the two Antonescus were escorted upstairs and locked in the King's strongroom.

Back in his study the King consulted with his advisors as to the immediate steps to be taken. The leaders of the political parties had to be informed of the arrests, the Allies had to be notified, the military plan for the coup had to be executed, but most important of all, a prime minister had to be named to replace Mihai Antonescu. In the absence of Maniu, it was decided to appoint General Sănătescu, who enjoyed the respect of the army. Ionniţiu typed out a decree to this effect, the King signed it, and the new prime minister set out for army headquarters to transmit the order for Romanian troops under Colonel Dămăceanu to take up positions at strategic points in Bucharest and to cease hostilities against the Soviet forces at the front. Proof that the army placed their loyalty to their supreme commander, the King, above that to Marshal Antonescu, was demonstrated by the fact that not a single senior officer disobeyed Sănătescu's orders and not one of them defected in support of the Marshal.

Since Maniu and Pătrăşcanu had failed to agree on a list of ministers, and neither was at the palace, the new government had to be formed on the spot from the King's advisors. Niculescu-Buzeşti was elevated to Foreign Minister, and General Aldea became Minister of the Interior, while the representatives of the four parties in the DNF – Maniu, Brătianu, Petrescu and Pătrăşcanu – were appointed Ministers of State without Portfolio. Ionniţiu was doubtless not alone in his feeling at the time that the politicians had, at this crucial moment, shown themselves to be 'a pathetic bunch'.[49]

The first of them to appear at the palace was Pătrăşcanu, who arrived shortly after 8 pm. He brought with him the King's proclamation, which was approved after amendments by Buzeşti and Sănătescu, and the texts of two decrees, previously agreed at meetings of the NDB, granting an amnesty to political prisoners and abolishing the internment camps in which many Communists and other political detainees had been held. At the same time,

Pătrăşcanu asked the King for the post of Minister of Justice. Since none of the other political leaders had cabinet seats, the King did not want to risk an accusation of partiality, but given Pătrăşcanu's legal background, his diligence in producing the draft proclamation and the decrees, and that he was the first member of the NDB to appear at the palace, the King offered him a compromise, Minister of Justice ad interim.

The fact that Pătrăşcanu, alone among the political representatives, secured this temporary position gave rise in accounts about the formation of this new government to the supposition that he was acting on orders from the Communist Party and this, in turn, helped to cement the fiction in Communist historiography of the dominant role of the Party in the coup. In the circumstances, it was the most immediately plausible appointment for Pătrăşcanu given the speed of events on the afternoon of 23 August and the lack of time in which to contact the leaders of the Communist Party.[50]

Pătrăşcanu was followed shortly afterwards by Titel Petrescu and then, an hour or so later, by Emil Bodnăraş who was presented to the King under the name of 'engineer Ceauşu' and head of a group of Communist-trained armed civilians known as the 'Patriotic Guards'. About an hour after the recording of the King's proclamation to the country was broadcast over the radio at 10.12 pm, announcing the coup and the immediate cessation of hostilities with the Allies, Marshal Antonescu, who was still locked in the palace strongroom, asked for paper and made his will. Another hour passed before Bodnăraş and a group of armed workers took charge of the two Antonescus and drove them away to a safe house in the Bucharest district of Vatra Luminoasă.[51]

A few hours later Antonescu's fellow ministers were taken into custody: General Constantin Pantazi, Minister of Defence; General Constantin Vasiliu, Under-Secretary of State at the Interior Ministry; and Colonel Mircea Elefterescu, head of Bucharest Police.[52] On 31 August, shortly after Soviet troops entered Bucharest, Lt. Gen. Tevcenkov, political chief of the Second Ukrainian Front, acting on Stalin's orders, went to the head of the Bucharest garrison, Iosif Teodorescu, to take Antonescu into Soviet custody.[53] Teodorescu invited General Aurel Aldea, the Minister of the Interior, and General Victor Dombrovski, mayor of Bucharest, to the garrison and they informed Tevcenkov that they were unaware of Antonescu's whereabouts. Tevcenkov insisted on finding out, whereupon Teodorescu phoned the government and after a while a man in civilian clothes arrived. He introduced himself as Bodnăraş, a member of the Central Committee of the Romanian Communist Party. Asked by Tevcenkov for information about Antonescu, Bodnăraş replied that he was being held by the Communists.

Tevcenkov and General Nikolai Burenin, the commander of Soviet forces in Bucharest, accompanied by some forty Soviet officers and men, were then taken by Bodnăraş to the two-storey house where Antonescu and his colleagues were being held. The Marshal occupied a room on the second floor while Mihai Antonescu, Pantazi, Vasiliu and Elefterescu were kept on the ground floor. They were guarded inside the house by ten armed civilians. There was no guard on the outside. Tevcenkov told Bodnăraş that because of the poor security he proposed to take the prisoners into Soviet custody. Bodnăraş preferred to keep the captives where they were but under a guard reinforced by Soviet soldiers. Tevcenkov rejected this proposal, accepting instead the continued presence of some of the armed Romanian civilians around the prisoners. Bodnăraş added that 'the [Romanian] government did not want Antonescu to end up in Moscow'. At 5 pm on the same day – 31 August – Antonescu and the others were taken to the headquarters of the Soviet 53rd Army.[54]

On the following day the group was visited by General Aldea and then taken by lorry to Urziceni. On 2 September they continued by road to a station on the Soviet side of the frontier where they were put on a train for Moscow. After a three-day journey they reached the Soviet capital from where they were driven 'in comfortable vehicles' to a castle some 60 km away. According to an account written by Pantazi's son, they were well treated.[55] Each member of the group had his own room and was allowed to walk in the park. Nevertheless, on 8 November the Marshal tried to hang himself with a noose made from strips torn from his bedsheet, but he was discovered in time by Vasiliu. Subsequently, a Soviet officer was billeted with the prisoners.

With the entry of the Red Army, the advance units of which arrived in Bucharest on 30 August, the country came under Russian control. Romania's external position immediately after the coup was that of a state waging war against its former allies on the side of its former enemies, with whom its relationships were covered by the Armistice Agreement between the Allies and Romania signed in Moscow on 12 September 1944.

2
Setting the Scene: Problems of Cohesion, 1918–1938

Romania came out of the First World War with double its former population, territory and industrial capacity – 7.3 million Romanians had by 1919 increased to 16.2 million, but they still lived mostly on the land. The economy was characterized by agricultural overpopulation and low productivity per acre – about half that of Western Europe. The newly enlarged provincial Romania with its legacy of a different historical experience, coupled with the diverse ethnic mix of the significant minority Hungarian, German and Jewish populations which it contained, posed major problems of harmonization and consolidation which, in the brief interlude of the inter-war period, the country's leaders had little time, capacity and will to address. A failure to solve these issues blighted the country's progress towards modernization and the exercise of genuine democratic rule.

There were contrasts in the pattern of economic development. Transylvania had benefited from Austrian and Hungarian investment until 1914, but the rest of the country remained underdeveloped. Although it possessed great natural wealth, with fertile soil and raw materials such as natural gas, lignite, oil, metals and forests, Romania lacked the industrial capacity to use these resources to the full. Industrial development was confined to an east-west axis from Timişoara to Braşov in Transylvania, and a north-south axis from Sighişoara in Transylvania to Ploieşti and Bucharest in Wallachia. This left the country predominantly agriculture-based, with great variation in standards of living between town and country.

According to the 1930 census, almost 80 per cent of its working population lived on the land in villages that were poorly served by transport and communications. Its total population in 1939 was calculated to be just over 19.9 million.[1] Few villages had piped water or electricity, health services were primitive, especially in the more backward regions of Moldavia and Bessarabia, and in such conditions it is hardly surprising that with a live birth rate of just 17 per cent, Romania had the highest infant mortality rate in Europe.[2] Only 13 per cent of the adult population were employed in industry, commerce and transport.[3] The 1930 census registered this number as 947,739 persons.[4] The corresponding German figures were 42 per cent in industry and 26 per cent in agriculture (1930). In 1936 there were 440,000 persons in state employment in Romania compared with only 250,000 in Germany.[5] Whereas illiteracy in Germany had virtually disappeared by 1900, Romania's census of 1930 registered an illiteracy rate of 43 per cent amongst those over the age of seven.[6]

These problems were of a complexity which would have taxed the most far-sighted government and the most thoroughgoing cadres of administration. In the interwar period Romania had neither. The greatest discrepancy, from a Western point of view, lay in the gulf between word and deed. Behind the facade of political institutions copied from the West the practice of government was subject to patronage and to narrow sectional interests. Under the constitution of 1923 the king had the power to dissolve parliament and to appoint a new government. The monarchy, which under King Carol (1881–1914) and King Ferdinand (1914–27) had won the trust and affection of the Romanian population, soon lost much of its prestige through the antics of Carol II, who returned to the country from exile in 1930. Hugh Seton-Watson, a gifted young contemporary analyst of Carol's exploits, described him thus:

> Superficially brilliant and basically ignorant, gifted with enormous energy and unlimited lust for power, a lover of demagogy, melodrama and bombastic speeches, he was determined to be a Great Man, the Saviour and Regenerator of his country. His impressionistic mind was filled with admiration of Mussolini, then still the most picturesque figure on the European political stage, and he set himself to imitate him. In his untiring work, which lasted ten years, he combined a little of the terrorist methods of the Duce with much of the well-tried Balkan procedure of corruption and intrigue.[7]

Institutionalized corruption was matched by examples of a personal variety. The exploitative rule of foreign princes in Wallachia and Moldavia in the eighteenth and early nineteenth century had helped to create a culture amongst the dominant elite in which rapacity was regarded as proof of dexterity and cunning, and therefore corruption of principles had become widespread. This culture had been assimilated by the small, bureaucratic middle class who expected to rely on unofficial remuneration in the form of favours to supplement their meagre salaries. There was no native economic middle class to act as a check upon the elite since commerce had fallen principally into the hands of the largely disenfranchised Jews who were barred from public service.

Idealism was scorned and those who searched for it, the young, were driven to the sole parties which seemed to have any on offer, those of the Right. Although a radical land reform programme was introduced soon after the First World War, many peasants were unable to afford the loans necessary to buy agricultural machinery. The economic recession of the 1930s ushered in a decade of instability in which the xenophobia of the impoverished peasantry was exploited by right-wing movements, principally by the Iron Guard, and directed against the Jews. The latter's position as alcohol suppliers, money-lenders and middle-men in the timber trade made them disliked by the peasants, themselves vulnerable to any force capable of mobilizing them. Disillusion with the failure of parliamentary government – represented principally by the National Liberal and National Peasant parties – to solve economic problems fuelled support for the Guard, with its promise of spiritual regeneration and its programme of combatting 'Jewish Bolshevism'.[8]

Combatting 'Jewish Communism' was one of the slogans produced by the Iron Guard, a movement created and dominated, even after his death, by Corneliu Zelea Codreanu.[9] As one scholar has concluded, 'there can be no understanding of the Iron Guard without a thorough understanding of Codreanu', who was dubbed by his followers *Căpitanul* (The Captain).[10] It was Codreanu who inspired the Guard with his invectives against what he saw as 'the Judeo-Bolshevik' threat, against the drive for modernization through imitation of Western political and economic institutions, and against a corrupt ruling elite.

Codreanu was born in 1899 in the northern Moldavia town of Huşi. His father, Ion Zelinski, had come to the town from Austrian Bukovina shortly before Corneliu's birth with his German wife Elisabeth Brunner. Ion was engaged as a teacher at the local secondary school and in 1902 romanianized his surname to Zelea and added a second one, Codreanu, in recognition of his forester lineage (*codru* meaning 'forest' in Romanian). Between 1910 and 1916 Corneliu attended the military school at Mănăstirea Dealului in Wallachia, housed in a monastery, and it was in these surroundings that a respect for discipline and reverence for God were inculcated in him.

At the end of the First World War he enrolled at Iaşi University where he attended the lectures of Professor Alexandru Cuza, who presented Communism as a Jewish conspiracy against 'Christian' Europe. In 1923 Cuza founded the League of National Christian Defence (LANC)[11] with an anti-Semitic programme, the principal point of which was the application of a *numerus clausus* for the admission of Jews into the professions. But Codreanu, who aligned himself with Cuza, was not interested in pursuing this aim solely through the ballot box; it was to be imposed through violence, as events of 1923 were to show.

In October 1923 Codreanu organized a plot to shoot politicians who had supported an amendment to the Romanian constitution granting Jews the right to citizenship, but the scheme was betrayed and Codreanu and a few of his friends were arrested and tried, but acquitted. On leaving custody Ion Moţa, one of the conspirators, shot dead the man suspected of having betrayed the plot.

A second event linked to the conspiracy highlights another aspect of Codreanu's movement, namely its missionary role. In his autobiography Codreanu described how he received a vision of the Archangel Michael in the prison chapel and was urged by him to dedicate his life to God. After his release, Codreanu returned to Iaşi and set up the Brotherhood of the Cross (*Frăţia de Cruce*), an organization for young men designed to foster a national revival. He appointed Moţa as head of the Brotherhood. The very name suggested a mystic communion amongst its members whose ritual required them to take a formal vow pledging their life to Codreanu and the Brotherhood. In this respect the Guard sits uneasily in a 'fascist' context, if only, as one scholar has put it, 'in that Codreanu's theories were derived from the Book of Revelation. He made a practice of going up in the mountains to pray. One does not hear that of Hitler or of Mussolini. The Guard was much more akin to the Russian *narodniki* than to any western model.'[12]

The first task they set themselves was to build a student centre but Codreanu's notoriety led the local prefect, Constantin Manciu, to break up the student group with great violence, binding them with ropes and dragging them through the streets of the town. Codreanu took his revenge by shooting Manciu and two other officials in the Iaşi courtroom in October 1924. His personal popularity led the government to put him on trial far from Moldavia in Turnu-Severin, near the Yugoslav border. Still the jury acquitted him, returning their verdict with LANC emblems in their lapels.

Cuza was becoming unnerved by Codreanu's violence and to avoid a rift in the LANC Codreanu and a close friend, Ion Moţa, left for France. They returned in the spring of 1926 to contest the elections in which the LANC secured ten seats in parliament. Codreanu was not amongst the successful deputies and attacked the LANC for having sold out to the Jews. On 24 June 1927 he founded his own movement, the Legion of the Archangel Michael (*Legiunea Arhanghelului Mihail*). Its aim was to engender a spiritual regeneration amongst Romanians and to create 'a new type of man'.

The Legion began slowly, its first public meeting being held in December 1929.[13] In April 1930 Codreanu created a militant political wing of the Legion which he christened the Iron Guard (*Garda de Fier*), in order to combat 'Jewish Communism'.[14] Early in 1931 both the Guard and the Legion were banned by Iuliu Maniu's[15] National Peasant government but this did not prevent them from contesting the elections of that summer as the 'C. Z. Codreanu Group'. They failed to win a seat but in a by-election Codreanu was returned and his father won a second by-election in the following year. Outlawed again in 1932 they still contested general elections and in July won five seats.

A propaganda policy of working without accepting payment was initiated by the Legion but its value was often offset by the violence directed by some legionaries against their political opponents. The fear of unrest during an election campaign led I. G. Duca's Liberal government to dissolve the Guard yet again on 10 December 1933, and in the agitation that followed several Guardists were killed and hundreds arrested. On 29 December, nine days after a fresh election victory, Duca was shot dead by three Guardists on Sinaia station. The assassins were sentenced to life imprisonment, but Codreanu was cleared of involvement and emerged from hiding to continue the Legion's communal work. In December 1934, Codreanu persuaded General Gheorghe Cantacuzino to found a new party called 'All for the Country' (*Totul Pentru Țară*) which was based on the infrastructure of the Legion and which acknowledged Codreanu as its spiritual leader.[16] The Legion's increasing appeal to industrial workers was reflected in the foundation in 1936 of a Legionary Workers' Corps which attracted 6,000 members in Bucharest alone.[17]

Codreanu's autobiography appeared in that same year. In it he laid out the Legion's programme which, in part, was conceived like a monastic order. The Legion was endowed with a spiritual mission to change Romanians by creating 'the new man', one bent on social justice. There was no place for the bourgeoisie. His opposition to democracy was expressed in a virulent anti-Semitism. The Legion's articles of faith dictated a pathological hatred of Jews whom Codreanu saw as the fount of Communism. Democracy was not good for the Romanians because it 'breaks the unity of the Romanian people, dividing it into parties, stirring it up and so, disunited, exposing it to face the united block of Jewish power in a difficult moment of history'. A multi-party system was, in Codreanu's view, incapable of ensuring continuity in development: 'It is as if', he wrote, 'on a farm the owners changed yearly, each coming with different plans, doing away with what the predecessors did.'[18]

The deaths of two legionary volunteers in Spain at the beginning of 1937 provided an opportunity for the Guard to put on a display of strength in Bucharest. An appeal was made to students to attend the funeral of Vasile Marin and Ion Moța: 'The entire Romanian Christian body at the university, academies and senior schools in Bucharest regards it as a duty of honour regarding the sacrifice made by the two legionaries, former student leaders and heads of the generation of 1922, to be present on 11, 12 and 13 February for the funeral rites.'

At the head of the cortège, which included the German Minister Wilhelm Fabricius and his Italian colleague, marched several detachments of legionaries while the funeral service, held the following day, on 13 February, was conducted by four prelates of the Orthodox Church, Metropolitan Bishop Gurie of Bessarabia; Nicolae Bălan, Metropolitan of Transylvania; Vartolomei, Bishop of Râmnic; and Veniamin, the vicar of the patriarchate.[19] In his funeral blessing for the two legionaries, Bălan gave thanks to the Lord 'that you have considered our people worthy enough to choose from their midst faithful warriors for your work, who from beyond the grave send us their mission and the confession of their faith, following the words of your great disciples from the earliest of times which rang out around the world: "That is how I understood my life's duty. I loved Christ and I went happily to my death for him!".'[20]

The December 1937 elections were a turning point for democracy in Romania. On the expiry of its term of office in November the Liberal government of Gheorghe Tătărescu resigned. King Carol invited Ion Mihalache to form a National Peasant government but Mihalache objected to the inclusion of a political rival in the government and refused. Carol therefore went back to Tătărescu. During the election campaign Maniu took over as head of the National Peasant Party and in order to overturn Tătărescu he made a pact with Codreanu and Gheorghe Brătianu, the leader of a dissident Liberal group.

Maniu's action surprised friends of democracy in Romania and abroad.[21] Politically, he had nothing in common with the Guard; he merely wanted to use the organization to dissuade the Liberals from the use of intimidation during the campaign. No common lists of candidates were drawn up; the signatories simply agreed to support free elections.[22] Nevertheless, the Guard gained respectability from association with Maniu's name, while Maniu stifled the cause of democracy at a time when it was struggling for air, especially as the pact prevented his party from criticizing the Guard during the campaign. 'Above all', as Henry Roberts argued, 'it showed the National Peasants' own loss of confidence in themselves or their ideas, and was in the sharpest contrast to their refusals to make any deals on the road to power in 1927 and 1928.'[23]

The 'All for the Country' Party emerged with 66 seats (15.6 per cent of the vote), the third strongest party behind the Liberals (152 seats, 35.9 per cent) and the National Peasants (86 seats, 20.4 per cent). For the first time in the history of Romania a government had fallen in an election, for the Liberal Party failed to receive the 40 per cent of the votes that it required to stay in power.[24] Tătărescu resigned on 28 December and on the same day Carol turned to the Transylvanian poet Octavian Goga, head of the National Christian Party, formed in 1935 from an alliance of Cuza's LANC with Goga's National Agrarian Party, to form a government, despite the fact that Goga's party had received less than 10 per cent of the vote (39 seats). By propelling the anti-Semitic National Christian Party into power Carol hoped to draw off support from the Guard.

Carol promoted anti-Semitism for political expediency. Under the Goga government anti-Semitism was raised to the level of state policy. One of Goga's first steps was to suppress, on 30 December 1937, the 'Jewish' newspapers *Dimineaţa*, *Adevărul* and *Lupta*, so-called because their editors or owners were Jewish, on the grounds of their 'destructive tendencies... which had ruined the country's moral health'.[25] Newspapers in the major provincial towns were also closed 'because they were run by Jews'.[26] Goga cancelled licences held by Jews to sell alcohol and tobacco, and placed a ban on the employment of Jews and foreigners in cafes and restaurants, while the Bucharest bar association suspended its 1,540 registered Jewish lawyers from practising in Bucharest.[27] Istrate Micescu, the Foreign Minister who was responsible for leading the campaign to exclude Jewish lawyers from the Bucharest bar, whilst defending the anti-Semitic programme to the British and French Ministers in Bucharest as necessary to avoid an Iron Guard government and promising moderation in its application, was at the same time telling the German Minister that 'anti-Semitic measures would be intensified'.[28]

This wave of discrimination culminated in a Decree on the Revision of Citizenship, promulgated on 21 January 1938, which targeted all Jews who had obtained Romanian naturalization, whether on the basis of their own declarations, or following a court decision. The Jews were required to submit documentary proof of their right to citizenship within thirty days, a condition that most could not meet since they could not obtain the necessary documents in time. As a result of the revision, completed on 15 September 1939, 225,222 Jews had their rights as Romanian citizens withdrawn.[29] The decree was intended to persuade Jews to emigrate, and Carol demonstrated clearly what he had in mind for them when he gave an interview to a correspondent of the British *Daily Herald*, A. L. Easterman, which was published on 10 January 1938.[30]

Public opinion in Britain was unnerved. The British Minister in Bucharest, Sir Reginald Hoare, transmitted his government's concern to Goga over the anti-Semitic measures.[31] The French Minister, Adrien Thierry, followed suit. Jewish and foreign business concerns ceased trading in protest against the government, thus threatening economic collapse. But anti-Semitism had become such a powerful card in Romania that no government could afford to ignore it. This was recognized by Franklin Mott Gunther, the US Minister to Bucharest, in a prophetic cable to his Secretary of State dated 20 January:

> I regret to report my conviction that even if this [Goga-Cuza] Government should not survive the elections the issue of [anti-Semitism] itself is now so much to the fore that it will have to be espoused by any succeeding government or even dictatorship in response to a determined insistent public demand.[32]

New elections were called by Carol against a background of conflict between Cuza's supporters and those of Codreanu. At the urging of the Germans, who backed Goga, and of General Ion Antonescu, Minister of Defence in the Goga cabinet, Codreanu and Goga came to an understanding on 8 February 1938 whereby the former would run for office but not campaign. Carol clearly saw this arrangement between the ultra-nationalists as a threat to his power to manipulate and on 11 February he promptly dismissed Goga whose final words in his farewell address to the nation were 'Israel, you have won!' On 20 February, Carol abolished the constitution and instituted a royal dictatorship.

A puppet government under the Patriarch Miron Cristea was sworn in, with Armand Călinescu, Codreanu's avowed enemy, as Minister of the Interior. Widespread arrests of Guardists were ordered in March and in the following month Călinescu moved against Codreanu, ordering his arrest on 16 April on charges of insulting a minister in office. Codreanu had accused Nicolae Iorga, the historian and journalist, of 'spiritual dishonour' in denigrating the Guard's attempts to set up workers' canteens and Guardist-run shops. Codreanu was sentenced to six months imprisonment and then hastily retried in May for conspiracy to take over the state. In a trial considered to be prejudiced against him, Codreanu was found guilty and condemned to ten years' hard labour.

Călinescu then ordered the rounding-up of hundreds of Guardists, among them Codreanu's intended successor, Gheorghe Clima. Some of the other leaders went underground, including Horia Sima, a thirty-one-year-old school teacher, and they organized squads to hit back at their opponents.[33] A Jewish lawyer was shot dead, Jewish shops were looted, and synagogues set ablaze. Then, on 24 November the Rector of Cluj University, a friend of Călinescu, was shot and wounded. Carol's patience with the Guard was finally exhausted. Codreanu, the three murderers of Duca, and ten other Guardist assassins, were taken from their prison and strangled in woods to the north of Bucharest on the night of 29–30 November. Their bodies were taken to the prison at Jilava and buried in the grounds. A communiqué of 1 December announced that they had been shot 'while trying to escape'.

News of the murders was met by the general public with disbelief and contempt. They were particularly disgusted by their cold-blooded nature and felt shame that their monarch could have been behind such a deed. Carl Clodius, the German economic specialist handling Germany's commercial relations with Romania, noted:

> The murder of Codreanu and his followers has changed the situation considerably. Condemnation of this murder is equally strong in almost all circles of the population. I encountered no Romanian politician who even attempted to defend the murder to me. Even members of the government have tried only hesitantly and with very weak arguments to motivate and explain the murder as a political necessity. The embitterment in the Iron Guard is tremendous ... The murder of Codreanu has shaken [Carol's] moral position in the country to such an extent that he will recover from it only very slowly, if at all.[34]

The violence of the measures taken by Carol against the Guard seems to have been driven by his fear of it as a tool of Hitler. The wave of arrests of

Guardists had taken place soon after the *Anschluss* between Germany and Austria in March 1938, and the murder of Codreanu and thirteen other Guardists occurred immediately after Carol's visit to Hitler, when the Führer had urged their release and the formation of a Guardist government.[35]

The Guardists underground swore revenge. Horia Sima planned a coup but the plot was uncovered and he fled the country on 8 February 1939 for Berlin.[36] Assassination teams were set up but they were uncovered by the police. Eventually, on 21 September 1939, a group of six managed to ambush Călinescu, now Prime Minister, in Bucharest and shot him dead. Brutal reprisals were now taken against the Guard on Carol's order. Not only were the six Guardists responsible shot, and their bodies left for several days on the spot where Călinescu fell, but in each county prefects were ordered to select three members of the Guard for execution, while in the prison camps between 60 and 90 Guardists were shot. The British Minister to Bucharest reported that some 400 Guardists were victims of Carol's revenge.[37]

Carol appointed Tătărescu again as Prime Minister in November 1939 in the hope of encouraging the National Liberals and National Peasants to join a national alliance, but both Brătianu and Maniu refused. D. J. Hall, a British propaganda representative, provided an acute analysis of the political situation in March 1940:

> The King has now gained such authority that his Ministers have no say whatsoever in the Government of the country. Many of them have, at one time or another, been engaged in questionable activities and the King's power is such that he is able to employ them as puppets. The Prime Minister, M. Tătărescu, is purely a mouthpiece for the King. The Foreign Minister, M. Gafencu, while sound enough in the theory of his foreign policy, and in his affection for the allied cause, has not the courage to withstand any demand made of him. M. Giurescu, the Minister of Propaganda, is pro-German in his inclinations, and all other members of the Government are dominated by fear. In fact, it may be said that if any explanation is ever required of any action of Romania, it can be found in that one word – 'fear'. Anyone who opposes the regime is a marked man. The secret police system has been developed to such an extent that there is no man of any importance, either in politics or commerce, who can do or say anything without being immediately observed. Many of the houses of these people have microphones fitted in them, and they are too frightened to have them removed.[38]

As German successes in the war alerted Carol of the advisability of German friendship, he became more conciliatory towards the Iron Guard. Carol had ordered the release of a number of Guardists from detention in January 1940. In May, Horia Sima, the Guard's new leader who had fled to Germany during the previous year, re-entered the country. Upon the fall of France in

June, Carol established by decree the Party of the Nation (*Partidul Naţiunii*), a single party totally subservient to the King, and within days Sima issued a manifesto calling upon the Guardists to join it. This outward sign of national unity proved irrelevant in the face of momentous events on the international stage.[39]

In economic terms Romania was of vital importance to Hitler's war machine. At the time she possessed significant exploitable reserves of oil. As late as 1937 Germany's share in Romania's foreign trade was no greater than it had been in 1929.[40] It was the change in the European political balance rather than direct economic penetration which enabled what had already started to be more comprehensibly realized: an increase in Germany's influence. The *Anschluss* with Austria in March 1938 started the ball rolling south-eastwards and paved the way for German dominance of Romania's economy.[41] This was sealed by the signature on 23 March 1939 of the Wohltat Agreement. This treaty and the oil agreement of May 1940 increased Germany's share of Romania's imports to 51 per cent and of her exports to 44 per cent in 1940.[42]

The measures taken by the Germans to improve railways lines, to increase the numbers of locomotives and tank-cars, and to improve loading and unloading facilities along the route between Romania and Germany began to bear fruit in spring 1941, with the result that deliveries of oil to the Reich reached their height in that same year. After supplies had been interrupted by the freezing over of the Danube in the winter of 1940–1, and then again in April 1941, and because of the destruction of bridges and the danger of mines, stocks of oil had reached record levels in Romania at Giurgiu on the Danube and Constanţa on the Black Sea. From early summer exports of oil on a prodigious scale were resumed. Between July and October some 500,000 tons of fuel were delivered to Germany. During the whole year 3.9 million tons of petroleum products were exported by Romania, of which 2.9 million went to Germany and the German armies in Russia and in the Balkans. The rest was exported to Italy, Sweden, Switzerland and Turkey.[43]

In return for his territorial concessions made in summer 1940 Carol obtained Hitler's guarantee of protection but Romania was carved up to meet the Führer's needs and demands and it was too late to save his throne. One third of Romania's 1939 area was severed in 1940 and with it Romania's population fell from 19.9 million to 13.3 million.[44] In economic terms the territorial losses were crippling: 37 per cent of the arable land, 44 per cent of the forest land, 27 per cent of the orchards, and 37 per cent of the vineyards. Of the area given over to wheat (as of 1939) Romania lost 37 per cent, to maize 30 per cent, to sunflower 75 per cent, to hemp 43 per cent, and to soya 86 per cent.[45] On a human scale the loss of a population of whom half – some three millions – were ethnically Romanian, was too much for most Romanians to stomach.

Protests organized on 3 September by the anti-Semitic Iron Guard – which had never forgiven Carol for the assassination in November 1938 of its leader Corneliu Codreanu – led to the seizure of government buildings. Fearing a breakdown of order Wilhelm Fabricius, the German Minister in Bucharest, informed Berlin on 5 September that he had advised General Ion Antonescu, a former Minister of War, to demand dictatorial powers from the King.[46] We should not infer from this that the Antonescu regime was imposed by Germany. In fact, Antonescu's rise to power was brought about not by Fabricius but by 'German-friendly' elements among the ministers and royal councillors who surrounded the King.[47]

Fabricius' advice to Antonescu illustrated most clearly the degree to which Romania had fallen within the orbit of Germany. Carol accepted Antonescu's demand and on 5 September granted Antonescu, who enjoyed the respect of the Army, unlimited powers in the hope of restoring order and saving his throne. The Iron Guard was not satisfied and called for the King's abdication. Antonescu was driven to echo the demand and on the following day Carol gave way in favour of his son King Michael. On the same day, the new king, Michael, issued a decree granting Antonescu unlimited powers as the Leader of the Romanian State (*Conducătorul Statului Român*), thereby relegating himself to the position of a ceremonial figure. A further decree, signed by Michael two days later, defined Antonescu's powers. The *Conducător* had the authority to initiate and promulgate all laws and to modify those already in force; to appoint and dismiss ministers; and to conclude treaties, declare war and make peace.[48]

In order to govern, Antonescu turned to the principal political parties but both the major democratic parties – the National Liberals and the National Peasants – refused to participate. He was therefore thrown back on the Iron Guard for support, sympathy for which had grown considerably following the disasters of the summer, and whose political profile had been given a major boost when Carol included it in the Gigurtu government of 4 July.[49] A National Legionary State[50] was proclaimed on 14 September and in the cabinet formed on the following day Horia Sima, the leader of the Guard, was appointed Deputy Prime Minister. Five other ministries were given to Guard members, among them the Foreign Ministry and the Ministry of the Interior. A distant relative, Mihai Antonescu, was made Minister of Justice.

Antonescu made an extremely favourable impression on Hitler when he met the Führer for the first time in Berlin on 21 November 1940, according to Paul Schmidt, Hitler's interpreter, despite the Romanian leader's two-hour rant against the Vienna Award.[51] He was not afraid to express his bitterness over the Award, while in subsequent meetings his experience as a military commander sometimes put Hitler on the defensive. The Führer's personal regard for Antonescu contrasted sharply with the reservations he had for the bombastic and militarily-inexperienced Mussolini. Yet behind this respect for the Romanian leader lay a more pragmatic assessment, expressed by

Hermann Goering: 'One must be very cautious with Antonescu. He is quite a stubborn mule but the only one in Romania who sticks to a pro-German line.'[52]

General Antonescu's alliance with the Iron Guard was basically a matter of convenience.[53] It was not long, however, before the Guard's lack of discipline, its penchant for violence, and its rigid anti-Semitism sowed the seeds of discord between Antonescu and Sima, and exasperated the Germans by compromising their attempts to increase their stranglehold over the Romanian economy. The Guard's pledge to revenge its murdered leader Codreanu was honoured when they stormed into the cells of Jilava prison on the night of 26–7 November and massacred 64 ministers, and senior police officers whom they held guilty of murdering Guardists. This lawlessness dismayed Antonescu and disquieted Hitler. Romania was of vital strategic importance in the Führer's plan to attack the Soviet Union and he wanted order and stability in the country.

Antonescu himself, concerned about the Guard's activities, requested a meeting with Hitler and he travelled to Obersalzburg to meet the Führer on 14 January 1941. Hitler told the Romanian leader that he was the only person in Romania who could cope with any situation but that it would be impossible to govern the country with the Iron Guard providing opposition. Antonescu would ultimately have to become the leader of the Guard and the best thing would be for this proposal to be put by Antonescu to the Guard itself.[54]

Antonescu felt sufficiently encouraged by the Führer's support for him to act against it. The opportunity was provided by the murder of Major Doering, an officer attached to the German Military Mission, on 19 January in Bucharest. Antonescu used the murder as the justification for the dismissal of the Guardist Minister of the Interior on the following day. At the same time he removed the Guardist head of the police, the chief of the Bucharest police, and the chief of the *Siguranţa*, the security police. All three refused to obey Antonescu's decree and on the following day, 21 January, the latter two barricaded themselves in the *Siguranţa* headquarters, together with a group of about fifty Guardists, and opened fire on the troops who had been sent to eject them. The shots marked the beginning of the Iron Guard uprising.

The revolt was largely confined to Bucharest but the Guardists did not limit themselves to defending their positions in public buildings. During the morning of 22 January, they moved against defenceless Jews, looting and burning their homes, and cold-bloodedly murdering 120 of them.[55] That same afternoon Antonescu ordered the army to use tanks against the barricaded Guardists and by the evening most of the buildings had been retaken. Twenty-one soldiers were killed in the operations. Acting through Hermann Neubacher[56] with Antonescu, Sima accepted Neubacher's dictation of cease-fire terms to which Antonescu also agreed. Some Guardists laid down their arms, while others took refuge in the houses of German officials from where they were smuggled to Germany. Sima, according to the Romanian Secret Service, was hidden in Neubacher's car and driven to the German legation in Sofia, from where he was taken to Germany in an army truck.

On 27 January 1941, after unsuccessfully approaching the National Peasant Party leader Iuliu Maniu, and the National Liberal head Constantin Brătianu, Antonescu appointed a new cabinet formed almost entirely of officers. By bringing military discipline to government he hoped to avoid the rifts of the past. Precisely the Guard's indiscipline, and its treachery, ruled it out as a partner. A decree-law was introduced on 5 February outlawing any unauthorized political organization. The death penalty would apply to any person found in possession of arms without authorization. The National Legionary State was dissolved on 14 February and a massive operation was launched to round up those who had taken part in the uprising. To all intents and purposes a military dictatorship was established under Antonescu and was given the rubber-stamp of a popular plebiscite at the beginning of March 1941.

3

The Drift into Germany's Orbit: Romania, 1938–1941

Romania was driven into alliance with Nazi Germany by fear of the Soviet Union. 'Nothing could put Romania on Germany's side', remarked a member of the Romanian Foreign Ministry to the British Minister Sir Reginald Hoare in March 1940, 'except the conviction that only Germany could keep the Soviets out of Romania.'[1] That conviction was quick to form after the collapse of France in May 1940, the Soviet seizure from Romania of Bessarabia and Northern Bukovina at the end of June, and the loss of Northern Transylvania to Hungary under the Vienna Award in late August. One third of Romania's 1939 area was ceded in 1940 and with it Romania's population fell from 19.9 million to 13.3 million. The loss of the three territories led King Carol II to accept Hitler's frontier guarantee, one which he gave only after Carol's agreement to the Vienna Award.

In a broader sense, Romania's alliance with Germany between 1940 and 1944 was generated by the disintegration of the European order established after the First World War and by the threat posed by the Soviet Union to Romania's territorial integrity.[2] That threat became reality when Romania bowed to a Soviet ultimatum, issued on 26 June 1940, for the annexation of Bessarabia and Northern Bukovina on pain of the use of force.

The First World War had given Romania a chance to gain the predominantly Romanian-populated province of Transylvania, then under Hungarian rule, and the region of Bukovina[3] which Austria had acquired in 1775. The Allied Powers offered both territories to Romania in return for her entry into the war on the side of the Entente. This she did in August 1916, and it says much about the strength of character of King Ferdinand that he signed a declaration of war against his country of birth. Romania was duly rewarded at the Paris Peace Conference with Transylvania and Bukovina, despite her defection from the war in April 1918 when she was forced to sign a peace treaty with Germany. Two months earlier Romanian troops, profiting from the disintegration of the Russian army in the wake of the Bolshevik revolution, had occupied the province of Bessarabia, annexed by Russia in 1812. The union of Bessarabia with Romania, proclaimed by representatives of the

Romanian majority in the province on 27 March 1918, was confirmed by the Paris Peace Treaties. It was not, however, accepted by the Soviet Union.

The enlarged Romanian state, *România Mare* (Great Romania), encompassed virtually all ethnic Romanians. It also included, however, significant Slav, German, Hungarian and Bulgarian minorities. By the same token, Romania's leaders linked the integrity of her new borders to the maintenance of, and respect for, the new international order consecrated by the Peace Settlement. Defence of the European status quo thus became the cornerstone of inter-war foreign policy pursued by all Romanian governments until the Munich agreement of 1938. There were three bases to this policy: alliance with the other post-1919 states that shared a common interest with Romania in opposing frontier revision; collaboration with France, the strongest Western continental military power; and support for and participation in the League of Nations which guaranteed the territorial integrity of its members.

These three features of Romanian foreign policy were harmonized by Nicolae Titulescu.[4] In doing so he demonstrated that a small country's interests could be defended just as effectively with accomplished diplomacy as with military power. On being appointed Foreign Minister in October 1932, Titulescu's experience of, and faith in, the League guided his hand in his conduct of Romanian policy – he had been elected President of the 11th Ordinary Session of the League on 10 September 1930 and re-elected in 1931. Convinced that his country's security was dependent on the maintenance of international order he sought to consolidate the Little Entente, formed in 1921 by Romania with Czechoslovakia and Yugoslavia as a deterrent against Hungarian revisionism.

'Revisionism means war' became a catch-phrase of Titulescu, uttered with increasing frequency after the rise of Hitler who advocated revision of the Versailles treaties. Hitler's challenge to the status quo encouraged Hungary to press her claims to Transylvania and it was to counter the danger posed by Hitler to European peace that Titulescu then took action. He advocated the creation of a system of collective security based on France, which had the largest army in Europe, and the Soviet Union, and it was he who helped to bring about the mutual assistance pact between Moscow and Paris in May 1935. Titulescu hoped that this agreement would form the nucleus of a large coalition of anti-revisionist states to hold Hitler in check and to this end he took Romania down the road to an alliance with the Soviet Union.

The main stumbling block to such an alliance was the Bessarabian question. Soviet intransigence mollified sufficiently for Moscow to sign the Kellogg-Briand Pact in 1928 which outlawed war as an instrument of national policy. On the initiative of the Soviet government a supplementary protocol was signed in Moscow on 9 February 1929, by which the Soviet Union and its western neighbours, including Romania, agreed to put the pact into effect at once, without waiting for the other states to ratify it.

In June 1934 an exchange of letters between Titulescu and Maxim Litvinov, Soviet Commissar for Foreign Relations, marked the resumption of diplomatic relations between the two countries and paved the way for Titulescu to seek a defensive alliance with the Soviet Union. Consequently, in September 1935 Titulescu began discussions with Litvinov over the conclusion of a Soviet-Romanian Treaty of Mutual Assistance.

The international situation, however, turned against him. Titulescu's condemnation of the Italian invasion of Abyssinia in the autumn of 1935 and of the German occupation of the Rhineland in March 1936, as violations of the Covenant of the League of Nations, made him an enemy of both these states, and led Mussolini to call for his dismissal. To add to Titulescu's problems, the Rhineland occupation exposed France's weakness. It denied French forces easy access to the Danube, which underwrote Romania's security, and caused Romanian politicians to question the wisdom of pursuing an alliance with the Soviet Union which, because of the feebleness of France, might bring Romania into dependence on her powerful eastern neighbour.

Titulescu was himself aware of this danger and therefore when he and Litvinov agreed, on 21 July 1936, upon the general principles of the Soviet-Romanian pact, the question of its subordination to the Franco-Soviet alliance was the only article that divided the two foreign ministers. Titulescu argued that the pact should come into force only if France acted on the Franco-Soviet Treaty, but Litvinov disagreed. Titulescu was unable to extract from Litvinov *de jure* recognition of Romania's sovereignty over Bessarabia and before he could proceed further he was dismissed by King Carol II who shared his ministers' concern about a close association with the Soviet Union. Romanian foreign policy, with its principal pillar of France severely undermined and its architect of an accommodation with the Soviet Union removed, now sought to navigate its way between the competing interests of the Western allies and Germany.

The blows delivered by Mussolini and Hitler in 1936 to the prestige of the League of Nations, and to the principles of collective security and defence of the post-war territorial settlement, were only the first shocks to the European order upon which Romania had based her interwar foreign policy. The event which shattered that order was the Munich Agreement of 30 September 1938, as a result of which Hitler succeeded in imposing his own revision of European frontiers. The occupation of Prague in March 1939 allowed Germany, through its takeover of all Czechoslovak commercial and foreign investments, to extend its economic dominance throughout South-East Europe, a dominance which it had achieved through the *Anschluss* via the Austrian banking system. Romania's contracts with the Skoda arms company made Germany, at a stroke, Romania's principal arms supplier. Furthermore, since these arms were supplied from German-controlled Czechoslovakia, there was no need for Hitler to divert output to the Romanian army from German factories.[5]

During Carol's state visit to London in November 1938 he tried unsuccessfully to counter German economic influence by putting forward proposals to the British for assistance to Romania based on credits and investments, but the British did not consider these economically sound. On his way back to Romania Carol visited Hitler in order to assure him of his country's equitable policy. The King wanted good commercial relations with Germany but was concerned about Germany's position regarding Hungarian claims to Transylvania. Hitler, too, was anxious to extend trade between the two countries, but remained evasive about the Transylvanian question, realizing that German support on this issue gave him a vital lever of influence over both Hungary and Romania. Carol also discussed with Field Marshal Goering proposals for long-term economic collaboration between Germany and Romania and in contrast to his failure with the British, found the Germans only too anxious to take matters further.[6]

Romania thus found herself in a position of uncertainty after Munich. She was exposed to growing Hungarian pressure over Transylvania, was apprehensive of the Soviet Union's motives concerning Bessarabia, and, given the weakness of France, could no longer rely on the security of the Little Entente. Defenceless against German pressure, King Carol sought to come to an accommodation with Hitler by making economic concessions. This shift in policy, discernible following the Munich Agreement, was confirmed by the appointment of Grigore Gafencu as Foreign Minister in December 1938. He was determined to pursue a German guarantee of Romania's territorial integrity in return for Romanian economic concessions.[7] Hence, in February 1939, Helmuth Wohlthat went to Bucharest to open negotiations on a German-Romanian economic agreement. In order to strengthen the Romanian bargaining position Gafencu, using a decision in February of the British government to follow up Carol's November visit by sending a limited economic mission to Romania, suggested to the Germans that Britain was a serious rival to them. On 10 March Wohlthat submitted new, tougher proposals which were tantamount to the subordination of Romanian industry and agriculture to the economic needs of Germany.

Alarmed by the hardening of the German position, and by the entry of German troops into Prague on 15 March, Viorel Tilea, the Romanian Minister to London, informed the Foreign Secretary Lord Halifax on 17 March that his government had been asked to give Germany a monopoly of Romanian exports and to adapt industrial production in return for a guarantee of the country's borders. 'This', opined Tilea, 'seemed to the Romanian government something very much like an ultimatum.'[8] Fearing that Germany would seize Romania's oil both Britain and France gave guarantees to Romania on 13 April.[9] The Anglo-French guarantee was, as Carol and Gafencu had wished, unilateral in nature. It obliged the West to protect Romania against aggression provided Romania defended herself in the event of attack, but the Romanians were not bound to help Britain or France if they were attacked.[10]

The Anglo-French move was primarily political. German preponderance in Romanian affairs was confirmed by the signature on 23 March of the German-Romanian economic treaty which bound the Romanian economy more closely to that of Germany and under the terms of which the Germans undertook to supply the Romanian armed forces with arms and equipment and to provide assistance to Romania in cultivating foodstuffs and oilseeds, and in establishing new industries for processing agricultural products, all of which were of interest to the German economy. As far as possible, Romania 'struggled to keep the Reich from obtaining too favourable a rate of exchange and to retain as large a share as possible of its exports for the free world market'.[11] The agreement did not prevent Gafencu from professing his continued faith in a policy of neutrality or 'equilibrium', as he liked to term it, in a speech before the Chamber of Deputies in Bucharest on 29 June 1939:

> It is a principle with us not to seek the support of one of the two great neighbouring Powers in turning against the other, in order to give no pretext for conflict on our frontiers or on our territory. This principle is of service to our interest, to those of our neighbours, and to the general interests of peace. A strong and independent Romania is, for the States that surround us, a guarantee of security.[12]

The maintenance of that 'equilibrium' rested on the tension between Nazi Germany and the Soviet Union, for the states of Eastern Europe represented a buffer zone between the two great dictatorships and the status quo of the area was dependent on the mutual suspicion felt by Hitler and Stalin. That status quo, the underpinning of Romanian policy, was shattered by the signing of the Nazi-Soviet Pact of Non-Aggression, also known as the Molotov-Ribbentrop Pact after the names of the German and Soviet Foreign Ministers who signed it on 23 August 1939. Under the terms of the Pact Hitler claimed to have 'definitely sealed' the peace between the German Reich and the Soviet Union by establishing 'precisely and for all time' the respective zones of interest of the two Powers.

Hardly had the ink dried on the document before first Hitler, on 1 September, and then Stalin, sixteen days later, attacked Poland and partitioned it. With their country on its knees, the Polish government and army command withdrew to Romania where King Carol had given a promise of sanctuary. During the early hours of the following morning, Marshal Edward Smigly-Rydz, the head of the armed forces, crossed the Czeremosz bridge onto Romanian territory and was placed in confinement in Craiova. The Romanian government allowed seventy tons of gold belonging to the Bank of Poland to reach the port of Constanţa where it was loaded into a ship and transferred to France via Syria.[13] President Ignacy Moscicki was sent to Bicaz and other members of the government to isolated localities such as Slanic and Băile Herculane.[14] They were joined by some 26,000 Polish citizens, 15,000 of whom were civilians, according to Romanian archival sources.[15]

On 30 November 1939 the Soviet Union attacked Finland. The latter's defeat in the middle of March 1940 added further weight to those in the Romanian government who advocated still greater ties with Germany as a guarantee against attacks on their territorial integrity. At the same time, the provisions of the German-Romanian economic treaty of 23 March 1939 were beginning to be translated into action. Several German-Romanian companies for the exploitation of Romania's resources were founded.[16] Gafencu still sought equilibrium. He urged the government to 'save by all our means our political and economic neutrality, and in the same way as we have managed for many months, not weaken our positions whether by imprudent or provocative words and attitudes towards Germany, or by unfriendly words and postures towards the Western Powers, or by renunciation of any valuable element of our independence'.[17] But the re-opening of the issue of Bessarabia by the Soviets and events in Scandinavia took the ground from under his feet.

Two further events persuaded many Romanians that the writing was on the wall regarding their sovereignty. First, on 29 March 1940, Molotov, the Soviet Commissar for Foreign Relations, officially rekindled the Bessarabian question by declaring before the Supreme Soviet that the Soviet Government had never recognized the occupation of the province by Romania, and second, on 9 April the Germans invaded Denmark and Norway, two more neutral countries which, like Romania, had tried to come to an understanding with Hitler. King Carol's neutrality was becoming more precarious under the impact of German military successes and Soviet pressure, and also because of Anglo-French efforts to disrupt oil supplies to Germany by acts of sabotage on the Danube which constituted an infringement of Romania's neutrality. The bungling of these attempts in April, made with the acquiescence of some members of the Romanian General Staff, compromised the Romanians in German eyes and exposed them to the risk of an invasion against which the British and French were powerless, in Romanian eyes, to provide help.[18]

The French, nevertheless, did contemplate military aid. At the end of March General Weygand, commander of French forces in the eastern Mediterranean, sent a representative to Bucharest to sound out the Romanians about the possibility of sending a French expeditionary air force. This project was vague and uncoordinated with the British. The French troops were in Syria and the Turkish government was disinclined to allow them to cross Turkey. The logistical problems were horrendous. The whole idea alarmed the Romanian General Staff who feared that the Germans would act pre-emptively against them. Gafencu responded by reassuring the

Germans that he would resist all Anglo-French efforts to draw Romania into the war and that the Germans need not invade Romania to secure their supplies of oil.[19]

The German offensive in the West on 10 May 1940 against Holland and Belgium, in violation of their neutrality, radically changed King Carol's assessment of his position and marked the end of Romanian neutrality. The choice was no longer between Germany and the Western Powers. The rapid German victories in Holland, Belgium and France stunned the Romanians who regarded every defeat for the Allies as an argument for closer association with Germany. From the middle of May, Hungary and the Soviet Union began deploying troops along their borders with Romania and the Romanian High Command responded in kind. Bereft of any hope of Anglo-French help against his neighbours' territorial pretensions, King Carol turned decidedly towards Germany.

On 15 May he told Wilhelm Fabricius, the German Minister to Bucharest, that 'Romania's future depended solely upon Germany' and five days later Prime Minister Gheorghe Tătărescu let Fabricius know that Romania was ready to align its foreign policy with Germany in return for an assurance against Russia.[20] On 24 May Baron Manfred von Killinger, Hitler's special envoy to Bucharest, had a meeting with Colonel Mihai Moruzov, head of the Romanian Intelligence Service (SSI). Killinger's mission was to follow the activity of the British Secret Service in South-East Europe and Moruzov was a person with whom he felt he could collaborate.[21] The opinions expressed by Killinger to Moruzov were his own and no instructions had been given to him to bring them to the attention of the Romanian government. Yet given his status, he must have known that they would be passed on by Moruzov to Carol. Killinger recognized that

> there is, on the one hand, a climate of opinion which is very favourable to Britain and France since the abiding conviction is that the creation of Greater Romania [Romania post-1918] is due exclusively to these countries and that, in the future, the fate of Romania will also be in the hands of the allies. On the other hand, there is an atmosphere which is unfavourable to close relations with Germany, either because of memories of the last war, or because of certain intentions which are attributed today to Germany.
>
> I am convinced, however, the reality is different. In the first place, although Britain and France perhaps contributed to the national claims of Romania, I see no possibility of their helping Romania today. On the contrary, by entering a war alongside the allies, Romania can only lose out. Romania is today surrounded by enemies: Hungary, Bulgaria and the Soviet Union. If it can deal with the first two on its own, there is no way it can cope with the Bolshevik torrent.
>
> [...]

> Germany considers that there are two enemies. Enemy number 1: The allies who will attack the oil fields and installations from the air from bases in Greece or Turkey, from a distance of two or three hours' flying time. Enemy number 2: the Soviet Union which, in order to realize the pan-Slav idea, will attack Romania not only to retake Bessarabia, but in order to unite with the Slavs in the Balkan peninsula. In this scenario Romania will be devastated, including the oil fields, of course, if these have not already been destroyed by the Romanians. Obviously, in both cases, Romania will not be able to offer resistance for long. The only course is for the conclusion of an official bond with Germany which is both correct and certain, and which is the only one which can absolutely guarantee Romania's territorial integrity.[22]

On 28 May Tătărescu informed Fabricius that its friendly relations with Germany were 'based on active collaboration with Germany in all domains' and expressed 'the hope of the Romanian government that the framework of friendly collaboration with the government of the Reich would be extended'.[23] He drew the Reich's attention to the recent concentrations by its neighbours of troops on Romania's frontiers which threatened the peace of the region. The German reply of 2 June was a momentous blow. Instead of offering advice, Joachim von Ribbentrop, the German Foreign Minister, asked the Romanians whether they would be ready to make territorial concessions to their neighbours, particularly to the Russians.[24] Carol was taken aback. While expressing willingness to enter into discussions with the Soviet Union over the conclusion of a pact of non-aggression, Carol was unwilling to consider the cession of Bessarabia and underlined this by stressing, through Tătărescu on 20 June, the importance for Germany of a strong Romanian state, guardian of the River Dniester and of the mouths of the Danube.[25]

What Carol did not know, of course, was that Germany had already recognized the Soviet claim to Bessarabia in the supplementary secret annex to the Nazi-Soviet Non-Aggression Pact. Article 3 of the annex read: 'with regard to South-Eastern Europe, the Soviet side emphasizes its interest in Bessarabia; the German side declares complete political *désintéressement* in these territories'.[26] Hitler's magnanimity in conceding the Soviet interest in Bessarabia was founded on an optimistic assessment of German power and Soviet weakness in South-Eastern Europe, a view reflected in the prediction made by the German military attaché in Bucharest in December 1939 that 'the Russians will not occupy Bessarabia as long as Germany is strong enough. However, should we suffer a serious setback, or have all our forces engaged, Russia might take advantage of a rare opportunity which might not occur for a long time.'[27]

The accuracy of the attaché's forecast was borne out by events. Shortly before midnight on 26 June, when German forces were completing their victorious sweep through France, Molotov summoned the Romanian Minister in Moscow, Davidescu, to the Kremlin and presented an ultimatum demanding that Romania should cede Bessarabia and Northern Bukovina to the Soviet Union. The Soviet note called for a reply from the Romanian government within 24 hours. The Romanians appealed to the Germans for help but Berlin responded by advising Bucharest to accept the conditions set by Moscow. Carol had before him the example of Poland where war against either the Soviet Union or Germany might lead to the intervention of the other and to the partition of the country. Most of the King's advisors were against resistance and he acceded to the Soviet demands.

From the lost provinces, Bessarabia in particular, came tales of humiliation and injury inflicted on the retreating Romanians by the Russian population and especially by the Jews who had scores to settle with their former masters over anti-Semitic legislation. In the summer of 1938 General Nicolae Ciupercă, commander of the Third Army, and as such responsible for law and order in Bessarabia, had forbidden the use of Russian in public in Chişinău. He did this on the spurious grounds that only the Jews used Russian.[28] In fact there were in Chişinău nearly as many Russians eager to use their own language as Jews. The resentment Ciupercă and his kind had sown through their intolerance towards non-Romanians in Bessarabia – the Romanian mayor of Chişinău banned samovars from the teashops of the city in July 1938 – was now visited, indiscriminately and with interest, on Romanian troops, officials and civilians as they hastened to leave the province. Passions were stoked by the major Romanian dailies which ran emotional eyewitness accounts of events in the Bessarabian capital. An example was the report carried by *Universul* on 1 July from its Bessarabian correspondent:

> Thursday [27 June], at 6 am I was at the headquarters of the Third Romanian army corps... At 7 am it was announced officially 'Soviet troops will enter at 2 pm.' In the town, it was difficult to find any means of transport to the station, which was about four kilometers from the centre of town. Columns of refugees, each with a bundle of belongings in their hand, mothers carrying children in their arms and dragging others, their eyes clouded with tears, hastening their steps with a single objective in mind: the station.

The correspondent, Elefterie Negel, took the last train out of Chişinău the destination of which was Galaţi. His portrayal of the events en route was coloured with religious overtones redolent of a holy war between Christianity and Communism:

> Before entering the first station after Chişinău, thick columns of smoke rose in sacrifice towards the heavens... We picked out the Mazarache church, with its Romanian heritage. It was thus that the Jewish

> Communists began their wicked deeds against the holy sites. In the compartment next door a women is on her knees uttering prayers accompanied by curses against the pagans who had been cosseted for so long at the generous breast of the [Romanian] people.[29]

Emphasis was given in Romanian military bulletins to the behaviour of Jewish Communists as the Soviet army arrived in the two provinces. Romanian officers in Soroca were 'stripped of their insignia of rank by Jews while Soviet soldiers looked on'.[30] The commander of the frontier troops in Cernăuţi informed his superiors in Bucharest that at the moment the order for Romanian withdrawal was given, 'the Jews launched themselves into anti-Romanian protests, tearing and spitting on the *tricolor* and climbing onto the monument to union with Romania where they hoisted the red flag'.[31]

Other army reports came in of water and refuse being thrown at the departing Romanians, of Romanian officers being spat upon, of having their epaulettes ripped off, and in some cases of being beaten by Jews. The head of the Soviet police in Chilia Nouă was 'the Jew Dr Rabinovici'; the Soviet newspapers which appeared in Chişinău after the Soviet occupation were run by 'Jewish editors'; at Ismail, 'the millers and bakers all Jews, refused to produce bread the day before the Soviet ultimatum, spreading the rumour immediately after the announcement of the ultimatum that the shortage of bread was due to the fact that the flour had been requisitioned by the [Romanian] army'. In Bukovina, the arms dump in Rădăuţi was attacked 'by a group of Jews', and at Gura Humorului, 'the Jews confiscated cars to prevent the Romanians from leaving'.[32]

Carol II reflected the reactions of many of his subjects as reports of the withdrawal reached Bucharest. In his diary entry for Friday 28 June he wrote:

> The first items of news to reach us are very sad, the behavior of the population in Bessarabia, especially that of the Jews, leaves much to be desired. The columns of refugees and trains were attacked by Communist hordes, which delayed even more the opportunity – ridiculously short as it was – for evacuation.[33]

Two days later he noted: 'The news from Bessarabia is still sad ... Many of the leaders of the Front for National Revival [Carol's party] have shown themselves to be completely Bolshevized, being the first to have received the Soviet troops with red flags and flowers'.[34] That most of the local officials who turned Communist after the Soviet annexation were Romanian is borne out by Romanian army investigations which showed that before the Soviets began their campaign of deportations from the province, there were 505 Communist officials who were Romanian, and only 69 Jews.[35] Such evidence points to a broader range of sympathy for Communism in Bessarabia;

it undoubtedly attracted support from amongst Jews, but it also found favour amongst the Russian, Ukrainian, and even Romanian populations. In a number of towns the local minority populations were reported by the army to have joined in the humiliation of the Romanian troops:

> In Bolgrad, people gathered in groups at the appearance of Soviet aircraft and demonstrated their support. The same thing happened in other places in Bessarabia, the minority population being encouraged by the Russian motorized troops. The Bulgarian population in Bolgrad attacked the Romanians left in the town.[36]

These facts were completely overlooked in the Romanian press and in Romanian military reports where it was solely the Jews who were blamed for the victimization of the Romanian army. Also ignored was the destruction by the Communists of shops in the two provinces which were owned by the predominantly Jewish middle class. Instead, official opprobrium and popular hostility was heaped upon Jews, irrespective of whether they had Communist sympathies or not. As a result, anti-Semitic feeling reached new heights, causing the General Staff to express its concern over 'reprisals' by Romanians against the Jews. In Bucharest, bars and cafes were closed early on government orders to avoid anti-Jewish 'excesses' by segments of the population. The potential for violence was recognized in a US legation telegram to the State Department of 12 July which advised that 'Rumanians in general seem to wish to wreak their wrath either actively or passively on the Jews for the events which have taken place in Bessarabia'.[37]

It was in the ranks of the Romanian army itself that vengeance had first been unleashed on the Jews. Inflamed by the reports of the humiliation visited upon the retreating troops, some Romanian soldiers exacted their revenge on 1 July 1940, when fifty-two Jews were shot in Dorohoi town by Romanian troops as they withdrew from the district of Herţa. An official investigation into the deaths revealed that the shootings took place during the burial of a Romanian officer in the local Christian cemetery and whilst a number of Jews were at their own cemetery burying a Jewish soldier. At a certain moment a salvo of shots was heard at the Christian cemetery which the mourners took to be in honour of the fallen officer, but the gunfire increased in intensity, creating panic since those assembled thought the Russians had arrived. Everyone dispersed, leaving the coffin in the middle of the cemetery.

In fact, the shots had been fired by soldiers from two regiments retreating from Herţa who, allegedly humiliated by Jews there, were out to exact their revenge by shooting at the mourners in the Jewish cemetery. The investigation surmised that the 'reprisals' had been planned because some soldiers went straight to the houses of Jews after the first shots were fired, whilst in the houses of Romanians ikons had been placed in the windows or crosses painted on the walls in various colours as a signal to the soldiers not to fire. According to the report, forty-seven bodies had been identified; fifteen were found in the Jewish cemetery, those of five Jewish soldiers were found nearby, while the rest were scattered throughout houses and on the streets.[38]

Isolated incidents of reprisals against Jews also occurred in Moldavia. On 30 June a Jewish soldier was murdered by other soldiers. On the following day, four Jews were shot by a gendarmerie officer in Şerbăuţi. On the same day, seven Jews were seen leaving Dolhasca station under the escort of two soldiers and a junior officer – after entering a wood the Jews were shot. Several more were thrown from trains between Paşcani and Lespezi on 2 July – four were killed and five were badly injured and the perpetrators were not identified.[39] It was not only Jews who were the target of hostility: a Romanian soldier of Russian background was also cast out of a train.[40]

While most Jews in Bessarabia and Northern Bukovina were doubtless pleased to see the back of the Romanians, in the rest of Romania the Jewish population found itself saddled with a sense of guilt. The cession of the two provinces separated the Jewish population of Romania by placing it in two states hostile to each other. The shameful retreat from the two provinces inflamed anti-Semitic feeling in the country, forced the abdication of Carol, and the ascent to power of the Iron Guard. Shortly after the withdrawal, the leaders of the Jewish community strove to protect its members from an expected wave of violence by dissociating itself from the Jews of Bessarabia and Northern Bukovina, and issuing fiery declarations of loyalty to the Romanian state. Horia Carp, the secretary general of the Jewish community, wrote in an editorial:

> We only know from rumours ugly deeds which allegedly occurred during the withdrawal from Bessarabia and northern Bukovina, deeds committed by some of the inhabitants of the evacuated territories, amongst whom there were also allegedly Jews. We do not know to what extent the rumours are true, nor to what degree the Jews of Bessarabia participated in the reprehensible events that were committed there. But whatever the truth, what blame do we bear for these acts of wild madness, perpetrated by people who were born and lived under a different rule, who did not have time to bind themselves spiritually to the [Romanian] people and the country, and with whom we do not have, and cannot have, any sympathy in deeds which are alien to our faith and to our historical tradition, in any time and in any place destiny has cast us?[41]

The official expression of the Jewish community's attitude regarding the loss of Bessarabia and Northern Bukovina appeared under the signatures of Wilhelm Filderman, the President of the Jewish Federation, and of the Chief Rabbi, Alexander Şafran. It placed the accent on the Jews' sacrifices for and contribution to the creation of the Romanian nation state:

> The Jews in the Old Kingdom – native Romanian Jews – born and raised in generations on the land of Romania, are and remain bound

> wholeheartedly to the Romanian soil, soil generously watered with the blood of their best sons, fallen in the War of Independence of 1877, in that of 1913, and in the Great War of 1916–1918. Their ideals have always meshed with those of all Romanians, and whatever may happen, and whatever they may endure, as always they are ready to be alongside the Romanian people, in understanding of their destiny which binds them inextricably to this land.[42]

True as these details were, they had little impact on the officers and men of the Romanian army of 1940. The whole anti-Semitic argument rested on a total denial of these facts. The army's experience in Bessarabia in late June completely undermined the efforts of the Jewish community in Romania proper to create a bond. Even before the territorial losses of summer 1940, the leaders of the community had launched a subscription campaign for the army, publishing in each issue of their newspapers *Curierul israelit* and *Tribuna evreiască* an appeal for money 'for equipping the army' and a series of observations critical of those who were slow to respond.[43] As a result of the hostility shown towards it during the withdrawal – a hostility ascribed by the army solely to Jews – the army become totally infused with anti-Semitism. As if the supine surrender of the two provinces was not sufficient humiliation, the troops had to endure the insult and injury inflicted by Communist activists and sympathizers in the two provinces; within a year, several in the ranks of the army were to seize the opportunity to play out their prejudices in murderous fashion.

The Soviet ultimatum of 26 June amounted to international blackmail. Her annexation of Romanian territory under the threat of using force implied a readiness to commit acts outlawed by the two conventions for the Definition of Aggression, signed on 3 and 4 July 1933, to which both the Soviet Union and Romania were signatories.[44] Romania acquiesced to the Soviet demands in an exchange of notes. The new status of Bessarabia and Northern Bukovina, irrespective of all preceding legality, was therefore, from an international legal standpoint, based on a formal agreement contained in this exchange of notes, consenting to the retrocession of Bessarabia and the cession of Northern Bukovina.[45] What was not consented to by the Romanian side was the Soviet Union's annexation of the district of Herţa in Northern Moldavia, for it was not mentioned in the text of the ultimatum, nor her occupation of four islands at the mouth of the Danube in autumn 1940.

Attached to the ultimatum was a small map on which the ceded territories were marked by a thick red line drawn in pencil. Not only did the thickness of the line (covering a seven-mile wide band on the map) cause confusion as to which localities fell on the Soviet side, but the roughness of the pencil stroke cut across the north-eastern corner of Moldavia and the town of Herţa. Despite Romanian protests that this area was not mentioned in the ultimatum, the Soviet representatives on the Romanian-Soviet Commission established in Odessa to supervise its application insisted that the town, which hosted a strategic railway link, was part of the ceded areas and Soviet troops occupied it.

The frontier imposed upon Romania by the Soviet Union was by no means the ethnic line between Romanians and Ukrainians and the claim in the ultimatum that Bessarabia was principally peopled by Ukrainians was wildly inaccurate. Even the census taken in 1897 – while the province was under Russian rule – could not be adduced to bring the slightest support to the ultimatum's contention.[46] The Soviet claim to that part of Bukovina 'where the predominant majority of the population is connected with the Soviet Ukraine by common historical destinies' was less spurious, despite its formulation which invited the charge of writing history backwards. Although Bukovina had never formed part of the Russian Empire, and its total population, according to the 1930 Romanian census, contained a majority of Romanians,[47] in the northern part demanded by the Soviet Union there was an absolute Ukrainian majority.[48]

The total area ceded by Romania to the Soviet Union covered 50,762 square kilometres and contained a population of just under 3.78 million, of whom more than half, 2.02 million, were Romanian.[49] Losses of men and equipment were communicated to London by the British military attaché, Lt. Col. Geoffrey Macnab. He concluded that the 'withdrawal was in general very poorly executed and many units never received orders'. As a result, there had been 'about 75 court-martials of officers for cowardice and inefficiency', the only details of which to emerge were the dismissal of the Commander of the 21st division, and the reduction to half pay of Ilcuş, the Minister of Defence.[50] Fearful of what might befall them under Soviet rule, most of the civil population took the painful decision to leave with the Romanian troops but because of the short deadline given by the Soviets for the withdrawal of the army, they were forced to abandon their belongings. Even with the possessions they had, some of the Romanian refugees were attacked by armed groups of local Communists and robbed.

The first steps to provide aid were taken by the Romanian Red Cross. It instructed its local branches – there were fifty-four throughout the country – to set up canteens in the stations and on the routes along which the refugees were directed. Those from southern Bessarabia were placed in temporary encampments in the region of Topoloveni to the north-west of Bucharest and in the county of Prahova; those from the northern part were quartered in the area of Târgu-Ocna and Bacău, while the refugees from Bukovina were sheltered in the region of Piatra Neamţ. A nationwide appeal was made for money, clothing and food to which private companies and institutions, as well as members of the public, contributed generously. On 6 July the government set up a refugee committee to work under the auspices of the Ministry of Internal Affairs. Special offices were set up in prefectures and town halls to register refugees, to designate encampments for their shelter, and to give them help in reaching their destination. The Ministry of Health was charged with ensuring adequate sanitation in the camps.[51]

In the meantime, the refugees were placed in schools, hostels, small hotels and rooms requisitioned from the public. Clothing and shoes were distributed by the Red Cross to the needy. Medical assistance and medicines were dispensed free of charge. Some idea of the scale of support given can be gained from the work of the Red Cross office in Iaşi which organized a canteen in the main railway station in the town. During the seven weeks from 25 June to 9 August it provided light meals for 6,577 refugees and gave first aid to over 2,000 people.[52] The plight of the refugees proved relatively short-lived. After the reconquest of Bessarabia and Northern Bukovina by the German and Romanian armies in July 1941, the great majority returned to their homes.

In the changed power configuration of 1940 the Soviet Union felt able to disregard the Romanian frontiers which had been decided by the Allies at the Paris Peace Settlement. Stalin looked to improve his defence position against Germany before Hitler made Romania a client state and advanced his defence line to the River Prut. But the rapacious and cynical manner in which the Soviet Union exercised its claim to Bessarabia and Northern Bukovina drove Romania into Germany's arms by leading King Carol to fear that Stalin might encroach further upon Romanian soil. He therefore quickly declared Romania's solidarity with Germany before obtaining a guarantee from Hitler of his country's territorial integrity.

On 1 July the Romanian government renounced the Anglo-French guarantee, its membership of the Balkan Entente and of the League of Nations, and Carol informed Fabricius, the German Minister in Bucharest, of his desire for a political agreement with the Reich, telling him that without German protection 'Romania is incapable of any action and is subject to Soviet Russian influence'.[53] On the following day, the King requested that a German Military Mission be sent to Romania to help train the army and air force.[54] Hitler now cleverly exploited his position. In a letter of 13 July he reminded Carol of his acceptance of the Anglo-French guarantee and made German protection conditional upon the settlement of the outstanding territorial disputes with Hungary and Bulgaria over Transylvania and Dobrogea which had been triggered by the cession of Bessarabia and Northern Bukovina.

At the height of the crisis over the Soviet ultimatum Carol had called in the German Minister von Killinger to protest at the pressure being placed upon him, not only by the Russians, but also by the Hungarians and Bulgarians:

> I fully realize that Germany can give me no support against Russia. But one thing she can do, and one act of friendship is worth another for

> the oil has continued to flow without interruption precisely during your Western offensive – namely call off Hungary and Bulgaria.[55]

Hungary's revisionist ambitions were closely linked with those of the Third Reich. Like Hitler, Hungary's leaders had never accepted the 'injustices' of the Paris Peace Settlement and therefore Hitler's advocacy of revision of the Versailles Treaty encouraged Hungary to press her claims to her lost territories. The first success of Hungary's pro-German policy was gained in November 1938 when, under the terms of the First Vienna Award, Hungary acquired part of southern Slovakia from Czechoslovakia. In March 1939 she was awarded Carpatho-Ruthenia and then concentrated her attention on Transylvania. Hungarian strategy was to coordinate the claim to Transylvania with Soviet agitation over Bessarabia.

A month after the issue of Bessarabia was raised in the Soviet press, the Hungarian chief of staff, General Henrik Werth, advised his government in a memorandum dated 12 December 1939 that in the case of a Soviet attack on Romania, Hungary should act to recover 'the whole of Transylvania'. He also instructed General Gabor Faragho, the Hungarian military attaché in Moscow, to discuss with the Soviet authorities the possibility of a coordinated attack against Romania.[56] Not content with its amputation of Romania by annexing Bessarabia and Northern Bukovina in June 1940, the Soviet Union backed Hungary's claims to Transylvania. On 11 July the Hungarian Minister to Moscow sent a report to Budapest of a discussion he had had with Molotov during which the Soviet Foreign Minister had made clear that the USSR considered Hungary's territorial demands towards Romania to be justified, and offered its support for them should a conference be called to resolve the issues.[57]

Hitler's stance over Transylvania was dictated by his need for stability in preparing Operation *Barbarossa* which was conceived with both Hungarian and Romanian participation. Whilst warning the Hungarian Prime Minister on 10 July not to expect any help from Germany should Hungary attack Romania, Hitler was worried about a joint Russian-Hungarian move against Romania which would threaten the oilfields and thus endanger his plans for Russia. He therefore offered his offices as mediator and negotiations between Hungary and Romania began on 10 August at Turnu-Severin. After ten days of stalemate Hitler imposed a settlement. The German Foreign Minister Joachim von Ribbentrop and his Italian counterpart, Count Galeazzo Ciano, invited both sides to Vienna and told them to accept the result of their arbitration.

On the question of the future of Transylvania, Romanians were virtually unanimous that it was in political, cultural and economic terms more important to the cohesion of the Romanian state than Bessarabia, notwithstanding the painful consequences of the loss of the province. This view was conveyed by Ion Gigurtu, the Romanian prime minister, in a letter to

Ribbentrop on 27 August 1940. Gigurtu explained that while Romanian public opinion had recognized the need to accept the Soviet ultimatum over Bessarabia and Northern Bukovina, on German advice, in order to avoid war with the Soviet Union, the cession of part of Transylvania was a completely different matter. 'Transylvania', he wrote, 'was always considered by us as a fortress of Romanianism, in which our nation... developed'. The decision to cede Bessarabia had been taken, he argued, in order to deflect revisionist claims on Transylvania where the Romanians 'have lived for eighteen centuries'.[58]

Carol and his ministers were concerned that rejection of arbitration would lead to a Hungarian attack and German occupation of the oilfields, which might in turn provoke a Russian invasion of eastern Romania. The King convened a Crown Council in which members of the Iron Guard and other pro-German ministers were now present, and it voted 19 to 10 with one abstention for the acceptance of arbitration. Those against preferred defeat to disgrace, those in favour stressed the need to prevent the complete disintegration of Romania. Carol cast his vote with the latter.

Ribbentrop was instrumental in drawing up the terms of the Award and he was driven by German strategic interests in doing so. By pushing the border of Hungary, which at this time was more closely linked to Germany than Romania, to the south-east Carpathian ridge, he gave the German army a natural defensive wall. At the same time, the new frontier ran only a few kilometres from the Romanian oilfields around Ploieşti, which were vital to Hitler's plan to attack the Soviet Union.[59] On the announcement of the Ribbentrop-Ciano adjudication on 30 August 1940, Mihail Manoilescu, the Romanian Foreign Minister, fainted on the table.[60] Under the terms of the Second Vienna Award, as it came to be known, Transylvania was virtually partitioned. Hungary received an area of roughly 43,000 square kilometres in the north of the province representing roughly 40 per cent of its area and a population of 2.6 million.[61]

The partition triggered an exodus of Romanians from northern Transylvania. According to figures compiled by the official body set up to give assistance to these refugees, some 110,000 passed through its hands up to September 1943. Most were former employees of the Romanian state who overnight found themselves without jobs, including university and school teachers. Many were soon placed in new positions in their respective ministries and in the educational system. Others were sent before local committees formed from the prefect, mayor and representatives of the Red Cross who were given the authority to requisition dwellings to house them. Every refugee was given a special identity card and assistance benefits until they found work. In order to qualify for continued receipt of the benefits after a period of ninety days, they were required to show that they had sought employment. Those who refused to take up a job offered were denied further assistance.[62]

Unlike the refugees from Bessarabia and Northern Bukovina, who were able to return to their homes in autumn 1941, those from northern Transylvania remained in exile until the return of the area to Romanian rule in spring 1945.[63] The plight of the peasant refugees was in many cases alleviated by the generosity of family and friends. This is not to say that they were forgotten by the Antonescu regime. In cabinet meetings measures addressing their problems were discussed and agreed, but they often proved ineffective. The situation of refugees in the county of Iaşi explains why. While the prefect managed to settle 1,719 out of 1,861 families of refugees in the period 1 July 1940 to 31 March 1941 (the vast majority from Bessarabia and Northern Bukovina, but 110 were from northern Transylvania), he was not able to rent out land to them. The land in question had been confiscated from Jews under the law. Of the 2,922 hectares involved, only 254 hectares were being farmed by refugee tenant farmers. The reason, the prefect explained, was the inability of the prospective tenants to raise the necessary funds, which was due in turn to the difficulties they faced in obtaining loans from the state.[64]

The Bulgarian territorial claim was settled without controversy. Southern Dobrogea, an area of almost 7,000 square kilometres where only about twenty-five per cent of the population was Romanian, was returned to Bulgaria under an agreement signed on 21 August and ratified by the treaty of Craiova on 7 September. The return was accompanied by an exchange of population: Romanian subjects of Bulgarian origin in the counties of Tulcea and Constanţa in northern Dobrogea were transferred to Durostor and Caliacra in southern Dobrogea, while the Romanians in the latter counties were moved in their place. Bulgaria also undertook to compensate the departing Romanians for their loss of property.[65] According to the figures of the joint Romanian-Bulgarian commission for the transfer, 103,711 Romanians were moved from southern Dobrogea and 62,278 Bulgarians settled from northern Dobrogea.[66]

The territorial losses sustained by Romania in summer 1940 defined the strategic goals set by Antonescu on his accession to power in September of that year. At his third meeting with the Führer in Munich on 12 June 1941 – the first had taken place in Berlin on 21 November 1940 and the second at Obersalzburg on 14 January 1941 – Antonescu repeated his declaration made at the previous meetings that the Romanian people were ready to march unto death alongside the Axis since they had absolute faith in the Führer's sense of justice. The Romanian people had bound its fate to that of Germany because the two peoples complemented each other both economically and politically, and they had a common danger to confront. This was the Slav danger, which had to be ended once and for all. It was Antonescu's opinion that a postponement of the conflict with Russia would prejudice the chances of an Axis victory. The Romanian people, he continued, wanted the moment of reckoning with Russia to come as soon as possible so that they could take revenge for all that they had suffered at the hands of the Russians.[67] Ten days later Antonescu got his chance to regain Northern Bukovina and Bessarabia when Operation *Barbarossa* was launched.

Antonescu's motive was not solely revenge. He saw the German attack as an ideological crusade against the infidel of Communism and his participation in it as an act of Christian righteousness. In an order of the day Antonescu told his troops that the hour had arrived for the fight against the yoke of Bolshevism. The fact that Romania joined Germany in the attack on the Soviet Union without a declaration of war, albeit in order to regain the territories annexed by the Soviet Union, meant inevitably that Britain and the United States would brand it an enemy state.

The Romanian public regarded the retrieval of Bessarabia and Northern Bukovina as legitimate war aims. General Antonescu recovered these provinces, as defined by their boundaries prior to the Soviet seizure in June 1940, by 27 July 1941 at a cost of 4,112 dead, 12,120 wounded and 5,506 missing.[68] Yet some Romanians had misgivings about going further. Iuliu Maniu and Constantin Brătianu,[69] respective leaders of the National Peasant and National Liberal parties, urged the General not to let Romanian troops go beyond Romania's historical frontiers.[70]

Antonescu did not heed this advice. His reasoning was strictly military – as one would expect from an officer. He recognized that Bessarabia was only secure as long as Germany defeated the Soviet Union. Of even more importance was his belief that the road to northern Transylvania lay through Russia and allegiance to Hitler. After all, if the German leader had awarded northern Transylvania to Hungary in large part to pre-empt a war between Bucharest and Budapest, and then guaranteed the new border of Romania to ward off a possible Soviet intervention that would have threatened Romanian oilfields, he might be amenable to changing his mind once the Soviet threat had been eliminated.

A close analysis reveals that Ion Antonescu was a complex and inconsistent figure. Under his leadership Romania joined the Tripartite Pact on 23 November 1940 as a sovereign state, participated in the attack on the Soviet Union on 22 June 1941 as an equal partner of Germany, and was never occupied by the *Wehrmacht*. Yet Antonescu *inherited* the Axis alignment, which is not to say that he saw an alternative to it, and he bore no responsibility for the internal political chaos he was called upon to manage in September 1940. This is one major paradox of his regime. There were others. He was a war criminal, sending tens of thousands of Jews to their death in Transnistria, and yet he refused to send other Romanian Jews to the death camps in Poland. He was an anti-Semite and yet, despite the deportations to Transnistria, more Jews survived under his rule than in any other country within Axis Europe. While up to 300,000 Jews were victims of Antonescu's policies, some 375,000 are estimated to have survived, principally in Wallachia, Moldavia and southern Transylvania.[71] He led for five months a Fascist-style government, yet in January 1941 he removed that government in three days of street fighting and replaced it with a military dictatorship.

Antonescu enjoyed Hitler's personal respect. He headed the third-largest Axis army in the European war – 585,000 Romanian troops participated in the attack on the Soviet Union in June to October 1941.[72] Under his rule Romania sustained the German war effort with oil and other raw materials. All of this places Romania on a par with Italy as a principal ally of Germany and not in the category of minor Axis satellite.

Antonescu's predicament on the eve of the war was that of a state caught between two totalitarian giants who considered they had the right to impose their interests upon continental Europe. Had Romania defied the Soviet Union in June 1940 she would probably have gained, like Finland a year earlier, widespread sympathy, but little else. Germany could not help her since her hands were tied by the Molotov-Ribbentrop Pact. When Romania did go to war against the Soviet Union in the following year she did so as Germany's ally and thus incurred the enmity of Britain. Romania's alliance with Germany was not embodied in any treaty, merely signified by adherence to the Tripartite Pact. She was not a totally voluntary partner, as the opposition of Maniu and Brătianu demonstrated, but she was a partner and not vassal, and remained under the control of a Romanian ruler.

Although Antonescu remained master of his own country, any attempt to withdraw from the war before 1944 invited German occupation. But by 1944 the attrition of German forces deprived Hitler of the force necessary to punish Romania for doing just that. As long as Romania was able to preserve her internal cohesion and some military might, she was able to retain her freedom of action. This she did until the invasion of the Red Army in spring 1944.

4

The Prelude to Hostilities: Projecting Britain in Romania

During the years leading up to Britain's declaration of war upon Romania, cultural diplomacy was a principal means of projecting British influence and involvement in Romanian life.[1] The British Committee for Relations with Other Countries – soon afterwards to be known as The British Council – came into being on 5 December 1934 and drove this effort. It was the brainchild of Reginald Leeper, a senior figure in the News Department of the Foreign Office (he became its head in 1935), and it was largely due to his vision and pertinacity that the Council, with the support of senior figures in the Foreign Office, was established. Its main objective was to win friendship and respect for Britain abroad through cultural and educational activities.[2]

The greatest impetus to the Council's work came with the appointment in September 1937 of Lord Lloyd as its Chairman. Sir Harold Nicolson described him thus:

> He was a man of quick intelligence, abounding energy, persuasive persistence, great personal charm, and dominating will. Restless and indeed impatient, he delighted in travel: he would fly from capital to capital, interviewing kings, dictators and ministers... He was impressed by the fact that in many Balkan and Asian lands there was what he called 'a hunger for our help'.[3]

These attributes of Lord Lloyd were no better exemplified than in his dealings with Romania where the Council was quick to seize an opportunity to support the British cultural presence. It did not, however, have to operate in a void. Two Anglo-Romanian societies were already in existence. In 1923 Viorel Tilea, a fervent champion of the British and later Romanian Minister to London (1939–40) set up an Anglo-Romanian society in Cluj, and four years later a similar society was established in Bucharest.[4] They provided a firm basis for partnership.

In October 1937 Sir Reginald Hoare, the British Minister to Romania, inaugurated a School of English with 150 pupils, organized by Dr D. Mateescu,

Honorary Secretary of the Anglo-Romanian Society. John Amery, a young independent teacher of English who had come out to Bucharest for a year under the auspices of the British Council, was interviewed by Mateescu and appointed Principal of the School. In a desire to consolidate the work of the School, and to put it on a firmer footing, Amery sent a memorandum to Hoare early in 1938 enlisting his support for the position of Principal to be made permanent and for the Council to assist in this matter, and Hoare, in his turn, gave his backing to Amery in a letter to the Council dated 12 May 1938. In his letter Hoare quoted extensively from Amery's memorandum and in the process gave some idea of the work of the School:

> I accepted the post of Principal of the School of English because I considered it the most effective medium for raising the standard of English in Bucharest. Thanks to Dr Mateescu I was able to initiate two English literature courses, an outline course from Chaucer to Wordsworth, and a modern course from Tennyson to the present day... Examinations have been introduced for second- and third-year classes throughout the School. I began a dramatic society which was very promising... In fact, every effort has been made, within the time at our disposal and under existing conditions, to give the School not only an academic status but a corporate life of its own. The first aim has already been achieved because the way had been carefully prepared for many years by Dr Mateescu, the second will be achieved if we have permanent premises and a permanent staff.[5]

Hoare added some detail of his own about the School:

> Its success was immediate and by the end of the year [1937] the School had 350 pupils and could have had many more had the accomodation been greater. This year [1938] more extensive but otherwise unsatisfactory premises were secured in conjunction with a French school and a thousand pupils are now being taught. It is understood that the number could easily be doubled... The premises at present occupied are about to be demolished, hence the low rent...
>
> We are all agreed here that so long as there is a really eager desire to acquire a knowledge of English, far the most effective propaganda, taking the long view, is to give all possible encouragement to would-be students; conversely there could be no more effective anti-British propaganda than the knowledge, which would undoubtedly be widespread, that the Anglo-Romanian School had had to close down, or at any rate restrict its activities, through the lack of a few hundred pounds. From figures supplied by Amery it appears that 65% of the pupils at the School are either school children and students or persons requiring a commercial knowledge of English. It appears to me that the young and business people are exactly the persons whom we want to get into our net.[6]

Hoare's letter reached the desk of Kenneth Johnstone, one of the two newly created Deputy Secretaries-General of the Council, whose full-time services had recently been made available by the Foreign Office. Johnstone gave enthusiastic backing to Hoare's suggestion that Amery be offered full-time employment as Principal of the School; in a memorandum of 17 May to the Council's Secretary-General Colonel Charles Bridge, Johnstone wrote:

> It looks as if we had a magnificent opportunity here and I suggest that we ought to seize it with both hands... I suggest that we should telegraph to Sir R. Hoare a) authorizing him to offer Amery £500 a year, of which £140 would continue to be paid by the Anglo-Romanian Society; b) requesting an estimate for a school of 2,000 pupils, on the assumption that the Council would be willing to provide a second teacher to work under Amery. This money would of course have to be found from the Council's reserve fund: it would be impossible to cut down the relatively small amount we are spending in Romania.[7]

Johnstone's recommendation received Bridge's approval and he wrote to H. L Farquhar at the British legation in Bucharest, requesting an estimate of the expenditure involved in the proposed enlargement of the School of English. Farquhar's reply gives an indication of the differences between British and Romanian expectations which coloured the setting up of the new School: 'Although Mateescu is an official of the Ministry of Finance I have had considerable difficulty in explaining to him what a budget is, and in a conversation which I had with him over three weeks ago he showed a curious reluctance to produce any detailed statement.'[8] In the meantime, steps were taken to appoint two assistant teachers for the School, and after interviews conducted by Farquhar and Amery two men, Michael Sheldon and J. H. Vinden were selected and arrived on 23 September.

Lord Lloyd followed these developments closely and decided to add his personal imprimatur by making a private visit to Romania and renewing his friendship with King Carol, whom he had received as Governor of Bombay province during Carol's visit to India, as Crown Prince, in April 1920. The Council was already sponsoring a number of lectures by eminent British visitors to the country as part of a drive to strengthen a British presence in South-Eastern Europe in the face of rising German influence.[9] The Council's support was given formal recognition when on 12 October 1938, Lord Lloyd opened the British Institute in Bucharest, which was in fact the School of English in enlarged but decrepit premises at Strada Slătineanu 20.

King Carol showed a keen interest in this move and received Lord Lloyd, an old friend from the 1920s. Following their meeting the King requested the Mayor of Bucharest to present a suitable plot of land to the Council for a building for the Institute. But while its future looked bright, validation of the Institute by the Council raised a question mark over the status of Professor

John Burbank who had been appointed on a two-year contract by the Council in April 1937 to occupy the newly founded chair of English at Bucharest University. Colonel Bridge, the Council's Secretary-General, followed Lord Lloyd out to the Romanian capital to investigate these and related issues.

In a long, plaintive letter to Lord Lloyd, sent from the legation on 28 October 1938, Colonel Bridge confessed that the situation in Bucharest was so complicated as to make it almost impossible to settle and to sort out in three days. On the question of Burbank, Bridge told the Professor that the Council was willing to extend his contract for a further year and this Burbank accepted. With regard to the British Institute, Bridge reported that it had 2,300 students organized in 75 classes [by comparison, the British Institute in Rome had 1,000 students]. The average size of the classes was 40 pupils, which he deemed far too large, and the premises too small. 'There are, of course', he added, 'a large number of Jews, I think 40%, and this tends to keep the good class Romanians out. I am not sure what the solution of this problem is, but I think some limit must be set to the number of Jews admitted and I will discuss this with Mateescu.' Bridge shows a startling lack of sensitivity to the predicament of the Jews in Romania at this time, given the fact that they were the object of anti-Semitic legislation introduced by the Goga government earlier in the year, and that most of the Jews attended the Institute in order to improve their English in the hope of emigration.

On the staff Bridge commented: 'Amery has 10 teachers, who are all English bar two, and these two Romanians are probably the best. Two of the English teachers are unsatisfactory, and Amery is anxiously awaiting the arrival of the two teachers we are sending out.' Finally, Bridge discussed the relationship between the Anglo-Romanian Society and the Institute, about which he had had an inconclusive talk with Mateescu. Bridge confessed: 'I found it almost impossible to get him to understand that although the British School here is called the British Institute, it is in fact not an institute in our interpretation of the term. I told him that if and when the Institute and Society moved to the new building, the Society will become absorbed in and subordinate to the Institute, but whether he understood or not I am not clear.'[10]

Although the British Council had taken major strides to secure the teaching of English in Romania by the autumn of 1938, it is useful to put its achievement into perspective. The Council was providing the salaries of four teachers in Bucharest – Amery, Burbank, Seldon and Vinden, and of two teachers in the provinces – Mr F. Y. Thompson at Cernăuţi University and Mr A. C. Crawley at Iaşi.[11] By contrast, the French authorities were funding fifteen university posts in French in Romania, and the Italian government respectively ten.

One of the two new teachers awaited by Amery and referred to by Bridge in his letter to Lord Lloyd was Reginald (Reggie) Smith, husband of Olivia Manning who presented an unflattering portrait of her husband as

Guy Pringle in her *Balkan Trilogy*. Kenneth Johnstone announced Smith's appointment in an internal memorandum to the Council on 1 December 1938, advising the accounts section that Smith's salary was to be £325 per annum. Smith advised an official of the Council that he would be taking works by the following authors to Bucharest:

(1) Standard poets – Chaucer to Browning, with some critical works of the period.
(2) Modern writers:

    (a) Poets: Auden, Spender, Eliot, Graves, Yeats, MacNeice, Plomer, Greene, Van der Post.
    (b) Criticism: Eliot, Richards, Lewis.
    (c) D. H. Lawrence and Lawrenciana.
    (d) Wyndham Lewis, and a few modern novelists (unpolitical).

(3) Translations and foreign texts:
Flaubert, Baudelaire, Verlaine, Tolstoy.
(4) Some standard grammar books, works on language and some psycho-analytic works.
(5) *Certain volumes which you may object to.*
Although they are all fiction: Andre Malraux, Proletarian Literature in the USA, and modern history (scientific, literary, historical scholarship).[12]

Smith's warning about the 'possible objection' to certain volumes proved prophetic, although the source of the criticism was not the British Council but the Bishop of Southwark whose complaints – unascribed – were passed on by a Mr Boyd Tollinton of the Council to John Amery:

> One or two criticisms in regard to the Council's work in Bucharest have recently been voiced to us. We were told that some of the teachers at the Institute are unpunctual at their classes and fraternize too closely with their pupils. Will you let me know whether there is any truth in these remarks and take steps to avoid further criticism?
>
> Criticism has also been raised as to certain recent lectures given under the Council's auspices in which undue prominence was given to James Joyce's *Ulysses* and the works of D. H. Lawrence. It is said that this might give offence to the more serious sections of Romanian life.[13]

Lord Lloyd reviewed the position of the building for the British Institute at a meeting of the Executive Committee of the Council held on 19 December 1938. He reported that the Mayor of Bucharest, acting on King Carol's instructions, had agreed to present to the British Council land for the Institute building or, if no suitable land was available, the equivalent in cash. He anticipated that, to compete with the Italians, who had an impressive building in the centre of Bucharest, and to house all the activities of the Council in one building, an expenditure of £25,000 would be involved. Lord Lloyd justified this by emphasizing the importance of the Council's work in Romania and the success attending its activities there.[14]

The Treasury refused funds for the construction of the Institute until reminded that King Carol had personally donated the site, and then rapidly sanctioned the expenditure.[15] The land offered by the King was known as 'proprietatea Cesianu', situated on the corner of Calea Victoriei and Strada Sevastopol, and right in the centre of Bucharest. It had always been understood on both sides that the Anglo-Romanian Society would share the new premises with the Institute and it was the Society, in the person of the architect Prince Cantacuzino, that the British legation contacted.

The initial estimates supplied by the Prince were considered too high by the Council and discussions dragged on for over a year.[16] It was only in March 1940 that the Treasury sanctioned expenditure of £25,000 for the building in anticipation of fresh plans from the Prince but political events were swiftly making these redundant. King Carol's abdication in September 1940, and the appointment of the pro-German Ion Antonescu as virtual dictator, led to a rapid deterioration in relations between Britain and Romania and at the end of the month the Romanians ordered most of the British who had not already left to go. On 27 October Hoare telegraphed to the Foreign Office from Bucharest that the Institute was to be closed in view of the withdrawal of the teachers. In the following year the activities of the Anglo-Romanian Society were finally suspended.[17]

5
Challenging German Ambitions: Clandestine British Military Operations in Romania, 1939–1941

Romania began to figure in British calculations about Hitler's intentions in Central and Eastern Europe after the *Anschluss* of March 1938.[1] It was generally believed in the War Office that Germany would seek to impose its will on the area before turning its attention towards Western Europe. Given Romania's geographical position there was little Britain could offer her. The brutal fact of British-Romanian relations, bluntly expressed by one historian, was that 'Germany is inconveniently in the way: opportunity, proximity of manufacture and the logistics of supply all told in favour of the Third Reich.'[2] This held, of course, for military as well as economic matters. In these circumstances the British concluded that their only weapon against German ambitions in countries which fell into Hitler's orbit were military subversive operations.

In April 1938 Admiral Sir Hugh Sinclair, the Head of the British Secret Intelligence Service (SIS or MI6), approved the creation of a special unit, Section D, which would plan sabotage in enemy-occupied lands.[3] The unit was given the cover title of the Statistical Research Department of the War Office. Chosen to lead it was Major Laurence Grand, a thirty-seven-year-old sapper and graduate of Cambridge. Grand was recommended for the post to Sinclair by Stewart Menzies, head of Section II, the military section of SIS. Appointed as his assistant was Major Montague Chidson, an intelligence officer with a distinguished record who had served as SIS head of station in Bucharest between 1931 and 1936. Grand obtained a large Victorian mansion, The Frythe, in Hertfordshire and trained a small number of men in the practice of sabotage, in particular in the use of explosives, as well as preparing papers on the benefits of 'irregular warfare' carried out by well-organized and well-armed partisan groups.[4]

Grand and Section D were not alone in the intelligence community to be engaged in such activity. In October 1938 another sapper, Major John Holland, was appointed to a small section of the War Office known as GS(R) (General Staff (Research)), created two years earlier as a 'think tank' to look into specific subjects of interest to the Army Council. Holland's brief was to study the characteristics of guerrilla warfare with special reference to recent operations in China and Spain. At the same time, he was given secret instructions by the Deputy Chief of the Imperial General Staff to report on the possibility of providing British support for insurgency in any country of Central and Eastern Europe overrun by the German Army.[5]

To avoid duplication of effort, the Director of Military Intelligence, General Henry Pownall, agreed that Holland and Grand should coordinate their research and Holland moved into Grand's Section D premises. In January 1939 Holland was authorized by the Foreign Secretary, Lord Halifax, and the Chief of the Imperial General Staff, Lord Gort, to expand GS(R) by the addition of two officers: an expert on demolition and explosives, and an officer to be in charge of organization, recruitment and training. For the first position he chose another sapper, Major Millis Jefferis, and for the second, Lieutenant Colonel Colin Gubbins, who had seen service in Russia, Ireland and India.

Hitler's occupation of Prague in March 1939 gave even greater urgency to the work of Holland and Grand. With Gubbins established as his assistant (since April 1939), Holland expanded his section, recruiting more officers and earmarking personnel for training in sabotage. The latter were commissioned in the Officers' Emergency Reserve (OER) in advance of general mobilization. At the same time, it was decided that GS(R) should be placed under the supervision of the Director of Military Intelligence and be renamed Military Intelligence (Research) (MI(R)).

In the economic sphere Romania had been brought into the orbit of Germany by the signature on 23 March 1939 of the German-Romanian economic treaty, under the terms of which the Germans undertook to supply the Romanian armed forces with arms and equipment in return for Romanian goods. Fearful that Germany would seize Romania's oil both Britain and France gave guarantees to Romania on 13 April.[6] When the guarantee was announced British military planners were deep in debate about Romania's role in case of war with Germany.[7] From Bucharest, Sir Reginald Hoare, the British Minister, pointed out that the indispensable condition of Romania's participation on the side of Britain and France was an Allied army of 100,000 backed by a strong air force in Cyprus.[8] The military attaché, Lt. Col. Geoffrey Macnab, supported this view.[9] While admiring the qualities of the Romanian soldier, he was less complimentary about the Army's command which he considered as lagging behind in appreciation of modern developments and plagued by slackness in administration. He concluded:

> In another eighteen months the Army may well become a force to be reckoned with seriously. At present it has every hope of success if called to fight any of its neighbours, but in a conflict with a western power its chances of protracted resistance are not worth betting on.[10]

MI(R) recognized that Romania's oil was particularly tempting to Hitler and considered the problem under two rubrics – destruction of the oilfields and the interdiction of supply routes by the Danube and the rail network.[11] Gubbins visited Romania secretly and talked with engineers of oil companies with a British shareholding whose expertise was vital to the success of any sabotage of the oilfields. As the granting of the Anglo-French guarantee necessitated close military cooperation with the Romanian General Staff, the British and French military attachés, respectively Macnab and General Delhomme, opened discussions with them which included the feasibility of destroying the oil wells should Germany invade Romania. The Romanian Prime Minister, Armand Călinescu, supported an Anglo-French proposal to draw up such plans. In June, three new recruits to MI(R), Commander Dymock Watson of the Royal Navy, Major Young and Major Walter, prepared an appreciation and plans under the supervision of Holland.

The appreciation considered that if destruction was to be certain, a British military occupation was necessary, and that German communications were more important than the oilfields as targets for sabotage. Plans were not, however, prepared for military occupation but were drawn up for: (a) destruction of oilfields in conjunction with the Romanian General Staff and the Romanian Army; (b) partial destruction by British oilfield engineers assisted by a field company of sappers; and (c) destruction of communications with the assistance of the Romanian Army. During July and August reconnaissance missions were carried out and the appreciation and the plan came before the Chiefs of Staff in August who approved them.

On 25 August Commander Watson went to Bucharest to meet a French engineer, Leon Wenger, who had been sent by the *Deuxième Bureau* to represent his country's interests in the discussions with the Romanian General Staff on demolition of the oil wells. Their first meeting – held without the Romanians – was also attended by Lt. Col. Gubbins who, in the face of the German attack, had had to make a hasty withdrawal from Warsaw to Romania together with several other MI(R) officers almost as soon as they arrived. It was agreed that whatever assurances the British and French received from the Romanian government, the chances of the latter carrying out covert operations under war conditions and with any efficiency were slight. It was therefore decided that the British and French should prepare subsidiary plans of their own to make certain that all items of vital importance were destroyed under their direction. These plans foresaw a role for French troops from Syria should the Romanian General Staff baulk at playing its part. The existence of this 'back-up' plan was not to be disclosed to the Romanians.

Official plans with the Romanian General Staff were agreed by the British and French at the end of August. Operational liaison devolved on Colonel Leonida of the General Staff and Major J. V. Davidson-Houston, a sapper officer who had served in China and Russia, and who arrived in Bucharest in July 1939. Their task was to destroy or put out of action the oilfields in Ploieşti. A field company of Royal Engineers was to be despatched from Egypt. Additional personnel were to be sent to Astra Română, the Shell associate company, to work in Ploieşti as 'oilfield trainees'. With the outbreak of war in September, considerations of Turkish neutrality became a major factor in planning the transport of the company – some two hundred men and eight officers. The number of trips required by air would make it impossible to conceal the movement of the men from the Germans and for this reason the sea route was chosen.[12]

Commander Watson, with the assistance of Edward Masterson of the Unirea Oil Company, recruited a number of oil engineers for the demolition parties in Ploieşti. They were enrolled in the Territorial Army reserve by Lt. Col. Macnab, given uniforms, assigned by Watson to work with Major J. V. Davidson-Houston of the Royal Engineers and five OER officers recruited by MI(R) in London, and then despatched to Bucharest in August. Amongst the latter were Captains Geoffrey Household, Stanley Green and Herbert Watts. They were joined by William Harris-Burland from an MI(R) mission to Poland.[13] Demolition parties were thus formed from these engineers and officers and each one prepared detailed plans for sabotage in the area allocated to it. Under the supervision of Watson and Masterson instructions were issued to the teams for destroying wells, pumping stations and refineries.

The outbreak of war in September 1939 changed the nature of the relationship between Britain and Romania. Germany was now a declared enemy of Britain, but remained a potential ally of Romania. Germany concluded economic agreements with Romania on 29 September and 21 December 1939. Under the terms of the first agreement Romania undertook to export cereals and oil to the Reich in quantities as great as its transport capabilities would allow, receiving in turn war material of Polish origin, while the second agreement stipulated an increase in the exchange rate in favour of the Reichsmark and the 'political' undertaking of the Romanian government to guarantee under any conditions the annual export of 130,000 tons of oil to the Reich.[14]

King Carol consequently told the German air attaché, Colonel Alfred Gerstenberg, of a British plan to sabotage the oilfields but that he had rejected it. The 'oilfield trainees" arrival shortly afterwards 'cast some doubt' on Carol's claim and was observed by the German deputy-consul in Ploieşti who passed the information on to Colonel Wahle, the German military attaché.[15] Denial to Germany of Romania's oil became even more urgent. Explosive material was introduced into Romania by various means, including the diplomatic bag. Equipment for the use of the company of Royal Engineers and for training selected oil company employees and Romanian officers was brought in by the *Fouadieh* – chartered by British Middle East Headquarters in Cairo – from Alexandria, unloaded at Galaţi docks in October 1939 under the supervision of Davidson-Houston, and stored at an artillery barracks at Vlădeşti near Câmpulung. Charges and weapons were also concealed in the military attaché's office. At the same time, a flying-boat arrived at Constanţa with a Captain Davies on board with further demolition stores which consisted of limpet mines and pressure switches. Commander Watson met the plane at Constanţa and, after a hurried consultation with Captain Davies, it was decided that it was 'not good for the Romanians to know about limpets and pressure switches'. The boxes containing them were accordingly marked 'STORES FOR THE BRITISH LEGATION, BUCHAREST' which enabled them to be rescued and transferred direct to the legation.[16]

The Germans were on their guard against sabotage.[17] In August 1939 a German Military Intelligence (*Abwehr*) residence designated 'Kriegsorganisation Rumänien' was established in Bucharest.[18] Admiral Wilhelm Canaris,[19] the head of the *Abwehr*, sent Lt. Col. Erich Pruck to Bucharest in October 1939 to conclude an agreement with Mihail Moruzov, head of the Romanian Secret Service (SSI), which empowered the *Abwehr* to protect supply routes to Germany.[20] On 14 December 1939 Canaris gave the order for the creation of a body to ensure the security of the installations and storage facilities both within the oil region as well as in ports, and of communications, especially of the railways and on the Danube.

This body, composed of officers, non-commissioned officers and carefully selected soldiers, belonging to the special unit OKW/Amt Ausland Abwehr, 'Baulehrbataillon z.b.V. 800', which became on 1 June 1940 'Lehrregiment Brandenburg z.b.V 800', was coordinated by *Abwehr II* (Sonderaufgaben) sabotage and special missions.[21] The bulk of the battalion was placed near the Iron Gates,[22] while two hundred and fifty officers and men, disguised as *Reichsbund* Sports Groups, were posted to the Bulgarian port of Ruse, opposite the oil terminal at Giurgiu on the Romanian side of the Danube.

In late December 1939, a detachment of twelve officers and men led by Captain Kurt Drögsler (a chemist with the code name 'Victor Luptar') was sent to the oil region of Ploieşti to act under various covers and Romanian code names. At the same time, the Romanian Secret Service set up in early January 1940 the so-called 'Ploieşti' agency, headed initially (January–December 1940) by Lieutenant Constantin I. Antonescu and later (December 1940–2) by Major Gheorghe Filimon, with the mission to cover the activity of the German agents and to prevent acts of sabotage in the entire oil region. Within the 'Ploieşti' agency special supervisory teams were set up, formed from experienced agents of the Romanian Secret Service and placed under the command of Gheorghe Untăreanu (code-named 'Gheorghe Albu' or 'B. Dănilă'), who served also as the assistant head of the 'Ploieşti' agency and who worked closely with the members of the detachment of Kurt Drögsler. Thus two joint Romanian-German teams were formed to protect the strategic assets mentioned above against sabotage.[23]

The second detachment, placed under the command of Captain Heinrich Verbeek, was given the mission of ensuring the security of river traffic on the Danube against sabotage by the Allied secret services. Its members acted under different forms of cover (tourists, sportsmen, customs officers) with the tacit approval of the Romanian and Bulgarian authorities, on board vessels on the Danube or in the ports situated along the river. Verbeek's detachment also received an important mission from *Abwehr II*. Being preoccupied with the danger of an Allied landing in Romania in order to occupy or sabotage the oil region, *Abwehr II* drew up in April 1940 sabotage plans against a possible Allied landing on the Romanian Black Sea coast. According to the plan (code-named 'Operation *Sigmaringen*'), Verbeek's detachment was to blow up the Cernavodă bridge and block the Sulina channel in order to delay the advance of the Allied forces towards the country's interior.[24]

By spring 1940 the training of the British demolition parties was complete. The British Army HQ in Cairo chartered the SS *Deebank*, a merchant vessel, to transport the Royal Engineers – the 54th Field Company under Captain G. Young – which left Alexandria on 25 May. They arrived off Kilia, on the west side of the entrance to the Straits of Marmora, three days later, to the embarrassment of the neutral Turkish authorities. At the same time, the collapse of France, which had a shattering effect on the Romanian spirit, led King Carol to reconsider the wisdom of participation in the sabotage plans. With the prospect of British defeat in his mind, he was unwilling to do anything to provoke the Germans. For the British, Italy's entry into the war, on 10 June, increased fears of an Axis attack on Egypt. Concern that the engineers might be interned, when they were likely to be needed back in Egypt, led the British army to recall them and they turned back to Alexandria on 28 June.[25]

Plans for denying oil supplies delivered by barge along the Danube centred on blocking the points in the Kazan defile (Iron Gates), either by blockships or by detonating the cliffs on the Yugoslav side. They were directed by Section D's representative in Belgrade, Julius Hanau but ended in failure.[26] They were to be supplemented by the pre-emptive chartering of all available river vessels and the creation of a shortage of pilots at the Iron Gates by offering them – through the Goeland Transport and Trading Company, set up in January 1940 by the British government with Harris-Burland as general manager, to concentrate under one management measures of economic warfare – extended paid holidays.[27] The plans to block the Danube by sinking barges had been drawn up by Section D and Naval Intelligence in September 1939 and were to be coordinated by the naval attaché in Bucharest, Captain Max Despard.

Towards the end of November, Despard arrived to take up the position of naval attaché, Bucharest, Belgrade and Budapest. On 2 January 1940 Commander Watson returned to London. Whilst there he discussed the despatch of personnel for manning river craft which were to be filled with concrete and sunk at the Iron Gates. On Watson's return the five OER officers were sent to Egypt for a month's attachment to the Field Company. On returning to Britain on the orders of the Admiralty, Watson reported the unsatisfactory state of financial negotiations on compensation for the destruction of the oilwells for the Romanian government. Eric Berthoud, first secretary at the British legation in Bucharest with responsibility for oil matters, reached agreement with the Romanian government but the latter refused to sign the papers until the necessity for destruction became imminent.

During February and March preparations for placing British personnel with armaments and ammunition stores in the Goeland fleet operating on the Danube were made, and a number of Iron Gates pilots were bought off so they would not work for the Germans. The operation was in the charge of Despard. On 29 March 1940 the SS *Mardinian*, out of Liverpool, berthed at Sulina (with sixty-eight officers and ratings) and a cargo of ninety-five cases invoiced as Chrysler spares to the Chrysler agent in Budapest. The cases passed customs control without a hitch – Despard had been supplied with £1,500 'to ensure the cooperation of Romanian personnel' – and were handed over to his men. They contained thirty tons of arms and ammunition, including three Vickers machine guns, limpet mines and six hundred pounds of high explosive, and were transferred to the lighter *Termonde*. Other vessels, acquired by the Goeland Company and flying the British merchant marine flag, gave the flotilla a commercial appearance. The crews were made up of seamen from the Royal and Royal Australian Navies, and local personnel with experience of the Danube. The expedition was led by a Royal Navy officer, Commander A. P. Gibson.[28]

It left Sulina on 1 April, shadowed by a steamer chartered by German military intelligence. Two days later, it reached Giurgiu to take on fuel but the port captain delayed permission for the tugs to go to the oiling berth long enough for a search to be made of the cargo on the insistence of a German officer. Romanian officials searched the main tug and found uniforms, arms and some £500 in *lei*. The latter were impounded but on the protest of the British legation they were returned. On 5 April, the *Termonde* itself was inspected.[29] The discovery of the explosives confirmed German suspicions. Wilhelm Fabricius, the German Minister to Bucharest, told the Romanian Foreign Minister, Grigore Gafencu, that Germany would suspend arms' deliveries if the flotilla were allowed to proceed, a threat that was referred to King Carol. Carol gave way and the vessels were ordered to return to Brăila, without their cargo. This, the British could have access to later, since Romania was neutral. The ships eventually left individually – their departure had to be negotiated separately with Admiral Nicolae Păiş, Deputy-Minister of Air and Marine – for Istanbul between the end of May and 20 June.

With the failure of the Danube operation and the aborted sabotage attempt using the Royal Engineers, Commander Watson proposed in June as a last-ditch measure that the Ţintea oilfield, which was owned by the British subsidiary Astra Română, be destroyed.[30] Sir Reginald Hoare, the

British Minister in Bucharest, supported the idea. In the case of this high-pressure field, demolition could be effected more rapidly and separate plans, undisclosed to the Romanians, had been drawn up by the manager Leslie Forster. A night was fixed for the attempt by the teams which included an oil engineer whom the company guards would obey, but 48 hours before the operation the guards were withdrawn and the Romanian army moved in.[31] On 1 July the Prime Minister Ion Gigurtu announced the reorientation of Romania's foreign policy, in consequence of which the Romanian government renounced the Anglo-French guarantee, its membership of the Balkan Entente and of the League of Nations. On the following day King Carol asked Hitler for a Military Mission.

The new alignment ruled out any hope of destroying the oilfields or installations. Furthermore, the Romanians' hand had been forced by the discovery among secret documents of the French General Staff, captured by the Germans on 19 June in a train at Charité-sur-Loire, of the Anglo-French plan to carry out sabotage in the oilfields and a list of the personnel involved.[32] The captured documents showed clearly both the duplicity of King Carol II in 1939–40, as well as the extent of the Allied sabotage networks in the Ploieşti region.

Berlin, therefore, applied pressure in Bucharest to expel the British and French subjects who were still active in the oil industry. Mihail Moruzov, head of the Romanian Secret Service, placed in a delicate position after the discovery of the French documents, was forced to accede to a German request of 1 July for the expulsion of thirty British and French subjects suspected of 'undertaking a secret mission to carry out possible acts of sabotage' in the oil region.[33] Seventeen British subjects resident in Ploieşti were ordered to leave by 9 am on 4 July. Among them was W. R. Young, and with his departure coordination of subversive activities in Romania passed to Alfred George Gardyne de Chastelain,[34] with the exception of clandestine work organized by John Toyne, who was working under direct orders from London.[35]

A large number of French engineers were also expelled. In a German wireless paper of the time, Commander Watson, Major Davidson Houston, Colonel Gubbins and members of the OER were all mentioned as being engaged in Romanian oilfield sabotage.[36] Of the seventeen British expelled, eleven had been involved in the sabotage planning. Hoare concluded:

> Avowed Axis policy of Romanian Government must mean that Germany and Italy will obtain all the oil they can transport, that transport will be organized in their favour and oil exports directed in accordance with their wishes.[37]

His prediction was accurate. As the war developed, Romania came to provide about forty per cent of German requirements for oil.[38]

Continual supervision by the *Abwehr* of the remaining British engineers, coupled with their harrasment by the irregular police of the Iron Guard, drove the majority of the British subjects in the oil region to leave Romania in the second half of September 1940. Furthermore, seven British citizens[39] accused of sabotage of German oil cars – some of them being indeed SO(2) agents – were arrested between 24 September and 3 October 1940 on the grounds of being part of a spy network, according to the reports sent to Berlin by the German legation in Bucharest, led by the British military attaché Lieutenant Colonel Geoffrey Macnab. The arrests and interrogation were carried out by the Iron Guard police together with the SD (*Sicherheitsdienst*) and Gestapo representatives in Romania.[40]

Those engaged in the sabotage were enlisted by Major Young of MI(R). Principal among them were J. E. Treacy (Canadian), manager of an oil well supply business in Ploieşti, A. C. Anderson, an oil engineer living near the oilfields, E. Boaden, drilling superintendent of the Unirea Company, and Reginald Young, refinery engineer of Româno Americană.[41] The activities of the sabotage team covered several refineries, the principal marshalling yards of Ploieşti, and a few of the shunting stations in Transylvania.[42]

The remainder of the sabotage team continued to operate successfully until September 1940:

> The first indication that their work was becoming known was provided by an attack on Treacy's house in Ploieşti with an incendiary bomb thrown by individuals who were recognised as couriers between the German Legation in Bucharest and the Consulate in Ploieşti. Representations to the Roumanian authorities gave no satisfaction, and it was evident that little support would be forthcoming in the event of further trouble. Despite this incident, which by chance caused comparatively little damage as Treacy had moved his bedroom for security reasons, Treacy continued to operate until his arrest in mid-September 1940. Anderson and Treacy were badly tortured by members of the Iron Guard, Mrs Treacy was beaten, and the others received blows with the butt of a revolver in an attempt to make them disclose the nature of their work. Unfortunately, considerable quantities of sulphuric acid, powdered emery, special grease guns for injecting emery-treated grease into the reciprocating parts of locomotives, and blueprints of locomotive and truck bogies were found in Treacy's house and office.[43]

From Ploieşti those arrested were taken to Bucharest and imprisoned; they were released only later in October following strong diplomatic protests made by Sir Reginald Hoare to General Ion Antonescu and after a certain amount of bribery of officials by Ion Popovici (code name 'Procopius')[44] using SOE funds.[45] Immediately after their release they were sent to Istanbul where Treacy and Anderson were obliged to undergo medical treatment.

By this time more than 400 British subjects, including workers and engineers, had been either expelled or forced to leave Romania, which effectively put an end to SOE plans of sabotage in the country.[46]

In July 1940, in response to defeat in continental Europe, MI(R) and Section D were merged with Electra House (a semi-secret propaganda section of the Foreign Office) to form SO(2) (Special Operations 2), part of the Special Operations Executive (SOE) created in that month on Churchill's orders with a brief 'to set Europe ablaze'. A cabinet directive of 22 July 1940 made Hugh Dalton, the Minister of Economic Warfare, chairman of SOE. Sir Frank Nelson, a successful businessman who had worked for the Foreign Office in Switzerland up to the fall of France, accepted the role of executive head. SOE's propaganda side was christened SO(1) and responsibility for subversive operations was given to SO(2). SOE's role was to promote sabotage and subversion in enemy occupied territory and to establish a nucleus of trained men tasked with assisting indigenous resistance groups. SO(2)'s actual strength in personnel is unclear. Grand was made head of SO(2) and his second-in-command was Charles Hambro. In August 1941, after a dispute with the Ministry of Information and the Foreign Office, the bulk of SO(1) was transferred to the newly created Political Warfare Executive (PWE), under the control of the Foreign Office, where it was amalgamated with parts of the Foreign Publicity Department of the Ministry of Information and the European Section of the BBC. SOE remained as a purely planning and operations organization until it was disbanded after the end of the Second World War, in 1946. During this time, the principal focus of SOE's operations was on occupied Europe, but it also performed with varying degrees of intensity in North Africa, the Middle East, South Asia and the Far East.

It was indeed under the auspicies of MI(R) that original SO(2) collaborators had concentrated on the more unobtrusive forms of sabotage of oil trains proceeding to Germany in spring 1940: 'Effective action against this traffic was taken by cutting brake couplings and filling axle boxes with sulphuric acid, which had the effect of emulsifying the lubricating oil, causing hot boxes. The principal Romanian engineer involved in this activity was Gogu Constantinescu, recruited from the Orion Refinery in Ploieşti.'[47] He had numerous Romanian assistants, but their names were never disclosed to SO(2) for security reasons.

In March 1940 a propaganda department of Section D had been inaugurated under de Chastelain with H. Paniguian as adviser.[48] 'Subversive and anti-German propaganda was prepared, duplicated each in several thousand copies, and distributed. When the volume of material became too great to handle comfortably by the duplicating process, a printing press was acquired which operated during normal working hours on legitimate printing business and at night printed SO(2) material.'[49]

Popovici[50] soon became the principal collaborator in connection with the printing press, which had been obtained

> with the assistance of Bondi Kalman of the J. Walter Thomson Company, and Max Fischer, a printing and lithographic expert, who had associations with the *Scrisul Românesc* printing press of Craiova (owned by the brother of Tătărescu, ex-Romanian Prime Minister). Both Kalman and Fischer gave their services voluntarily, and until his departure from Romania in late 1940 Fischer was responsible for the purchase from various sources of paper and ink. He also took delivery of the finished material and handed it over at clandestine meetings with de Chastelain.[51]

In Romania, the attempt to set the country ablaze had been comprehensively extinguished by the failure of operations to blow up the oil wells. SO(2) now turned its attention to building an anti-German resistance within the country. With the consolidation of Romania's alignment with Germany after Antonescu's advent to power in September 1940, SO(2) concentrated on developing contacts with pro-British members of the political opposition.

At this point it should be made clear that resistance in Romania, either to the Antonescu regime or to his German allies, cannot be discussed in the same terms as in the cases of France or Yugoslavia. The circumstances of Antonescu's accession to power, his maintenance of Romania's sovereignty during the period of alliance with Germany, and his pursuit of the war against a Communist Russia considered a predator, meant that any armed resistance to his rule was viewed by most Romanians as treachery. It followed from retention of sovereignty that a Romanian resistance movement must engage in resistance not against an oocupying power, but in insurrectionary action against its own national government, in conditions of hostility to such a movement itself.

The resistance offered was small in scale – there were no organized operations of the kind conducted by the Maquis in France, or by Mihailovici and Tito in Yugoslavia. Those partisan groups that took to the mountains of Romania in the summer of 1944 took action not against German troops but against the Red Army, which they saw not as their 'liberator' from 'Fascism' but rather as an instrument of Soviet Communism. This is not to dishonour the few Romanians whose anti-Axis convictions led them to undertake clandestine activities in favour of Allied – particularly British – military intelligence, nor the handful of Communists who carried out isolated attacks on the Romanian rail network designed to hinder the Axis war effort against the Russians. But the Communists were seen by most Romanians as traitors by virtue of their allegiance to Moscow, and by their continued subservience to the Comintern line justifying the Soviet annexation of Bessarabia and Northern Bukovina. There was no major public opposition within Romania to Antonescu's rule, only spasmodic letters of protest from individual Romanians.[52] Resistance, in the Romanian context, meant political opposition and the figure to whom the British – who took the lead in these matters during the war – turned was the pro-British National Peasant Party leader Iuliu Maniu.

In September 1940 de Chastelain met Maniu in the house of Rică Georgescu.[53] Plans were discussed for the Peasant Party leader to travel to London to set up a Free Romanian Committee. Maniu agreed and decided that his Committee would consist of Virgil Madgearu,[54] ex-Minister of Finance and a leading economist; Ion Mihalache,[55] Maniu's deputy; Nicolae Titulescu, then in Switzerland; with Mr Carol Davila as his representative in the United States. Unfortunately Madgearu was assassinated by the Iron Guard on 27 November 1940, Titulescu was in poor health and died a natural death at Cannes on 17 March 1941, and Mihalache refused to leave the country. In their place Maniu sent abroad in December Cornel Bianu to replace Madgearu, and Ştefan Neniţescu to act as his secretary. Pavel Pavel also left with the approval of Maniu 'but in no way as his representative'.[56]

Georgescu enlisted the support of his uncle, General Alexander Manolescu, ex-aide de camp to Prince Nicholas, and a person well connected in military and Palace circles. Manolescu also accepted a fund of one million *lei* 'to cover entertainment expenses to be incurred in furthering our [SOE's] interests'.[57]

On 30 September 1940 de Chastelain was obliged to leave Romania on the insistence of Sir Reginald Hoare who was concerned about his safety following the collapse of the plan to sabotage the oilfields. De Chastelain handed over the SOE organisation to Herbert Watts but Watts, too, became a victim of the rapidly-deteriorating state of British-Romanian relations and was obliged to leave the country after only a few weeks. His role was assumed by R. Hazell 'who until then had been collaborating with the Polish organisation in Romania'.[58]

The principal thrust of SOE activity in Romania during this period was provided by the propaganda effort, directed by SO(1) – in August 1941 to become the Political Warfare Executive (PWE) – and in this respect Ion Popovici and Rică Georgescu were the mainstays. Both supervised the work of the printing press and amongst those who assisted them was Max Davidovici 'who was also supplying very valuable military information to the military attaché covering most provinces of Romania'.[59] The press produced material for Chalmers-Wright of the Ministry of Information as well as on behalf of *Ardealul*, the first 'black' propaganda radio station set up by SOE in London in October 1940.[60]

The station's first team was formed by Robert William Seton-Watson,[61] Viorel Virgil Tilea, the former Romanian Minister to Britain,[62] and Dan Dimancescu, a former counsellor at the Romanian legation in London.[63] Known variously in British circles as R.1, 'Romanian Brethren' (*Fraţi Români*), or Independent Romania (România independentă), it was commonly referred to by the Romanian name for Transylvania (*Ardealul*) on account of its cover, an anti-Antonescu group allegedly based in Romania.

During its early broadcasts it was charged with creating an 'atmosphere of transmission by Roumanians in Roumania for Roumanians'.[64] The principal aims of the station were to dissuade Romanians from supporting military and economic assistance to Germany, to disrupt economic activity, and to encourage opposition to Antonescu and to the Iron Guard. Propaganda on behalf of *Ardealul* was printed by a group coordinated by Ion Popovici, Rică Georgescu and Iosif Păsătoiu,[65] with finance provided by de Chastelain.[66]

Colonel Bill Bailey, SO(2) representative in Istanbul, sent a policy statement to headquarters dated 21 December 1940 upon which he based his discussions immediately after Christmas with the British Minister Sir Reginald Hoare in Bucharest on the agency's plan to create a local pro-Ally organization comprising the residue of Maniu's party, dissident Iron Guardists, and 'other suitable elements'.[67]

AIMS:

A. To ensure that, should Germany undertake a campaign in south-eastern Europe, Russia or Asia Minor, *using Roumania as an advanced base*, the maximum of interference and resistance inside the country could be at once produced.

B. To ensure that, before this strategy becomes necessary, a campaign of agricultural and industrial sabotage, aimed against Germany, is instituted and maintained. Should Germany *not* undertake a military campaign as foreseen, then this sabotage work will be extended and intensified.

OPERATIONS

Therefore the following operations are essential to the realization of the above aims:-

General:

1. The securing to the British cause of the effective support of all anti-German elements in Roumania.
2. The coordination of the activities of these elements to ensure that we derive maximum advantage.

Specific:

3. The establishment of contact with representatives of all such elements, and the organisation of lines of communication to enable contact to be maintained should the British Diplomatic Mission to Roumania be withdrawn.
4. The encouragement of mutual contact and cooperation between individual parties and groups.

5. The provision of financial and material assistance for our contacts where required.

Note:

(i) S.O.2 has already been engaged on this work for about four months. Experience gained during this period suggests that we can most easily realise our aims in the following manner.
(ii) With the exception of the Legionary Party, which was reinstated in September 1940, all political parties in Roumania have been dissolved since February 1938, and can now maintain their structure and existence *only* illegally.

6. The National Peasant Party provides a strong basis on which to graft illegal organisations, such as

   a) Ardealul (the organisation which operates the Roumanian Freedom Station).
   b) Frontul Plugarilor – the Ploughman's Front.
   c) Dissident factions from the original Iron Guard, whom we are organising from outside the country.
   d) The anti-Legionary University movement.
   e) Other suitable elements that we may be able to recruit in the course of our work.

7. This alliance of anti-German elements can be led by only one man – Doctor Iuliu Maniu. It is essential that his personal safety be ensured, and he must therefore be evacuated from Roumania. He has already selected certain collaborators who will leave the country with him, and appointed deputies who will represent him inside the country during his absence, and also arranged the necessary liaison with other groups.
8. S.O.2 is already working with representatives of the other groups, both within and outside Roumania, with the knowledge and approval of Doctor Maniu.
9. The above provides the necessary man-power and executive for the work.
10. The work itself, already in hand, consists of:-

    a) Preliminary organisation, particularly in centres of military importance. This is chiefly concerned with the building up of the necessary 'cells'.
    b) Dissemination of propaganda, verbal, printed and radio.
    c) Training of personnel for sabotage and para-military operations.
    d) Formations of arms and explosives dumps.

e) Installation of W/T [wireless transmitter] units and provision of codes for communication between cells and with us outside the country.

11. It is desirable that contact between Roumanians and British *inside Roumania* be kept to an absolute minimum. The S.O.2 representative already installed in the Legation should suffice. Main contact between S.O.2 and Roumanians will be made *outside* the country.
12. It is estimated that about two months are required to complete the operations listed in paragraph 10 a), b) and e). This work will be greatly facilitated if we are assured of the advice and general assistance of the British Legation in Bucharest. Therefore it is imperative that *no* major acts of sabotage or other subversive, which might result in rupture of diplomatic relations, be indulged in, or directed, by British agents during this period; the more so, since any conceivable isolated acts of sabotage which we feel we could execute involve risk out of proportion to the results which they might produce. It is most improbable that any such acts, if successful, could do more than cause the enemy very temporary inconvenience, while the recent entry of Gestapo agents into Roumanian police departments renders it virtually impossible for British subjects to carry on subversive activities without grave risk of detection. S.O.2 policy, as recently modified in London, provides its Balkan representative with full powers to abandon sabotage projects if he feels that such operations will prove prejudicial to political work.
13. Commercial activities beyond the scope of operations outlined in this report are also to be avoided, as non-success in this direction may also result in rupture of diplomatic relations.
14. In conclusion, it should be stated that the policy outlined in this memorandum coincides in principle with that pursued by S.O.2 in Jugoslavia and Bulgaria. Corresponding elements are already working with us in these countries. This state of affairs provides the possibility of organising concerted action in all three countries at a later stage in the development of our plans.

Istanbul:

21st December, 1940.[68]

In a minute written in Belgrade and dated 3 January 1941, Bailey reported that 'complete agreement' had been reached in Bucharest with Hoare and with Ian le Rougetel, the political advisor at the British legation, as to the programme which SO(2) should carry out in Romania. Owing to the fact that his visit had taken place immediately after Christmas he had been able to see only Ion Popovici among SO(2)'s Romanian contacts who convinced him that the agency's activities were 'yielding fruit'. The most satisfactory aspect of his visit, he wrote, was that he managed to persuade Hoare to allow his (Bailey's) deputy, Alfred George Gardyne de Chastelain, to go to Bucharest as a diplomatic courier.[69]

De Chastelain returned to Romania on 15 January and took the opportunity of re-establishing contact with all individuals and organisations then collaborating with SOE. Under Hazell's direction a large war chest had been accumulated and handed over to Popovici to finance Maniu and *Ardealul*. De Chastelain made a second, final, trip to Bucharest immediately after the Iron Guard rebellion of 22–5 January 1941 and reached final agreement with Maniu as to procedure once the British legation had left the country. By this time the Minister and certain of his secretaries were well informed of SOE's plans and consequently decisions were taken in agreement with the Minister, SOE and Maniu. Maniu claimed to have made arrangements for an important amount of sabotage which could be put into effect by the end of February. This sabotage, however, was conditional upon the bombing by the RAF of oil refineries and certain rail targets in Romania. It was in fact on the understanding that such bombing would be carried out that Sir Reginald Hoare concurred in the breaking of diplomatic relations with Romania.[70]

Among the final arrangements made with Maniu was a signal plan for the W/T set which was to provide communications between Bucharest and Istanbul after the departure of the British diplomatic mission. De Chastelain used two visits in January and February to contact the Romanians with whom SO(2) planned to work after the legation left, principally Maniu, Rică Georgescu and Ion Popovici.

On 8 January 1941 SOE submitted a memorandum to the British Chiefs of Staff on 'Interference with German Oil Supplies'. The supplies in question were those from the oilfields and refineries as well as stocks coming from Russia across the Black Sea which were landed at the Romanian port of Constanţa and the Bulgarian port of Varna. The oil was transported by two means, river and rail. During the last months of 1940 it was estimated that 130,000 tons per month were being transported up the Danube, and some 70,000 tons by rail. When the Danube reopened for navigation after freezing over during the winter months, SOE calculated that the river capacity could be increased to 200,000 tons per month, and the carrying capacity of the railways raised similarly to 200,000 tons by June.[71]

Whilst recognizing the impossibility of destroying the oilfields, the memorandum argued that 'fairly serious damage' could be caused to the oilfields and refineries by persistent bombing which would set the wells on fire and 'very likely' destroy the refineries. The traffic in Russian oil across the Black Sea could be attacked by destroying the tankers carrying the oil and by destroying the oil depots. SOE revealed that sabotage was being carried out in Romania by SO(2) agents in the form of derailment of oil trains, occasional rail-cutting, insertion of acids into axleboxes of tank cars and engines, and the blowing up of pipelines. Large-scale sabotage involving attacks on bridges, tunnels and marshalling yards was considered to be 'very difficult to arrange under present conditions with any frequency or continuity'.[72] One bridge was of particular interest, however, that over the River Ialomiţa, between Bucharest and Ploieşti, across which all oil supplies from the Romanian fields destined for transport by the Danube, and a small part of those for transport by rail, had to pass. Destruction of the bridge would interrupt this traffic.

Experience had shown that small-scale attacks on tugs and barges, undertaken in Yugoslav waters in autumn 1939 and in spring and summer 1940, were 'quite useless'. SOE proposed air attacks on fields and refineries, marshalling yards and harbours, but these were not 'within its sphere'. Where it did feel it could act was in trying to produce an internal upheaval in Romania, by blowing up the Ialomiţa bridge, and by blocking the Danube at points in the Kazan defile (the Iron Gates) in Yugoslavia.

Regarding the former, SOE had aimed at raising 'serious trouble' only in the event of a complete German military occupation. It had, nevertheless, 'the necessary connections with various organizations in Romania, such as the Peasant Party, the Communists and certain sections of the Iron Guard, which could be used to produce an upheaval as quickly as possible'.[73] Plans for mining cliffs in the Kazan defile and blocking had been prepared in September 1939 and were well on the way to completion by the middle of December 1939 when the Yugoslav government intervened, stopped the work and took over the mines which had already been laid. Blocking the Kazan defile would, in SOE's estimation, be 'likely to deal the Germans a really crippling blow', but it could only be carried out with the help of the Yugoslav General Staff and 'the only condition on which they [the Yugoslav government] would possibly agree to complete the work is that it should be done as a precautionary measure of defence against the German invasion and that the charges would only be fired after Yugoslavia had been attacked'.[74]

SO(2)'s plans for an 'upheaval' came to nothing; the RAF pleaded that it had no aircraft available for bombing the Romanian oilfields, and the proposed Kazan operation was aborted after the German invasion of Yugoslavia. The withdrawal of the British legation meant that there was no SOE officer to coordinate any sabotage action by the Romanians. On 10 February Hoare informed Antonescu by note:

> It has become abundantly evident that this country's Government which you have directed for six months has become entirely dependent on Germany. Not only actual facts but also numerous statements published by yourself confirm this. Some months ago you informed me that a small

number of German troops were arriving in Roumania in order to instruct the Roumanian Army in modern methods of warfare and that the necessary equipment was likewise being despatched from Germany for the re-armament of the Roumanian troops.

Some instruction has no doubt been imparted, but the essential development is that the German High Command is building up in Roumania all the elements of an expeditionary force, and is concentrating at various strategic points large supplies of munitions and oil fuel. Roumanian territory is thus being used by Germany as a military base in furtherance of her plans for prosecuting the war. These measures are being taken without one word of dissent from you. In these circumstances, His Majesty's Government in the United Kingdom have decided to recall me and to withdraw the diplomatic Mission and the Consular Officers under my control. I therefore propose to leave this country on the 15th February or as soon after as a ship is available to convey my party to Istanbul, and I have been instructed by His Majesty's Government to request that all the facilities and courtesies which are customary in the circumstances may be accorded to my Mission and the British Consular Staffs.[75]

On the eve of Britain's severance of diplomatic relations Hoare, admitting that 'the game is up', could do nothing more than agree with Maniu that the National Peasant Party should maintain contact with the British by radio.[76] And for almost three years radio and occasional courier were the means of contact with Romania. A wireless set was left with Valeriu 'Rică' Georgescu (code-named 'Jockey') and ten million *lei* from the coffers of the British-owned Unirea Oil Company to fund a resistance group of members of Maniu's party.[77] The Minister's final impression was that 'though Maniu's intentions are the very best, he is sadly lacking in inspiration... However, there is nobody else who could head a patriotic movement, and so at present it is Maniu or nothing.'[78]

SOE were of the same opinion.[79] At a meeting at the Foreign Office on 20 February, SOE representatives revealed that their programme in Romania was 'entirely dependent' on the support of Maniu and the Peasant Party on whom they would have to rely for their communications with Romania once the British legation had left.[80] Maniu had apparently promised both Hoare and de Chastelain that he, too, would leave shortly afterwards, but he did not and the trickle of messages forwarded by [Georgescu] gave no reason why.

The problems arising from Maniu's indecisiveness were not helped by scheming with Romanian emigré circles in London. Partly out of deference to Maniu the Foreign Office refused to support a 'Free Romanian Movement' in Britain. A second reason was that no other Romanian abroad was considered 'of sufficient calibre to command serious [domestic] support'. Finally, after June 1941 such a move was expected to dangerously complicate relations with the Soviet Union.[81] Without such an organization, Romanian émigrés allowed themselves to be riven by factionalism, thereby reducing their effectiveness as a political group to the Foreign Office and SOE. Viorel Tilea, the former Romanian Minister to London, proved to be particularly difficult. In early 1941 Tilea was allowed to establish a 'Romanian National Committee' but the Foreign Office withheld recognition or publicity.[82] Before long, a group of mostly Maniu's supporters broke away and formed a short-lived 'Romanian Democratic Committee' as they considered Tilea and his associates tainted by their past association with former King Carol.[83]

Nevertheless, Tilea continued his asociation with the radio station *Ardealul*. Following German implementation of Operation *Barbarossa* on 22 June 1941, *Ardealul* was directed to encourage Romania's disengagement from the war against the Soviet Union and to this end it adopted first the slogan 'stop at the Dniester', and then, 'withdrawal to the Dniester' after the pre-1940 boundary had been crossed.[84] On the thorny question of Romanian-Soviet relations, *Ardealul* contended that the former's security concerns would be better addressed if she withdrew from Soviet territory. The presence of the Romanian armies in Russia was attributed to a German plot to weaken Romania's ability to defend itself against Hungarian aggression. Later, *Ardealul* emphasized the scale of Romanian losses at Stalingrad and contrasted them to the much more modest Hungarian commitment to the Russian campaign.[85] Its message was that Romanian troops should be kept at home, ready for use 'against the Hungarian menace'.[86]

On 8 April 1941, the first message was received from Maniu's W/T set, known as Z.4.[87] It claimed to have been on the air for several weeks before this, but SOE Turkey possessed no W/T equipment of its own and was forced to rely upon the help of MI6 in Istanbul which had its hands full with its own traffic. Messages continued regularly from Z.4 until 23 June, the day after Germany and Romania attacked Russia.[88] The Romanian contacts proved an invaluable resource, penetrating even into the German High Command in Bucharest. As a consequence Popovici was able to let London know on 11 April 1941 that Germany would attack Russia on 15 June that year. This information was provided by General Alexander Manolescu, Rică Georgescu's uncle, from a source in the German High Command.[89]

Z.4 was used to exchange messages with advice from the British government over Germany's invitation to Romania to occupy the Serbian Banat:

> Maniu, and undoubtedly through him Antonescu, was warned that His Majesty's Government would regard as an enemy any country which sided with Germany against Soviet Russia. He was also informed by the emigré Yugoslav Government through HMG that the occupation of the Banat would be regarded as an enemy act subject to settlement at the

> Peace Conference, with inevitable bad effects on Romania's relations with Yugoslavia.[90]

Radio contact was broken when both Georgescu and his associates were caught by the Germans on 15 August 1941 and handed over to the Romanians.[91] Those arrested included Popovici, Badica Iaroslavici, Ion Beza (the operator of the W/T set),[92] Iosif Păsătoiu,[93] Ştefan Cosmovici, Alexandru Klamer, Ion Deleanu, Mihai Iaroslavici, Corneliu Radocea and Augustin Vişa.

The background to the group's arrest was given by Reinhard Heydrich, head of the Reich Main Security Office (RSHA), in a report to German Foreign Minister Joachim von Ribbentrop, dated 17 September 1941. The head of the SD in Istanbul, SS-Untersturmführer Emil Duplitzer, 'had managed to cast an eye' over a letter sent by one member of the MI6 network run by Archibald Gibson in Istanbul to another.[94] It emerged from the letter that its author, a Romanian citizen by the name of Constantin Mircea, had fallen out with Gibson over the latter's instructions to him to go to Palestine. Mircea intended to exact revenge upon Gibson over what he considered to be unjust treatment by handing over sensitive materials in his possession to the SSI, the Romanian intelligence service. With this in mind Mircea left Istanbul without informing Gibson. In order to prevent Mircea from handing over the material Gibson told another of his agents, Marin Iorgulescu, to follow Mircea and denounce him to the Romanian police as a British agent in order to ensure Mircea's arrest. Iorgulescu was said to have received 20,000 Turkish pounds from Gibson for this mission and was due to leave Istanbul by train on 1 August.

Duplitzer reached Bucharest before Iorgulescu and arranged for the SSI to arrest both Mircea and Iorgulescu. On the basis of information obtained from their interrogations, Ion Popovici was detained. He gave valuable details about what Heydrich called 'the British intelligence service':

> Given that Popovici knew how the service was organized as well as the names of the British officers involved, having at his disposal the sum of 47 million lei, he can be considered in all probability the head of the British espionage network in Romania. In particular, Popovici set up and used a secret W/T transmitter which, among other things, played a part in dissemination of propaganda on the question of Transylvania. The money and the radio have been confiscated together with the transmission codes. Popovici's revelations led to the arrest of a further ten persons. Immediately after his arrival in Bucharest SS-Untersturmführer Duplitzer gave a detailed briefing to minister von Killinger.[95]

One of those given up by Popovici was Augustin Vişa.[96] Profoundly moved by the loss of northern Transylvania to Hungary in August 1940 he offered his help to Popovici in the belief that only Britain could help Romania to regain the territory. In a memoir written more than thirty years after his arrest in 1941, but published only after the 1989 revolution,[97] he wrote that he had been asked by Maniu in November 1940 to get in touch with a nephew of his (i.e. of Maniu), Iuliu (Ilarie) Sache Bălan,[98] with a request that the latter build a wireless transmitter so that the Peasant Party leader could maintain contact with SOE after the departure of de Chastelain and his replacement from Bucharest. Bălan was head of the Bucharest repair shop at AEG, the German electrical manufacturer. Progress on the radio was slow and in an effort to speed things along Maniu instructed Vişa to collect from Popovici an additional sum of money for Bălan.[99]

The set was completed by mid-December and a few days before it was handed over to Vişa, Maniu gave him a cipher and a key with instructions from SOE in its use. It was Vişa's first experience of enciphering and he required several days of practice. The wireless transmission – by morse – was entrusted to an experienced telegraphist, Jean Beza, who worked for the Romanian LARES airline as a wireless operator. Beza was introduced by Popovici to Vişa and after Popovici took his leave the two of them picked up the transmitter from Bălan. They established contact with SOE, with de Chastelain, in early January 1941 during the latter's visit to Bucharest as a diplomatic courier. Among the messages composed by Maniu and enciphered by Popovici and Vişa was one addressed to Churchill which drew his attention to Carol II's 'damaging activity against Romania and King Michael'; another in which Maniu alerted Churchill that Serbs and Romanians in north-east Yugoslavia had asked the Romanian state to occupy the area temporarily until the end of the war to prevent it falling under Hungarian occupation; and a third in which a Soviet air raid in Bucharest was reported.[100]

Vişa was arrested in Sinaia and taken to Bucharest. He and his colleagues were transferred to the SSI prison called Malmaison on Calea Plevnei in Bucharest for interrogation. Vişa was questioned the next day by Captain Camil Bărbulescu[101] of the Romanian Military Police and by SS-Untersturmführer Duplitzer, about his links with Popovici, Beza and Bălan and asked to name other members of the group. Vişa denied that there were any other members. Maniu was not mentioned. Vişa was sent back to his cell and later Bărbulescu returned to see him on his own. He wanted to know who had built the radio transmitter, how he had come to know the other three members of the group, who had helped him with the encipering and deciphering, and what had made him 'become a spy'. He gave him a pen and paper and told him to provide answers by the following day.

Vişa, without mentioning Maniu, recounted how Bălan had constructed a transmitter, how he (Vişa) had found a skilled telegraphist in the person of Jean Beza, that he (Vişa) had a code with which he did the enciphering and decipering. No one other than himself knew the content of the messages transmitted and received. They had opened up contact in January

1941 when they sent a few preliminary messages to test the code and establish transmission times. They sent in total some six messages and received three or four. Vişa did not give details about the the Soviet air raid or the Serbian request, for fear of being accused of treason. He denied knowing Rică Georgescu. At further sessions with Bărbulescu he was asked about Iosif Păsătoiu and Constantin Mircea but, as with Georgescu, he said that he had never met them.[102]

Bărbulescu, in his report on his enquiries for the military authorities, revealed the circumstances surrounding the group's arrest.[103] It had been triggered by the arrival in Bucharest from Istanbul of a salesman, Marin Iorgulescu, who was suspected of being a courier for the 'Intelligence Service'.[104] A search of Iorgulescu's residence on 8 August 1941 produced nothing concrete but did confirm that he had contacts amongst the British and Romanian communities in Istanbul and that he knew the lawyer Constantin Mircea who had returned to Bucharest on 28 July 1941. Bărbulescu mentioned two British citizens who were 'forced to leave the country, as undesirables' the previous autumn, de Chastelain and Archibald Gibson,[105] and had settled in Istanbul. De Chastelain 'left behind numerous friends with whom he wished to maintain contact. The same can be said about the brothers Archibald and Harold Gibson who, like others in their temporary stay in Romania, reaped benefits while performing only modest labour. Suffice it to mention that de Chastelain received a salary at Unirea of £80, which was the equivalent of 200,000 lei.'[106]

Bărbulescu claimed that de Chastelain, on his arrival in Istanbul, had taken charge of the 'sabotage section' and Archibald Gibson, the 'espionage section' of the 'Intelligence Service', a fact which led him to conclude that both men had been engaged in spying during their residence in Romania. In an attempt to keep abreast of developments in Romania, both de Chastelain and Gibson met Romanians passing through Istanbul at a club called 'Taxim' which was part-owned by a Romanian citizen, Marin A. Iorgulescu. Bărbulescu pointedly remarked that Iorgulescu's partners were 'the Jews Stelescu, Minculescu and Komorovsky'.[107] Later the club was taken over by a Turk but Iorgulescu continued to play a leading role in the management. It became a regular haunt of the British colony in Istanbul as well as being a preferred venue for Romanians, among them the Peasant Party members Pavel Pavel, Ştefan Neniţescu and Cornel Bianu, all of whom were to move to London; businessmen such as Aurel Ştefanovici and Cornel Mihăescu; and the lawyer Constantin Mircea.

Mircea had studied in London and returned to Romania as a staunch Anglophile.[108] In May 1940 he married Lady Nelly Ford but the marriage soon fell apart. On 17 February 1941 they went to Istanbul where Mircea broke with his wife who went on to Australia. Mircea was well-known to both de Chastlelain and Gibson and he accepted 'their invitation to work for the British'.[109] He was asked to provide information about Romanians arriving in Istanbul, information that he conveyed in reports which he wrote in an office which Bărbulescu called 'the headquarters of British espionage, based in the British Inspectorate of Shipping in Missir Appartment'.[110]

Mircea performed this service for five months until he fell out with Gibson over a woman, Stella Penciu, a girlfriend of Gibson's. Mircea was offered a job in Palestine but he refused to go and instead returned to Romania at the end of July with Stella. His action unnerved de Chastelain and Gibson since Mircea was privy to certain aspects of British clandestine activities in Romania and they sent Marin Iorgulescu to warn Georgescu and his associates. Iorgulescu left Istanbul on 1 August with, Bărbulescu claimed, 20,000 Turkish pounds which he had received from either de Chastelain or Gibson 'to give probably to the British agents in Romania'.[111] Iorgulescu left at 9 pm by train, then travelled by car through Babeski-Svilengrad to Sofia, from where he caught a plane to Bucharest. When Iorgulescu's flat was searched in Bucharest, no trace of the money was found.

The report from Bărbulescu continued:

> It was from Constantin Mircea that we learned that Gibson and de Chastelain were kept informed about events in Romania by a wireless-transmitter in Bucharest, with which they were in contact almost very night... Among the persons suspected of being involved with the transmitter was Ion Popovici, a colleague of de Chastelain at the *Unirea* oil company. This character had cropped up in the spy scandal in which Henriette Sumpt and Maurice Negre were implicated since he had paid Sumpt 15,000 lei on behalf of de Chastelain... We can now establish that the the information which Sumpt and Negre sent to Istanbul also went to de Chastelain.[112]

Bărbulescu revealed that Popovici, in a fit of depression brought on by the news of his brother's death on the Eastern Front, had divulged under questioning a host of details about the transmitter, his own associates and his relations with the Georgescu group. The transmitter had been assembled by Iuliu Sache Bălan and functioned in his house on Strada Sabinelor no. 32. The messages were encoded using a cipher found in the office of Augustin Vişa and transmitted by Ion Beza, who received 60,000 *lei* per month from Popovici, with whom de Chastelain had left the sum of some 80 million *lei* to fund the activities of the group.[113] The principal informants were Mihai Iaroslavici-Bădică, a 'baptized Jew' in Bărbulescu's parlance; Ştefan Cosmovici, an unemployed engineer; Sandu Klamer, a 'Jewish police informer'; Miss Plesnilă, an employee of the Ministry of Propaganda; Ecaterina Levasz, a Hungarian by origin; Adolf Regenstreif (also known as Andrei Iliescu); and Adela Abramovici (also known as Didi Armof).[114]

Popovici declared in one of his (twenty-one) statements to Bărbulescu that de Chastelain had informed him in January 1941 that a radio transmitter, allowing communication with Istanbul, would soon be brought into operation by Rică Georgescu. Georgescu contacted Popovici to find suitable associates for their cause and Popovici brought in Augustin Vişa whom he had first met at a bar frequented by Transylvanians in Bucharest. They had seen each other again at the funeral of the economist Virgil Madgearu in early December 1940. Vişa was given the cipher left by de Chastelain in January 1941 and Ilarie Bălan had been paid to build the set.

The encoding and decoding was done in Vişa's appartment on Strada Poenaru Bordea no. 16 by Vişa and Popovici, on occasions by Vişa alone. It was Popovici who taught Georgescu and Iaroslavici how to use the cipher but the messages to be encoded were composed either by Georgescu or by others. Popovici authored a single message, one asking the British to enquire with the Russians about the fate of his friend Senator Leanca, the former prefect of Bălţi, who had been deported to Siberia. When asked by Istanbul how the sabotage was going, Georgescu gave fictitious replies, claiming that various targets – usually bridges – had been blown up.[115]

By dint of bribery through Maniu and Mihai Popovici, an associate, the trial of Ion Popovici and his group was indefinitely postponed but in the words of the SOE 'history', 'work suffered a great setback which accounted for many of the delays and disappointments subsequently experienced. With the W/T set gone, contact with Romania could be maintained only through American diplomatic couriers, neutral diplomats and the few reliable Romanians able to travel.'[116]

The most active of neutral diplomats was a Turkish subject named Satvet Lutfi Tozan, an armaments dealer and honorary Finnish Consul in Istanbul. In November 1941 Tozan met Iuliu Maniu and Mihai Popovici in the house of the Turkish Ambassador, Suphi Tanriover, in Bucharest. Tozan was at this time collaborating in Istanbul with Commander Vladimir Wolfson of Royal Naval Intelligence and soon gained the confidence of Maniu and Popovici.[117] They explained to him the predicament of the Georgescu-Popovici group, stating that funds were urgently needed if their lives were to be saved. Tozan reported this on his arrival in Istanbul to Wolfson. He agreed to return to Romania to obtain Maniu's agreement to a programme of activity drawn up in consultation between the London, Cairo and Istanbul offices of SOE. SOE used Tozan to send $40,000 to Maniu, which, as the SOE 'history' diplomatically puts it 'was probably vital in the indefinite postponement of the trial of our collaborators'.[118]

6
Clandestine British Operations in Romania, 1942–1943

Until 3 August 1941, when the Romanian army began crossing the River Dniester into the pre-1940 Soviet Union as a partner in Nazi Germany's Operation *Barbarossa,* launched on 22 June, Romania had been re-conquering its own territory annexed by Stalin under threat of war. Indeed, the British government had not protested when Romanian forces crossed the River Prut into Bessarabia and Northern Bukovina at the end of June 1941. However, after August, Romania started to conduct hostilities on pre-1940 Soviet soil. Following the fall of Odessa in mid-October, Moscow began to apply increasing pressure on Britain to declare war on Romania – Stalin urged Churchill to act because Romania, alongside Finland and Hungary, was effectively at war with the Soviet Union. Churchill was reluctant to do this and set out his reasons in a letter to Stalin dated 4 November:

> These countries [Finland, Hungary and Romania] are full of our friends: they have been overpowered by Hitler and used as a cat's paw. But if fortune turns against that ruffian they might easily come back to our side.[1]

Stalin continued to press the matter as the Germans advanced towards Moscow and Churchill, realizing the need to give the Soviet leader a public gesture of support, finally acquiesced. On 29 November the British government sent an ultimatum via the US legation to the Romanian government pointing out that for several months it had been conducting aggressive military operations on the territory of the USSR, an ally of Great Britain, in close collaboration with Germany, and warning that unless the Romanians ceased military operations in the USSR by 5 December the British government would have no option but to declare the existence of a state of war between the two countries.[2]

The Romanian government did not reply until the day after the expiry of the ultimatum. It offered a justification for Romania's military action against the USSR which, it was argued, was one of legitimate self-defence in the face of Soviet aggression which had begun in 1940 with the occupation of Bessarabia and Northern Bukovina.[3] 'The Royal Romanian Government', the reply continued, 'is firmly convinced that its military action is the only way in which it can ensure its salvation against the visible Russian threat.'[4]

On 6 December the US Minister, Franklin Mott Gunther,[5] addressed the following message to Mihai Antonescu, the foreign minister:

> On 29 November, His Majesty's Government in the United Kingdom sent the Romanian Government through the US minister a message according to which if, by 5 December, the Romanian Government did not cease military operations and did not withdraw effectively from any active participation in the hostilities against the USSR, His Majesty's Government would have no option than to declare the existence of a state of war between the two countries. Since the Romanian Government has not responded to this message and since, according to the information available to His Majesty's Government there is no indication that the Romanian Government intends to accept the conditions mentioned above, a state of war will exist between the two countries from 12.01 Greenwich Mean Time on 7 December.[6]

On the following day Britain's declaration of war was duly enacted and Antonescu, who had served as military attaché in London and had a great admiration for Britain, expressed regret in a radio broadcast that his people's centuries-old struggle to preserve its existence, its liberty and its unity had not been understood. Romania's present action was in continuation of that struggle:

> The declaration of war is without foundation. I regret that there has been so little understanding of the turmoil and tragedy which for centuries has enveloped the brave and ceaselessly tormented and unjustly-stricken Romanian people [...].
>
> Romania accepts this challenge in the firm belief that, in the struggle against Communism, she serves not only the national belief, the right to preservation and honour of the Romanian people, but also serves, as in the past, through her struggle and her sacrifice, the very civilization to which Great Britain is bound.[7]

On 12 December, the day after war was declared on the USA by Germany and Italy, the ministers of the latter countries, respectively von Killinger and Bova-Scoppa, went together to Mihai Antonescu and advised the Romanian government to consider itself at war with the United States under the terms of the Tripartite Pact. As a result, Gheorghe Davidescu, a senior official in the Foreign Ministry, handed Benton, the US chargé in Bucharest, the Romanian declaration of war.[8] A clear indication of where Antonescu's loyalties lay, despite these developments, can be gauged from his admission – made after the entry of the United States into the war following the Japanese attack on Pearl Harbor on 7 December: 'I am an ally of the Reich against Russia, I am neutral in the conflict between Great Britain and Germany. I am for America against the Japanese.'[9]

Broader considerations of relations with its new ally, the Soviet Union, dictated British policy towards Antonescu after Britain's declaration of war. The defeat of the Axis powers and, as a prequisite for this goal, the preservation of Allied unity, became paramount issues for Churchill and Roosevelt and remained so throughout the war.

Stalin's request for a political agreement with Britain had been made in a message to Churchill on 8 November 1941. Annoyed by Britain's unwillingness to declare war on Romania, Finland and Hungary, Stalin wanted a specific treaty with Britain recognizing Soviet pretensions in Eastern Europe. Britain's eventual declaration of war on the three countries went some way towards placating Stalin, and in order to maintain Russian morale Churchill approved a visit to Moscow by Foreign Secretary Anthony Eden. Eden and his officials in the Foreign Office were against discussion of peace aims, a view which was strengthened by the entry of the United States into the war and the need to consult President Roosevelt on the subject.[10]

The day after his arrival on 15 December, Eden was received by Stalin who told him that he expected the western frontier of the Soviet Union to be the frontier of 1941, which included the Baltic States, part of Poland, and Bessarabia and Northern Bukovina, and that Romania should give special facilities for bases to the Soviet Union, receiving compensation from territory now occupied by Hungary.[11] In a letter to Churchill, who was in Washington, Eden predicted that 'if the Russians are victorious they will be able to establish these frontiers'.[12] The Foreign Secretary's foresight explains the pragmatism of British policy towards Romania thereafter and its subordination to the wider interest of relations with the Soviet Union.

Churchill made clear in a message of 21 December to Eden that he was unwilling to approach Roosevelt for American agreement to Stalin's proposals and advised Eden not to be disappointed if he failed to get a joint declaration in Moscow. Eden's hands were tied and Stalin, anxious to avoid the failure to secure an agreement becoming public, agreed that Eden should return to London for consultations on the assumption that these would lead to the signing of an Anglo-Soviet treaty within two or three weeks. It soon became clear that the period of two or three weeks was optimistic. Churchill was opposed to acceptance of the 1941 frontiers, especially as it flew in the face of the principles to which he had just put his name, alongside that of the American President, in the Atlantic Charter. Despite this, the cabinet decided to put the case for accepting Stalin's demands to Roosevelt. The British argument was that refusal to recognize the 1941 frontiers might lead Stalin to attempt negotiations for a separate peace with Germany. Roosevelt, on the other hand, was not convinced. Acceptance of the Soviet position would establish the precedent that frontiers could be settled before the post-war peace conference and would signify condonement of Russia's seizure of the Baltic states, thereby undermining the principles of the Atlantic Charter.[13]

Roosevelt tried to persuade Stalin to postpone the frontier question until the end of the war but Stalin simply replied that he would take note of his views. Churchill, concerned about British defeats in the Far East, became more conciliatory. He sent word to Roosevelt that 'the increasing gravity of the war has led me to feel that the principles of the Atlantic Charter ought not to be construed so as to deny Russia the frontiers she occupied when Germany attacked her'.[14] Roosevelt would not be persuaded and Molotov, now negotiating in London, continued to battle for this clause to be approved. After a good deal of wrangling between Eden and Molotov, the latter agreed to accept the British draft of a treaty on 26 May 1942 and it was signed, but without the inclusion of the territorial clause.

Romanian attitudes towards the Western Allies were described by Archibald Gibson, *The Times* correspondent who resided in Romania between 1924 and October 1940:

> In the light of their own bitter experience of Russia, it seemed to the Romanians quite inconceivable that the British and Americans could trust the Russians. The Romanians either just could not understand our enthusiasm over Soviet concessions to Western scruples, like the dissolution of the Cominform or greater freedom for religion in the Soviet Union, or dismissed it as feigned. They saw these Soviet moves as tactical retreats which in no way altered Moscow's long-term plans of bringing about the downfall of capitalism throughout the world.
>
> Crediting us with knowledge as deep as their own, the Romanians questioned the sincerity of flattering references to the Soviet Union in British and American statements, broadcasts and books. To the Romanians praise of the Soviet system was quite incomprehensible.
>
> They knew conditions to be worse in the Soviet Union than they were in Romania. They were also aware that the standard of living in Britain and the USA was far higher than in Romania. This fact the Romanian authorities did not hide from the Romanian people, unlike the Kremlin which concealed the gulf dividing British and American living standards from those in the Soviet Union.
>
> Despite evidence of the tremendous efforts which Britain and America were making to send the Soviet Union supplies via Persia and by the treacherous sea-route to north Russia, the Romanians thought it was all part of some deep-laid plan to make use of the Soviet Union for as long as was convenient, but for no longer. It is perhaps no wonder that in this frame of mind the Romanians could delude themselves that they were

> rendering the British and Americans a service by fighting the Russians. Or that the Romanians seldom, if ever, pondered the enormity of finding themselves the allies of Germany who, for the second time in a generation, had set the world ablaze and had brought death and destruction to millions, Romanians included.
>
> The Romanians do not appear to have reflected on the fact that their oil had helped the Luftwaffe to blitz Britain and keep the Panzers in action in every campaign which Germany had fought against Britain and her allies. They also seemed unaware that Romania's rejection of Britain's ultimatum of 30 November 1941, which had given Romania a chance of withdrawal from the war, had not advanced her cause in the Allied camp.
>
> Yet the failure of Romanians to realize that their partnership with Germany had excited the anger of former friends did not, as time went on, prevent them from becoming more and more outspoken about the increasing irksomeness of their association with the Germans. Firm in their conviction that collaboration between the Anglo-Americans and the Russians could not endure, the Romanians did what they could to propitiate the Western powers and to vilify the Soviet Union. Romanian propaganda heaped abuse unsparingly on the Russians and parsimoniously – just for the sake of appearances – on the British and Americans.[15]

For the British, Iuliu Maniu, the leader of the National Peasant Party, was the pivotal point for any action against the Antonescu regime. The priority for SOE was to repair the radio link. They were helped by two members of the Romanian foreign service, Ion Christu, chief of the economic section of the Foreign Ministry, and Cătălin Vlădescu-Olt, a secretary in the diplomatic service. In November 1941 Christu travelled to Istanbul as head of a Romanian trade delegation, of which Vlădescu-Olt was a member. At a meeting with de Chastelain, Christu agreed to urge Maniu to revive the communications link with the British.

Satvet Lutfi Tozan (SOE code name 'Pants') returned to Bucharest in December 1941 where he contacted Maniu and secured his agreement to:

(a) accept sufficient funds as a war chest with which to reorganize work against the Axis;
(b) accept two new W/T sets with their respective signal plans and ciphers;
(c) organize a large-scale go-slow movement in Romanian industry and means of transport;
(d) answer a number of questionnaires dealing with political, military and economic matters in Romania and in Hungary.[16]

Tozan agreed to visit Romania a second time to hand over funds, W/T sets, questionnaires and ciphers, but did not leave until mid-March 1942.

In early January 1942 the Foreign Office and SOE were in agreement that 'Maniu is our best hope of starting an anti-Axis movement' and that 'a *coup d'état* would be the goal to aim at'; the implication was that he should therefore stay in Romania.[17] However, correspondence in mid-January between Foreign Office officials suggests that Maniu had decided to leave Romania 'for British territory', and SOE in Cairo was asked to issue travel documents for the party under English names.[18] Yet Maniu appears to have had second thoughts for he never took up the opportunity. He argued that he had to remain in Romania to lead his Party since he was the only person capable of doing so. He also claimed that, had he gone into exile, this would have damaged his standing in Romania.[19]

A minute dated 9 February 1942, which appears to have been written by de Chastelain in Istanbul, notes that

> Towards the end of December we succeeded in getting a friend [Tozan] into Roumania to contact A [Alecu code name for Maniu] with whom our Istanbul organisation had been in close relations before the Axis occupation of that country and a number of our friends who acted as intermediaries were arrested and at the same time we lost our W/T communication.
>
> (1) From the contact that our friend had with A it resulted that:
>
> (a) He was still our friend.
> (b) That he was still convinced that we could win the war.
> (c) That he continued to believe that his country should be ranged on our side and in the war now proceeding between ourselves and the totalitarians.
>
> (2) A stated that he and his followers which included a number of generals in the Roumanian Army and with the assistance of the Army itself are prepared to revolt against the Antonescu Government and to attack the German occupying troops providing he received an Anglo-Russian assurance that the Russians will not invade Roumania.
> (3) To start revolt A stated that he considered that his intention is to persuade Roumanian troops from proceeding to the Eastern Front. This he claims he can do.
> (4) A also stated that he required two W/T sets which he would install in order to be in communication with us.
> (5) A indicated that he would require funds for distribution among his 60 country organisations and also for acquiring available arms and munition.
> (6) For the success of his revolt A did not ask for any outside armed assistance but if the above mentioned guarantee were given he suggested that leaflets be dropped over Roumania coinciding with the revolt.
> (7) From the telegraphic correspondence we have had with London it would appear that the desired guarantee will not be forthcoming

> by the 14th February when PANTS [Savtet Lufti Tozan] according to present plans intends paying his next visit to A. Indeed we have no encouragement from London to believe that the guarantee will be given at any time.[20]

Tozan eventually left by car for Sofia en route to Romania on the morning of 14 March 1942:

> Prior to his departure, he had despatched one W/T set via the Finnish courier to the Turkish Embassy in Bucharest and another via a returning Finnish consul to the Turkish Legation in Budapest. With him he took two cars, one containing a large quantity of tobacco as a present to the Finnish troops on the Russian front, a large number of cigarettes in the boxes of which were concealed part of the material for Maniu, a quantity of precious stones and foreign currency, questionnaires, signal plan and cipher. Travelling as a Finnish consul, he possessed *laissez-passers* for all frontiers and was not subject to customs examination. He performed a few commissions in Sofia and arrived in Bucharest towards the end of March, where he succeeded in handing over to Maniu the W/T set, cash, precious stones, questionnaires, signal plan and cipher. From there he proceeded to Budapest where by misadventure he was arrested and imprisoned.[21]

Although Maniu was now equipped to reorganize and re-establish communications with Istanbul, the W/T set never came on the air, replies to SOE questionnaires were never received, and frustration with him built up in the Foreign Office.[22] According to an MI6 source de Chastelain sent two other W/T sets through Vlădescu-Olt whom Christu arranged to be appointed Consul-General in Istanbul from 1 April 1942, and member, without any special duties, of the Romanian legation staff in Ankara from 1 July. Dividing his time between Istanbul and Ankara, Vlădescu-Olt was able to throw agents of the Romanian Secret Service (SSI) off his scent and see de Chastelain on several occasions.[23] He used his visits to Bucharest to take the two wireless transmitters.[24]

Maniu's indecisiveness did not prevent Eden from presenting him to the Russians as the best chance of getting Romania to abandon the Axis. An aide-memoire handed by Eden to Maisky, the Soviet ambassador to London, on 21 March argued that the only person with whom negotiations over Romania's exit from the war could be conducted was Maniu.[25] Six days later, Eden enquired whether Maisky had received a response, and on 29 April he wrote again. It was only on 15 May that the ambassador told Eden that the Soviet government 'did not for the moment want to take any action with M. Maniu'.[26]

There was also an absence of positive action on Maniu's part. It was most obvious at the paramilitary level. If the British believed that a 'patriotic movement' headed by Maniu would undertake the kind of resistance operations undertaken by Mihailovici and Tito in Yugoslavia, then they were to be sorely disappointed. Indeed, Maniu's inaction in this regard was acutely embarrassing to the Romanian section of SOE and contrasted with the sabotage – albeit isolated – of German supply trains by a handful of Communists who plotted sporadic attacks on the Romanian rail network designed to hinder the Axis war effort against the Russians. But the Communists were seen by most Romanians as traitors by virtue of their allegiance to Moscow, and by their continued subservience to the Comintern line which sought to justify the Soviet annexation of Bessarabia and Northern Bukovina. Petre Gheorghe, the secretary of the Bucharest Ilfov cell of the outlawed Communist Party, was arrested by the Romanian Secret Service and accused with an associate Nicolae Atanasoff of espionage in favour of the Soviet Union.[27] In summer 1942 Ştefan Foriş, the general secretary of the Party, whose relations with Gheorghe were strained, was alleged by colleagues to have refused to give any legal aid to Gheorghe and Atanasoff. At a summary trial in Ploieşti lasting only a single day – 6 August – both were found guilty and sentenced to death. After a delay of several months both were executed by firing squad on 8 February 1943.[28]

Antonescu had given the order in summer 1941 that if any act of sabotage was carried out by Communists, 20 Jewish Communists and five non-Jewish Communists would be shot in reprisal. There were occasional arrests of persons distributing Communist propaganda against the Antonescu regime. In a report of 18 August 1942, the head of the Bucharest police, General Palangeanu, reported that five printers had been arrested in January 1942 for printing and distributing a Communist pamphlet deriding the Romanian government. The ringleader had been sentenced to death. At a later date a further eight printers had been arrested for printing and distributing a speech of Stalin. Two received the death sentence.[29]

On the propaganda front a second 'black' station *Vocea Constiinţei Româneşti* had been established in Jerusalem in autumn 1941. It attacked corruption in Romania and raised the issue of Northern Transylvania.[30] Several months later, in June 1942, de Chastelain and Lt. Col. Edward Masterson, the Romania country section head based in Cairo, proposed that a fictitious resistance organization be launched on radio waves.[31] Broadcasts would create an impression of gestation and activity of the movement by planting 'hints of extensive operations and unified leadership' in the press of neutral countries.[32] Thus a third 'black' station, known as both *Postul luptei de eliberare* and *Mişcarea Luptătoare* went on the air from Jerusalem on 27 July 1942. It purported to be the home-based, official station of an anti-German movement composed of smaller organizations. Its imaginary leader, 'Vlaicu', was named after Vladislav, a 14th-century prince of Wallachia and one of Romania's most venerated medieval rulers. 'Vlaicu' himself would never speak. The alleged cells in Romania would receive instructions 'over the air', in code or *en clair*.

The station's main theme was the imperative for Romania to cease supplying, supporting and hosting the Germans, and its most vigorous contributors were George Beza and Petru Vulpescu.[33] To assist Beza and Vulpescu as speakers over the 'Vlaicu' radio, Nicolae Marinescu, an employee of the Taxim Restaurant in Istanbul, was engaged in November 1942 and despatched to Palestine. Details of their propaganda theme and instructions to Romanians in the matter of sabotage and go-slow tactics were originally submitted to and approved by Colonel Tom Masterson.[34] The financing proper of the 'Vlaicu' movement inside Romania was organised by Lt. Col. E. C. Masterson with the assistance of the Greek brothers, Djavouris.

In November 1942 SOE Cairo reported that the scheme was having an effect inside Romania 'thanks to proper coordination between leaflets and radio'. One hundred thousand leaflets had been dropped, addressed to 'Vlaicu' and promising support. The latter's appreciation was then broadcast, together with a proclamation to the Romanian people, which was also dropped in leaflet form.[35] Evidence that the 'Vlaicu' operation caused embarrassment to the Antonescu regime was obtained from comment in the Romanian press and over the Romanian broadcasting service, and on the arrest of several collaborators by the Romanian authorities in July 1944.[36]

'Recurring difficulties' with the first 'black' station *Ardealul*'s Romanian team, and duplication with the other two stations led to its replacement with a fourth station *Porunca Mareşalului* (The Marshal's Order) which was launched on 21 July 1943.[37] A fifth station, *Prahova*, targeting oil production, began broadcasting from England on 18 October 1943. It advocated 'go-slow methods in order to conserve Roumanian oil-supplies' and thus reduce the flow to Germany.[38] By spring 1944 the rapid advance of the Red Army reduced the effectiveness of anti-German propaganda since in the minds of most Romanians the Soviet menace outweighed any disadvantages the continued alliance with Germany might bring. *Prahova* was consequently closed down on 30 April and *Porunca Mareşalului* suffered the same fate on 26 June 1944.[39]

Interruption of Romanian oil production remained a priority for the Allies. With action on the ground impractical, they turned to attack from the air. The first air raids on the oilfields at Ploieşti had been carried out by Soviet aircraft between 1 July and 18 August 1941, but they appear to have caused little damage.[40] Almost a year passed before the Western Allies were in a position to launch an attack, and then the opportunity arose more by accident than design. In May 1942 twenty-three B-24 Liberators of the United States Army Air Force (USAAF) under the command of Colonel Harry Halverson, left Florida for deployment in South-East Asia via the Middle East. Whilst in Khartoum, Japanese advances in China overran the bases from which Halverson was to operate. Halverson received new orders to attack the oil refineries at Ploieşti with fuel and bombs provided by the Royal Air Force. His force was moved to the Suez Canal base at Fayid and took off late in the evening of 11 June.

Their plan was a daring one and represented the first USAAF attack on a European target. Not one of the airmen taking part had been on an operation to an opposed distant target, and the USAAF had never tried the B-24 in action. Consideration of Turkish neutrality meant that the bombers had to be brought in over Constanţa, and since the range to the target was some 1,300 miles, the recovery airfields were to be in Iraq, which at that time was under Allied control. Thirteen aircraft took off, of which twelve aircraft reached Ploieşti but no bomb fell in the target area. No aircraft were lost to enemy action; six landed in Iraq, two in Syria, and four were interned in Turkey.

As one Romanian historian has concluded of Maniu's behaviour throughout 1942, in the eyes of the British the Peasant Party leader, while a perceptive political analyst, could not be relied upon to either make decisions or to give firm directions to his supporters.[41] Efforts were made to spur him into action by de Chastelain who developed contact with one of the Romanian Vice-Consuls in Istanbul, Cătălin Vlădescu-Olt, and his wife, both acquaintances of de Chastelain since the early days of the war in Romania.[42] This couple had collaborated with Ion Christu[43] of the Ministry of Foreign Affairs for ten years and were respectively his personal assistant and secretary when he was Minister of Foreign Trade in 1940.

Christu himself came to Turkey in November 1942 as Chairman of a Romanian economic mission to negotiate supplies of cotton in Turkey against deliveries of petroleum products. De Chastelain and Edward Masterson had long conversations with Christu, urging upon him the need for immediate action aimed either at the German war effort or the overthrow of the Antonescu regime. Before his return to Romania, Christu indicated his intention of angling for the appointment of Romanian Minister either in Ankara or in Sofia, in either of which positions he would be able to collaborate with the British. He made it a condition, however, that this should not be held against him by the British government at the end of the war. The 'history' of SOE states that Christu, on his appointment as Minister in Sofia, 'proved a great disappointment and failed to appreciate the solidarity of the military alliance between the Soviet Union and the Western Powers and Romania's guilt in her aggressive campaign against the Soviet Union'.[44]

Vlădescu-Olt, on the other hand, was judged to be a more active and sensible collaborator, and in the course of his meetings with de Chastelain made frequent trips to Bucharest to contact various groups of the opposition. In November 1942, following up arrangements made in the early days of the war between Tom Masterson and the managing directors of two oil companies, Coco Dumitrescu of Unirea, and Dumitru Gheorghiu of the Creditul Minier, Gheorghiu went to Istanbul ostensibly to negotiate with de Chastelain on behalf of Unirea for the sale of that company to the Creditul Minier. The real object of his visit, however, was to report from Maniu and another notable Romanian individual, Nicolae Caranfil. Maniu informed de Chastelain through Gheorghiu that 'for the first time in Romania's political history, all political parties, groups and important personalities had sunk their differences to form a coalition under his leadership'.[45]

Among the principal figures in this group, Gheorghiu listed Dinu Brătianu,[46] Gheorghe Brătianu,[47] Ion Lugoşianu,[48] Nicolae Caranfil,[49] George Caranfil,[50] Ion Christu, Alexander Creţianu,[51] Savel Rădulescu,[52] Radu Cruţescu and many others.

> It appeared that Caranfil was the motive power behind this group and, while appreciating Maniu's value as a symbol for a popular political movement, knew him to be too conservative for the action required. This coalition proposed placing key men in the more important ministries such as the Interior, War and Communications, as a prelude to staging a *coup d' état* as soon as they would judge German forces in Romania sufficiently weak to give their action a reasonable chance of success. They further conditioned this action, however, upon Allied (Anglo-American) troops being within striking distance of Romania's frontiers.[53]

Gheorghiu went back to Romania in December 1942 with instructions from de Chastelain to inform his friends that it was up to them to take action of whatever kind they could as quickly as possible and that they should not rely upon support from Anglo-American forces. He returned to Istanbul in March 1943, accompanied by Mircea Durma, as representative of the Romanian National Bank, but in point of fact as an envoy of Mihai Antonescu:

> Gheorghiu was urged to insist upon Maniu reopening W/T communications at the earliest possible moment, but in order to bridge the gap until this should happen, he was given a special figure cipher, called Cipher No. 5, with which it was proposed to transmit messages to Maniu over the BBC in the German broadcasts. Such messages began on 12 April 1943 and continued throughout the year, proving a very successful method of one-way communication.[54]

There remained a serious obstacle to any action by Maniu – suspicion of Russia's intentions in the event of a German-Romanian defeat. In September 1942 Maniu had communicated his concern to SOE: 'so long as we do not know positively... that the allied nations are willing to exclude a Russian invasion of Romania once the German front collapses... it is practically impossible for our opposition ... to come out against the Axis and organize anything with concrete effect'.[55] The Foreign Office was unwilling to raise this matter with Moscow, for fear of giving the Russians an opportunity to openly declare their interests in respect of Romania.[56]

By the end of the year, the idea of leaving Romania seems to have found favour once more with Maniu. At the same time he advanced the idea of an Allied (but not Soviet) airborne landing to back up a Romanian volte-face. Such overtly anti-Soviet initiatives worried the Foreign Office which remained convinced that no action regarding Romania should be taken without consulting the Russians, a view which they conveyed to the State Department in January 1943.[57]

In a reply to Sir Charles Hambro, head of SOE,[58] Sir Alexander Cadogan, Permanent Under-Secretary at the Foreign Office[59] explained the FO's position on 31 December 1942:

> The short-term advantages of cooperating with Maniu (i.e. sabotage, disruption of the army etc.) are too small and too problematic to justify the long-term disadvantage of committing ourselves in advance with regard to the political and territorial future of Romania. From his messages, it seems clear to us that Maniu is primarily interested not in working out immediate plans for sabotage and mutiny, but in formulating a policy for the future of Romania and in safeguarding as far as possible her position at the eventual peace settlement ... It is obvious that he is most anxious to induce us to guarantee the frontiers of Romania against both Hungary and the Soviet Union, and particularly against the latter.
>
> Since in the nature of things the Soviet Government have a special interest in Romania, we have always recognized that we cannot adopt a positive policy towards Romania without first consulting the Soviet Government. It was for this purpose that we offered last spring to put the Soviet Government in touch with Maniu. The fact that they declined our offer is, I think, proof that they intend to keep their hands free.
>
> If we now again raise the question with the Soviet Government and put forward definite proposals for the future territorial settlement and government of Romania on the lines desired by Maniu, we shall be making a beginning to which there is no visible end. Once started, these discussions could not possibly be limited to Romania, but would inevitably extend to the post-war settlement of the whole of the Balkans and of Central Europe. When the time comes to discuss these problems with the Soviet Government there will be trouble enough, quite apart from Romania, and it is even possible that in order to get what we want in other respects, we shall have to acquiesce in the Soviet Government's claim to dispose of Romania as they wish, and in order to save the rest of the Balkans, we may even be obliged to throw Romania to the wolves. You will understand, therefore, that it is politically impossible for us at present either

to formulate a positive policy with regard to the future of Romania or to tackle the Soviet Government on these lines.

As I have said above, we do not rate the prospects of effective sabotage in Romania very high, nor do we believe that Maniu is in a position to make a really substantial contribution to the war effort. Nevertheless on this point we are prepared to admit that we may be wrong. If Maniu really can bring about the disintegration of the Romanian armies in the Soviet Union, then it would of course be worthwhile paying him a fairly stiff price. In this, however, the Russians are mainly concerned. It is they who will be the chief gainers by such a move and they who will have to pay the price. Theirs must therefore, we think, be the decision. We would propose then, if you see no objection, to pass on to the Soviet Government some of the information contained in your papers and to ask them whether, in the circumstances, they now wish to get in touch with Maniu.[60]

The Foreign Office therefore temporized over a request from Maniu in the following month to send representatives to London, until they conferred with Moscow. In March 1943 the Russians reacted. Eden, who was visiting Moscow, received a personal letter from Molotov. Whilst declining any contact with Maniu themselves, the Russians supported continued British links: 'it is possible that in the course of negotiations a basis may be found for collaboration between this group and the British and Soviet governments'.[61]

With this green light from Moscow, SOE was given authority to prepare missions to Romania. The first, code-named 'Ranji', was dispatched in June 1943 to work alongside Maniu. Captain Thomas Charles David Augusten Russell MC of the Scots Guards was dropped into Yugoslavia together with a Romanian wireless operator Nicolae Ţurcanu on the night of 15–16 June, to be met by a reception committee arranged by a British Mission with Mihailovici's forces in the Homolje area.[62] This was the first British-led mission to be despatched by SOE to Romania since it had entered the war. The mission's task was to penetrate into Romania for the purposes of 'opening-up W/T communications, effecting contact with Maniu's organization, and establishing a reception area in the Romanian Carpathians'.[63]

This mission to Yugoslavia was led by Captain Jasper Rootham.[64] He described his new colleague thus: 'David Russell, tall, fair-haired and blue-eyed, with an infectious smile, instantly won all hearts, not least because he was the Serbs' idea of what an Englishman should look like.'[65] Rootham considered Russell's mission 'a madcap one' and hazardous,[66] an opinion shared by the local Chetnik commander Velja whose warning turned out to be sadly prophetic:

[Velja] said also that in his view it would be most unwise for Russell to go only with his wireless operator, and offered to provide a bodyguard of thirty men if we would arm them. There were, he explained, numbers

> of villages on the Romanian side of the Danube whose inhabitants were Serb; he had contact with them and would be able to organize a sort of base headquarters for Russell from which he could sally forth on his appointed task. Otherwise, said Velja with the utmost seriousness, he would not give much for Russell's chances. He would be murdered by some Rumanian peasant for his money.[67]

After a preliminary reconnaissance of the Golubac area, the 'Ranji' mission, augmented by a Romanian-speaking Serb Chetnik eventually crossed the Danube into Romania on 2 August. Towards the middle of the month they established themselves in a forest near Vârciorova, where they made contact with the Pitulescu brothers, one of whom was a prominent Peasant Party associate of Maniu, and from where they sent their first W/T messages from Romania on 12 and 13 August. It was in this forest that Captain Russell was murdered on 4 September, probably for the gold sovereigns he was carrying to use as payment. A post-war enquiry never succeeded in establishing by whom he was killed. Ţurcanu, who discovered his body, reported his death to SOE in Cairo on 20 September from Bucharest under the code name 'Reginald' using a Royal Navy cipher which he kept on a silk handkerchief.[68] Ţurcanu had taken shelter at the flat of an old friend, Captain Radu Protopopescu, who obtained false papers for him and told him of friends who were willing to take action against the Germans in Romania.[69]

Recent research based on SOE papers provides more details about Russell's death.[70] After crossing the Danube on 2 August into Romania the team moved some fifty miles, reaching Mehadia where the former mayor, Madgearu, was a well-known supporter of Maniu. They spent the night with him, after which Madgearu opined that they would be safer staying in one of his two vineyards. To reduce suspicions should they be discovered, he insisted that they left their weapons and uniforms with him so that he could hide them in his other vineyard:[71]

> As an afterthought, Russell asked him to stash the propaganda leaflets they had brought with them and to distribute them in the village two to three weeks later. Leaving them alone for the night, Madgearu disappeared and returning the next morning, completely drunk. When he had sobered up, he told them he had distributed the leaflets throughout the town. Not surprisingly a house-to-house search conducted by the gendarmerie, police and Gestapo was in full swing.
>
> 'Why did you distribute the leaflets?' asked the team in one voice.
>
> 'Why not? Did you want me to make soup with them?'[72]

Unnerved by Madgearu's indiscretions Russell and Ţurcanu sent him off to find a car to take them to Timişoara 'where they had important business'.[73]

With Madgearu out of the way, they found their way to the station, caught a train to Turnu Severin from where they returned to Vârciorova. Here they contacted Ion Pitulescu, the local National Peasant Party leader, but he did not have the authority from Maniu to negotiate with Russell. Pitulescu therefore made the long journey to Bucharest, only to discover that Maniu was being treated in hospital in Braşov, some 180 kilometres to the north of Bucharest.

> Forced to kill time for three weeks, the three-man SOE team kept to the woods close to the village. Towards the end of August, due to increased enemy patrolling, they moved to the far end of a heavily wooded valley called Fundul Vâdiţei, about 4 to 6 kilometres from the village, where they occupied an abandoned fishermen's hut dug into the ground and covered with branches. Here they encountered a local woodsman called Dumitru Burcu. Every day, Ţurcanu went down to the Pitulescu house to send messages (composed by Russell) while Russell and Petre Mihai remained at the hideout.[74]
>
> It was on one of these occasions – on Saturday 4 September 1943 – that Russell was killed in mysterious circumstances, found shot in the head from behind, less than a week after his twenty-eighth birthday. An investigation immediately started, both on the ground and back at SOE HQ in Cairo. According to Turcanu, who had been delayed at the Pitulescu house until the early hours of the morning of 5 September due to poor radio transmission conditions, he had returned to the hut and found Russell dead. Everything in the hut had been turned upside down. Both Russell's watches[75] were missing and Petre Mihai was nowhere to be found. Ironically, Pitulescu arrived back from Bucharest that same day with authority from Maniu to engage with Russell's SOE mission.[76]

Before his murder, Russell had hidden most of the mission's money (in gold sovereigns) and sensitive documents in a tree about fifty metres away from the hut. After retrieving them, Ţurcanu made his way to Bucharest with the radio and money where, after making contact with Maniu's supporters, he was settled in a flat and able to resume his transmissions. Petre Mihai (Nicolae Petra) arrived shortly afterwards in Bucharest and related his story to Ţurcanu:

> After you [Ţurcanu] left, we [Petre Mihai and Russell] bathed in the stream, ate, told stories and jokes and when evening came, drank a brandy and then went into the hut where we continued talking till we fell asleep. At about 9.30 or 10.30 pm, I woke up to the noise of crackling leaves (that is to say dried leaves trodden by somebody). I listened and heard the steps becoming louder and louder, then I stretched my hand to touch Thomas [Russell] to wake him but he was also awake and I said

> 'I hear'... I crawled out through the back of the hut... I see suddenly a flash of light, exactly like the light of a torch you had and at the same time I hear the shout 'Hands up or I shoot' and I could hear a number of shots being fired as if from an automatic rifle.[77]

In a report drawn up by Captain Silviu G. Meţianu of SOE on Russell's death, the author wrote that Mihai Pitulescu suspected very strongly that the woodsman, Dumitru Burcu, was connected with the shooting. He was spending money 'freely on his young woman' shortly after the incident. Mrs Pitulescu also had in her possession a long written statement by Petre Mihai but Meţianu could not decipher it since it was in Serbian.[78]

Nevertheless, SOE investigations into the murder to find the perpetrator could produce no hard evidence against anyone. Word had soon spread of the mission's presence in the area, attracting police and military patrols and several bands of cut-throat thieves including Serbian guerrillas. In a US Office of Strategic Services (OSS) report dated 3 November 1944, a source claimed that between 29 August and 19 September 1943, Romanian officials knew about a three-man W/T party. The information was highly accurate: Vella Nicolo Antonio, 'a soldier of fortune'; Albert Thomas, 'a British or American'; and Petre Mihai, 'a Serb Chetnik'. A forest ranger had reported them, noting that Thomas was in British Army battledress and Petre Mihai in Romanian peasant costume.[79]

In weekly Progress Report No. 61 for the week ending 23 September 1943,[80] the SOE desk officer wrote: 'in conclusion, it is pointed out that Russell probably undertook one of the most difficult of missions, bearing in mind that Romania is an enemy country and no reception arrangements could be made for him. The result of this mission is that we are now in W/T communication with Romania, which we have been trying to establish for the past two years.' Charles St George Maydwell, Russell's Commanding Officer informed the family.[81]

Ţurcanu had indeed reached Bucharest where he established contact with Dumitriu Gheorghiu and with an ex-collaborator of SOE under Harris-Burland, Radu Protopopescu. Protopopescu provided shelter for Ţurcanu and allowed him to operate his W/T set from his house until the latter's detection by German radio geometry on 14 July 1944.[82]

Amidst British efforts to goad Maniu into decisive action, interruption of Romanian oil production remained a priority for the Allies. On Sunday 1 August 1943, 178 B-24 Liberators of the 9th USAAF left Benghazi to bomb the Ploieşti oil refineries. Unknown to Allied intelligence, the Luftwaffe had placed a signal interception group near Athens which had broken the Allied code and was reading 9th USAAF transmissions. A short message to Allied forces in the Mediterranean alerting them of the mission, code-named 'Tidal Wave', was intercepted. As a result German aircraft were expecting the attackers. Of the B-24s launched, 163 actually bombed the target. Fifty-three

Liberators were lost, including eight interned in Turkey; 55 were damaged, and 310 airmen killed (about one in five of the 1,620 airmen who reached the target area). The Luftwaffe's losses were four aircraft over Ploieşti and two over Greece. The Romanian air force losses were recorded as two planes.[83]

A Romanian government communiqué, released the day after the attack, was remarkably frank:

> The raid lasted three hours. The American aircraft, which approached in single groups, made the Ploieşti district their chief target, avoiding Bucharest and flying over the summer resort of Snagov (over the lake of that same name) at a height of 200 metres. By a curious coincidence, Marshal Antonescu and the Vice-President Mihai Antonescu were sailing on the lake in a motor-boat, but fortunately for them no bombs were dropped there. The aircraft flew over the town of Ploieşti for more than half an hour at a low altitude, probably with the objective of making a reconnaissance and spotting their objectives. The attack then began in earnest and all important objectives connected with the oil industry were hit with such accuracy that only two bombs fell in the suburbs of the city near to the station, destroying four or five buildings and causing some casualties... The number of casualties is fairly low in view of the importance of the attack: 100 persons were killed and 200 injured, half of whom were women inmates of the Ploieşti women's prison.[84]

7
The 'Autonomous' Mission

In strategic terms, Romania's fate was settled at the Tehran Conference of Stalin, Roosevelt and Churchill at the end of November 1943. Soviet victories against the Germans had brought them to the western bank of the Dnieper River and convinced the American chiefs of staff of the wisdom of liberating Europe by invading Germany from the west, to meet the Red Army invading from the east. Churchill's preference for a strategy of liberation based on the Mediterranean was rejected, and with it any hope of getting US and British troops into the Balkans before the Russians. The insistence on the 'west-east' strategy ensured that Stalin would be in a position to impose his will wherever the Red Army advanced. The basic problem for Britain and the United States after Tehran was what limits would Stalin observe, or could be persuaded to observe, on his newly acquired freedom of action. Unlike Stalin, neither Churchill nor Roosevelt could call upon military force to support their arguments in respect of Eastern Europe. Their alternatives were therefore either to acquiesce to Stalin's demands, or to try to stay his hand by concluding agreements to which he could be held. In fact, they tried both.[1]

Within a month of the Tehran Conference Romania began to influence strategic decision-making. A second SOE mission to Romania had been planned in spring 1943. De Chastelain, the head of SOE in Istanbul, left Turkey for London and in July travelled to Canada in order to recruit native speakers for missions to Bulgaria, Hungary and Romania. He returned to London and went on to Egypt for parachute training in preparation for the mission to Romania, code-named 'Autonomous'. Radio contact was maintained through 'Reginald' with Rică Georgescu, code name 'Jockey', who despite being in jail in Bucharest, was given liberal visiting rights by the authorities and was allowed to roam at leisure inside the prison.[2] Originally, the mission had been conceived as a classical operation – to disrupt German communications – but Stalin unexpectedly agreed in November that Maniu should be allowed to send an emissary to the Allies to discuss operational details for the overthrow of Antonescu's regime and 'its replacement by a Government prepared to surrender unconditionally to the three principal

Allies'. The Soviet government insisted that a Soviet representative take part in the negotiations. 'Autonomous' now assumed a predominantly political purpose, de Chastelain's task being to inform Maniu personally of the apparent Soviet change of heart.[3]

On 22 November de Chastelain made his first attempt to parachute into Romania from Tocra airfield near Benghazi. After finding no signals at the dropping zone, the plane, a Liberator, turned back but an error in navigation over Albania caused it to run short of fuel and de Chastelain and the crew bailed out off the Italian coast near Brindisi. The place chosen for landing in Romania, an estate called Storobăneasă situated some twenty miles north of the Danube and south-east of the town of Alexandria, belonged to the Racotta family. Alexandru (Sandu) Racotta, a staunch Anglophile and close friend of Rică Georgescu, had visited Georgescu in prison and on one visit had been asked to help the 'Autonomous' mission. Racotta agreed. Racotta and 'Reginald' had been charged by Georgescu with waiting at the drop zone for de Chastelain but their car broke down and they were unable to get there.

De Chastelain's second attempt was made with Ivor Porter, a former English-language teacher in Bucharest, who had been recruited into SOE in spring 1941 after leaving Romania.[4] They took off on 5 December but failed to spot the ground signals giving them the all-clear to jump and returned to Egypt. On the third occasion, de Chastelain and Porter were accompanied by a Romanian sabotage expert, Silviu Meţianu,[5] recruited by Major Edward Boxshall[6] of SOE in London. At 00.30 hours on 22 December the three men were dropped in thick mist.

They landed some fourteen kilometres from the drop zone. With whistles to help them locate each other, de Chastelain and Porter soon met up but it took them over two hours to find Meţianu. They hid in a wood until daybreak and then set out to find the car which should have been awaiting them. De Chastelain asked a peasant woman for directions but on their way back they were seen by gendarmes and civilians with rifles who fired over their heads. They were escorted to the gendarmerie post in Ploşca, a village some 100 km to the south-west of Bucharest, where they were welcomed by the local dignitaries and given a hearty meal. Direction-finding equipment told the Germans about the presence of an aircraft near Ploşca and two German soldiers tried to reach the party but were turned away by the local officials. From Ploşca they were driven to Turnu-Măgurele and then on to police headquarters in Bucharest where they remained until their release on 23 August 1944. Their radio transmitter went with them.[7]

Having fallen into Antonescu's hands de Chastelain and Porter decided to inform the Marshal of the British government's attitude towards Romania and the latter's continuation of hostilities against Russia. They pointed out verbally and in writing to Antonescu through Generals Vasiliu and Tobescu that his first move should be to despatch envoys fully authorized to obtain armistice terms from the three Allies. The sequel to this was the departure from Romania to Turkey, and from there to Cairo, of Prince Barbu Stirbey in March 1944 and of Constantin Vişoianu some time later.[8]

During their internment in Bucharest, Berlin requested on several occasions that de Chastelain be handed over to them but Marshal Antonescu steadfastly refused. Two German officers were allowed to question the group, but under Romanian supervision. Senior Romanian officials interrogated the group independently, including General C. Z. Vasiliu, Deputy Minister of the Interior; Eugen Cristescu,[9] head of the Secret Service; and General Constantin Tobescu of the gendarmerie.[10] The prisoners were treated well, were taken for occasional drives, and de Chastelain was allowed to undergo dental treatment in town. At the end of March, Vasiliu, Cristescu and Tobescu visited de Chastelain in turn. They told him of their concern at the Russian advance and their fear for their own and their families' safety. Vasiliu toyed with the idea of fleeing to Istanbul, but only if de Chastelain accompanied him. The General was afraid of problems with the Turks, which he thought he would not be able to overcome without de Chastelain's help. Cristescu asked de Chastelain about prices in Istanbul. He seemed relieved to discover that he and his wife could live there for a year or two on the 4,000 gold dollars he had put by.[11]

Maniu wrote to the Marshal seeking better treatment for persons arrested for spying. Whether he had in mind the de Chastelain group or that of Rică Georgescu is unclear. Antonescu, in his reply of 19 February 1944, was diplomatically dismissive – he was also well-aware that Maniu was notoriously indiscreet in passing on details of exchanges between the two of them and was aware that his reply would reach the ears of the German legation:

> The Marshal is surprised that a former Prime Minister could propose to the authorities responsible for the country's destiny that they should break the law and create a special situation for persons who are subject to legal investigation and are required to be treated according to established procedures. The Marshal regrets that Mr Maniu is not aware of the serious consequences which would follow if the government resorted to acts which would show that it is in connivance with the spies and elements who were ready to endanger not only the country's security but also relations of friendship and alliance on which our security has been based and is still, to a large extent, based.[12]

The instructions for de Chastelain's mission included, as we have seen, advice to Maniu on the need for unconditional surrender. At the same time, the Foreign Office stressed that all approaches should be addressed to the Soviet and US governments, as well as to the British. It was in this spirit that the British ambassador to Moscow, Sir Archibald Clark Kerr, was instructed by the Foreign Office to inform the Soviets of contact made by a Romanian Colonel 'Black' with Cătălin Vlădescu-Olt, the Romanian consul in Istanbul, in summer 1943, whilst the latter was in Bucharest. Colonel 'Black' told Vlădescu-Olt of a plan by a group of Romanian officers to overthrow Antonescu and take Romania out of the war, but asked Vlădescu-Olt to keep his name secret, hence the use by SOE of the code word 'Black' for the colonel. According to 'Black', the group consisted of three generals – Nicolescu, Potopeanu and Sănătescu – but details of what forces they could count on were lacking.[13]

These details were passed on in Istanbul to de Chastelain by the Romanian Vice-Consul, Victor Caranfil, and in late October the Foreign Office told Clark Kerr that it saw no reason why they should not be communicated to the Soviet government.[14] At the beginning of 1944, Vlădescu-Olt was able to provide further details to SOE. The generals did not want to surrender directly to the Russians but preferred to capitulate before a token British force of one or two thousand parachutists, commanded by a senior British officer. Vlădescu-Olt claimed that the group could count on half a million men, but they were only lightly armed and had hardly any armoured vehicles.

It was only on 12 February 1944 that a memorandum from the British Embassy in Washington, dated 8 February 1944, was sent by the State Department to Admiral William Leahy, the coordinator of the US Joint Chiefs of Staff, about the planned coup.[15] The covering note from the State Department explained that the memorandum described a proposal made to the SOE through the Romanian Vice-Consul in Istanbul on behalf of certain military elements in Romania who professed to be prepared to overthrow Antonescu by means of a coup conducted in the name of the King. The memorandum indicated the desire of the British government to learn the views of the US government with regard to the proposal. The State Department was of the view that 'the time which has elapsed since the original proposal of the plan without bringing any crystallization thereof tends to throw doubt on the likelihood of its eventual maturity. Furthermore, consideration of the proposal poses the question of the compatibility of the Romanian stipulation regarding the use of token British forces with the principal of unconditional surrender.'[16]

The memorandum itself mentioned that the spokesman for the group of officers involved in the plan was a colonel in command of a regiment of 1,300 soldiers in Bucharest, and that two – not three – generals were connected with the plan. It was known, however, that several leading generals could not be counted upon for their support. The two backing the coup were ready to start the rebellion as soon as His Majesty's government agreed to send [a] high-ranking officer with a token force of 1,000 to 2,000 paratroops to the Eastern Front where, together with the Russian Command, they would receive the unconditional surrender of the Romanian Army: 'The generals insist on the presence of a token British force.'[17] SOE hoped to get into wireless contact with the group soon but the scheme, the memorandum went on, appeared 'embryonic'. Moreover, the arrangements for surrender seemed to postulate a Romanian-held sector of the Russian Front but the Germans were unlikely to allot a specific sector in this way until they were more forcefully pressed in the south. In spite of the weaknesses of the scheme the British government felt that the US government should be aware of its existence and solicited its view. In the meantime, the British would take no initiative beyond trying to establish wireless contact with the group.

The British misgivings were communicated on the same day – 8 February – to the Russians when the British ambassador Archibald Clark Kerr let the Soviets know of the 'Black' plan in an audience with Molotov's deputy, Dekanozov. The intended coup, the ambassador explained, was a purely military one, but His Majesty's government doubted its chances of success. Planning was at an initial stage and the figure of half a million men who might support the takeover seemed an exaggeration. Nevertheless, his government would be grateful to have the Soviet government's view of the desirability of supporting the coup. In the meantime, the British would take no action.[18] Indeed, wireless contact appears not to have been established with the group and the plan withered on the vine.

The Russian advance on the Eastern Front had made a deep impression on Churchill. The Prime Minister's position on Russia's western frontiers had changed considerably during the two years since January 1942. Minuting Eden on 16 January 1944 he admitted:

> Undoubtedly my own feelings have changed in the two years that have passed... The tremendous victories of the Russian armies, the deep-seated changes which have taken place in the character of the Russian State and Government, the new confidence which has grown in our hearts towards Stalin – these have all had their effect. Most of all is the fact that the Russians may very soon be in physical possession of these territories, and it is absolutely certain that we should never attempt to turn them out.[19]

Maniu failed to appreciate this change – as indeed did the two Antonescus. Maniu retained a pre-war image of Britain, coloured by a belief in Britain's imperial might and an assumption that Churchill would contest at every step Soviet ambitions in Eastern Europe. The British did little to disabuse him of his view. When Antonescu was summoned to Germany after the German occupation of Hungary on 19 March 1944, Mihai Antonescu sent a message to the British via Istanbul asking what Allied help Romania could count on. General Sir Henry Maitland-Wilson, Supreme Allied Commander, Mediterranean, responded by urging the Marshal not to visit Hitler and to order his troops to cease resistance to the Red Army. Antonescu could count on air support.

Maitland-Wilson had a message from Maniu on 20 March enquiring what assistance the Allies could give in the event of a coup. Wilson said that Romania's future was linked to her determination to overthrow the

Antonescu regime and that powerful air attacks would be directed against targets indicated by Maniu, but the sentence 'no land assistance can be given from this theatre' was removed by the Foreign Office from his draft, thereby laying the seeds of misunderstanding between Maniu and the Western Allies. Within seventy-two hours Molotov had told the British Ambassador in Moscow that the Soviet government was now ready to deal with both Antonescu and Maniu. He suggested that Wilson's reply should be supplemented by another telegram proposing that Antonescu appoint a competent person to liaise between the Soviet and Romanian high commands. This message was transmitted to both Antonescu and Maniu via 'Reginald',[20] and when he received it the Marshal asked for an independent line of communication between himself and Cairo via the 'Autonomous' transmitter held by the gendarmerie.[21]

Maitland-Wilson's message was received on 25 March, the day of Antonescu's return from his visit to Hitler. The reply was maudlin: 'Do not ask an old man and honest soldier to end his days in humility', Antonescu pleaded, addressing Maitland-Wilson as 'a great and glorious soldier' who should not force him to throw his people 'into the bottomless pit of shame and destruction. We are your friends not enemies.' No country with its forces almost intact 'as are ours' could capitulate 'without some serious guarantee of her future'.[22]

De Chastelain was asked to transmit it on the 'Autonomous' W/T set. He pointed out that the message as drafted was futile, that both Middle East and London were tired of hearing Romania's requests for guarantees, and suggested that the Marshal should redraft his message putting forward more practical suggestions. The sending of the message was delayed by the unexpected arrival of a German interrogating officer, Sonderführer (Specialist Leader) Alfred Petermann,[23] whose visit coincided with the signal time agreed upon for transmission. In consequence the despatch of the reply had to be delayed until 29 March when it was discovered that the crystals required for the Cairo wavelength had been stolen from the Gendarmerie headquarters.[24] In view of the urgency of the situation, de Chastelain informed Cristescu and Vasiliu that Maniu possessed a W/T which had been sent into the country in February 1942 and had never been used, and suggested Maniu be approached with a view to using this set for the transmission of Antonescu's reply, which indeed it was.[25]

De Chastelain, in his 'History' of SOE in Romania, takes up the narrative:

> On Sunday 2 April, de Chastelain was driven by General Tobescu in his private car to a small wood outside Bucharest where he met Maniu who had been brought to the rendez-vous by General Vasiliu. During a conversation lasting an hour and a half, Maniu was urged to lose no further time in taking action as the rout of the German army on the Romanian sector of the Russian front provided circumstances for a *coup d'état* more

favourable than were ever likely to occur again. Maniu confirmed his receipt of assurance of help from the Supreme Allied Commander in the Mediterranean (SACMED) and said that he proposed to put his plan into operation the following week.[26]

No such action from Maniu followed. On 13 April de Chastelain received via the 'Reginald' W/T set, Maniu and General Vasiliu the Allied armistice terms for Romania in cipher. They called for a Romanian volte-face against the Germans; the payment of reparations to the Russians; the confirmation of Bessarabia and Northern Bukovina as Soviet territory; the restoration of Northern Transylvania to Romania; and the granting to Soviet troops of unrestricted movement, although not occupation, throughout Romania during the period of the armistice.[27] The terms were rejected, despite a strongly worded memorandum prepared by de Chastelain in consultation with Porter which failed to convince Antonescu of his error in not accepting them.[28]

Antonescu's tolerance and use of the radio channel with Cairo underlined the significance to the British of the line of communication offered by the SOE presence in Romania. In psychological terms it provided an enormous boost to active opponents of the Antonescu regime but from a political perspective it shed no light on the intentions of the Western Allies towards Romania. To make good the setbacks suffered by the 'Autonomous' party, Lt. Col. Edward Masterson succeeded in smuggling in through Istanbul several W/T sets which had reached the possession of Alexandru Ştefănescu,[29] a well-known pro-British Romanian, and Grigore Niculescu-Buzeşti, the head of the Cipher Department in the Romanian Foreign Office.[30] These sets, together with 'Reginald', were employed for the exchange of messages between the armistice delegates, Ştirbei and Vişoianu, on the one hand, and Maniu on the other. Another set was installed in the Romanian legation in Ankara for use between Creţianu and Niculescu-Buzeşti.[31]

In the military theatre US and British airforces were sent in to dislocate enemy communications in Romania and to help Soviet troops who, by the beginning of April 1944 had entered Romania near Iaşi in Moldavia. In mid-April Stalin ordered the 2nd and 3rd Ukrainian Fronts to commence a coordinated invasion of Romania. His aim was to deprive the German and Romanian armies of their defence lines in Northern Romania, thereby facilitating a subsequent advance by the Red Army into the entire Balkan region. Furthermore, a successful invasion would deprive the Axis of its vital oilfields in Romania, and thus undermine Germany's ability to continue the war. It would also endanger the stability of the Antonescu regime and possibly force Romania to withdraw from the war, a move which would have the knock-on effect of persuading Bulgaria to break its ties with Hitler.[32]

In the event, this offensive failed. General I. S. Konev's 2nd Ukrainian Front was unable to break through the Axis forces in the Târgu-Frumos and

Iaşi regions in May and although Marshal R. Malinovsky's 3rd Ukrainian Front was able to take some bridgeheads across the Dniester River in early April, its efforts to expand those bridgeheads did not bear fruit: 'For the first time since late 1942, counter-attacking German forces in early May 1944 actually managed to inflict serious defeats on major Red Army forces defending bridgeheads across a major river.'[33]

On 4 April, 220 B-17 Fortresses and 93 B-24 Liberators of the 15th USAAF, escorted by 120 fighters, dropped over 860 tons of bombs on railway yards at Chitila in the north-west part of Bucharest. The raid began at noon. There had been a practice alert that morning and when the sirens went off for the real thing during the lunch hour, many people disregarded the warning. In the Gara de Nord marshalling yards, which the bombers successfully attacked, there were several trains packed with refugees from Moldavia. Many of these unfortunate souls were also victims. How many civilians lost their lives in the bombing is unclear but de Chastelain, in a wireless message sent to SOE on 19 April, put the figure at 3,000.[34]

The offensive on the oil industry was continued with a raid on Ploieşti on the following day. One hundred and thirty Liberators and 90 Fortresses accompanied by 150 fighters dropped over 580 tons of high explosives on railway yards there. On 15 April the Bucharest yards were attacked again by the 15th USAAF, and on that same night the RAF joined in the assault.[35] There were further attacks on Ploieşti throughout the summer. The smoke-screen and anti-aircraft defences used by the Germans made it one of the most heavily-defended Axis targets in Europe, and meant that the allied air forces had to return continually in order to disable the oilfields.

In an effort to hasten peace negotiations Maniu charged Constantin Vişoianu, a Romanian diplomat; Alexandru Racotta, an executive for the oil company Astra Română; Radu Hurmuzescu; and the business magnate Max Auşnit, with contacting the British directly in Cairo. The Racotta family estate to the west of Bucharest had been the original landing area for the 'Autonomous' mission of December 1943. Captain Constantin Ghica Cantacuzino,[36] a Romanian airforce pilot with close links to Maniu, stole a Heinkel 111 bomber on 17 June 1944 from Ianca airfield near the Danube port of Brăila but Vişoianu decided to travel by train and Ghica-Cantacuzino flew the rest of the group, code-named 'Yardarm', to Aleppo.[37] Under the auspices of the RAF Cantacuzino flew the Heinkel to Cairo where the group was held incommunicado until cleared by SIME (Security Intelligence Middle East[38]) after extensive interrogation, since Hurmuzescu's brother Dan had business relations in Romania with the British-born German agent Arthur Alfred Tester.[39] SIME, nevertheless, did not consider Radu to be a security risk but recommended that he not be employed by any Allied organization unless under supervision.[40] Auşnit, too, had a business relationship with Tester but was cleared, although he was not allowed to proceed to London to settle his affairs there.[41]

Some aspects of Auşnit's background and activities uncovered by the SIME interrogation were of an interesting nature, including sympathy for the plight of Jewish refugees in Romania, and that was how he became involved with Tester. On 24 July 1944 Auşnit stated that he had first heard the name in 1938 or early 1939 in connection with Tester's alleged interest in mining concessions, especially for gold. At the end of 1942 a friend of Auşnit, Constantin Bursan, told him that he was a partner with Tester in organizing the emigration of Jews by contacting shipping firms and government authorities. If Auşnit wanted to help the Jews, Bursan said he should see Tester. A few days later Tester and Bursan called on Auşnit. As he was working with the Germans Tester said that he was 'naturally an anti-Semite, but a civilized one who did not wish to stand in the way of Jewish emigration, but did not wish to mixed up with it'. He explained that a bank which he had set up would be willing to do a certain amount to help, but that the Jews would first of all have to pay off his original capital investment with the bank as the price for assisting their departure. This would amount to £5,000 to £6,000. Auşnit undertook to pay the required sum. The arrangements for Jewish emigration proceeded and a few hundred Jews were able to leave the country but difficulties of travel in the Black Sea prevented further emigration.[42]

Racotta was flown to the UK where use was made of his extensive and intimate knowledge of the Romanian oil industry. Cantacuzino was flown to Bari where he was taken on by the USAAF.[43] Auşnit and Hurmuzescu were allowed to circulate in Cairo but the former's lavishness with money attracted attention. Following the 23 August coup Auşnit and Hurmuzescu were flown back to Bucharest by the USAAF in September, and Racotta in October. Auşnit and Hurmuzescu were authorized by Christopher Steel, the Foreign Office representative in Cairo, with the endorsement of the State Department, to report to Lieutenant Commander Frank Wisner, Chief of the OSS Mission in Bucharest.[44]

Concern for aircrews shot down, and for de Chastelain's group, led SOE in Cairo to send in small two-man teams of Jewish volunteers to work with the Zionist leader A. L. Zissu.[45] Zissu's network was asked to locate all Allied prisoners and to assist their escape. The latter numbered more than a thousand and were being held in a camp in the Carpathian foothills at Timişul de Jos where, by their own account, they were generously treated.[46] The first of these teams, Sergeants Liova Bokovsky and Arich Fichman, took off under the code name 'Mantilla' in an RAF Liberator from Tokra near Benghazi in the evening of 30 September 1943, and were dropped over Lipova in western Romania early the following morning.[47]

They were picked up by the Romanian gendarmerie almost immediately and taken into custody, joining the aircrews in Timişul de Jos. Another team – Shaike Dan Trachtenberg and Menu Ben Efraim – was parachuted in undetected in June 1944 and reached Zissu.[48] Using his contacts with the

Romanian General Staff, Jean Cohen, a colleague of Zissu, provided a complete list of Allied prisoners and their whereabouts to Shaike Dan who passed them on to SOE and MI9.[49]

On 14 July, Ţurcanu, the operator of the 'Reginald' set was arrested, having been located through radio geometry by the German authorities independent of the Romanian secret police. Also detained were Alexandru A. Ionescu, a friend and collaborator of Rică Georgescu, who enciphered and deciphered messages for Maniu; Radu Protopopescu, who had housed the W/T set in the early period; and a Major Ouatu, who facilitated the entry and exit of messages into and from the prison where Georgescu, Popovici and the others had been held since their arrest in 1941.[50]

On 22 August, at eight o'clock in the evening, General Vasiliu informed de Chastelain that Soviet forces had broken through Romania's defences along the entire front from the north of Iaşi to the Black Sea; columns had already reached a point 50 miles south of Iaşi and were encountering little resistance from Romanian or German forces in the south. Faced with the imminent occupation of Romania by a hostile Soviet army, Mihai Antonescu, the Prime Minister, had decided – late though it was – to act independently of the Marshal, and wished to know if de Chastelain would be willing to fly to Cairo that night or the following morning with Antonescu to negotiate terms with the Allies. De Chastelain agreed under certain conditions which remained to be set out on paper, but which General Vasiliu did not wish to hear at the time, as he was due to report to the Prime Minister at nine o'clock that evening as to whether in principle de Chastelain was willing to accompany him.

The following morning – 23 August – de Chastelain drafted conditions, which were as follows:

(1) He should be allowed to have an interview alone with Maniu.
(2) He must be allowed to re-establish W/T contact with Cairo before his departure and have an exchange of messages in a cipher unknown to the Romanian authorities and which he possessed.
(3) The party must be accompanied by an officer from the General Staff fully acquainted with all details of Germany's battle order, reserves, etc. on Romanian territory.

At ten o'clock de Chastelain requested an interview with Tobescu to hand over the conditions, but received the reply that the General could not see him until five o'clock that evening. The conditions were then sealed in an envelope and sent down by hand of the NCO in command of the guard. De Chastelain never again saw Tobescu or Vasiliu.

On that same day, 23 August, King Michael arrested Marshal Antonescu (as described in Chapter 1). This was followed by the immediate arrest of Mihai Antonescu, the Prime Minister, General Vasiliu, and other members of the government. On 25 August Ivor Porter, Nicolae Ţurcanu and Rică Georgescu, all of whom had been released from their respective places of detention, found each other and were able to restore a channel of wireless communication with Cairo from the vault of the National Bank in Bucharest. The W/T used was Ţurcanu's set which upon his arrest had been taken to the Malmaison prison on Calea Plevnei. Georgescu had remembered this and brought it to the bank.[51] At 10.30 that night Michael broadcast his proclamation to the nation wherein he ended hostilities against the Allies and ordered his forces to support the Soviet troops.

The importance of radio contact with the West was highlighted immediately after King Michael's coup of 23 August against Antonescu, as de Chastelain himself recorded:

> At 10.25 pm that night [23 August] the King's proclamation was read over the Bucharest radio station, and about an hour later I was called along with my two companions to the Ministry of Foreign Affairs. We were taken straight to the palace, where we met the King, the Prime Minister, the Foreign Minister and members of the King's immediate entourage. The King was very worried about the failure of their wireless set to establish contact with Istanbul. This set had previously been operating from Snagov and was in working order up to 8.15 that evening. It had been moved over to the palace as it was feared that the Germans might block the Bucharest-Ploieşti road which, in fact, they did about midnight. Captain Porter and I stood by the wireless set at midnight, 1 a.m. and 2 a.m. but on each occasion failed to get through. As the King was obviously concerned at this lack of contact with the outside world, and as he was particularly desirous of having our bombing support and, if possible, support of other kinds as well, I suggested leaving Bucharest at once by aeroplane for Istanbul to report to Cairo and London, and to make arrangements for other W/T sets known to be in Bucharest to be contacted by Istanbul. Both the King and the Prime Minister considered the proposal very sound and provided me with a Romanian staff officer who would act as courier, carrying instructions to the Romanian minister in Ankara and to the two envoys in Cairo with regard to the signing of the Armistice.[52]

In agreement with the King and the new Prime Minister General Sănătescu, de Chastelain left by special aircraft for Istanbul accompanied by a Romanian staff officer, Colonel Ştefan Niculescu,[53] to inform Headquarters in Cairo and London of what had occurred and to request the urgent despatch of bombing support against specific German targets. Porter and Meţianu were left behind to liaise with the Romanian government, which they continued to do until the arrival of the spearhead of the British Military Commission in September 1944.

Before taking off from the airfield at Boteni, de Chastelain agreed with the airport commander upon a simple signal plan for the reception and despatch of messages between Boteni and Istanbul against the failure of other W/T sets to come into action.[54] This was used on several occasions in the early days following the coup d'état, but fortunately on 25 August Ţurcanu, who had been released from prison, succeeded in re-establishing contact with Cairo with his W/T set. The appeals sent over these various means of communication, added to the request sent from SOE headquarters Istanbul to Cairo for bombing support against the Germans, resulted in the despatch of a large aerial force on 25 August which effectively put out of commission the German-held airfields at Băneasa and Otopeni. This prompt action probably prevented the occupation of Bucharest by German forces who had attacked the capital from the north in considerable strength. In Bucharest itself the Romanian forces were estimated to have captured over 50,000 Germans and killed 5,000 more. The coup d'état was a complete success and no defection occurred in any part of the country.

All the American and British aircrews captured by the Romanians were transferred by Allied aircraft to Italy on 2 and 3 September. The US 15th Air Force's aircrew rescue unit, managed largely by officers of the Office of Strategic Services, sent a party to Popesti-Leordeni airfield to the south of Bucharest on 29 August to arrange for the repatriation of some 1,125 American POWs. Major Walter M. Ross of the OSS planned and directed this operation.[55] Virtually all the airmen had been held in Timişul de Jos, some 100 km north of Bucharest in the Carpathian mountains, and they praised the authorities for the benign treatment they received.[56]

8
MI6 and Romania, 1940–1945

The blanket of secrecy that covered MI6's activities during the Second World War has been partially removed with the publication of Keith Jeffrey's (2010) admirable history of the organization, yet in respect of Romania little has entered the public domain in Britain about the work of the MI6 network. It was active throughout the war in gathering and passing on information to the British authorities about Axis military operations in the area between the Rivers Dniester and Bug in southern Ukraine that was administered by Romania between 1941 and the early part of 1944. The restoration to history, therefore, of Alexander Eck and his network is overdue.[1]

Eck had had a truly international career, in keeping with his background. He was born on 16 December 1876 in the province of Polock in Poland, then under Russian rule, of a Swedish father and a Russian mother. His father was a baker and his mother took in washing. After attending junior school in Warsaw he attended the Pavel Galagan College in Kiev where he completed his secondary schooling in 1894. He returned to Warsaw and studied history and Slavonic philology at the university from which he graduated in 1898. His first post was as a teacher of Russian in a gymnasium in Warsaw, after which he moved to St Petersburg where he taught for a brief period in 1903 in a girls' high school.

While in Warsaw, although – according to an obituary – not a Jew, he became a member of the Jewish Social Democratic Association and in 1903, under the name of Muchin, he joined the Bolshevik (Leninist) wing of the Russian Social Democratic Workers' Party. In December 1905, under the name of Artem, he acted on the strike committee in Ekaterinoslav. At the beginning of 1906, he was arrested (for the third time) in Rostov-on-Don and in May sentenced to be deported to Tobolsk but managed to escape before the journey. From then onwards, until his exile in France in 1909, he was a member of the underground movement in Kiev and Lodz. In 1907 he went to London under the name of Budownicz, as a delegate to the Russian Social Democratic Workers Party congress. Two years later he left Russia and settled in France, living successively in Nancy, Nice and Paris.

On the outbreak of the First World War, Eck volunteered along with another eighty Russian political émigrés to join the French army. He served in 1915 as an intelligence officer at the headquarters of General Sarrail in Salonica, and after the armistice of 11 November 1918 was sent as part of the Allied Military Mission to Slovakia. He was demobilized in January 1920, in Paris.[2] Between 1921 and 1934 he lectured in Russian at the University of Ghent, from where he moved to the University of Brussels to become Professor of Byzantine and Slavonic Studies.[3] In 1939, after the outbreak of war, he re-joined the intelligence bureau of the French Army with the rank of captain and in February 1940 proposed to his superiors that he take advantage of an invitation from the eminent historian Nicolae Iorga to give a series of lectures at *Institutul de Istorie Universală* and at the University of Bucharest in order to gather intelligence about Romanian defences in Bessarabia, German spies posing as journalists, and German troop movements in the country. They agreed and on 28 February 1940 he arrived in Bucharest.[4]

After the fall of France in June 1940, Eck's offer to work for MI6 was accepted, it is claimed, by Winston Churchill himself, whom Eck knew personally.[5] His profession as a scholar of Byzantium afforded him cover for lecturing at *Institutul de Istorie Universală* and at the French Institute of Byzantine Studies[6] where its director, Professor Laurent gave him an office.[7] Eck's young female companion, Margareta Haller,[8] assisted Eck in his espionage activity by handling the reports that came in from the members of the network.[9]

Eck first met Haller in 1937 at the Belgian stand whilst attending the Paris International Exhibition and kept up a regular correspondence with her until he arrived in Bucharest in February 1940. Driven by a deep affection for Haller, he confided in her to reveal his anti-Axis sentiments and after the fall of France she agreed to help him gather information about German officers and civilians who visited the German factory 'Scherg' where she was employed. When she was dismissed in November 1941, as a result of the application of the law on Romanianization of enterprises,[10] Eck stepped in to secure her a temporary position as secretary to the commercial attaché at the French legation, after which she was made secretary of the French Red Cross in Romania. In addition to collecting information about German military units, Haller was tasked by Eck with delivering messages encoded by him and placed visiting-card envelopes to three Polish radio operators, Gałaczyński, Wieraszko and Czupryk, recommended by Captain Stopoźński, a Polish intelligence officer, to Eck when the British legation withdrew from Romania in February 1941.[11]

The MI6 network coordinated by Eck included French nationals resident in Romania who, after the fall of France in June 1940, committed themselves to the Allied cause. Among these were Jean Mouton, Charles Singevin, Michel Dard and Yves Augier, members of the former French legation; Pierre Guiraud, a teacher at the French Institute in Chişinău who had withdrawn to the French Institute in Bucharest after the annexation of Bessarabia by the Soviet Union in June 1940; Marcel Fontaine, director of the French Institute in Craiova; Georges Daurat who had served with the rank of captain as a machine-gun instructor on the French Military Mission to Romania led by General Henri Berthelot from 1916 to 1918; Pierre Boullen, the French consul in Timişoara; Seguinaud, the former French consul in Constanţa; and Vitalien Laurent, the director of the French Institute of Byzantine Studies in Bucharest.[12]

Eck added to their number several Romanian recruits, two of the most notable being Dan Brătianu, head of the Bucharest office of the Romanian Telephone Company, and George Tomaziu.[13] According to an undated report of the SSI, Charles Becher, a Swiss engineer working in Romania, acted as a mail box and paymaster for the network after the departure of the British legation in February 1941.[14]

Tomaziu was born in the northern Moldavian town of Dorohoi on 4 April 1915. Here he spent his childhood and youth, his artist's eye remaining permanently focused on the gentle rolling Moldavian landscape. His mother, Lucreţia, was a first cousin of the composer George Enescu who frequently spent days on end in the family home. Tomaziu was also Enescu's godson and his long discussions with his godfather instilled in him a passion for music. He even began to study the violin, but his vocation as a painter took priority – he painted his first self-portrait at the age of four. He was in fact a soulmate of Enescu's illegitimate daughter, Didica, who later became wardrobe mistress at the Bucharest Opera and whom Enescu often came surreptitiously to see. Throughout Tomaziu's youth, his bond with his godfather grew ever closer. The artist was ever-present at the musical evenings at Enescu's imposing house on Bucharest's elegant *Calea Victoriei*, evenings whose charm is evoked in one of Tomaziu's paintings purchased by the Enescu museum.

When Enescu's foreign tours separated him from Tomaziu they wrote to each other.[15] Between 1934 and 1936 Tomaziu made study trips to Vienna, Munich, and Dresden where, behind dealers' counters he discovered 'decadent art', the work of the major German Expressionist painters. He attended regularly the Salzburg Festival, writing music reviews. In 1935 he had his first exhibition in the Sala Mozart in Bucharest, and after taking his diploma in Fine Arts two years later, he was taken to Paris by Enescu. The latter introduced him to the French sculptor and painter André Lhote (1885–1962), with whom he worked from 1938 to 1939.

A fierce critic of German National Socialism, which he regarded as pure evil and whose face he had seen during his visits to Germany between 1934 and 1936, Tomaziu was one of the few Romanians who translated his convictions into deeds. He spent the period from autumn 1938 until April 1939 in Germany when he returned to Romania and lodged with his friend, the artist Dinu Albulescu. In autumn 1940 he met Mihnea Gheorghiu,[16] a fervent opponent of the Iron Guard, whom Tomaziu sheltered during the Iron Guard rebellion in January 1941. At this same time, a former fellow student at the Academy of Fine Arts, Irina Olszewski, told him that she was in touch with a supporter of General de Gaulle, and that the latter believed that Tomaziu could be useful in the fight against the Germans. Tomaziu agreed to meet this person who turned out to be Eck.[17]

Eck asked Tomaziu to deliver a letter to Marcel Fontaine, Director of the French Institute in Craiova, and to bring back the reply, and gave him money for the rail fare. Tomaziu carried out the task and Eck then told him that he was interested in information of any kind about the German positions in Romania and their troop movements. The preferred method for obtaining these details was personal observation. Tomaziu was instructed on how to identify German units by the colour of officers' epaulettes or collar-tabs and to recognize their transport by the letters on number plates and by the badges on their mudguards. As an artist, Tomaziu was adept at memorizing the latter and drawing them at the first discreet opportunity, either on a quiet street corner or in a coffee house. He followed units to their barracks in taxis to whose drivers he gave random addresses. From time to time he would check whether the same units were in the same barracks. Tomaziu wrote his information on paper impregnated with an inflammable substance so that it could be destroyed at the slightest touch of a light – from a cigarette, for example. These reports were then photographed and the negatives developed by Guiraud. The prints were then sent by a Turkish diplomatic courier to Istanbul, to the MI6 station there. It was also Guiraud who encoded information passed on by Eck to Istanbul, through the same channel.[18]

As a cover for seeing Eck regularly, Tomaziu went to Eck's house to paint a portrait of him. Eventually, Eck confided that he was not working on behalf of de Gaulle, although he was a French colonel, but for the British Secret Service, in which he was a captain.[19] Eck often travelled to the provinces, ostensibly in search of subjects for his painting, with a pass from the Romanian High Command where he had a relative who was a general. When Romania entered the war by joining the German attack on the Soviet Union in June 1941, Eck told Tomaziu that he was placing himself in great danger by working for the Allies but Tomaziu insisted on continuing his activity. The Olszewski sisters, however, withdrew from Eck's network. Eck asked Tomaziu to identity new recruits and he recommended his friends Mihnea Gheorghiu, Dinu Albulescu and Titi Grigorescu.[20]

In 1942, using a pass belonging to his father – who was also called George – Tomaziu visited Odessa, which was now under Romanian administration as the principal city of the province Transnistria, and met there Liviu Rusu who offered him a position at the Opera. Tomaziu worked as an artistic assistant on productions of *La Boheme* and *The Sleeping Beauty* whilst at the same time he passed on information to Eck about German troop movements and the preparations for the offensive in the Caucasus.[21] It was during this visit that he witnessed the massacre of a column of some 300 Jews in Brailov.[22]

Dissatisfied with the work he could do at the Opera, Tomaziu returned, with Eck's agreement, to Bucharest in autumn 1943 and settled down to painting again. Eck's radio-transmitter was moved to Tomaziu's house. It was operated, according to Tomaziu, by two Poles, Gałaczyński and Czupryk, who were living in Bucharest following their release from internment in Romania – thousands had fled to Romania in September 1939 after the German invasion of Poland.[23] The operators sent messages about Romanian and German troop movements in Morse code every other Sunday at a pre-arranged time. In the middle of a transmission from another location in January 1944 they were tracked down by German detector units, arrested by the Romanian police, and interned.[24] As soon as Margareta Haller got news of their arrest she instructed Tomaziu to destroy the radio in his house which he did by dismantling it and throwing the parts into the River Dâmboviţa.

Securitate papers state that Eck's network was betrayed by Constantin Poltzer.[25] In mid-June 1944 Polzer revealed his activity for Eck to Colonel Vasile Nicolau, head of the Military Statistical Bureau in Odobeşti, who then went to Bucharest with a number of subordinates to round up the network.[26] On 17 June 1944 Eck was arrested with Haller in Ciorogârla, on the outskirts of Bucharest, where they had taken refuge from the Allied air raids on the capital. Other members of his network, amongst them Pierre Guiraud and Tomaziu's friend, the painter Dinu Albulescu, were also picked up.[27] Tomaziu, too, was arrested at his home in Bucharest and was taken to Odobeşti where he was held under guard in an old farmhouse. He was beaten by his Romanian interrogators and went on hunger-strike. Two days later he saw Eck, Haller and other colleagues from his window. They were being held in an adjacent building (Eck was initially given a hotel room in Odobeşti where he was held under guard).[28] After nine days without food Tomaziu's interrogation was suspended. Eck gave a declaration in Tomaziu's presence that he was head of the MI6 network in Romania and Tomaziu admitted his own part. Eck consigned his declaration to paper at the request of the military prosecutor Captain Ion Săvulescu. As the most authoritative account of his network's genesis and structure it merits reproduction in full:

> At the beginning of this war I presented myself at the Ministry of War in Paris and enrolled in the army, having passed the age of automatic mobilization. At the same time Mr Nicolae Iorga, my colleague and friend whom I had known for a number of years and who had come (in 1937, I think) to the University of Brussels, renewed his request that I should come to Romania to give a series of lectures in Romanian universities. I informed the head of the Deuxième Bureau of the Army General Staff to which I was attached and my head urged me to accept Mr Iorga's request. He tasked me at the same time with assessing the defence potential

of Romania against the Soviet Union. To facilitate this latter task an arrangement was made with the newspaper *Le Jour-L'Écho de Paris* which designated me its correspondent in Romania.

After my arrival in Romania in February 1940, I had several meetings with Mr Iorga and then left to visit various parts of Bessarabia – Chişinău, Tighina, Cetatea Albă, Saba etc. I noted the extreme precariousness of Romania's defences in this region and drew up a report in this sense for Deuxième Bureau of the Army in Paris. With this mission accomplished, I gave some lectures at the universities of Cernăuţi and Iaşi and returned to Bucharest at the end of March 1940 where I began a series of lectures at the 'Nicolae Iorga' Institute of World History,[29] as well as at the Cultural League and later at the faculty of law in Bucharest. Later, in 1943–44, I gave some courses and led seminars at the faculty of letters in Bucharest; all of these courses and lectures were given on a voluntary basis; in May 1943, the Romanian Ministry of Education asked me to accept the position of academic advisor, a position which I still hold.

After the Deuxième Bureau of the Army in Paris had received my report I was given orders to remain in Romania at the discretion of the military attaché at the French legation, Lt. Col. [Jean] Neubanser, should there be military action by the French Army in the East, to which I was to be possibly posted.

After the signing of the armistice of 18 June 1940,[30] I handed in my resignation from the French Army and, with the approval of Lt. Col. Neubanser, presented myself to the British military attaché[31] in Bucharest with a request to enrol in the British Army, in conformity with the offer made by Great Britain to all French persons who wished to continue the fight. General de Gaulle did not have at that moment any military organization under his orders, and the French Army of the East was subject to the armistice. My request was immediately accepted by Mr Churchill (who already knew me) and I was charged with organizing an intelligence network directed against the German Army (a Romanian section of the Intelligence Service[32]). I was given complete autonomy regarding the recruitment of members of the network, the means of action, and the organizational structure. I submitted the aims and objectives which I proposed to follow and these were approved by London, namely:

(1) Members of the network were to be recruited solely amongst French persons who wished to continue the fight and amongst Romanian patriots fiercely sympathetic to France and Britain;
(2) Recruitment was to be made solely on a military basis, after approval by London of each of the candidates whom I proposed;
(3) The methods of gathering information were to be:

(a) Direct observation by network members;
(b) Information provided by disinterested or casual, or unwitting informers;
(c) The use of agents paid for raw information was to be strictly ruled out.

I received from London these general directives:

(1) A total ban on gathering information about the Romanian Army;
(2) A total ban on any other activity apart from gathering military, economic and political intelligence concerning Germany.

After the formation of military units under the orders of General de Gaulle, it was understood that the intelligence provided by my network would be regularly communicated to the General Staff of French Forces through the intermediary of a French liaison officer at the British embassy in Istanbul.[33] I began the recruitment of our agents in summer 1940, according to the principles laid out above.

The first member of the network accepted by London was Miss Margareta Haller whom I had known for some time, having met her in Paris and resumed acquaintance with her in Bucharest after my arrival there (she held at that time a position of trust as the chief cashier at the Scherg store in Bucharest). Her correctness and loyalty, her general culture, her attachment to France, her genuine patriotism for Romania and her very lively intelligence all represented precious qualities for the network. Her nomination was accepted by London with appointment to officer rank, and later she was awarded the Order of the British Empire.

At the end of 1940 or at the beginning of 1941 Misses Tatiana and Irene Olchewski, whom I had met at the end of one of my lectures, asked me if they could be of service to France or Britain in some way. Their moral qualities and their general culture were evident and I proposed to them that they should join the network and their applications were accepted by London under the same conditions as that of Miss Haller. On 22 June 1941, after Romania's entry into the war against the Soviet Union, the Olchewski sisters tendered their resignation and since then they have had no contact with the network, and equally our personal relationship has ceased. At the same time, Mr George Tomaziu, an extremely talented painter, offered his services. He was an excellent observer, an honest, cultivated Romanian patriot, a convinced pro-Allied and pro-French figure who was accepted by London, promoted subsequently to the rank of second lieutenant, and recommended for the Military Cross. A little later Mr Tomaziu suggested to me the recruitment of Messrs Albulescu, Grigorescu, and Gheorghiu (the latter had studied in Britain and showed pro-British sentiments). The first two were accepted by London, that is as regular members of the Service. As for Mr Gheorghiu, I did not receive a reply from London in spite of my repeated questions and I decided to use his services as an informer. I only knew personally Mr Albulescu who for a long time was ignorant of my role in the Service. Mr Gheorghiu only met me at the end of 1943, when he came twice in person to bring me information because I wished to know him personally after he provided certain inaccurate information. I never met Mr Grigorescu whose only contact was with Mr Tomaziu.

From the French side I encountered difficulty over the recruitment of members for the Service, since all the French who were partisans of General de Gaulle preferred to rejoin the French forces fighting in Syria, Egypt and French Africa. Messrs Lenseigne and Batty, after collaborating for several months, left for the Near East. In spring 1942, M. Pierre Guiraud, who was ignorant of my activity in the Service, was offered the position of a teacher in Hungary. I informed London and received the order to persuade him to leave for Hungary whilst accepting an *engagement* with the Intelligence Service, thereby serving in a very useful manner the allied cause. I then explained my mission in Romania to M. Guiraud and passed on to him the proposal from London. M. Guiraud accepted it, was enrolled in the Service with the rank of second lieutenant, and left for Budapest at the beginning of summer 1942. He acquitted himself very well in his mission and provided me in particular with information about the movements of German troops on the Hungarian-Romanian frontier for which I did not have an accurate observer in Romania. M. Guiraud received the Military Cross for his services in Hungary. In November 1943, second lieutenant Guiraud returned to Bucharest after his main collaborators in Hungary were arrested by the Hungarian authorities and he was advised to leave the country. After his return to Romania I was ordered not to use him further and isolated him completely from my network, to avoid compromising it. M. Guiraud was to await the arrival of allied troops.

At the beginning of 1941, at the time of the departure of the British legation from Romania, Mr Stopczyński, a captain in the Polish army attached to this legation, recommended to me three of his compatriots who had taken refuge in Romania: Mr Galaczyński, a former deputy prefect, Mr Wiraszka, a military radio operator, and a lieutenant Ciupryk. They were to assist me, after the departure of the British legation, in organizing a radio station to transmit information provided by me to London. These three persons were enrolled in the Service.

None of the regular members of the Service received any payment if they had a source of sufficient income. This was also the case of Misses Haller, Irina and Tania Olszewski, Messrs Tomaziu, Albulescu, Grigorescu, Gheorghiu and, during his mission in Hungary and after his return to Romania, M. Guiraud. All these persons were reimbursed only for expenses incurred by the Service – especially travel expenses. The rent for Mr Tomaziu's workshop was paid from November 1943 (at the earliest) since this workshop was used to draw copies of the distinguishing signs on German vehicles. Messrs Galaczyński, Wiraszka and Ciupryk each received a supplement to their income from their employment (each one had regular employment outside the service) to reach the overall sum of 40,000 *lei* each. Mr Galaczyński, who was married, received a supplement of 20,000 *lei* per month. I myself drew the regular salary of a captain since my resources (my personal income in France) could not reach me. The consideration of [*illegible text*] *lei* and later of 33,000 *lei* per month [*illegible text*] from the Ministry of Education in Romania since May 1943 was used by me for my personal well-being. The result was that all the members of the Service were driven by a total disinterest in monetary gain, having joined the Service for purely patriotic and ideological reasons.

The activity of the Service consisted of the following tasks:

(1) The identification of German troops (Wehrmacht and Luftwaffe units) passing through or stationed in Romania from their number plates and letters painted on the vehicles, as well as from the numbers and colours of the letters on their epaulettes. When the occasion presented itself, the same observations were made outside the territory of Romania.[34]
(2) Conversations with German soldiers passing through Bucharest in order to gather information about the situation in Germany (industry, food supply, units arriving in Germany from France for the Eastern front) and in Romania for the Balkans.
(3) Contacts with various persons in the diplomatic corps in order to gather information of the same nature as that brought by German soldiers, by civilians having contact with diplomats or from travellers from neutral countries travelling in Germany.

The means of transmitting the information gathered were the following:

(1) The radio set constructed by military engineer Wiraszka and made operational in summer 1942. This set operated until January 1944 when it was discovered by the Romanians. I aimed at setting up another set in lieutenant Tomaziu's studio, and the necessary adjustments to that end were made by Mr Wiraska to Mr Tomaziu's wireless receiver. However there was not sufficient time to get this second post up and running.
(2) A courier service was organized by the transmission centre in Istanbul for the transmission of drawings and more detailed intelligence: a person would introduce themselves to me with an agreed password,

> gave me usually a message from London and agreed a *rendez-vous* with me where I would hand him an envelope which was to be passed on to London. These couriers were usually different people on each occasion and I was totally ignorant of their identity. It is totally contrary to the truth that the diplomatic bag was used by the network to transmit messages, as is insinuated by certain interrogators from the Romanian military police. Such a method would have been absolutely impossible given the strict checks made on the contents of these bags by the heads of diplomatic missions in Bucharest, as well as in Istanbul and Ankara.[35] I myself was given the task in August 1941 of taking a diplomatic bag from the French legation in Bucharest to the French embassy in Istanbul and I was unable to use this suitcase even for carrying my own academic papers as no documents of a private nature were allowed in the case.
>
> On the whole, the network functioned for four years to the entire satisfaction of the British High Command, since it received on several occasions the thanks of the high command and of Churchill himself. Several members of the network were decorated and I myself received the Distinguished Service Order. My subordinates and I had the satisfaction of having served well the interests of the allied armies and of having rendered important service to Romania itself. Having acted as good soldiers and good patriots of our respective countries my colleagues and I take responsibility for our actions with our heads held high.[36]

There were no further interrogations and relations between the prisoners and their Romanian guards became relaxed and friendly. France's national day was celebrated with several bottles of wine, and even the Romanian commandant raised a glass to France with his prisoners. Tomaziu's father was allowed to visit him and told him that Marshal Antonescu had given his godfather, George Enescu, an undertaking that nothing grave would happen to him. Since Antonescu was in discussions with the Allies about a possible armistice he perhaps thought that his hold over the fate of a group of British agents could prove useful as a bargaining counter.

Guirard, who was also under arrest, had, in fact, got word to Colonel Traian Borcescu, head of the counter-intelligence section of the Romanian Secret Service, and warned him that if Eck and Haller fell into German hands the British would hold the Romanian authorities responsible.[37] A meeting was arranged between Borcescu and Georges Daurat in the office of Colonel Octav Rădulescu, the counter-intelligence officer in the telephone company. With Dan Brătianu acting as interpreter from French, Daurat revealed to Borcescu that he too was a member of the MI6 network and asked Borcescu to ensure the safety of Eck and Haller. Borcescu informed Eugen Cristescu, the head of the Romanian Intelligence Service, by telephone and sent

Brătianu to him to give further details.[38] On orders from above, once the interrogations at Odobeşti were completed, Eck's group was transferred on 20 July to Malmaison jail in Bucharest which came under the direct authority of the SSI.[39]

Tomaziu declared that there was a very relaxed regime in the prison – he was allowed visits, and he got to know Rică Georgescu, arrested in August 1941, who was able to listen to the radio. At 11.15 on the night of 23 August, just a few hours after King Michael's coup against Marshal Antonescu, Borcescu gave a note to Dan Brătianu, head of the Bucharest office of the Romanian Telephone Company and a member of Eck's network, for the officer in command of Malmaison. The note contained orders from Borcescu for the immediate release of Eck, Haller and the rest of the group. Brătianu was taken by car to the prison by one of his colleagues, Andrei Chrisoghelos, and together they collected Eck and Haller and took them to Brătianu's house in the early hours of the morning.[40] Two days later, on 26 August,[41] Eck and Haller left in a plane provided by Borcescu for Istanbul in the company of Brătianu.

The role of Dan Brătianu, an MI6 agent, and his connection with Borcescu, a servant of the Antonescu regime, requires explanation.[42] During the war Brătianu passed on details to Borcescu of telephone calls made by German officials in Romania. His most significant action in this respect was on the afternoon of 23 August 1944. He was contacted by Borcescu after Antonescu's arrest and asked to stay in his office. General Gerstenberg, the commander of German forces in Romania, had given an undertaking to King Michael to withdraw his troops from Bucharest in return for a guarantee of safe passage. Gerstenberg, however, telephoned Hitler who ordered him to arrest the king and to occupy Bucharest. At once, Borcescu asked Brătianu for details of German telephone installations in the capital and at 11 pm all German telephone links were cut. Without them, the Germans found it difficult to coordinate their resistance to Romanian forces in Bucharest and they were soon overcome.

Both Eck and Brătianu acknowledged the help received from Borcescu and his colleague Florin Begnescu in a declaration they wrote for him in Istanbul, dated 28 August 1944:

> We the undersigned, Dan M. Brătianu and Alexander Eck, captain in the British Army, hereby confirm that we have had the fullest assistance from Colonel Traian Borcescu and Lieutenant Florin Ion Begnescu, whose truly patriotic sentiment for Romania cannot be questioned for one moment. They cannot be suspected of seeking to shield Eugen Cristescu [the head of the Romanian Secret Intelligence Service] at any time. I gave them the task, during our absence in Istanbul, of re-establishing the radio link as quickly as possible with our agencies in Istanbul with the help of my assistant Lieutenant Guiraud. Any measure taken against them would

> only disrupt our activity, details of which can be obtained from the Foreign Minister and the Minister of War, General Racoviţă. On our return to Romania from our mission we can give the requisite supplementary information.[43]

Tomaziu never set eyes on them again.[44] In his memoirs Brătianu took up the story:

> I left by plane for Istanbul together with Eck and his secretary Margareta Haller, to hand them over to the British consul. There I met Major Arthur Ellerington, Eck's controller, who was married to a Romanian.[45] During my stay in Istanbul, from 26 August to 14 September, I met several employees of the British consulate and also an American, Frank Stevens, correspondent of the Christian Science Monitor, as well as some representatives of the French Resistance Movement. For a few days I stayed with Professor Eck in a flat on the shore of the Bosphorus and then I moved to the Romanian consulate, at the invitation of the consul, Alexandru Creţianu. I found an old friend of mine at the consulate, Bob Negulescu. None of us knew the exact conditions of the armistice concluded with the Russians. At the British consulate I also met Kim Philby, who was unmasked later as a Russian spy and who knew all about my collaboration during the war with SIS agents in Romania. As he was a faithful informer of the Russians, it was no surprise that I should be arrested in 1948 on the order of the Russians and sentenced to 15 years hard labour for 'high treason'.[46]

With the arrival of Soviet troops in Bucharest on 30 August 1944, and the subsequent Soviet occupation of Romania, MI6's target changed. Eck's departure did not mean that his network could not be revived. Indeed Tomaziu, after his release from prison on 24 August 1944, resumed his painting and also, on his own admission, in a declaration to the *Securitate* dated 8 August 1950, his intelligence activity for the British.[47] He met up with Guiraud who invited him to continue his clandestine activity, informing him that Eck's place had been taken by Ivor Porter.[48] Tomaziu agreed and was taken to see Porter, now in charge of the Press Office at the British legation. Guiraud also put Tomaziu in touch with Boullen, Eck's deputy, at the beginning of October 1944. Boullen was also working for the British, under Porter's supervision, and Tomaziu carried out missions for both men, often reporting back to Annie Samuelli, Porter's assistant at the Press Office.[49] Tomaziu and Samuelli helped Porter and Boullen to smuggle four Poles, members of Eck's network, out of the country at the end of September 1944.[50] They were dressed in French military uniforms and sneaked into a group of French prisoners who were being repatriated in a French military aircraft. Guiraud left Romania by the same flight.[51]

In March 1946 Boullen asked Tomaziu to visit Olteniţa to report on the defences there and the positions of Soviet troops. In the summer he received a similar request, this time to visit Giurgiu. Tomaziu told Boullen that he could not go himself but that he would ask a trusted friend, another painter, Victor Brătulescu, to travel there. Brătulescu reported on the progress in building a landing stage for ferries and noted the number plates of Soviet military vehicles. In spring 1947 Boullen, on learning that Tomaziu had personal business in Craiova, asked him to bring back information on Soviet troop emplacements in Slatina, Calafat and Craiova. Tomaziu found no time to do this whilst in Craiova and so turned once more to Brătulescu who was given his travel expenses and produced the information. Tomaziu also related how he was asked on one occasion, in early 1945, by Brigadier E. R. Greer, deputy-head of the British Military Mission, to travel to Galaţi to get information on Soviet troop movements in the area. Tomaziu, being otherwise engaged, suggested a friend, Ion Ghinea, who had accompanied him to Olteniţa on the mission for Boullen. Ghinea agreed to gather the information and passed it on to Tomaziu who relayed it to Greer. Before leaving Romania in 1947, Greer introduced Tomaziu to Colonel Turner, the British military attaché, but Tomaziu only saw him once, in spring 1948, when Turner told him that he had been unable to arrange the shipment of some paintings which Tomaziu wished to exhibit in London.[52]

Tomaziu was arrested on 22 March 1950 and found himself once more in Malmaison prison on charges of 'high treason'. In the following month he was produced as a prosecution witness in the trial of another 'espionage network', made up of employees at the British and American legations, and a journalist.[53] Tomaziu faced his own trial later that year and was sentenced on 22 November 1950 to fifteen years' hard labour for 'high treason' on the grounds that he carried out espionage for the British.[54] He passed through the major prisons of the Romanian gulag: Aiud, Piteşti and Gherla. In 1963, when he was released following a general amnesty of political prisoners, his parents had died without his knowledge. He lived thereafter from the money he received from paintings commissioned by foreign diplomats.[55]

The achievements of MI6 in the period 1944 to 1945 in Romania were notable, and were due principally to the courage of its agents, the great majority of whom were Romanian and French. A handful of Poles, soldiers from the Polish army that escaped the German and Soviet partition of September 1939, also played a valiant part. But it was the Romanian agents who paid the highest penalty. Whilst Eck, his French colleagues, and the Poles – who had been interned when caught – were able to leave Romania because of their status as foreign nationals, their Romanian associates remained to continue their cooperation with British intelligence, at the cost of arrest by the Communist authorities on charges of treason and long terms of imprisonment.

9
The Eradication of Opposition to Communist Rule

Romanian history is composed of many layers of tragedy but one of the most significant is the imposition of Communist rule. The new dominant force in Romanian politics after the 23 August coup was the Communist Party. Its leaders set out under Soviet direction to effect a Communist revolution, in furtherance of which they were driven by ideology to purge institutions of those who had served not only the Antonescu regime, but also those of the pre-war governments.

The traditional view of the transition to Communism in Soviet-occupied Eastern Europe after 1945 is teleological: Soviet domination is presented as the imposition of a new system which forced the region to look away from the West and turn towards Moscow.[1] It is implied that the imposition of Communism forced a deviation from an inexorable development towards functioning democracy, despite the fact that most of the democratic countries in the region in the interwar period were unable to provide economic and political stability.

After the collapse of Communism in the late 1980s and early 1990s, broadly speaking, a fresh approach was offered in order to explain the post-war Communization of Eastern Europe. The emphasis shifts from the impact of Soviet domination to the part played by indigenous political parties, notably the domestic Communist parties.[2] Certainly, the role of the latter should not be overlooked; on the one hand, these parties sought to take control of existing institutions, such as the secret police, and on the other they created new ones, such as the judicial organs. Yet such an approach should not obscure the role of the Soviet Union in the region after 1945, nor call into question the postulated premeditated design of Soviet domination which Stalin harboured for the region, nor overlook the coercive methods employed by the local Communist parties, supported by a Soviet military occupation, to impose Communist rule.

As part of the Armistice Agreement, signed in Moscow on 12 September 1944,[3] the British suggested to the Soviet Foreign Minister Veaceslav Molotov that an Allied Control Commission be set up to oversee the implementation of the terms but the Soviet determination to have the main say in this matter was carried through in their armistice draft of 31 August which stated that the terms would be implemented 'under the control of the Soviet High Command, hereinafter called Allied (Soviet) High Command, acting on behalf of the Allied powers'.

Stalin used the Armistice Agreement to subvert the effects of the 23 August coup which had threatened to wrest the initiative in Romanian affairs from him. In order to regain that initiative the Soviet leader fashioned from the armistice a legal framework for securing a dominant political and economic interest in Romania. Since the Soviet Union had a monopoly of its interpretation, the Armistice Agreement became the mechanism for the takeover of Romania.[4] Stalin's policy in Romania was designed to exact retribution for the Romanian invasion of the Soviet Union and to provide for permanent military security – a notion implying not merely disarmament and treaty guarantees but also the abrogation of the political power of those who had launched the invasion.[5] Articles 13 and 14 provided for the arrest of war criminals and the dissolution of 'Fascist-type' organizations.

In practice, the Control Commission functioned under statutes drawn up by the Russians, under which, until Potsdam, American and British officers were treated as delegations to the Commission, not structurally part of it. Hence rights formally granted to the Allies under the Armistice Agreement were defined and enforced by the Russians. Stalin, therefore, had two satisfactory instruments for pursuing his objectives in Romania: a Communist Party which was an acknowledged part of the country's political structure, and an agreement with his Allies giving the Red Army all the scope it needed.[6]

The takeover of Romania resulted from the interaction between the two: while fighting was still in progress, the Red Army, as any army, required order behind the front, but in Romania the only order acceptable to the Russians was that guaranteed by the Romanian Communist Party (RCP). The Party's role was to prevent the post-coup regime from establishing order on any other terms. That requirement implied, first, neutralizing the existing means of maintaining the social order, namely the army, judiciary and police and redesigning them to the Soviet model; second, creating mass support, which the RCP totally lacked, and which would provide the new regime with the necessary theoretical legitimation. Both activities involved reliance on fear, and both could be relied upon to destroy any vestiges of support for the monarchy and for 'Western' democracy.

SOE found itself hamstrung by British sensitivity to Soviet sensibilities. The 'History of SOE' in Romania states that de Chastelain 'was not allowed to return to Roumania despite his promises to the King and the Prime Minister, and was called to Cairo and to London to report to General Paget, Commander-In-Chief Middle East, Lord Moyne, Minister Resident in Cairo, and in London to Sir Orme Sargent at the Foreign Office, Clement Attlee,

Acting Prime Minister, and Hugh Dalton, President of the Board of Trade, who offered de Chastelain employment on the Allied Control Commission in Romania, in the interests of the Department of Trade'.[7] The Foreign Office, anxious not to further upset the Russians who believed that the purpose of the 'Autonomous' mission had been to conclude a separate peace with Antonescu behind their backs, counselled against de Chastelain's return.[8] With the arrival of the British Military Mission in Bucharest in September 1944, both Ivor Porter and Silviu Meţianu were ordered to drop forthwith all contact with previous SOE collaborators, 'who were thus left without any form of support either moral or financial'.[9]

British and American diplomats did not consider the armistice conditions unduly harsh although Averell Harriman, US ambassador to Moscow, had serious doubts about Soviet intentions and predicted that the terms would 'give the Soviet command unlimited control of Romania's economic life' and, more ominously, 'police power for the period of the armistice'.[10] Both the British and US governments endorsed the agreement without demur; indeed their acceptance of Moscow as the place of signature was a tacit admission that their eastern partner, as the principal belligerent ally in Eastern Europe, had earned the right as victor to dictate its terms to the Romanians. That the Soviet Union should adopt this position was accepted as inevitable by Churchill in a speech to the House of Commons delivered on 26 September 1944. The Prime Minister admitted that

> the armistice terms agreed upon for Finland and Romania bear, naturally, the imprint of the Soviet will – and here I must draw attention to the restraint which has characterized the Soviet treatment of these two countries, both of which marched blithely behind Hitler in his attempted destruction of Russia, and both of which added their quota of injuries to the immense volume of suffering which the Russian people have endured, have survived, and have triumphantly surmounted.[11]

Against Churchill's statement, made when the Red Army was still fighting its way across Eastern Europe, must be set the belief of King Michael and his ministers that his coup against Antonescu and the volte-face against the Germans had earned Romania the right to be treated not as a defeated enemy, but as a new co-belligerent. Such a view received no sympathy from Stalin, who was unwilling to forgive Romania for its contribution to Operation *Barbarossa*. Yet ironically, King Michael's action, by facilitating the Red Army's advance in the Balkans, was to seal his country's consignment to the Soviet sphere of influence and Stalin's domination. With Soviet troops pouring into Romania and Bulgaria, Churchill was determined to save Greece and possibly Italy from a Communist takeover, and this spectre was to haunt Churchill's policy towards Romania.

By the time that Churchill decided to divide up responsibility in the Balkans with Stalin by talking to him personally, Britain had few cards to play. The Russians were already in occupation of much of Romania and Bulgaria and so Churchill, when he flew to Moscow at the beginning of October 1944, got straight down to business and proposed the now notorious 'percentages agreement', struck on the evening of 9 October.[12] Although Churchill maintained in his memoirs that 'only immediate wartime arrangements' were under discussion, he knew that Stalin could not be dislodged by force from the position of influence which he had gained. Thus in proposing the deal, Churchill was merely being pragmatic; he was recognizing Soviet preponderance in the Balkans, one which was restricted only by the Red Army's own operational problems.[13] Stalin interpreted the 'percentages agreement' as he chose, and the absence of any Western forces, not just in Romania, but in the whole of Eastern Europe, ensured that the exercise of Soviet authority in the area remained unrestricted.

In the caretaker government of General Sănătescu (23 August–2 November 1944), set up to direct Romania's new war course, the majority of ministerial posts had gone to military officers, with only the Ministry of Justice being secured by the Communists in the person of Lucreţiu Pătrăşcanu. Both Maniu and Brătianu preferred not to participate in government, proposing other members of their parties instead. While several senior officers of the Intelligence Service, were arrested in September 1944, the committee charged with screening the 600 personnel of the SSI employed nationally concluded, in a report of 20 October, that they could find only two officers against whom charges could be levelled and these were 'abusive behaviour and unseemly conduct'.[14] The personnel of the Ministry of the Interior and of the security police, the *Siguranţa,* remained largely unchanged.[15] It was the failure to replace these figures that provided a pretext for the Communists to set about torpedoing the Sănătescu government. At the same time the Soviet authorities set about weakening Romania's army and police force.

On 2 October the Soviet High Command demanded the reduction of the police force from 18,000 to 12,000 men. On 6 October it forced the resignation of General Gheorghe Mihail, the Chief of the Romanian General Staff, because of his opposition to the Soviet order that all Romanian units should be disarmed, except for the twelve divisions fighting alongside the Russians. Mihail's successor, General Nicolae Rădescu, consented under protest to the Soviet demand (26 October) that the Romanian army in the interior be reduced from thirteen full-strength to three skeleton divisions with a total complement of 10,000 men, and that the numbers of frontier guards and gendarmerie be cut from 74,086 to 58,018. This process was continued over the next three years, leading to a fall in the strength of the Romanian Armed forces from 419,000 in May 1945 to 136,000 in December 1947.[16]

These actions by the Soviet authorities ensured that the Communist Party could proceed without fundamental interference. Its first task was to broaden its bridgehead in government. That in itself demanded admission to crucial ministries – Interior, Defence as well as Justice – and the creation of mass support which could be used to demand radical political change. On 2 October the Communist Party and the Social Democratic Party joined forces to form the National Democratic Front (NDF). Members of the Front threatened workers at the major factories in Bucharest and elsewhere with arrest by the Soviet army if they refused to vote out the old works' committees and elect NDF representatives in their place. The new committees then took charge of the workers' canteens and the rationing procedures and soon the NDF had much of industry in its grip, forcing workers to accede to its will under pain of the withdrawal of rations and special ration cards.

In industry and elsewhere, the threats were given weight by the 'Guards of Patriotic Defence', enlarged from the nucleus of armed workers who took charge of Antonescu after his arrest. Enlargement, in September 1944, was supervised by the Soviet Security Service, the NKGB, and placed under the command of Emil Bodnăraş. It provided the ideal cover for the training of agents and thugs who were to be infiltrated into the police and security forces when the Communists gained access to the Ministry of the Interior. The 'Guards' were used to root out 'Fascists' and encourage recalcitrants to see the error of opposition. When necessary, they enjoyed the logistic cooperation of the Russian command. Their recruits included jailbirds and former Legionnaires, whose intimidatory skills had, of course, been honed in the late 1930s.[17] On 15 January 1945 the Prime Minister, General Rădescu, ordered the Guards' disbandment, but Teohari Georgescu, the Deputy Minister of the Interior, and Bodnăraş simply ignored the instruction. With the truncated Romanian army absent or disarmed, the Government had no countervailing power.

The Armistice Agreement had stipulated the dissolution of 'all pro-Hitler organizations (of a Fascist type)' (Article 15). This, widely drawn, was liberally interpreted. In early September the Foreign Minister, Niculescu-Buzeşti, and Ion Mocsony-Styrcea, the Marshal of the Palace (both leading figures in the coup of 23 August), called for the immediate establishment of a tribunal for the trial of war criminals and of pro-Germans holding responsible positions. Maniu raised legalistic objections and the proposal was dropped.[18]

The liquidation of Fascism fell to the Russians and to their local minions. It should at this point be recalled that the war against the Axis still in progress was widely accepted as an 'anti-Fascist' crusade; that there were many in Romania who, in some sense or other, qualified as 'Fascist' and that the governments immediately after the coup appeared to be dilatory in dealing with them. So, an agitation to get rid of Fascists could count on some popular support. Events soon demonstrated that, in practice, 'Fascist' came to mean what the Communists said it was. And they could say it through 'spontaneous' demonstrations and through a press which was rapidly being brought under control.[19]

On 8 October the NDF organized its first mass meeting in Bucharest, at which some 60,000 demonstrators called for the resignation of the Sănătescu government for having failed to remove 'Fascists' from public life. On the following day General Vinogradov, the head of the Russian Military Mission, demanded that the government arrest forty-seven Romanians as war criminals, among them two cabinet ministers, General Gheorghe Potopeanu, the Minister of the National Economy who had served for a brief period as Military Governor of Transnistria, and General Ion Boiteanu, the Minister of Education. The slowness with which Sănătescu acted against Antonescu's officials merely provided grist to the mill of the Communist Party and to the Soviet authorities. Both accused the Romanians of not respecting Articles 14 and 15 of the Armistice. In their defence Romanian officials argued that the bureaucracy would not be able to function if large scale purges of the kind demanded by the Russians were implemented.[20] Confirmation of the Communists' charges came from an American OSS (Office of Strategic Services) report of February 1945 which stated that during the first six weeks after the August coup the Sănătescu government dismissed only eight Romanian officials.[21]

Demonstrations also focused on specific political figures whom the Communists wanted removed. One such was the new Minister of the Interior, Nicolae Penescu, a National Peasant Party member who was vehemently anti-Soviet. Mass demonstrations were organized to shout 'Down with Penescu'. At the end of November the NDF seized upon a suburban brawl as a pretext for demanding his resignation.[22] A group of drunken Romanian soldiers shot dead two trade unionists, for whom the NDF organized a huge funeral. The Communist press raged about 'Hitlerist Fascist bullets from automatic rifles of the Fifth Column supported by leaders of the National Peasant Party'. The Peasant Party ministers and their National Liberal colleagues withdrew from the cabinet of Sănătescu which they felt was too tolerant of the Communists' harassment. On 2 December the King asked General Nicolae Rădescu, formerly Chief of the General Staff and a non-party figure, to form a cabinet.[23]

Rădescu received strong backing from King Michael, who on 4 December warned Andrei Vishinsky, the Soviet Deputy Foreign Minister, that the Communists' activities threatened to throw the country into anarchy. Among these was an unremitting press campaign in the Communist Party newspaper *Scânteia* condemning the Romanians' alleged failure to fulfil the principal conditions of the armistice. *Scânteia* reprinted (6 December 1944) Soviet charges that the Romanian Government had systematically shirked from honouring its direct debt and had openly supported the administration that sabotaged the Armistice Convention. The leaders of the so-called 'historical parties' in Romania, the National Peasant and National Liberal Parties who were widely represented in the Sănătescu government, were responsible. The conclusion was ominous: 'The Soviet Command in this part of the

Soviet-German front is displaying the utmost patience which is being abused by those Romanian politicians who have transformed this region of the front into an area of intrigue which is undermining the mobilization of the forces of the Romanian people and basic order in the country.'[24]

The King told Vyshinski, the Soviet Deputy Minister of Foreign Affairs, that if the Soviet Union continued to support the Communists in this way, he would find himself forced to abdicate and leave the country. Vyshinski was said to have been surprised by the King's boldness and denied any Soviet responsibility. In the government reshuffle the Communist-dominated NDF had hoped to secure the Ministry of the Interior, but Rădescu reserved the post for himself. Thereupon the RCP leaders, Ana Pauker and Vasile Luca, refused even to discuss NDF participation in the new government. However, under instructions from Vyshinski, they now backed down.[25] Rădescu did, however, concede the position of Deputy Minister of the Interior, to the Communists, appointing Teohari Georgescu, a member of the Party's Central Committee; his Communist colleagues in the cabinet were Pătrăşcanu, Minister of Justice, and Gheorghe Gheorghiu-Dej, Minister of Communications and Public Works.

Vyshinski's decision throws some light on Soviet intentions at this time. The short-term priority was to conclude the war against Germany as quickly as possible. Instability in Romania would compromise that aim. Furthermore, the Romanian Communist Party was still not strong enough to take over the administration of the country where the bulk of the population was hostile to Communism; therefore, should the King abdicate, the Russians were likely to have to assume part of the administration themselves. Such a move would raise questions in Britain and the United States about their motives. Consequently, Vyshinski lowered the temperature in Romania. He left the country as he had come, without notice, on 8 December.[26]

So, for a brief period, NDF meetings and street demonstrations ceased, but Communist penetration of institutions continued unabated. Teohari Georgescu installed his own men in nine of the sixteen prefectures in the provinces with strict orders to avoid government instructions and to do only his bidding. He also ignored an undertaking to Rădescu to disband the 10,000-strong Communist militia and introduced into the *Siguranţa* agents trained in the 'Patriotic Guards'. On 19 December Maniu addressed a letter to de Chastelain drawing his attention to the 'development of a new reign of terror in Roumania' and endeavouring to persuade him to return.[27]

The truce ended with the publication of the NDF New Year's appeal to the people in which they condemned the Rădescu government for failing to fulfil the terms of the Armistice, and called for agrarian reform within six weeks of all property exceeding an area of 50 hectares.

It was soon evident that the RCP's moves were Soviet-orchestrated. On 4 January 1945 Stalin received Ana Pauker, Gheorghiu-Dej and Gheorghe Apostol in his dacha outside Moscow. According to Gheorghi Dimitrov, the

Bulgarian Communist Party leader who spent the war years in Moscow, Stalin advised the Romanian delegation to focus on agrarian reform and to use the Tudor Vladmirescu infantry division as internal support for the NDF.[28] The actions of the NDF bore this claim out. The NDF attacked its National Liberal and National Peasant partners in the government, denouncing them as 'Fascists' who opposed the will of the people. On 29 January the NDF published its government programme. It was clearly directed against its National Liberal and National Peasant partners in the government, denouncing them as 'reactionaries' who opposed the will of the people, and called for a new government, immediate agrarian reform, and the democratization of the army.[29] When the Liberals and Peasants attempted to answer these charges, their newspapers ceased to appear owing to the refusal of the Communist-controlled printing union to produce them.

Acting on instructions from Vyshinski, Gheorghiu-Dej approached the dissident liberal leader Gheorghe Tătărescu with an invitation to enter the NDF in order to give it the appearance of a broader base. On 31 January Gheorghiu-Dej told the NDF council of the talks which he had had with Tătărescu who said that he was ready to enter the NDF. 'There are opinions', Gheorghiu-Dej stated, 'in very competent places [i.e. Moscow], which indicate to us the need to bring Tătărescu close to us and not to reject him.' Vasile Luca agreed; for him Tătărescu 'represented economic power'. Lothar Rădăceanu, however, was less enthusiastic. He criticised Tătărescu's tolerance of the Iron Guardists and the fact that 'he was their greatest protector'. Gheorghiu-Dej saw the attraction of Tătărescu not merely in the advantages he could bring to the NDF but also in terms of the damage he could do to Maniu: 'Maniu wants to get rid of him [Tătărescu] as a dangerous adversary... Let us think seriously of breaking the National Peasant front', Gheorghiu-Dej concluded.[30]

The Communist press accused Rădescu of sabotaging the armistice by allegedly failing to cleanse Romanian public life of 'Fascism' but omitted to point out that it had failed to put its own house in order in the case of those ministries headed by Communists. Teohari Georgescu sent an open letter to the press accusing Rădescu of having hindered the 'decontamination' of the Ministry of the Interior. In a stormy cabinet meeting on 14 February, Rădescu requested Georgescu's resignation for acts of insubordination. Georgescu, supported by his Communist colleagues in the cabinet, refused to go and the Prime Minister responded by publishing on 16 February three circulars, dated 13 and 28 December 1944, and 20 January 1945, calling on the commission charged with compiling the list of officials liable for dismissal to complete its task. Rădescu was able to point out that the commission for purging the Ministry of the Interior, of which Teohari Georgescu himself was a member, had taken three months to examine 75 cases out of 300, and that following the General's intervention 137 cases had been dealt with in twelve days. In fact, under the Rădescu government 780 officers (i.e.

employees of the Interior Ministry) out of a total force estimated at 14,000, were purged.[31]

Aware of the power which Georgescu and Bodnăraş were amassing, Rădescu ordered the disbandment of the 'Patriotic Guards' on 15 January but the two Communists simply ignored his instruction. Still Georgescu refused to leave his post. He continued to go to his office and issued a telegram to prefects, informing them that 'in compliance with the decision of the NDF council', he would remain in office. 'I advise you most emphatically', he continued, 'not to carry out orders directed against the people, given by General Rădescu, who has proved himself by his dictatorial action to be the enemy of our people.'[32] In the meantime the Deputy Prime Minister Petru Groza, a tool of the Communists, was encouraging peasants to anticipate agrarian reform by seizing the land of the large estate owners. An article in *Scânteia* of 13 February 1945 reported the expropriation of estates by peasants in the counties of Prahova and Dâmboviţa. Two days later Rădescu accused Groza at a cabinet meeting of preparing civil war. Both Rădescu and King Michael feared that the Left was preparing a coup amidst reports that the Russians were sending NKGB troops to Bucharest.

The NDF staged demonstrations in several towns, among them Brăila, Constanţa, Craiova, Roman and Târgu-Mureş, calling for the resignation of the Rădescu government. Although many of the participants came of their own accord, the NDF also used blackmail to mobilize demonstrators. Workers who did not join trade unions were refused ration cards. A police report of 4 February stated that in many factories works' committees were paralleled by so-called 'sacrifice committees' composed of members of parties of the Left. These committees were set up to ensure that the workers followed the orders of the Communist Party and did not join any other parties or non-Communist organizations.[33]

Any hopes that the Romanian people might have had from the Declaration on Liberated Europe, issued at the Yalta Conference, that 'sovereign rights and self-government' would be restored 'to those peoples who have been forcibly deprived of them' were soon dispelled. Organized thuggery was practised by the 'Patriotic Guards' in support of the NDF committees whose hold over several key factories in Bucharest was challenged by non-NDF workers. This particular campaign of Communist-inspired violence began at the ASAM defence works early in February and spread to the Official Gazette and Stella works where the NDF committees were thrown out. At the union elections at the ASAM shops only 14 of the 600 workers voted for the Communist candidates while 180 voted for the non-party list (the remainder abstained).

On 6 February sixty members of the 'Patriotic Guards' and two NKGB soldiers drove to the ASAM works, beat up those who had voted for the independent list, and took eleven of them away to the NKGB headquarters. On 19 February 3,600 of the 5,500 employees at the Malaxa steel and armament works in Bucharest signed a resolution calling for the resignation of the NDF committee headed by Vasile Mauriciu, a former Iron Guardist. Voting on the resolution on the following day was interrupted when the NDF committee called on railwaymen and tramway employees to defend them at the factory. Fighting broke out between the Malaxa workers and the outsiders during which several workers were killed and the Communist labour leader Gheorghe Apostol was wounded. After the affray all those whose identity cards showed that they had voted were arrested and taken to NDF branches.[34]

Travesty was added to injury. *Scânteia* accused Rădescu of attempting to foment a civil war; its attacks were echoed by *Graiul Nou*, the Red Army newspaper in Romania, and *Pravda*. Anatoli Pavlov, the Soviet political representative on the Allied Control Commission, followed the script by advising the chief American on the Commission that unless the Rădescu government 'rid itself of... Fascist elements... the people themselves can be expected to take necessary corrective action'.[35] Matters came to a head on 24 February. At the end of a large NDF demonstration, the crowd moved into the palace square in front of the Ministry of the Interior where Rădescu had his office. Shots were fired and several people were killed. On orders from Rădescu the Romanian troops guarding the building fired into the air to disperse the crowd. The American historian Henry Roberts

> watched the procession and was in the crowd no more than fifty feet from the first shots. Yet at that time and since I have been unable to discover precisely what happened. I do know that government had kept Romanian troops off the streets that day to avoid inciting trouble. The crowd did move toward the Ministry of the Interior building, although it showed little signs of direction. The first shots were fired from a small piece and from somewhere in the crowd, but by whom and for what purpose I do not know.[36]

What was clearly established later by a joint Romanian-Russian commission of doctors was that the bullets extracted from the victims were not of a calibre used by the Romanian army, but these findings came too late for Rădescu. Unable to contain his anger at the provocation, the Prime Minister broadcast to the nation and denounced the Communist leaders, Ana Pauker and Vasile Luca, as 'hyenas' and 'foreigners without God or country', a reference to their non-Romanian origins and their atheism.[37] The Russians now intervened. Vyshinski arrived unexpectedly in Bucharest on 27 February and went straight to the Palace to demand that Rădescu be replaced. King Michael hesitated and told the Russian that constitutional procedures had to be respected. On the following afternoon Vyshinski returned and demanded to know what action the King had taken. When Michael again announced that he was consulting political leaders, the Deputy Minister shouted his dissatisfaction and gave the King until six that evening to announce Rădescu's dismissal. The King was intimidated into consenting.

Michael turned to the British and American representatives for help and advice, but despite the lodging of Western protests in Bucharest and Moscow at Vyshinski's behaviour, the Deputy Foreign Minister continued to force the pace:

> All the truly democratic forces in Romania must be represented in the government and such a government will be able to ensure order and peace in Romania, which is behind the front of the Red Army, whilst at the same time ensuring the honourable and conscientious fulfilment of the armistice conditions.[38]

Military pressure was soon added to political. On 28 February Colonel General Ivan Susaikov, the Deputy Commander of the Southern Group of Armies, replaced Lieutenant General V. Vinogradov as Deputy Chairman of the Allied Control Commission.[39] Without consulting his British and American colleagues, he ordered some Romanian units stationed in and around Bucharest to the Front and disbanded others. Their place was taken by Soviet tanks and troops who occupied the Prefecture of Police, the Central Post Office and the Romanian General Staff Headquarters. Two Romanian bomber groups and two fighter squadrons based in the capital were disbanded, and the rest of the Romanian air force was grounded. Hundreds of plain clothes and uniformed police were dismissed and Soviet troops patrolled the streets of Bucharest, checking the documents of pedestrians and of drivers and their vehicles, and using this opportunity to commandeer even more Romanian vehicles.

On 1 March Vyshinski informed the King that Petru Groza, Rădescu's deputy and a trusted nominee of the Russians 'was the Soviet choice'. Michael reluctantly gave Groza the go-ahead to form a government but the Liberals and Peasants refused to join a government controlled by the NDF. Groza's first cabinet was rejected by the King. On 5 March Vyshinski informed Michael that unless a Groza government was accepted he 'could not be responsible for the continuance of Romania as an independent state'.[40] Fearing a coup the King acquiesced on the following afternoon. Thereafter, the Communist takeover of Romania proceeded rapidly.[41]

Susaikov later explained to the British and American representatives, respectively Air Vice-Marshal Stevenson and Brigadier Schuyler, that the Groza government was indeed imposed by force on the orders of Marshal Malinovsky who feared a Romanian military uprising in the rear of his troops at the Front. Susaikov had been sent to Bucharest to prevent a Romanian volte-face by disarming Romanian troops and bringing in Groza.[42] This argument is not entirely without substance. Soviet sensitivity to disorder behind the lines had been conveyed to Schuyler at the time by Pavlov, the Soviet political representative. At a meeting of the Allied Control Commission on 14 February 1945, Pavlov had told Schuyler that 'no disorder can be permitted to occur in the rear of the Soviet armies... nor can any Fascist activities within the state of Romania be permitted'.[43]

From the archival evidence now available, there seems to have been some disagreement within the Communist Party leadership over the composition of the Groza government. The decisive voice in the matter appears to have been Vyshinski. In a note dated 21 January 1945 to Serghei Dangulov, Senior Assistant to the Head of the Political Department of the Allied Control Commission, Vyshinski told him 'to maintain contacts and relations with Gheorghe Tătărescu', a former Prime Minister under King Carol and a dissident Liberal.[44] Vyshinski's influence with Gheorghiu-Dej persuaded the latter to reject calls late in February from the National Liberal representative Constantin (Bebe) Brătianu for the Communists to continue to work with the National Liberals and National Peasants in government. Instead, Gheorghiu-Dej pressed for an alliance both with Tătărescu and with a dissident National Peasant faction led by Anton Alexandrescu. At an NDF council meeting held on 26 February, Gheorghiu-Dej made his position clear. He had told Brătianu that he did not have a mandate to hold discussions with him and told him bluntly that his proposal [for continued cooperation] was unacceptable: 'We see no reason for the present government to carry on.' Reviewing the current political situation, Gheorghiu-Dej said that although the NDF had consolidated its position in the government, it had not succeeded in resolving the political crisis:

> What we proposed was to enlarge our political base. The forces which today make up the NDF are not sufficient, new alliances must be found. We have found these in the progressive elements among the National Peasants [...] and secondly in the political grouping of Tătărescu. We can no longer make the same kinds of combinations with the representatives of the so-called 'historical' parties as we have made to date.[45]

Gheorghiu-Dej's views were not shared by other leading Communists. Vasile Luca, speaking at a meeting of the NDF council held on 5 March, insisted that despite the NDF's dislike of holding talks with the National Liberals and National Peasants 'we must do everything that is humanly possible to form a government in a constitutional manner in the interests of the country and in the current international context, [and] we must not, in our haste, destroy everything'.[46] Ana Pauker was, according to Anton Alexandrescu, in favour of a new government formed in collaboration with Maniu and Brătianu and had allegedly received the backing of General Susaikov.[47]

The optimism felt in British and American quarters at the measure of agreement secured amongst the Allies at Yalta was largely dispelled by Soviet conduct after the conference, in particular in Romania. The imposition of the Groza government engendered a sense of hopelessness in Clark Kerr, British ambassador to Moscow, who in a paper on Soviet policy dated 27 March 1945, described Soviet policy in Romania as 'the sheerest power politics, entirely out of harmony with the principles enshrined in the Crimea declaration'. He went on to say that there had been

> no attempt to consult with us or with the Americans and we have been expected to condone and, indeed, to associate ourselves with the decisions imposed upon King Michael by M. Vyshinski. When we quote the Yalta declaration to the Russians we meet with the reply that our arguments are not in accordance with the Statutes agreed upon for the Allied Control Commission. In other words, the Yalta declaration is being treated by the Soviet government as little more than a sedative which cannot be allowed to interfere with what is, in the eyes of the Russians, their established right, fully admitted by us, to do as they like in Roumania. When our protests become more urgent, no time is lost in starting a minor press campaign against General Plastiras and his Administration in Greece, as if to remind us that Russian forbearance as regards that country is measured by ours in Roumania.[48]

Clark Kerr's explanation for Soviet actions was that 'at Yalta the Soviet leaders no doubt confirmed their impression that they could pursue their own ends in the Balkans without fear of serious opposition, provided always that they stopped short at Greece...They must feel pretty sure that, until Germany is finally beaten, we shall not strongly oppose Soviet action in such countries as Roumania and Bulgaria.' With the Red Army in occupation of both countries, the Russians had a unique opportunity to bend internal developments there according to their will, especially as the pre-war social systems had been completely disrupted. 'Such an opportunity', Clark Kerr argued, 'may not recur, and they are determined that, when society crystallises again in those countries bordering upon the Soviet Union, the social structure, although not necessarily identical to, will be in harmony with that of the Soviet Union, and that all potential hostile influences will have been eliminated.' He concluded that Britain would 'make little headway with the Kremlin so long as we conduct fruitless arguments with them over such countries as Roumania or Bulgaria'.[49]

Clark Kerr's advocacy of concessions to the Soviets over Romania and Bulgaria was not shared by Sir Orme Sargent, Assistant Under-Secretary at the Foreign Office. In a minute of 2 April 1945 on the need to reconsider policy towards Russia, he argued that concessions to the Soviets were justified until the invasion of France but no longer in a situation where Anglo-American forces were moving rapidly into the heart of Germany. In Sargent's view, the Soviets had reacted with truculence to the Western Allies' recent successes against the German armies.

An example of this truculence was the imposition of the Groza government and the subsequent refusal of the Soviets to discuss it with the British and Americans. This change of attitude was out of keeping with Soviet willingness to cooperate shown at Yalta: 'Instead of the Russians being in a position from Berlin to dictate their terms to their Allies, the latter are meeting them on equal terms in Germany, and indeed the terms on which they meet may end by being more favourable to the Western Allies than to the Russians.' He believed that a deal on spheres of influence by which Poland, Romania and Bulgaria would be sacrificed to the Soviet Union in return for Czechoslovakia, Yugoslavia, Austria and Turkey was inconceivable because not only could the British never be sure that Stalin would observe such a bargain, but it would appear in the eyes of the world as the cynical abandonment of the small nations whose interest Britain was pledged to defend.[50]

This last point had been recognized by Churchill himself when signing the 'percentages agreement' with Stalin in Moscow in October 1944. He admitted that the 'agreement' tied his hands in protesting at the imposition of the Groza government:

> On the very evening when I was speaking in the House of Commons upon the results of our labours at Yalta the first violation by the Russians both of the spirit and of the letter of our agreements took place in Roumania. We were all committed by the declaration on Liberated Europe, so recently signed, to see that both free elections and democratic governments were established in the countries occupied by the Allied armies... I was deeply disturbed by this news, which was to prove a pattern of things to come. The Russians had established the rule of a Communist minority by force and misrepresentation. We were hampered in our protests because Eden and I during our October visit to Moscow had recognized that Russia should have a largely predominant voice in Roumania and Bulgaria while we took the lead in Greece. Stalin had kept very strictly to this understanding during the six weeks' fighting against the Communists and ELAS in the city of Athens, in spite of the fact that all this was most disagreeable to him and those around him.[51]

The new Groza government was dominated by the NDF, which held fourteen of the eighteen cabinet posts. Communists controlled the Ministries of the Interior, Justice, War, and the National Economy. Dissident Liberal and Peasants held the other four portfolios, the most notorious being King Carol's former Prime Minister Gheorghe Tătărescu, once an opponent and now a sycophant of the Soviet Union, who was made Deputy Prime Minister and Foreign Minister. Teohari Georgescu was elevated to the position of Minister of the Interior. Immediately after his appointment Georgescu announced that 'in order to carry out its tasks... the Ministry of the Interior must rely on a powerful police apparatus that had been purged of all Fascist, collaborationist or compromised elements who had been perverted by anti-democratic and venal customs and practices'.[52] Of the 6,300 Ministry of the Interior personnel employed on 6 March 1945, 2,851 were placed on the reserve and 195 dismissed. In their place were brought in 'honest, democratic and capable elements'.[53]

The police, the *Siguranța*, the gendarmerie, and the Corps of Detectives were reorganized, the latter body being given the special task of tracking down and arresting members of the Iron Guard who were still active.[54] Under the direction of an NKVD agent, Alexandru Nicolski, the Corps was to provide the nucleus of the *Securitate*.[55] Georgescu's colleague, Emil Bodnăraş, was promoted to secretary-general to the Prime Minister. Bodnăraş occupied a key position, for various strands in the Communist takeover intersected in his office. He was also an agent of the NKVD and reported faithfully to his masters in Moscow on the attitudes of senior figures in the new government as well as on the manoeuvring within the RCP.

On 7 March Groza announced that there would be a purge of 'Fascists' from public life and on 2 April the Party daily *Scânteia* declared that several hundred police and counter-espionage officers who were 'guilty of the disaster which had befallen the country' (Communist jargon for the alliance with Germany) had been arrested. The arrests were carried out on 20 March by Bessarabian-born Soviet agents, newly conscripted into the police. Most of them had been captured by the Romanian authorities during the interwar years and had been released from jail after 23 August. To complete Soviet control over the forces of repression Groza signed an order on 27 April giving the secretary-general control of the intelligence service, the SSI. The danger of any opposition to the Soviet and Communist presence by trained and armed forces was eliminated, and the new instruments for Communizing Romanian society were in place.

The establishment of the Groza government brought with it the total subordination of the forces of order to the Communists. Citizens' committees were to assist the police, which had been reduced by Soviet order on 28 February and purged, and these arrogated to themselves the right to check people's documents in the street, to search homes for goods allegedly removed from the Soviet Union during the war or which had formerly belonged to Germans and Hungarians, and to inspect houses with a view to billeting refugees or Soviet officers. There was no legal supervision of these random intrusions into people's lives and the rapidity with which the police degenerated into a force of repression under Groza generated a widespread fear of authority.

In order to obtain the verdicts that he required Vyshinski ordered Pătrăşcanu, the Minister of Justice, to dismiss more than 1,000 magistrates in April 1945 and replace them with pliant zealots.[56] It was not just the retributive aspect of these purges that was important but also the instrumental use of them. The two were linked: the threat of retribution was deployed to pressure people to become tools of the Communists. Groza himself told the British journalist Archie Gibson on 23 May 1945 that 'he had at one time 90,000 Romanians under arrest, which figure had later fallen to 2,300. Another source, quoting Pătrăşcanu, the Communist Minister of Justice, put the number at 60,000 in mid-April.'[57]

For some there were good grounds for arrest, as in the case of Nicolae Sturdza and Nelly Ostroveanu, two members of an Iron Guard group who were found to be housing nineteen German soldiers living under assumed names in Bucharest and who were arrested in March. For others the opposite was true; thirteen Poles were held in the internment camp at Caracal without being questioned. Persons convicted of atrocities during the Romanian administration of Transnistria were harshly punished. People's Tribunals were introduced by Pătrăşcanu to try alleged war criminals and on 22 May twenty-nine individuals found guilty of this charge, including Generals Nicolae Macici, Constantin Trestioreanu and Cornel Calotescu, were sentenced to death, and eight others to various terms of imprisonment.[58] The death sentences were commuted to life imprisonment on 5 June.[59] In August 1945 the discovery of two 'terrorist' plots led to the arrest of about twenty 'hirelings of ex-Premier Rădescu', and of a second group of seventeen people who had allegedly plotted 'against the unity of the Romanian nation'. Both groups included National Peasant Party members.

The young King was greatly unnerved by these developments and appealed to Britain and the United States for help, invoking the principles of the Atlantic Charter and the Yalta Declaration. On 2 August, at the end of the Potsdam Conference, both countries announced that they would sign peace treaties 'only with recognized democratic governments', a stipulation which gave some hope to the King and the opposition leaders, Maniu and Brătianu.[60] The latter discussed plans to remove the Groza government and on 20 August the King asked for Groza's resignation but the Prime Minister, with the backing of General Susaikov, refused. King Michael, in retaliation, boycotted the government; he declined to see any of its ministers and to sign decrees.

The stalemate lasted for over four months. It was broken at the Moscow Conference of the Foreign Ministers of Britain, the United States and the Soviet Union, held between 16 and 26 December, where it was decided that a commission, composed of ambassadors Clark Kerr, Harriman, and Deputy Foreign Minister Vyshinski, should go to Bucharest to advise King Michael on the inclusion in the government of one representative each from the National Peasant and National Liberal Parties. After this reorganization it was also agreed that free elections would be held 'as soon as possible on the basis of universal suffrage and secret ballot'.[61]

The commission's visit coincided with the mission of Lt. Col. Boxshall to liquidate SOE affairs in Romania. After the collapse of the Antonescu regime, Rică Georgescu and the members of his groups had been released from prison.[62] As de Chastelain admitted in his account of the 'History of SOE in Romania', 'their first reaction, of course, was to seek support from those who had engaged them, and in this they were disappointed'.[63] It was only in February 1945 that it had been agreed that Lt. Col. Harris-Burland – by that time in Romania as Ministry of War Transport (MWT) representative on the Allied Control Commission – should attempt the liquidation of SOE affairs 'in his spare time',[64] but after a few months it became clear that Harris-Burland's duties with the MWT rendered the attempt impractical. The War Office therefore cabled the British Military Mission in Bucharest in September to request approval of the Allied Control Commission for a visit by Lt. Col. Boxshall to finalize outstanding liquidation matters.[65]

Boxshall arrived in Bucharest by air from Bari on 22 December 1945. After consultations in early January 1946 involving Ian Le Rougetel, the political officer at the British legation, Colonel Forster, head of the economic section, and Harris-Burland, Boxshall brought up to date the SOE liquidation accounts prepared in London. These provided for settlement of monies administered by Harris-Burland in the running of the Goeland Company in 1940, by Major Ivor Porter in running SOE affairs after 23 August 1944, and small payments, on the recommendation of Rică Georgescu and Alexandru Ionescu, to certain Romanians who had assisted SOE during the war. Alexandru Ştefănescu was repaid the sum of £1,923, the balance of sums which he had advanced to the British legation from the assets in Romania of J. P. Coats, the thread company.[66] In the conclusion to his report Boxshall stressed that he fully endorsed the views of Le Rougetel, Forster and Harris-Burland that 'both Rică Georgescu's and Ştefănescu's integrity is beyond doubt. They both – but especially Georgescu – continue to render great service to the British cause in Romania.'[67]

The resolution of another financial matter proved more problematic. Boxshall sought the approval of the Head of the British Military Mission, Air Vice-Marshal Stevenson, at the end of December to enlist two British officers to assist him in the retrieval of 'the 255 gold sovereigns and $2,000 allegedly remitted by REGINALD (our W/T operator) [Nicolae Ţurcanu, a member of the 'Ranji' mission] to some of his relatives'. Stevenson flatly rejected Boxshall's request on the grounds that the likelihood of success in obtaining the money was negligible and that any attempt to do so at that time might easily lead to complaints to the Romanian Secret Service or to the Soviet authorities by the people concerned, which could possibly 'inconvenience' the British Military Mission. Boxshall himself appears not to have been fully convinced of the allegation against Ţurcanu since in his own opinion the two sums should have been written off. He went on in his report, 'I am strengthened in my belief by the fact that Reginald's wife has repeatedly called on the Mission for assistance; it is known that she is living in exceedingly straitened circumstances, which would obviously not be the case if the money had, in fact, been handed to his relatives by Reginald.'[68]

The Moscow Conference agreement was the final step for the Soviets in getting the West to recognize their dominance of Romania.[69] Had the agreement been respected to the letter, it would have represented a victory for King Michael's defiance, but as events were to prove, it merely allowed the Western Allies to disguise their impotence. Groza went through the motions of implementing the terms, accepting Emil Haţieganu of the Peasant Party and Mihai Romniceanu of the Liberals into his cabinet as Ministers without Portfolio, and undertaking, on 8 January 1946, to hold early elections, and to guarantee access to the radio and the media to all parties. On the basis of these assurances Britain and the United States expressed their willingness to recognize the Groza government at the beginning of February in the expectation that the elections would be held at the end of April or early May. In the event Groza procrastinated. On 27 May both Britain and the United States protested to Groza at his failure to honour his pledges, and eventually his government produced an electoral law which was heavily weighted in its favour. All parties of the Left were to run on a common list, including the Social Democratic Party which the Communists had succeeded in splitting.

A new wave of arrests took place in May 1946. Among those detained was General Aurel Aldea, the Interior Minister in the first Sănătescu government who was arrested on 27 May and charged with 'plotting to destroy the unity of the Romanian state' on the grounds that 'in the summer of 1945 he had brought together various subversive organizations under his own central command' in a 'National Resistance Movement' (*Mişcarea Naţională de Rezistenţă*). Initially, these groups had acted independently, the most important of them being *Haiducii lui Avram Iancu* (The Outlaws of Avram Iancu), which had been set up in Transylvania on 1 December 1944 by leading figures of the National Peasant Party, among them Iuliu Maniu's nephew. An offshoot of this group was *Divizia Sumanele Negre* (The Black Greatcoats Division) which also had its centre of operations in Transylvania.

In a declaration to the *Siguranţa*, Aldea revealed that he had established links in autumn 1945 with these groups and brought them under his command. In fact, the National Resistance Movement was a paper tiger: its principal activity was the distribution of primitive anti-Communist propaganda. Its actions largely consisted of attacks on Hungarians by members of *Haiducii lui Avram Iancu* in revenge for murders of Romanians by Hungarian policemen during the period of Hungarian rule of Northern Transylvania, and it was these which caused the greatest concern to the Soviet authorities for they raised the spectre of civil war in Transylvania. Aldea was tried along with fifty-five 'accomplices' on the eve of the polls in November and sentenced on 18 November to hard labour for life.[70]

In September 1946 Maniu appealed to de Chastelain for easier access to British officials and the Foreign Office reluctantly agreed, but Christopher

Warner, the desk officer for Romania, wrote that Maniu was 'a tiresome, perhaps at times even a silly old man'.[71] Adrian Holman, who succeeded Le Rougetel in April 1946, had little time for the Peasant Party leader and in May of the following year Maniu complained to him that the British appeared to have completely forgotten the historic parties.[72]

Opposition meetings were frequently interrupted during the election campaign by gangs of hooligans and when the American political representative in Bucharest, Burton Berry, protested, Groza told him that

> when the Anglo-Americans agreed to the Moscow decision they were thinking in terms of free elections such as were held in England or America, whereas the Russians were thinking in terms of free elections such as were held in Russia. In view of the presence of the Russian army in Romania, the coming elections would likely be held according to the Russian interpretation of free and unfettered.[73]

The results of the elections, held on 19 November, came as no surprise to the Foreign Office and to the State Department. The government bloc claimed almost five million votes (84 per cent), while the National Peasants were awarded 800,000 and the Liberals less than 300,000. A total of 414 deputies were elected to a single chamber Parliament, of whom 348 represented the government parties and 66 the opposition. In the view of Western diplomats and press correspondents the results were faked, and consequently Dean Acheson, the acting US Secretary of State, declared that his government would not recognize them. In the House of Commons Hector McNeil, the Under-Secretary for Foreign Affairs, said that the elections were neither free nor fair. During the campaign the opposition parties were, he argued, denied full freedom of speech, and the arrangements on polling day were such as to permit wholesale fabrication of the results. These assessments have been confirmed by documents from the Romanian Communist Party's own archives.[74] Yet despite this condemnation of the results, the British government, on advice from the Foreign Office, decided not to support an American protest to the Russians calling for new elections, on the feeble grounds that Moscow would simply prevaricate.

King Michael threatened to postpone the opening of Parliament but Burton Berry, the American representative in Bucharest, to whom he appealed for support, was unable to give him any encouragement. Yet more arrests followed the signing of the Peace Treaty with Romania on 10 February 1947. Its political clauses were so lacking in definition that the Ministry of the Interior could interpret the phrases 'organization of a Fascist type' and 'war criminal' as arbitrarily as they wished. On 20 March, 315 members of the opposition parties were arrested and on the night of 4 May, another 600. There was no legal basis for these arrests; those in May were made under the provisions of a top-secret order of the Ministry of the Interior and the persons detained were sent to prisons in Gherla, Piteşti, Craiova and Miercurea Ciuc. Some of the 596 persons sent to Gherla were peasants who had opposed collectivization; others were teachers, doctors and priests who had campaigned on behalf of the opposition parties in November 1946. Many did not know why they had been arrested. Several managed to escape and most were released after six months but the Communist authorities had achieved their aim: to intimidate the population and to prepare the ground for the liquidation of the opposition parties.

Such was the atmosphere of fear that even Tătărescu, the Deputy Prime Minister, was moved in May to send a memorandum to the cabinet, arguing that

> preventive arrests must cease so that the atmosphere of insecurity may be dispelled. The security police should be continually on the alert, but it should act only against offenders. The guilty persons should be punished without mercy, but only within the letter of the law. All illegally detained persons should be released.[75]

Tătărescu's argument fell on deaf ears, for the campaign to eliminate the opposition parties, approved by Stalin and coordinated by Vyshinski, had entered its final stage. Instructions were given to Pintilie Bodnarenko, a senior NKGB agent in Bucharest who was made responsible for overseeing the *Siguranţa* attempts to compromise the Peasant Party leadership. Bodnarenko achieved this by employing an *agent provocateur* to persuade Maniu's deputy Ion Mihalache to attempt to flee the country in a plane provided by him. The plan succeeded and on 14 July 1947 Mihalache and several prominent figures in the Peasant Party were arrested as they were about to leave for Turkey from Tămădău airfield (about 50 km from Bucharest).

A few days later Maniu was detained and the whole leadership of the Party was put on trial on 30 October before a military tribunal for plotting against the security of the state.[76] More specifically, it was alleged that secret negotiations took place in Bucharest in September 1946 between Maniu's representative, Grigore Niculescu-Buzeşti, and 'representatives of the US Secret Service' for the carrying out of a coup, according to which 'a clandestine organization was set up in the country, armed, equipped and financed by the Americans'. In the second half of 1946, under the direction of Maniu and Mihalache, it was alleged that a 'plotting centre' had been established abroad, under their leadership and that of Grigore Niculescu-Buzeşti and Victor Rădulescu-Pogoneanu, designed to discredit the Romanian government's foreign policy. Maniu was further accused of the systematic gathering of information of a political, economic and military nature, and of conveying it to representatives of the US and British Missions in Romania. Finally, 'with a view to setting up a "government" of impostors abroad, the prisoner Maniu prepared and attempted to carry out the treacherous flight from the country of the prisoners Mihalache, Penescu, Ilie Lazăr and Carandino'.[77] Maniu admitted that he had supported the decision of Mihalache and others to flee the country; both men were found guilty and sentenced to solitary confinement in jail for life on 11 November. Neither man was ever seen in public again.[78]

Holman showed no sympathy whatsoever for Maniu and his colleagues. His view was that Britain could not protest because the National Peasant Party leadership had broken the law by attempting to flee, a subtle admission in itself that Romania was no longer a free country in the Western understanding of the term. The Foreign Office had to remind him that the trial was about the suppression of the opposition as with the trial of Nikola Petkov in Bulgaria.[79] Holman dug his heels in and refused to accept the Bulgarian analogy, displaying a good measure of *schadenfreud* in opining that the US mission had been shown to be deeply implicated in the alleged 'plot'. He was of the view that the defendants could be found guilty in an English court and on 12 November, in a telegram reporting the sentences, wrote that 'every defendant was, I think justifiably, found guilty legally on one or more of the charges'. In a despatch penned the same day he claimed that facts had come to light about the National Peasant Party at the trial 'which definitely establish it as a "fascist" organization by East European standards'.[80]

The final obstacle to complete Soviet domination of Romania was King Michael. Even in 1945 the continuation of the Romanian kingdom within the Soviet orbit appeared, in the circumstances, to be an anomaly.[81] The young monarch had valiantly wrestled with the Soviet tentacles which were slowly throttling the country's independence, often with only half-hearted support from Britain and the United States, but the stage-managed trial of Maniu was a clear sign that the King's struggle was in vain. Nevertheless, the Romanian people clung to him as the last symbol of hope for a sane and settled future. In September 1947 Foreign Minister Tătărescu had been compelled to dismiss several hundred members of his ministry who were regarded as pro-Western, and on 7 November he and other Liberal cabinet members were removed from their posts at Groza's insistence. The King felt obliged to accept the Communists Ana Pauker and Vasile Luca as respectively Foreign Minister and Minister of Finance. By Christmas the Communist Party had taken over every significant ministry, including the Ministry of Defence to which Emil Bodnăraş was appointed on 23 December.

When the King went to London on 12 November with the Queen Mother for the marriage of Princess Elizabeth, Groza and Gheorghiu-Dej, now the First Secretary of the Communist Party, hoped that he would renounce the throne and not return. Indeed Michael asked for American advice on this subject and the US ambassador in London considered that his return 'would serve no useful purpose'.[82] Nevertheless, the King, who while abroad had announced his engagement to Princess Anne de Bourbon Parma, took the bold decision to return with the Queen Mother on 21 December. Nine days later the Communists acted. Groza and Dej asked the King to come to Bucharest from his mountain retreat at Sinaia and presented him with a ready-made abdication statement. When he refused to authorize it the two men gave him half an hour to consider his position. In the meantime troops were brought in to surround the palace. Still the King declined to sign, whereupon Groza threatened civil war. Faced with the possibility of bloodshed Michael gave in. With his signature ended the Romanian kingdom and the country's possibilities of independent action. On that same day, 30 December 1947, the Romanian People's Republic was declared.

A unique, authoritative account of the immediate events leading to the King's abdication is given by Ivor Porter who was serving at the time as a second secretary at the British legation in Bucharest. In a memorandum dated 26 February 1948 for the Foreign Office, providing a summary of the principal political events in Romania during 1947, Porter wrote:

> The King had been accorded normal courtesies when he had left the country to attend Princess Elizabeth's wedding, and although received on his return with less than the customary ceremonial had been met by all members of his Government. When he raised the matter of his engagement to Princess Anne of Bourbon-Parma, the Government were unable to give him an immediate answer and the King then left for Sinaia. On the evening of the 29th, however, he received a telephone message from the Prime Minister asking him to return to Bucharest on urgent business, and even then neither he nor any of his suite were able to guess that a crisis had occurred. On returning to Bucharest early next morning, he noticed that the palace was surrounded by troops of the Tudor Vladimirescu division and that there were a large number of civilian police in evidence. Dr Groza and Mr Gheorghiu-Dej were received by him almost immediately and they presented him with an abdication decree for signature. When he asked for some respite to think over the matter, it was pointed out to him that if he did not sign forthwith there would be bloodshed and nothing would be gained. He therefore signed at about fourteen hours on 30th December, and left the country with his suite soon after the New Year. It is now well-known that the King did not abdicate on account of his Government's refusal to allow him to marry. It seems clear that the decision of the King to return to Romania in spite of all the pressure against such a course which was without doubt exercised by those around him must in itself have been somewhat disconcerting for the Government. What is more important, however, is that when the question of his marriage was raised, Moscow most probably felt that to agree and then operate an abdication at a time when a popular young Queen, and possibly an heir,

were already installed in the country would be very much more difficult. A sudden decision appears therefore to have been taken, and as there was no time to develop an issue on which the King would have been compelled to abdicate, resort was made to a simple *coup d'état* supported by armed force.[83]

10
Condemned but not Forgotten: The Fate of Pro-British Activists in Romania, 1945–1964

With the imposition of Communist rule in 1945, Romania was forced to turn its back on the West and face eastwards. This meant that anyone with a link to the West, especially those Romanians who had assisted SOE, became suspect in the eyes of the new regime. Such figures, having played their part in the defeat of Nazi Germany, now found themselves to be the targets of the Western Allies' erstwhile partner, the Soviet Union, and its surrogate Romanian Communist Party. Those deemed to be opponents of the new Communist order attracted particular attention. Contact with the West became a cardinal sin with which the leaders of the established democratic parties could be charged, tried and removed from the political scene. Such was the fate of Iuliu Maniu, the head of the National Peasant Party, of Constantin (Dinu) Brătianu,[1] the head of the National Liberal Party, and of Titel Petrescu, the secretary-general of the Social Democratic Party.[2]

For many Romanians, Maniu and his close associate, Ion Mihalache, were synonymous with the National Peasant Party. The respect enjoyed by both amongst much of the Romanian electorate, and their suspicion of Soviet intentions, coupled with Maniu's wartime links with SOE and his close post-war contact with officials at the British and United States' legations in Bucharest, marked them out as major obstacles in the eyes of the Communist authorities in the transition to the creation of a single mass party and of a Communist state. Romanians with pro-Western sentiments also became targets of the security police, amongst them the local Romanian employees of Western legations and institutions. They, too, became victims of the regime.

The cards of Anglophiles were marked, in Gheorghiu-Dej's eyes, for two reasons: first, because Gheorghiu-Dej, who had not enjoyed a formal education, was envious of those who had (including his own colleagues); and second, since Britain was a major power, and had been a significant influence in the cultural and commercial lives of many Romanians, contact with the country and its culture identified them as adversaries of the Communist regime. Anything British was regarded by the Communists with suspicion, and anything that was both cultural and British attracted the special attention of the Romanian secret police, the *Securitate*.

Despite the Communist mistrust of the British, the Foreign Office was quick to show interest in a renewal of British Council activities in Romania and the position of the Anglo-Romanian Society after the signature of the Allied Armistice Agreement with Romania in Moscow on 12 September 1944. However, as discussed in Chapter 9 the Soviet determination to secure their own political and economic influence in the region had resulted in a rewriting of the Agreement in their favour and under their terms. As if to stress the point, Molotov, the Soviet Foreign Minister, in conversation with the American ambassador to Moscow, Averell Harriman, implied that the Western Allies could only have political contact with the Romanian government through the Russians. The same was to be true of cultural contacts. Since the Soviet Union had the monopoly of its interpretation, the Armistice Agreement became the mechanism for the takeover of Romania.[3] The British and the Americans, who both sent Military Missions to Romania, were reduced to the role of spectators.

On 14 November 1944, H. J. Seymour of the Foreign Office wrote to Ian Le Rougetel, British Political Representative to the Allied Control Commission in Bucharest, for his views on the Anglo-Romanian Society and the prospects of a resumption of British Council work. Le Rougetel, who only received the letter on 26 January 1945, sent a detailed reply on 28 February which highlights the constraints imposed by Soviet control:

> So far as the Society is concerned, no public meetings have been held as yet and it has been felt that the best way in which the Society's aims could at present be achieved is by the loan of its books to an English Library under the control of this Mission.
>
> Under the Armistice Convention the dissemination of all propaganda material is subject to the direction of the 'Allied (Soviet) High Command'. We have therefore felt that, rather than to raise the whole question of British propaganda in this country, our first step should be to announce the foundation of the Library and to invite both Romanians and Russians to take advantage of its facilities... We hope in this way to be able at the same time to fill a crying need among the Romanians and allay any suspicions that the Russians might entertain regarding our propaganda activities. We are confident that the Library, when it is opened next month, will attract a large membership and when it has been open for a few weeks, we shall be able to judge better of the advisability of extending its activities and perhaps of resuming the meetings of the Anglo-Romanian Society.
>
> The only other activity which we are launching out on at present is films. We have received several news reels with Romanian commentaries

> and these have been most successfully shown, with the addition of Russian sub-titles, in Bucharest and the provincial towns.
>
> Our whole approach to the question of British propaganda in this country must, of course, be radically different now that Romania is within the Russian sphere of operations. The Romanians are in an embarrassingly Anglophile mood at present and we are at pains to discourage them from assuming that we are here as their protectors and invariably insist that the future of this country depends on straightforward and practical cooperation with Russia.
>
> It is therefore obvious that our publicity work here cannot be aimed exclusively at the furtherance of Anglo-Romanian cultural relations.[4]

Further information about the newly created English Library was given by Ivor Porter, serving as Major in the Press Office of the British Military Mission, to the Council in a letter dated 2 May 1945. Porter's letter was sent to F. Y. Thompson, the former British Council lecturer in Cernăuţi who was now working in the Council's headquarters. His efforts to satisfy the Romanian thirst for English literature are chronicled thus:

> In view, however, of the great demand for English literature of all kinds with which we were confronted, we decided to put the books of the 'Anglo-Romanian Society' into circulation. The Mission took these books on loan from the 'Anglo-Romanian Society' and named them the 'English Library'. A small committee, consisting of Prof. Oprescu, Mr Chrissoveloni and myself has been formed. Miss Pantazi is librarian and has two assistant librarians, Miss Donici and Mr Catargi. The library is in two sections, a lending library and a reference library and there are reading rooms for students. We have another room for British newspapers and periodicals. The library, which is housed in Strada Biserica Amzei 7, is in no way, of course, a society or club. The library of the Bucharest Faculty of English Language and Literature was burnt out during the bombing last year and their work was almost immobilized. We have, therefore, lent them some 770 books from the English Library, consisting chiefly of the Eckersley courses and anthologies of verse, essays and plays. We intend to let the University of Iaşi have some 100 books of the same kind. We have given about 80 books to the Russian Mission for Russians who are learning English.[5]

Several members of the Romanian staff of the British legation, of the British Press Office,[6] and of the British Military Mission, were arrested on charges of espionage in 1949 and 1950.[7] These persons were sentenced to long periods of incarceration by the Communist authorities, but they were not forgotten by successive British Heads of Mission. Those of the Press Office who were arrested in summer and autumn 1949 were Constantin (Costica Mugur),[8] a cashier; Annie Samuelli, assistant to the head; Eleonore Bunea de Wied,[9] Mugur's assistant and a cousin of King Michael; Maria Golescu, a librarian; Angela Rădulescu, a clerk; and Ion Vorvoreanu and a Mrs Cremniter, both translators. The latter died shortly after her arrest.

Mugur, Samuelli and de Wied were part of a group accused of being 'enslaved to Anglo-American imperialist interests and driven by their embittered hatred towards the democratic regime installed in our country who carried out – with the help and under the direction of members of the Anglo-American missions and later legation – high treason, thereby threatening the security and independence of our state, the Romanian People's Republic'.[10] Their trial was given significant publicity in Romania, doubtless in order to intimidate. The accused were found guilty and sentenced on 28 April 1950. The other members of the group were Annie Samuelli's sister Nora, an employee at the American Information Service, and Liviu Nasta, correspondent of the *New York Times* in Romania after 1945.[11] Mugur was sentenced to hard labour for life, Annie and Nasta to twenty years' hard labour, and Nora and de Wied to fifteen years' hard labour.[12]

Maria Golescu was arrested during the night of 24 October 1949.[13] She was accused of acting as a conduit for reports from Ştefan Neniţescu, an associate of Iuliu Maniu, about the effects of the measures taken by the regime to communize the country, to Herbert Marchant, John Bennett's successor as Head of the Press Office.[14] These reports were brought to Golescu at the Information Office by Magdalena Cancicov. Both Golescu and Cancicov were amongst a group of seventeen persons tried in secret for various offences against the regime, found guilty of high treason and sentenced on 28 December 1950 by a military tribunal in Bucharest. In both cases the sentence received was the same: twenty years' hard labour.[15] Golescu was held in Jilava prison from October 1949 until 22 February 1951 when she was moved to Mislea women's jail north of Ploieşti where she remained until 21 June 1956. On that date she was transferred to Miercurea-Ciuc women's prison in Transylvania and it was from this jail that she was released on 19 June 1962, having benefited from a pardon under decree number 482 of the State Council of 11 June of that year.[16]

On 4 March 1950 the Bucharest legation notified the FO that 'three Roumanian members of the staff of the American Legation disappeared last night and were no doubt arrested. The librarian of our Information section, Mrs Constantin, and her husband who has no official connexion with the Legation, also disappeared during the night.'[17] In fact, the fate of Mr and Mrs Constantin was shared by more than sixty local staff from Western legations in Bucharest during the following four years and suggests a pattern both of intimidation aimed at sapping the morale of Romanians working for these legations, and of hampering the activities of foreign missions in those areas where a fluent knowledge of the Romanian language was essential.

A review of the arrests and releases of local employees at the British legation, dated 21 December 1955, listed fifteen names: Mr and Mrs Constantin, Valentin Sarry, Paul Bandu, Mrs Bunea (Eleonora de Wied), Annie Samuelli, Constantin Mugur, George Balică, Răileanu, Emil Godeanu, Mrs Wassilko (Alexandra Greaznov), Nicolae Parău, Rose Sussman, Gheorghe Bobincă and Ludwig Pîrvu.[18]

Mr and Mrs Constantin were released in February 1951. Valentin Sarry was employed in the consulate at Constanţa as a messenger and Paul Bandu was a university student used by the consular representative as a courier to carry private mail between Constanţa and Bucharest.[19] Their trial was reported to the Foreign Office in June 1950. Sarry's mother received assistance from the legation and in November 1955 she indicated in a letter that her son was still in prison. Nothing further was known about Bandu. George Balică disappeared on 8 February 1951 and it was later ascertained that he had been arrested. He was released and returned to his home on 23 April 1953 and was employed from October 1953 as an assistant to the administration officer of the legation. Răileanu, a locally-employed chauffeur, was detained at his home on 21 July 1951 and released in July 1955. He was given a temporary job in the legation and then taken on as a driver by the US legation from 1 November. Godeanu was legal adviser to the British legation. He was arrested at his house on 20 March 1952 and no further information had been heard of him although the review reported that there had been persistent rumours during 1955 that he had been released and seen in Bucharest.[20]

Mrs Wassilko, a clerk in the legation administration office, was arrested on 3 December 1953 but in December 1955 had yet to come up for trial. Nicolae Parău, a telephone operator, was also arrested, on 31 December 1954, and returned to the legation on 15 October in the following year, the remainder of his three years sentence having been remitted under an amnesty of October 1955.[21] He was re-employed as a telephonist in the legation. Rose Sussman was similarly re-employed, in the consular section, having been arrested on 25 February 1954. She returned to the legation on 4 October 1955. Two domestic employees, Gheorghe Bobincă and Ludwig Pârvu, both butlers employed by diplomats at the legation disappeared respectively on 2 December 1952 and 29 March 1954, and although the former had since been released, there was no further information to hand about Pîrvu.[22]

It should be stressed that the legation consistently raised the arrest of these persons with the Romanian Ministry of Foreign Affairs, despite that fact only one of them, Mrs Sussman, was a dual national and that even in her case the *locus standi* of the British in international law was extremely weak, the Romanian state having primacy where their citizens were concerned.[23] Indeed, these were the grounds upon which Romanian ministers rejected the British representations. Nevertheless, diplomatic correspondence contains much evidence of the efforts made to ascertain the fate of local employees who had suddenly disappeared. These included a proposal to pay bail.

In March 1954 William Sullivan, Head of Mission in Bucharest, reported on a meeting with Gheorghe Preoteasa, the Deputy Minister of Foreign Affairs, where

> I was enabled to develop my case fully without interruption and began by referring back to the arrests of Mrs Wassilko (Greaznov) and of Parău, leading up to that of Mrs Sussman, and pointing out the curious fact that the last of the arrests had coincided with the departure of my administration and consular officer on leave. I was not prepared as an abstract proposition to dispute the Roumanian claim that under international law I was not entitled to concern myself with the regime's dealings with their own nationals, but I asserted that the right of a legation to carry out its duties without let or hindrance was no less valid and important from the international law angle. These arbitrary arrests, without previous explanation or consultation, seriously hampered the work of the legation and could only be bad for our mutual relations.[24]

Two weeks later, Sullivan, who was about to complete his tour of duty, asked Harry Hohler, the head of the Northern Department at the Foreign Office if he would authorize him, in his farewell interview with Preoteasa, to offer

> (a) Substantial bail (say ten thousand lei per head) for provisional release and return to duty of the four members of my Roumanian staff arrested during my tour (since April 1951), namely the chauffeur Răileanu, Mrs Wassilko, telephonist Parău and Mrs Sussman.
> (b) Assurances binding on my successors that these persons will not be given political asylum and that the course of 'justice' will not otherwise be impeded.
>
> If not, can you suggest anything else I could do, before I leave, for these unfortunate people?[25]

Hohler replied that 'on both political and legal grounds, I cannot authorise the step you propose'. He went on: 'You might, however, at your farewell interview, raise again the general question of arrests and stress that while not disputing the legal rights of the Roumanian authorities in these matters, you wish to emphasize the harm which they do to Anglo-Roumanian relations.'[26]

Activity on behalf of SOE led a number of Romanians to be charged by the Communist authorities with 'high treason'. One such victim was Dan Hurmuzescu who was arrested in March 1950. He was accused of passing on information after 23 August 1944, as an official of the Romanian Ministry of the National Economy responsible for supplying provisions to the occupying Soviet army, to 'the British Intelligence Service led by Ivor Porter', about the nature and deployment of Soviet troops in Romania. He was tried in January 1951, found guilty and sentenced to twenty years' hard labour.[27] His appeal against the sentence, on the grounds that he was merely providing information of a non-confidential nature to a fellow Allied Power of the Allied Control Commission, was rejected on 12 May 1951.[28]

Another collaborator of the British, arrested in 1951, was Andrei Ion Deleanu.[29] He was arrested in 1951 as a 'suspect element' and sent without trial to a labour camp on the Black Sea where he was held until 1953.[30] It was more than a decade before the FO was in a position to consider a request for assistance from him.[31] Indeed, The FO's stance over the arrest and imprisonment of local employees of the legation, invariably on charges of espionage, was flaccid. In March 1951, when the question of human rights appeared on the agenda of the imminent Four-Power talks on the Balkan Peace Treaties, Paul Mason, the British Minister in Sofia, in a letter to N. J. A Cheetham of the Southern Department of the Foreign Office, wrote:

> I do rather view with dismay the prospect of flogging again the dead horse of human rights in the satellite countries. There is frankly nothing we can do about it here, it merely exasperates the local governments who quite plausibly (though incorrectly) regard it as an intervention in their internal policies, and it makes it much more difficult for us to establish any kind of reasonable relations with them.[32]

At one point concerns about the fate of local Romanian staff seem to have been overshadowed by considerations of trade with Romania. Hohler, in a letter of 12 March 1954 to the Board of Trade, made it clear that a trade agreement with Romania 'should not be made dependent on satisfaction of a political demand, however justifiable'.[33] He had conveyed the same sentiments to the Romanian chargé in London, a Mr Vianu, who called to see him at the latter's request on 8 March 1954. In a minute sent to William Sullivan, Head of Mission in Bucharest, Hohler reported that he had told Vianu that if Britain and Romania were to have decent relations

> it was essential that our Legation in Bucharest, as the Roumanian Legation in London, should be able to function in a satisfactory manner. Recently, however, the Roumanian authorities had arrested a number of members of the staff of H.M. Legation at Bucharest. Of these two were Roumanian citizens and the third was a dual national. I accordingly did not in any way dispute the right of the Roumanian authorities to arrest these persons. At the same time I wished to point out that it was very difficult for our Legation in Bucharest to function effectively if we were deprived of the services of employees with local knowledge and with a knowledge of the Roumanian language. I knew that police in all countries were anxious to arrest people, but I suggested that Mr Vianu might put the following considerations to his Ministry. If the Roumanian authorities had really serious charges to bring against the three persons, they were, of course,

> entitled to arrest them, as we should have done in similar circumstances. Nonetheless, it would have been courteous to have sent for H.M. Minister and to have explained the circumstances to him.[34]

In the cases of Maria Golescu, Eleonore Bunea de Wied and Liviu Nasta, disquiet over their welfare was expressed to the Foreign Office by family and friends. On 28 February 1956, Robin Turton, the Minister of Health in the Conservative government, wrote to Lord John Hope, a fellow MP and Minister of State at the FO, enclosing a letter which he had received from his cousin, Countess Vera Lecca. The Countess expressed feelings of guilt about 'not having made an effort to try and find some way of helping our greatest and dearest friend... Miss Marionra [*sic*] Golescu'. Turton asked Lord Hope if he could 'get our ambassador in Bucharest to do something about Miss Golesco'.[35] Lord Hope passed the letter on to Hohler who informed the Head of Mission in Bucharest, Mr D. MacDermot, of its contents. Countess Lecca 'states that Madame Golescu is still in prison, and that she has recently had two pathetic letters from Madame Golescu's mother who is now 86 and may never see her only child again'. Hohler continued,

> I know it was agreed, when we last corresponded on this subject,[36] that it might not be helpful to take up the cases of such employees, particularly while we were still hammering away at the cases of Mrs Sarry and Mrs Placa. Mr Turton has, however, expressed the hope that it might be possible for you to slip in a timely and delicate hint, informally, in an attempt to secure Miss Golescu's release. I should be grateful to know, therefore, whether you think that anything can be said. It might be preferable not to treat Miss Golescu as an isolated case but this is a matter which I leave entirely to your discretion.[37]

What action MacDermot took over Maria Golescu is not clear from the records; what is certain is that she remained incarcerated for a further six years.

Her friend and colleague at the British Information Office, Eleonore Bunea de Wied, was also the subject of representations, in this instance from her family. Her brother, Karl Viktor Prinz zu Wied, in a memorandum submitted to the British consulate-general in Munich dated 17 April 1956, gave the following details of her background. Marie Eleonore Bunea, born Princess of Wied, had become a Romanian citizen through naturalization in 1937. Her first husband, Prince Alfred of Schönburg-Waldenburg, died in March 1941. Throughout the war Princess de Wied had served in the Romanian Red Cross Organization, at first as a nurse, later as an officer. Her father, Prince Wilhelm of Wied, former Prince of Albania, died in the Romanian mountain resort of Predeal in April 1945. After his death Eleonore moved to Bucharest where she became an employee of the British legation.[38] In February 1949 she married a Romanian, Ion Bunea. In July, Karl Viktor went on,

> she apparently attempted to leave the country illegally, together with her husband and seven other people. The attempt failed, the nine persons involved – described by Roumanian officials as 'smugglers and black-marketeers' – were arrested. The Roumanian government then claimed that this abortive attempt had been organized and assisted by the British chargé d'affaires, Mr Roderick Sarrel.
>
> Yesterday I received a letter from the daughter of our former Bucharest lawyer, telling me that my sister is suffering from tuberculosis. The letter ends (in French), 'C'est le moment ou jamais pour l'aider.'[39]

In his covering letter, addressed to the Secretary of State, the Right Honourable Selwyn Lloyd, the Consul-General, J. S. Somers Cocks, assumed that 'Her Majesty's Government would wish to take an interest in the fate of a former employee of theirs in an Iron Curtain country such as Roumania'.[40] In the reply to the Consul-General, written on behalf of Lloyd,[41] it was stated that 'no opportunity will be neglected to intervene informally on Madame Bunea's behalf'.[42] Unfortunately, the interventions made were to no avail and the Princess died in Miercurea-Ciuc prison on 29 September 1956.[43]

A family member also took up the case of Liviu Nasta with the Foreign Office. William Deakin, the Warden of St Antony's College, Oxford, called up E. F. Given of the Northern Department in April 1956 to bring his attention to the case of Nasta who was his father-in-law.[44] Deakin believed that part of the accusation against Nasta was that his daughter was married to a man who had worked in a literary capacity with Churchill.[45] Churchill himself wrote to Gheorghiu-Dej, General-Secretary of the Romanian Communist Party, in October 1956 asking for his intervention to secure the release of Nasta. Alan Dudley, the Head of Mission in Bucharest, was asked to hand the letter personally to Gheorghiu-Dej and intended to take it with him when he called on the Romanian leader but the latter left Bucharest at short notice and Dudley had to content himself with sending it. He enclosed with it a letter from Nasta's daughter.[46] Once again, these representations proved fruitless and shortly afterwards, on 6 December, Nasta died in Văcăreşti prison hospital at the age of 65.[47]

Robert Scott Foxe, who arrived as Head of Mission in May 1959, continued to focus on the question of the legation employees in his meetings with high-ranking Romanians. In May 1961, at a meeting with Corneliu Mănescu, the newly appointed Foreign Minister, he reiterated the point that the continued imprisonment of the legation employees was an obstacle to improved relations. In June, Scott Foxe raised the matter again with Gheorghiu-Dej at his last meeting with him before returning to London. Gheorghiu-Dej was in a good mood and promised that the legation employees would be released and would be able to go to Britain if they wanted. As the British Head of Mission recognized, it was most unusual for the regime to make such a significant concession so quickly.

James Dalton Murray, when presenting his credentials as British Minister in 11 October 1961, wrote that he had a conversation with Gheorghiu-Dej about Romanians who had helped the UK and had been sentenced on that account. He admitted that, as they were Romanian citizens, Britain had no legal standing, but considered it had a moral duty insofar as helping the British had entered into the indictment. Murray pressed the cases of four men: Constantin Agarici, Alexandru Văsescu, Modest Grigorcu and Constantin Raşcanu. Murray added that the first two had been openly attached to the British Mission (without identifying which one) and the last had, in fact, worked for British security. Gheorghiu-Dej gave assurances that imprisoned ex-employees of the legation had been released and encouraged Murray to take up the cases of the four with the Romanian Ministry of Foreign Affairs. This he did, but progress over the cases was exceedingly slow.

On 21 January 1964 Murray provided Charles Thompson of the Northern Department with an update on the situation:

> As I reported in my Despatch number 10 of January 16,[48] M. Gheorghiu-Dej also agreed that it would be appropriate if I were to bring forward for fresh consideration to the Ministry of External Affairs the exit permit cases in which we are interested, and I now enclose a copy of the communication on this matter which I handed today to M. Macovescu, the Deputy Minister in charge of the Ministry of Foreign Affairs.
>
> As you will see from the enclosures, I decided to go the whole hog because it seemed that this opportunity was too good to miss. Even if there is some crossing of wires over the cases about which Jakober is negotiating, my feeling is that an indication of the Embassy's interest can, in the present euphorious [*sic*] state of Anglo-Rumanian relations, only do good and not harm to the prospects for the departure of the individuals concerned.[49]

Going 'the whole hog' signalled the intention on Murray's part to go beyond the representations made on behalf of former political prisoners, imprisoned for their association with the British Military Mission and/or legation and to link three categories of applications for permission to leave Romania for British territory, the 'euphorious [*sic*] state of Anglo-Rumanian relations' being the recent decision to conduct them at embassy rather than legation level. In the enclosures referred to by Murray, three lists were presented, marked A, B and C. List A covered persons who were British nationals under British law, though in nearly every case also possessing Romanian citizenship; List B was mainly composed of 'old cases' which were familiar to the Romanian authorities from representations made over a number of years; and List C covered other cases, some of which 'had only recently come to the knowledge of the British authorities, which in the opinion of my Government deserve sympathetic consideration'.[50] List A contained five cases, List B six, and List C seven. Only one person – on List C – had any connection with the British authorities[51] while three cases on the same list were former employees of the Shell Petroleum Company (Astra Română) and their families.[52]

It was Shell which had turned to the services of the Mr Jakober, mentioned by Murray in his letter to Thompson. Henry Jakober, a British businessman with commercial links to Romania, acted as the conduit for payment to the Romanian authorities of monies given by private individuals in the West for exit visas for their relatives in prison in Romania. The ransom demanded varied according to the status of the prisoner but was between $4,000 and $6,000. The procedure was as follows: Jakober was approached at his address at 55 Park Lane in London and given the name of the person to be ransomed. He then gave the name a reference number which was quoted in all correspondence and took the details to Bucharest. There a ransom fee was fixed by the Romanian authorities and communicated to Jakober who, on his return to Britain gave instructions to those paying the ransom to deposit the sum into Jakober's account at the Credit Suisse Bank in Lucerne, Switzerland. The monies were only paid over to the Romanian authorities after the ransomed person had arrived in the West.[53]

Maria Golescu, who had been given a sentence of twenty years' hard labour on 28 December 1950 for high treason, was allowed to leave Romania with her elderly mother following payment of a ransom through Jakober in September 1962 in the following circumstances. Eric Tappe, a lecturer in Romanian Studies at London University, who had known Maria from his service on the British Military Mission in Bucharest between 1944 and 1946, took the initiative in organizing the payment. Tappe had been alerted about the ransom avenue by Maria's friend and colleague at the British legation, Annie Samuelli, who herself had been released from jail by the same means in the previous year.[54]

Tappe contacted Maria's cousin Alexandru (Sandu) Racotta, who had worked for the oil company Astra Română until his escape from Romania in June 1944,[55] and had subsequently been given a position with the Shell oil company in Mexico. Tappe arranged to meet Jakober at his London address and negotiated an original sum of $5,000 down to $4,200.[56] The bulk of the money was given by Sandu and by a friend of Maria's, Sybil Pantazi, who lived in Canada. Tappe provided £300. According to Tappe the Foreign Office refused to make a contribution, despite his request for one. It did, however, agree several months later to award her 'an *ex gratia* payment, equivalent to one year's salary at the time of her arrest, of £770.14.0d'.[57] Jakober confirmed

Maria's release in a letter to Tappe of 26 September 1962 and she was allowed to travel to France with her aged mother, with a visa for entry to Britain.[58] Maria was granted a small sum in National Assistance each month by the British government which was regularly supplemented by monies given by Tappe and Sandu Racotta, and both she and her mother Zoe lived out the rest of their lives in Eastbourne.[59]

As regards Constantin Agarici, Alexandru Văsescu, Modest Grigorcu and Constantin Raşcanu, the four persons whose cases were taken up by Murray in autumn 1961, it was only on 1 September 1964 that Murray was able to tell the FO that all four had been released. Whether their freedom was secured as a result of Murray's representations, or of the amnesties of 1963 and 1964, is not stated. Murray commented pointedly, 'It is, of course, characteristic of the Rumanians to tell us nothing officially about the fact that the four Rumanian citizens in whom Her Majesty's Government had expressed an interest were free.'[60]

Agarici called at the British embassy on 12 October 1964 and was seen by Miss E. A. Urquhart. He told her that he had been released from prison on 28 July that year and had been given employment as a technical clerk at a building site on the outskirts of Bucharest. This was the type of work he was doing, he said, immediately after the war. He did not wish to go to Britain as he had no family there and his closest relatives were living in Romania. Miss Urquhart thought Agarici was 'poorly dressed and rather thin, but his teeth seemed to have survived better than those of most of the released political prisoners'. She went on, 'I suspect that he had been directed on what to say to me about his treatment while in prison, since it follows very closely to the remarks made by the other released prisoners I have interviewed. All of them are careful not to comment adversely on their treatment and shrug their shoulders with a "water under the bridge" aside.'[61]

Văsescu also saw Miss Urquhart, presumably around the same time (her record of the interview appears to have been removed). She was clearly moved by his situation. In her report to the FO she noted, 'Although we have not received an authority to give Colonel Văsescu any money, he seemed in such dire straits that I decided to give him Lei 1000 (£29.15.3d) from our Benevolent Fund, as a gift from the UK based staff.'[62]

On 21 October 1964 Andrei Ion Deleanu called at the British embassy to see the ambassador, J. Dalton Murray, whom he told of his wartime work for the British. He also made a request for translation work to supplement his meagre income. Murray passed on this request to D. Thomas of the Northern Department who sought confirmation of Deleanu's background from Colonel Edwin Boxshall. Boxshall minuted that documentary evidence existed proving that Deleanu had been an SOE collaborator who 'ran the pro-Allied newspaper *Ardealul*. Colonel Harris-Burland who, as a member of the British Military Mission in Rumania, helped in the winding up of

SOE's commitments in that country, reported on 20 April 1945 that Deleanu was hard up and in need of assistance. He recommended that Deleanu be granted financial aid. Subsequent political events prevented this.' The embassy suggested that an ex gratia payment be made to Deleanu since it was unable to give him translation work and Boxshall reported on 2 December that 'the friends[63] have now given full consideration to the embassy's suggestion' and that 'a sum of up to a maximum of £200 (two hundred) has been approved'.[64]

What the British officials were unaware of was that because of Deleanu's involvement with the *Ardealul* group, funded by SOE, which had collapsed with the arrest of its leader Rică Georgescu in August 1941, he had been kept under surveillance by the *Securitate* between 1956 and 1959 and occasionally brought in for questioning. During these sessions he had shown himself willing, according to a *Securitate* report, to cooperate with the *Securitate* by incriminating those hostile to the regime, cooperation which was consolidated by his handwritten undertaking (*angajament*) to act as an informer, given on 8 April 1959.[65]

In his declaration he recognized his membership between 1940 and 1941 of a 'British espionage group led by Engineer Ion Popovici' and 'would make every effort to unmask hostile activities carried out by various elements who conspire against this [Communist] regime... including close relatives and friends'. Deleanu was given the code name 'Alexandru Dumitrescu' and later that of 'Dinu'.[66] In a supervisory report of 18 August 1960, Lieutenant N. Orbu of the *Securitate* reported that 'throughout his collaboration agent "Alexandru Dumitrescu" had shown seriousness and conscientiousness in carrying out the tasks assigned to him'. These included a promise by Deleanu to contact Romanian friends living abroad, amongst them 'Adela Călinescu and Mihai Iaroslavici, suspected of being British agents'.[67]

'Dinu' was well placed to report on the Romanians whom the British cultural attaché invited to events in the Romanian capital, as he was a regular guest at such functions. A *Securitate* note of 5 January 1974 gives the names of 'targets' assigned to 'Dinu', among them 'Ted', a British professor who the incidental information in the note indicates was Eric Tappe, Professor of Romanian Studies at the School of Slavonic and East European Studies, University of London.[68] The note also reveals that 'Dinu' was given a mission to report back on Doreen Berry, the Deputy-Director of the Great Britain–East Europe Centre, who had worked for the BBC Romanian section during the Second World War.[69] It is ironic that it was under the auspices of this centre that Deleanu was able to attend the Shakespeare Festival in Stratford-upon-Avon in 1964.

The experience of the Romanian 'local' staff of the British legation, of the British Press Office, and of the British Military Mission demonstrated that although sentenced to prison by the Romanian authorities, they were not condemned to oblivion by successive British ministers and ambassadors. The latter, with mute contempt, refused to admit the spurious charges levelled against their local staff and place themselves in a defensive position vis-à-vis the Communists, for they knew full well that it was the Communists themselves who regarded silence as an admission of guilt or at least as proof of an inability to deny.

Conclusion

'Shattered illusions' might be the best description of the sentiments held by the British authorities and the Romanian opposition to Axis rule regarding Romania's fate during the Second World War and its aftermath. During the war the military facts were never conducive to a defection strategy for Romania, but the fact that the British failed to dispel the illusion held by Romanians that there was a chance of surrender to the Western Allies played into the hands of the Germans and their anti-Soviet friends in Romania, and weakened the position of the Romanian opposition.

If the success of British military clandestine activities in Romania is to be judged by their effectiveness in fulfilling their principal purpose – the destruction of the oilfields and the interdiction of supply routes by the Danube and the rail network – then the verdict can only be one of failure. Although in the period 1940 to1944 there were a few isolated rail accidents, fires and explosions which might have been ascribed to sabotage, the importance of these in the context of oil production and export to the Reich from Romania was minimal. In fact, the battle for 'the black gold' waged by the *Abwehr* with the British and French intelligence agencies was won in 1940. Victory ensured the continued supply of fuel to the German war machine until interrupted by Allied air raids in the period from April to August 1944. The destruction of the British and French sabotage networks in the oilfields removed any possibility of the interruption of Romanian oil exports to Germany. Foreseeing this defeat, the British diplomat Robin Hankey, the head of chancery at the British legation in Bucharest, had noted in September 1940 that 'for the future our hopes of stopping oil seem to rest almost entirely on air operations, supplemented by anything that can be done of a less regular character'.[1]

Less disappointing results came from the task assigned to the MI6 network. It managed to transmit details of Axis military activity in Transnistria, and of troop movements in Romania, between 1940 and 1945. On a political level, the efforts of SOE to persuade Antonescu, through Iuliu Maniu and Romanian public opinion, to abandon the Axis camp were inconclusive.

The increasingly frequent Anglo-American air raids on the oilfields around Ploieşti and on Bucharest in April 1944 were a more effective reminder to all Romanians of the cost of the alliance with Germany, but it was the advance of the Red Army on Romanian territory and the beginning, on 20 August, of the Soviet offensive that concentrated minds and prompted King Michael and the anti-Antonescu opposition to decide to take action. The result was the coup three days later.

It is tragic and ironic that precisely the opposition to the Antonescu regime which had been nurtured by SOE found itself the target of Britain's wartime ally after the coup. What Maniu and his colleagues had feared regarding Stalin's designs upon Romania proved to be justified. Yet in London Maniu's stock was low. His indecisiveness in early 1942 and unwillingness to take firm political decisions was to hang over him in the Foreign Office after the coup and undermined confidence in him. Officials were highly critical of what they saw as Maniu's failure to appreciate that Romania was at war with Britain as well as with Russia. Ian Le Rougetel, the British Political Representative in Romania, while sympathetic to Maniu, thought that he should have participated in government after Antonescu's arrest.[2] His refusal to do so proved in retrospect to be a major tactical error, for the National Peasant Party was more easily relegated to the sidelines as the Soviet Union imposed its will with increasing severity on Romania. The suppression of the democratic process required the elimination of the 'historical' parties and Maniu to a certain degree opened the door to such an eventuality.

Exasperation with Maniu was widespread in the Foreign Office and in SOE. Shortly before the fall of the first Sănătescu government on 2 November 1944, an official minuted that 'if the machinery of government in Roumania breaks down, nobody will be more responsible than Mr Maniu with his endless intrigues'. Even Le Rougetel lost patience with the Peasant Party leader and was driven to conclude that the Soviets would be justified in imposing a military government.[3] A minute from a senior Foreign Office official, dated 3 November, stated that 'Air Vice Marshal Stevenson [Head of the British Military Mission] was perfectly correct in refusing to see M. Maniu and it is a pity that he did not refuse to see Maniu's intermediary. Maniu seems to be nothing but a drivelling old fool and I can quite sympathise with the Russians if they are trying to get rid of him by fair means or foul.'[4]

Frustration with Maniu was expressed by no less a person than de Chastelain in a letter he sent from London dated 1 February 1945 to his close friend Rică Georgescu:

> I imagine Alecu [one of the SOE code names for Maniu] is feeling depressed at the way events have developed since the *coup d'état* of 23 August, and while I sympathise with him, I cannot help feeling that his over-cautious policy is partly responsible for what has occurred. You will realise that during the last four years we have had so many promises

> of action from Alecu in one form or another, none of which came to anything, that the result of this was a gradual reduction in interest on the part of the departments concerned in London until Alecu finally reached a point where he was almost disregarded as a political factor. This may sound unfair and perhaps untrue, but were you to read through our files from 1940 to August 1944, you would soon see my point. It was with the greatest of effort that a few of us managed to maintain interest in Roumanian affairs.[5]

For Maniu, on the other hand, the suspicion that Romania had been abandoned by Britain preyed on his mind. Maniu's words, reported to London on 1 December 1944, that he would quite understand it if the British government wanted Romania to cast in her lot with Russia rather than the West, but would be grateful to receive word from them to this effect, stung the Prime Minister into minuting to Eden, 'Surely we are not called upon to make such an admission'.[6] Maniu begged repeatedly to be told whether Romania had been traded into the Soviet sphere of influence, and each time British representatives were instructed to deny this. Several years later, Archibald Clark Kerr, the British ambassador in Moscow who visited Bucharest in the spring of 1945, confessed that one of the most distasteful things he had ever been asked to do was to lie to a man like Maniu.[7] These lies led Maniu, and other democratic leaders in Romania, to compromise themselves unwittingly in the eyes of the Soviets in actions which were to cost them their liberty and which were to condemn them to spend their final years in prison.

The appearance of legitimacy which Britain and the United States gave to the Soviet-imposed Groza government of March 1945 was compounded by the conciliatory attitude shown by both towards Soviet actions in Romania. After the fraudulent elections of November 1946 both powers could have declared that the provisions of the Moscow Agreement had not been honoured, thereby invalidating any legitimacy claimed by the Groza government and thus rendering their signature of a peace treaty unjustifiable. Instead, British officials seemed at times to invoke Maniu's admittedly intransigent attitude towards the Soviets as an excuse for their own flaccidity in confronting Soviet designs. Judging from the published record few attempts appear to have been made to maintain close contact with Maniu after the 23 August coup. In a 'hands-on' society such as the Romanian one, such contact would have allowed a sensitive interlocutor to counsel a more nuanced approach by Maniu – he was seventy-one years old and in fragile health – to the political situation facing his country while the Red Army, with Romanian support, was still fighting its way westwards. Whether such advice would have been heeded is, nevertheless, open to grave doubt, given the incompatibility of Britain's stance towards the Soviet Union with that of the democratic parties in Romania.

Upon the conclusion of the war the British and Americans were faced with a Soviet Union in military occupation of much of Central and Eastern Europe. Their thoughts turned to damage-limitation, but without an effective lever of sanction, apart from the military option which no senior politician in the wake of a long war was prepared to countenance, they were reduced to the role of spectators in the Soviet colonization of the region. Yet in the eyes of many in Eastern Europe, the West had compromised its own principles. By failing to honour the pledge in the 'Declaration on Liberated Europe', made at the end of the Yalta Conference in February 1945, to 'foster the conditions in which the liberated peoples may exercise…the right of all peoples to choose the form of government under which they will live', Britain and the United States gave the appearance of legitimacy to what Churchill himself called 'force and misrepresentation'. It was this failure that damaged the West most in public opinion in the eastern half of Europe during the period of the Cold War; and in the minds of most of its inhabitants events today in the region conjure up ghosts from that past.

Appendix 1: Note of an interview between King Michael and a British intelligence officer made by Henry Spitzmuller, a French diplomat who remained in Romania after the fall of France

On 26 November 1943, at 14.05, the Marshal of the Royal Household, Baron Mocsonyi-Styrcea, ushered me and Mr House into his office in the royal palace in Bucharest. Every precaution had been taken to ensure that our arrival at the palace should pass unobserved. At 14.10, the King, accompanied by the Queen Mother, entered the room. After Mr House was presented, he explained to the King that he was a British journalist attached to Allied Newspapers, a group of British papers belonging to Lord Kemsley. He related briefly that he had spent the last three years in Denmark and that having managed to escape he was making his way to Turkey; thanks to his French friends he had a French passport with all the necessary visas, and had every chance of getting to Turkey on 2 December.

At that moment other persons arrived: the private secretary of the King, Mr Ioaniţiu, and Mr Niculescu-Buzeşti, head of the office of the Foreign Minister... and a close associate of Mr Maniu, charged with maintaining links between the King and the National Peasant Party leader. Mr House then explained to the King that, thanks to the friends present at the interview, he had been brought completely up to date with the political situation in Romania and said that he was ready to present an objective picture of it to the British Government, to which he could pass on a personal message from the King if he so wished. The King replied that his greatest wish was the British Government be informed as fully as possible about the political situation in Romania and on his own personal position. The Queen Mother concurred with this and both declared that the Allies should be in no doubt about their sincere wish to cooperate with them in Romania's interest, and that their own sentiments, which had never ceased to be favourable to the Allies, would be the guarantee of that.

'Did you know', the King told Mr House, 'that Marshal Antonescu declared war without even forewarning me, and that I learned about this deed from the radio and the newspapers?' Then the King and Queen Mother described the scene that they had had with the Marshal who had been incredibly insolent towards them...

Returning to the subject of our conversation, the King said: 'I needed a great deal of self-control to put up with what I have since Marshal Antonescu took over the government, violating the Constitution. I have withstood the greatest insults and have done so out of duty to the country. Be assured that I do not lack courage, nor the sense of sacrifice. I have often drawn up plans with my faithful colleagues to overthrow this odious regime which is currently oppressing the country. But what would be the point of a *putsch* when we lack the means to take it to its logical conclusion? Such a move would merely play into the hands of Antonescu and the Germans. As regards the Marshal, any chance of compromise is out of the question. 'You might say', the King added, 'that he is mad in the medical sense of the term and that he considers himself greater than Mussolini at the height of his power.'

The Queen Mother then remarked that she and Marshal Antonescu were at daggers drawn and said that he considered her to be the evil genius behind the King. At this the King added that he did need to be influenced in order to comprehend the situation.

Mr House then asked whether, in these circumstances, it would not be better for the King to contact the Allies in order to plead his cause. The King replied that his departure, especially in the present circumstances, would damage both Romania's interest and the Allied cause. He considered that, in the light of this, it was better for him to stay in Romania in order to support with his authority, when the time came, Romania's collaboration with the Allies. Moreover, his departure might be considered flight in the face of danger and of his own responsibilities. He therefore believed that he should only decide to flee as a last resort, and when he was only left with the choice of escape or captivity in Germany.

'All I can do', the King went on with bitterness, 'is to await events, as long as the Allies are unresolved to come to my aid in one way or another. Do not forget to explain that consideration for my country's future does not blind me to the fact that the Allies' policy is based on cooperation between the three Powers and I therefore understand that Russia and Romania must come to some kind of agreement.'

Mr House then remarked that the Allies had repeated most recently that unconditional surrender remained the essential condition of any armistice. 'I know', the King replied, 'but it is not because of this formula that I would refuse to negotiate if the occasion arose. Without underestimating its importance, I consider and hope that even the framework of this formula would permit interpretations which would allow me to accept it.'

The conversation then concentrated on the possibility of a *putsch* linked to an approach by the King to the Allies. The King and all those present explained to Mr House that such a move would result in the complete and immediate occupation of the country by the Germans, who would then have all the resources of Romania at their disposal. The King and his counsellors again explained to Mr House that the situation in Romania at that moment was unique in the sense that Marshal Antonescu's government represented only a tiny minority which, having taken power and maintained it with the support of the Germans, had imposed and continued to impose on the country a policy which was contrary to its wishes and its interests. A new government which would truly represent the people's wishes could only come to power through a *putsch*, which was impossible at the present moment without close cooperation with the Allies.

'If the Allies made a landing in the Balkans', the King said, 'everything would be simpler. The peninsula is practically undefended, but if Romania were to be occupied by the Germans the situation would immediately become less favourable.'

Mr House then put several questions to the King about his ideas and intentions concerning the government which would succeed that of the Marshal. The King replied that he would charge Mr Maniu with this task. Mr House would draw up a separate report about Maniu and his party's position. 'Maniu is an honest man', the King said, 'and the great majority of the population are behind him. If he is slow and very ponderous in the eyes of some, he still has great qualities. Our relations are characterized by mutual trust. I will give you a photocopy of a letter from Maniu which will show you that he has authorized me to speak in the name of his party, which represents a very large majority of the Romanian nation, in negotiations on foreign policy issues. It is, therefore, natural that I should designate him now as head of the future government. At the same time, since I wish to rule in the spirit of democracy, the Romanian people will be the ultimate arbiter of whether Maniu should remain in power. In my opinion, he has a good chance of retaining the country's trust; for my part, I hope that he does.'

The interview lasted one hour and thirty-five minutes.

Signed, Spitzmuller.

Appendix 2: Biography of Emil (Emilian) Bodnăraş (1904–1976)

There are many questions marks over Bodnăraş' real loyalties. According to his party file he was born in Colomeea (now in the Ukraine) on 10 February 1904 of Ukrainian-German parentage (I am grateful to Claudiu Secaşiu of the Consiliului Naţional pentru Studierea Arhivelor fostei Securităţii (National Council for the Study of the Archives of the former *Securitate* (CNSAS)) for this information).

Bodnăraş studied law at Iaşi University where, according to his official obituary, he first came into contact with Marxist groups. He then joined the Artillery School in Timişoara where he passed out on 1 July 1927 (*Anale de istorie*, Vol. 22(1) (1976): 189). His obituary says nothing about the following seven years until his arrest and his sentencing in 1934 to ten years hard labour. The gap has been filled from other sources.

In 1927 he was posted to Craiova with the rank of lieutenant and later transferred to a barracks at Sadagura in Northern Romania only thirty kilometres from the River Dniester and the border with the Soviet Union. From there he defected to the Soviet Union through the town of Hotin. Two questions arise at this point. Why should Bodnăraş, with his Ukrainian background, be posted so close to the Soviet frontier? Was he, perhaps, recruited by Romanian military intelligence and his defection planned? Information from the KGB archives now offers answers to these questions. It reveals that it was as the military intelligence officer of the 12th artillery regiment based in Sadagura that Bodnăraş was sent into the Soviet Union in 1931. He was turned, however, by the Soviets and was trained as an agent at a school in the town of Astrakhan (G. Iavorschi (1994), 'Pentru cine a lucrat "inginerul Ceauşu"?', *Magazin Istoric*, Vol. 28(9) (September): 18).

Bodnăraş' fluent knowledge of German allowed him to be used on various espionage missions by the GRU in Poland and the Baltic republics before being sent to Bulgaria in 1934. En route through Romania he was recognized in the Gara de Nord station in Bucharest and arrested. He was tried on 13 October 1934 in Iaşi for desertion, for stealing documents, and for crimes against the country's security, and sentenced to 10 years imprisonment.

Other questions arise. Why was he sent by his Soviet masters to Bulgaria by train through Romania, with all the risks of recognition that the journey entailed, when he could have travelled direct by boat from Odessa to Burgas? Was he sent deliberately by train in the hope that he would be caught by the Romanians as a Soviet spy and imprisoned with the Romanian Communists whom he could infiltrate on behalf of the GRU? Was he, in fact, a double agent?

His mission from the Soviets may well have been to evaluate Gheorghiu-Dej because the latter, unlike other leading figures in the RCP, had not studied in the Soviet Union. Serghei Nikonov, the Soviet-trained head of the SSI (the Romanian Intelligence Service) from 1946 to 1951, expressed the conviction in a conversation in 1988 with Titu Simon, a former officer in Romanian military intelligence, that Bodnăraş had been recruited in the 1920s by an officer in the SSI named Florin Becescu (cover-name 'Georgescu') to penetrate the NKVD and that this was the purpose of his mission to the Soviet Union.

In 1947 information was passed to Bodnăraş by the Soviets that Georgescu had worked as a double agent, for both the Romanians and the Soviets, and Bodnăraş gave orders for his liquidation before Nikonov could investigate the charges. The reason for Bodnăraş' haste, Nikonov believed, was to prevent the emergence of any details of his recruitment by Becescu (T. Simon (1992), *Pacepa: Quo Vadis?* (Bucharest: Odeon), pp. 77–8). Simon's account of Bodnăraş' hand in Becescu's death is corroborated by Traian Borcescu, head of the counter-intelligence section of the SSI between 1941 and 1944.

Becescu joined the Communist Party after 23 August 1944 and was appointed head of counter-intelligence in the SSI (he had held this post until 1941). However, he released information about Ana Pauker's private life as a young woman and lost the confidence of Bodnăraş. It was for this indiscretion that Bodnăraş, according to Borcescu, ordered Becescu's removal. While travelling to attend a meeting in Sinaia on the orders of Bodnăraş, Becescu's car was ambushed and he was shot dead by Communist agents (author's interview with Traian Borcescu, 8 March 1995).

Bodnăraş served his sentence at Doftana, Aiud, Galaţi and Braşov according to the official obituary. He was also held at Caransebeş jail, for he was seen there by a fellow inmate Mircea Oprişan, in 1942 (letter to the author from M. Oprişan, 29 August 1994). In Doftana, Bodnăraş formed a close friendship with Gheorghiu-Dej and became a member of the Communist Party. He was released from prison on 7 November 1942 at the suggestion of the SSI and settled in the town of Brăila near the mouth of the Danube. It was here that, in return for payments made to Rânzescu, the local inspector of police who was a friend of SSI head Eugen Cristescu, he was able to wander freely around the town and its outskirts and consequently to pick up instructions dropped by Soviet planes on the outskirts of town.

Using the cover of a commercial representative for a small company based in Brăila and the name of 'engineer Ceauşu', Bodnăraş travelled freely, albeit under the surveillance of the *Siguranţa* (security service), and he was a frequent visitor to Bucharest. There Bodnăraş collected information from an agent named Kendler, a timber-merchant, who on instructions from Bodnăraş paid a sum of 30,000 *lei* monthly in 1943 to Colonel Enache Borcescu, a member of the Romanian General Staff, for information about Romanian and German troop movements. Kendler's regular meeting place with Borcescu was a Greco-Catholic church in Bucharest (author's interview with Traian Borcescu, 8 March 1995).

Bodnăraş was also a frequent visitor to Târgu-Jiu where, by suborning Colonel Şerban Lioveanu, the commandant of the internment camp, he was able to consult Gheorghiu-Dej on several occasions. Drawing on secret Communist Party funds, Bodnăraş bought weapons from German soldiers based in Romania in order to arm Communist detachments which he formed in Bucharest in the early summer of 1944. This activity did not escape the attention of the Gestapo who requested his arrest but Colonel Traian Borcescu, the head of counter-intelligence in the SSI, resisted in the belief that Bodnăraş 'could be of use in Romania's exit from the war' (interview with T. Borcescu; see also Iavorschi (1994), p. 19).

After the establishment of the Groza government in March 1945, Bodnăraş was appointed secretary-general to the prime minister and in the following month he was given control of the intelligence service, the SSI. As a faithful servant of Moscow, he played a key role in consolidating Communist rule and eliminating opposition to it. He became a member of the Central Committee in 1945, a position he retained until his death in 1976, and a member of the Politburo (1948–65), Minister of the Armed Forces (1947–56), and Vice-President of the Council of Ministers (1954–65).

According to Khrushchev's memoirs it was Bodnăraş who, as Minister of War, first raised the question of the withdrawal of Soviet troops from Romania during Khrushchev's visit there in August 1955. Khrushchev was convinced that the matter had already been discussed by the Romanian Party leadership and Gheorghiu-Dej chose Bodnăraş to broach the subject because of his impeccable credentials. These were his past services to the Soviet Union, the confidence and respect which Khrushchev acknowledged he enjoyed amongst the Soviet leaders; and his senior position – he was one of the three deputy prime ministers. Khrushchev records that Bodnăraş justified the subject by pointing out that there was little threat to Soviet security interests because Romania was hemmed in by other Socialist countries and that there was 'nobody across the Black Sea from us except the Turks'. The international situation in 1955 did not permit the Soviet leader to act on the suggestion straightaway but the idea of withdrawal had been planted in his mind and he used it three years later at a time he regarded as more appropriate.

Bodnăraş was appointed a vice premier and remained close to Gheorghiu-Dej until the latter's death in 1965. Upon his elevation to the party leadership in that year, Ceauşescu offered Bodnăraş the position of vice president of the state council in return for his total obedience. Bodnăraş honoured the agreement, leading a largely withdrawn life – he was divorced – until his death in 1976. In conformity with his will, his body was not buried near Gheorghiu-Dej's in the Heroes' Monument in Bucharest but in his native village churchyard in northern Moldavia (Dennis Deletant (1999), *Communist Terror in Romania: Gheorghiu-Dej and the Police State* (London: Hurst), pp. 41–3).

Appendix 3: Rudolf Pander – interrogation report 7 December 1945, Military Intelligence Center USFET, CI-IIR/35

NARA, Rudolf Pander – interrogation report 7 December 1945, Military Intelligence Center USFET, CI–IIR/35, RG 165, Entry (P) 179C, Box 738 (Location: 390: 35/15/01), pp. 5–6 [My thanks to Ottmar Traşcă for putting me on the track of this report].

Of the various channels used by the Poles for communication with supreme HQ in London, Pander is best informed of the route which led from Poland through Rumania to Turkey. Agents crossed the Polish-Rumanian frontier with the help of the 'Green Border', a chain of five to seven outposts. Each of these outposts, spaced at 5–20 km intervals, consisted of two sections – one on each side of the border. They determined the locations best suited for crossings and kept a close watch on German frontier controls. Some of the outposts were not active, but constituted a reserve in case some of the active units should be discovered.

Relay stations were at Kolomea and Lwow in Poland, and at Czernowitz and Bucharest in Romania, where the Polish element of the Bukovina population assisted the agents.

Between Rumania and Turkey the following channels were used by Poles: by ship from Constanţa through the Black Sea to Istanbul; by courier via Sofia to Istanbul (this route was not very successful, Pander states, but HQ in Istanbul insisted that it be used); and contacts placed in various neutral embassies and the Red Cross in Bucharest. In the latter category were some Polish priests at the Papal Legation who sent their messages through the diplomatic mail. Until the Polish organization in Sofia was destroyed in Spring 1942, a Polish girl employed at the Swiss Legation there served as a contact. In Istanbul messages were transmitted by Polish monks in a Catholic monastery.

Another route led through Hungary and Jugoslavia. Results were poor because of transportation difficulties and the long distances to be covered in German-occupied territory.

Along the border between Hungary and Rumania an arrangement similar to the 'Green Border' was established with the Rumanian starting point located at Turda...

Pander was amazed at the perfection of Polish deception methods and equipment. Fifty typewritten pages could be reproduced on microfilm small enough to fit into the handle of a shaving brush. Passports and identification papers were perfectly forged in Warsaw. It was impossible to penetrate the Polish counter-espionage system since the Poles were loyal and extremely well-trained. The first step in the destruction of the system began with the capture of two Polish agents who, although in possession of apparently authentic papers, aroused suspicion by some careless questions at a control point in Lemberg. They justified the German suspicions by attempting to escape. Upon recapture they admitted that they were to be contacted by unknown persons at the Bucharest railroad station by means of signs and passwords. The attempt to use these at the appointed time and place failed to reveal any other agents. However, the Germans knew that one of the agents had been in Bucharest before and traced his contacts.

Soon thereafter, what was thought to be the HQ in Bucharest was raided after careful preparation and with the aid of the Rumanian Secret Police. A Polish couple residing at the supposed HQ proved to be innocent but the activities of a young Pole who had rented a spare room in the house aroused suspicion. He would appear in town from time to time to charge batteries and to meet individuals in the house; he would then return to some point in the nearby countryside. Pander deduced from this the presence of a W/T station in the area, and a raid on a particular farmhouse resulted in the capture of the station and two agents – one the head of the regional net, and the other, the aforementioned young Pole. Equipment, voluminous correspondence covering a two-year period, and codes were seized and immediately exploited.

Continued surveillance of the house in town led to the capture of two more agents. Every member of the system except one was ultimately captured. Arrests in Czernowitz and along the Rumanian-Polish border were delayed because the Rumanian Government claimed to have an agreement with the Poles pending at the time.

Notes

Introduction

1. Maurice Pearton (2005), 'British-Romanian Relations during the 20th Century: Some Reflections', in Dennis Deletant (ed.), *In and Out of Focus: Romania and Britain, Relations and Perspectives from 1930 to the Present* (Bucharest: British Council, Cavallioti), pp. 1–10 (1).
2. This phrasing owes much to Pearton, ibid.
3. The comments of one visitor give a sense of the atmosphere prevailing in early 1965, a few months before my own first trip to Romania in July of that year to attend a Romanian language summer school: 'Rumania irritates one from the start. Together with Czechoslovakia, it is the most rigid of the satellite countries. As a visitor, you are compelled to have a guide, and the guide dogs your every step. When you emerge from your bedroom in the morning, he is waiting for you. He bores you the whole day long. He is informative by nature, but humourless, tends to be didactic and knows everything. I could not escape the impression that shrewd dissimulation and a reactionary mentality are widespread' (Quoted from F. Bondy, 'Rumanian Travelogue', Survey, No. 55 (April 1965), p. 22).
4. See Biographies of Key Figures.
5. David Walker (1942), *Death at my Heels* (London: Chapman and Hall), pp. 24–5.
6. Patrick Maitland (1946), *European Dateline* (London: Quality Press), pp. 74–5. Patrick Francis Maitland, 17th Earl of Lauderdale (1911–2008), Conservative Member of Parliament for Lanark, 1951–9.
7. Archibald Gibson took over as head of station of MI6 in Bucharest in August 1936; see Keith Jeffrey (2010), *MI6: The History of the Secret Intelligence Service 1909–1949* (London: Bloomsbury), p. 273).
8. Quoted from Harold Gibson's CV, mentioned above.
9. Ibid.
10. František Dastich (born 1896, Olomouc, Moravia; died 17 February 1964, New York) also served with the French Foreign Legion during the First World War. He was a military attaché in Paris from 1920 to 1924 and a senior military attaché in Moscow from 1934 to 1938. After the Communist coup d'état in 1948, he fled to the United States.
11. František Moravec (born 23 July 1895, Čáslav; died 26 July 1966, Washington, DC).
12. Details taken from Frantisek Moravec (1975), *Master of Spies: The Memoirs of General Frantisek Moravec* (London: Bodley Head), pp. 123–50.
13. All of these officers were based in the British consulate in Istanbul (author's interview with William Harris-Burland, 10 August 1984). Harris-Burland was an SOE officer in Romania from 1940–1 and served in the British Military Mission to Romania, a component of the Allied Control Commission, from September 1944 until 1946.

14. Harold's first wife, Juliet Rachel Kalmanoviecz, whom he had married in 1921, died in 1947. He met his second wife in Istanbul where she ran a dance school. Ekaterina was from a White Russian family which fled to Bucharest after the October revolution. Measures were taken by the Romanian *Securitate* in 1959 to find out from Ekaterina's sister, Valentina Alfimova, who lived in Bucharest, details about Harold's activities (Arhiva Consiliului Naţional pentru Studierea Arhivelor Securităţii (hereafter CNSAS), Fond I, 163560, ff.32–5) but they appear not to have borne any fruit. The CNSAS was established by law in 1999 to administer the archive of the Communist security police, the *Securitate*, custody of which was taken over by the post-Communist security service, the SRI (*Serviciul Român de Informaţii*) in 1990. The archive includes reports of the pre-Communist security service, the *Siguranţa*.
15. *The Times*, 26 August 1960 and personal communication from Kyra Gibson, widow of Archibald Gibson, October 1983.
16. My own notes taken from a personal memoir of Archibald Gibson loaned to me by Kyra Gibson.
17. Quoted from my own notes on Gibson's personal memoir, returned to the possession of Mrs Kyra Gibson.
18. Author's interview with William Harris-Burland, 10 August 1984.
19. An archivist who took my call at *The Times* library was distinctly unhelpful and even denied that Archibald had ever worked for the newspaper, a denial which Maitland laughed off as 'ridiculous'.
20. *Serviciul Secret de Informaţii*.
21. Dennis Deletant (1985), 'Archie Gibson: *The Times* Correspondent in Romania, 1928–1940', *Anuarul Institutului de istorie şi arheologie 'A. D. Xenopol'*, Vol. XXII :135–48.
22. Through his daughter, in fact, who contacted me during a visit of mine to Bucharest and told me that her father would like to talk to me.
23. For details about Borcescu see Biographies of Key Figures.
24. I hereby offer my thanks to Claudiu Secaşiu of CNSAS and Ottmar Traşcă of the 'Gheorghe Bariţiu' Institute of History in Cluj-Napoca, for sharing copies of Eck's files with me.
25. Jeffrey (2010), pp. 414–15 and 505–6. Eck is identified by name in the paperback edition of the book following my communication to Professor Jeffrey of a draft of my article 'Researching MI6 and Romania, 1940–49', *Slavonic and East European Review*, Vol. 89(4) (October): 662–88.
26. I am grateful to an anonymous reader of the manuscript for his/her constructive suggestions on the chapter presentation.

1 Mission Accomplished: The Coup of 23 August 1944

1. This is a revised and augmented version of Chapter 10 of my book *Hitler's Forgotten Ally: Ion Antonescu and his Regime, Romania 1940–1944* (Basingstoke: Palgrave Macmillan, 2006).
2. Mihai was a very distant relation of the Marshal.
3. Hugh Gibson (1946) (ed. and trans.), *The Ciano Diaries 1939–1943* (Garden City, New York: Doubleday), p. 568.
4. Ibid., p. 572.
5. Ibid.
6. Ibid., p. 573.

7. Lya Benjamin (1996) (ed.), *Evreii din Romania intre anii 1940–1944*. Vol. II. 1940–1944: *Problema Evreiască în Stenogramele Consiliului de Miniştri* (Bucharest: Hasefer), Doc. 160, p. 501.
8. Vasile Arimia, Ion Ardeleanu and Ştefan Lache (1991) (eds), *Antonescu-Hitler: Corespondentă şi întîlniri inedite (1940–1944)*, Vol. II (Bucharest: Cozia), pp. 68–73. See also Dinu Giurescu (1999), *România în al doilea război mondial* (Bucharest: All), pp. 189–90.
9. Arimia et al. (1991), p. 80.
10. Spitzmuller joined the French legation in Bucharest as First Secretary in April 1938. For several of his reports to Paris, see Ottmar Traşca and Ana-Maria Stan (2002), *Rebeliunea legionară în documente străine* [*The Iron Guard Rebellion in Foreign Documents*] (Bucharest: Albatros).
11. My attempts to identify 'Mr House' were unsuccessful, the name being possibly a pseudonym.
12. Gheorghe Buzatu (1990), *Mareşalul Antonescu în faţa istoriei*, Vol. 1 (Iaşi: Editura BAI), pp. 388–91. For the complete text of the interview in English see Appendix 1.
13. Antonescu gave his reasons for rejecting an armistice at his trial in May 1946: 'In the first place I was afraid of losing the benefits of the Atlantic Charter and the benefit we derived from the public declarations made in the British parliament by Mr Churchill and Mr Eden ... The Atlantic Charter stated categorically "we will not recognize at the end of the war any change of frontier which has not been freely agreed". Somewhat later – that was in August 1941 – somewhat later Mr Eden repeated the same declaration in parliament and said: "We will not recognize frontiers which have not been freely agreed" ... Then the Russian armistice comes. What were the conditions laid out in this armistice? That we should accept the cession of Bessarabia and Bukovina. Acceptance would have meant the loss of the benefits of the Atlantic Charter and of Mr Eden's declarations. And so I, Marshal Antonescu, without any political party behind me, with only two plebiscites as political authority, could not assume the historical responsibility in the face of the present generation and in the face of past ones, that I had ceded Bessarabia ... Both Mr Maniu and Mr Mihalache, and Mr Dinu Brătianu and all the other politicians asked me on several occasions to conclude an armistice and I said, "I cannot conclude an armistice because of that problem, I cannot conclude an armistice because it requires me to turn my arms against Germany and I am a soldier and a man of honour and I cannot do that" ... I offered to turn over control of the state to them ... I told His Majesty the King several times ... I got a negative reply. All the time I was told that I must conclude the armistice. So I gave up [on offering to hand over power]' (Marcel-Dumitru Ciucă (1995–8) (ed.), *Procesul Mareşalului Antonescu. Documente*, Vol. 1 (Bucharest: Editura Saeculum, Editura Europa Nova), pp. 213–14.
14. The source of the memorandum is unclear. It is unsigned but bears the stamp of the Romanian Intelligence Service (SSI) certifying that it had been catalogued. In parts, it seems to be a verbatim record of a conversation between Antonescu and Maniu.
15. ANIC, Ministerul Afacerilor Interne (Ministry of Internal Affairs). Trial of Ion Antonescu, File 40010, Vol. 34, pp. 140–3.
16. Arimia et al. (1991), p. 144.
17. The plan for the occupation of Hungary was code-named 'Margarethe I' and that of Romania 'Margarethe II'; see Klaus Schönherr (1999), 'Die Auswirkungen der

militärischen Situation 1944 auf die Deutsch-Rumänischen Beziehungen', *Revue roumaine d'histoire*, Vol. 38(1–4): 176, note 71.

18. Benjamin (1996) (ed.), p. 557.
19. Ciucă (1995–8) (ed.), *Procesul Mareşalului Antonescu*, p. 211. Antonescu's assertion that he had never been to Germany before August 1944 on his own initiative overlooks his request to meet Hitler in January 1941 to express his concern about the Iron Guard's activities. He travelled to Obersalzburg to meet the Führer on 14 January 1941.
20. It should be emphasized that no one on the Romanian side, be it the Marshal, Mihai Antonescu or Maniu, was able to secure the joint agreement of the Americans, British and Russians to the conditional armistice proposals which it made between December 1943 and April 1944 in Stockholm (to the Russians) and in Cairo (to all three Allies). Eventually, agreement on armistice terms was reached with Britain and the US in Cairo in April 1944 and confirmed by the Russians through the Stockholm channel in June. However, no Romanian representative was empowered by Antonescu to sign them.
21. I. Ardeleanu, V. Arimia and M. Muşat (1984) (eds), 'Report of Lt. Col. A. G. G. de Chastelain on the "Autonomous" Mission, dated September 1944', in *23 August 1944. Documente*, Vol. II (Bucharest: Editura Ştiinţifică şi Enciclopedică), p. 802.
22. National Archives and Records Administration of the United States, College Park, Maryland (NARA), General Records of the Department of State (RG 59), European War, 74000119, EW 1939/2057. Reproduced in Ardeleanu et al. (1984), Vol. I, doc. 456.
23. The Soviet official in question was a man named Spitchkine whom the Special Operations Executive surmised was acting independently of his Minister, Madame Alexandra Kollontay (Elisabeth Barker (1976), *British Policy in South-East Europe in the Second World War* (London: Macmillan), p. 229).
24. *Foreign Relations of the United States* [*FRUS*] (1966), *1944, Vol. IV, Europe* (Washington DC: US Department of State), p. 170. The terms were also passed to the Romanian minister in Stockholm by the Soviet chargé who transmitted them on the same day (13 April) to Bucharest; see Buzatu (1990), pp. 418–20 and Ivor Porter (2005), *Michael of Romania: The King and the Country* (London: Sutton), p. 94.
25. Barker (1976), p. 233.
26. Ion Scurtu (1978) (ed.), *Culegere de documente şi materiale privind Istoria României* (6 September 1940–23 August 1944) [*Collection of documents and materials regarding the History of Romania*] (Bucharest: University of Bucharest), pp. 219–20 (I thank Viorel Achim for showing me this anthology).
27. Barker (1976), p. 140.
28. Ibid., p. 237.
29. Ibid., p. 238.
30. Interview with Corneliu Coposu, 31 October 1991. In a paper presented at a symposium in Paris on 22 May 1994, Coposu disclosed, in his capacity as Maniu's secretary and the person responsible for enciphering and deciphering Maniu's telegrams in the British code sent via Ţurcanu to Cairo, that in response to Novikov's suggestion to Vişoianu that the Romanian opposition should involve the section of the Comintern in Romania, Novikov was told that the number of Communists in Romania identified by the SSI (Romanian Intelligence) was 845, of whom 720 were foreigners. In reply, Maniu was told that it was common knowledge that a section of the Comintern in Romania did not exist but

that public opinion abroad had to have the impression of the existence of a homogeneous opposition embracing all social and political categories. Maniu said that, in that case, he had nothing against the enlargement of the opposition. However, none of the Communists contacted in Romania claimed to be the true representatives of the Romanian Communist Party. With some satisfaction, Maniu cabled Novikov for his direction as to who was the official representative of the Comintern in Romania and Novikov replied: 'Lucreţiu Pătrăşcanu' ('Exilul Românesc: Identitate şi Conştiinţă istorică', *Lupta*, No. 232 (7 October 1994): 5). According to Communist historiography, the meeting of 4 April in Târgu-Jiu is alleged to have instructed Pătrăşcanu, Bodnăraş, and Ion Gheorge Maurer to join the other political parties in an effort to extract Romania from the war with the Soviet Union. A few days later, Pătrăşcanu negotiated an agreement with Titel Petrescu, the leader of the Social Democratic Party, to set up a United Workers' Front. Bodnăraş made his first appearance at a sub-committee charged with the preparation of plans for the defence of Bucharest on 13 June although according to one account the main purpose was to discuss future relations with Moscow (Ioan Hudiţă (1994), 'Pagini de Jurnal', *Magazin Istoric*, Vol. 28(7) (July): 41).

31. Iosif Şraier, the Communist Party's legal representative, conducted negotiations with Iuliu Maniu and Prince Ştirbey in preparation for the 23 August coup. One source claims that he received full authority from Moscow in his conversations with Maniu which initially he conducted alone. Later he acted as Lucreţiu Pătrăşcanu's liaison in the negotiations between the Communist Party and the other members of the National Democratic Bloc. Before the Groza cabinet was reorganized in January 1946 he hoped to become Minister of the Interior but with his political ambitions frustrated, he left Romania later that year ('List of Roumanian Personalities, 1947', Report No. 262, 3 November 1947, TNA, FO/371/67272 B).
32. Deletant (1999), pp. 41–3. For Bodnăraş' biography see Appendix 2.
33. On 11 June 1941 the Minister of the Interior, General D. Popescu, transmitted Ion Antonescu's order to General E. Leoveanu, Director General of Police, that the gendarmerie should be prepared to arrest all Communists between 15 and 20 June (Ministerul Afacerilor Interne, File 40010, Vol. 11, p. 87.)
34. Porter (1989), p. 175.
35. The Racotta family estate to the west of Bucharest had been the original landing area for the 'Autonomous' mission of December 1943.
36. For Vişoianu's journey to Cairo see Bickham Sweet-Escott (1965), *Baker Street Irregular* (London: Methuen), pp. 210–11.
37. TNA, HS 5/835, 'Minutes of a Meeting held at 1100 hrs on 20 June 1944 at No. 10 El Gezera, Cairo'.
38. Barker (1976), p. 239.
39. Titus Gârbea; see Buzatu (1990), p. 487.
40. Arimia et al. (1991), p. 173.
41. The southern offensive was launched from Tiraspol and aimed at Izmail, Constanţa and Bulgaria.
42. Baron Ion de Mocsonyi-Styrcea was born at Cernăuţi on 16 May 1909. He graduated from Cambridge with a degree in modern languages in 1932 and joined the Romanian Foreign Ministry two years later. Between 1 April and 11 August 1942 he was Private Secretary to King Michael and Head of the Royal Chancery, and from the latter date until 1 April 1944 served as acting Marshal of the Royal Court. On 23 August 1944 he was made Marshal of the Court, a position from

which he resigned on 4 November 1944 for health reasons, but he remained on the roll of the Foreign Ministry until the purge of non-Communist employees on 6 March 1946. He spent much of the period between September 1947 and November 1962 in prison on charges fabricated by the Communists. He was allowed to leave Romania on 4 September 1964 and settled in Switzerland (letter from Mocsonyi-Styrcea to this author, 4 August 1984).

43. Porter (1989), pp. 192–3.
44. Letter from Mocsonyi-Styrcea to this author, 4 August 1984; see also Porter (2005), p. 104.
45. See Nicholas Baciu (1984), *Sell-Out to Stalin: The Tragic Errors of Churchill and Roosevelt* (New York: Vantage Press), p. 147. The courier in question, Neagu Djuvara, made it quite clear to his audience at the fiftieth anniversary symposium on '23 August 1944 in the History of Romania', held in Bucharest on 8–9 October 1994 (to which King Michael had accepted an invitation but was refused entry to Romania by the authorities), that Mihai Antonescu, with the Marshal's approval, had merely told Nanu to approach Madame Kollontay to ask whether the earlier conditions given by the Russians were still valid or would have to be negotiated. At the same time, Djuvara revealed, Mihai Antonescu instructed Nanu not to tell the British and Americans of this approach to the Soviets. Mihai Antonescu did not, as Nanu later claimed, tell him that the Marshal was ready to withdraw from the war and had given Mihai a free hand to sign the armistice (F. C. Nano (1952), 'The First Soviet Double-Cross: A Chapter in the Secret History of World War II', *Journal of Central European Affairs*, Vol. 12(3) (October): 236–58). As Djuvara remarked, the events in the three-month period since the issue of the Russian conditions had rendered many of them irrelevant and the mere raising of the question as to whether they were still valid showed how out of touch with reality the two Antonescus were.
46. At his trial in May 1946 the Marshal recalled his meeting with Brătianu: 'And I said then, to Mr Gheorghe Brătianu: "Look here, Mr Brătianu, I have abandoned the idea of not concluding an armistice, I shall conclude it, but I need these letters of guarantee because I cannot assume the historical responsibility for destroying the Romanian people... So, commit yourselves, accept your responsibility in writing, not verbally in words which are forgotten and which can be denied tomorrow." And then Mr Brătianu replied: "I'll go and bring you the letters, both of them, from Mr [Dinu] Brătianu as well, at 3pm." He did not come at 3pm, I went to the palace' (Ciucă (1995–8), p. 215).
47. This account of events on 23 August is taken from M. Ionniţiu (1991), '23 August 1944. Amintiri şi reflecţiuni', *Revista istorică*, Vol. 2(9–10): 557–75, and Porter (1989), pp. 198–202.
48. Porter (2005), p. 109.
49. Ionniţiu (1991), p. 570.
50. This is the view of Ionniţiu.
51. On Strada Sighişoara. Among this group of armed civilians was Ştefan Mladin, who for a period after 23 August was one of those responsible for acting as a bodyguard to Gheorghiu-Dej.
52. General Dumitru Popescu (Minister of the Interior), Eugen Cristescu and Radu Lecca were also arrested later.
53. The order was transmitted by General (later Marshal) Rodion Malinovski, Commander of the Second Ukrainian Front and therefore of Soviet operations in Romania, to his deputy Lt. Gen. Ivan Susaikov.

54. Details taken from a report addressed to Stalin by Malinovski and Susaikov on 2 September 1944; see Ciucă (1995–8), pp. 18–19. In an unsigned handwritten note in the Romanian Intelligence Service files, an eyewitness reported that 'on 31 August 1944, around 5 pm, as I was walking along Vatra Luminoasă street to catch the no. 26 tram, I was overtaken by a convoy of five vehicles. The first was an open-topped car and carried two civilians wearing the Romanian tricolor armband, and a Soviet officer. The second car had its roof up and had a Soviet soldier seated next to the driver. In the back sat Ion Antonescu and Mihai Antonescu. The third car carried General Pantazi, General Vasiliu and Colonel Elefterescu. The fourth car was open and had three Soviet officers. The fifth vehicle was a large lorry with Soviet troops armed with machine-guns. The convoy went off on Iancului street in the direction of Pantelimon' (ANIC, Ministerul Afacerilor Interne. Trial of Ion Antonescu, File 40010, Vol. 34, pp. 219–20).
55. Ion Pantazi (1980–1), 'O mărturie indirectă despre 23 august', *Apoziţia* (Munich): 20–30; see also the same author's *Am trecut prin iad* [*I passed through hell*] (1992) (Sibiu: Constant), pp. 307–10.

2 Setting the Scene: Problems of Cohesion, 1918–1938

1. *Anuarul Statistic al României, 1939 şi 1940* (1940) (Bucharest: Institutul de statistică), p. 41.
2. Armin Heinen (1999), *Legiunea 'Arhanghelul Mihail': O contribuţie la problema fascismului internaţional* [*The Legion of the Archangel Michael: A Contribution to the Problem of International Fascism*] (Bucharest: Humanitas), p. 32, note 5.
3. Ibid., p. 39.
4. *Anuarul Statistic* (1940), p. 362.
5. Heinen (1999), p. 40, note 48.
6. *Anuarul Statistic* (1940), p. 92.
7. Hugh Seton-Watson (1962), *Eastern Europe between the Wars 1918–1941* (3rd edn.) (New York, London: Harper Row), pp. 203–4.
8. For a study of the Iron Guard leader see Constantin Iordachi (2004), *Charisma, Politics and Violence: The Legion of the 'Archangel Michael' in Inter-war Romania* (Trondheim: Trondheim Studies on East European Cultures and Societies, No. 15).
9. The Iron Guard (*Garda de Fier*) was the military wing of the Legion of the Archangel Michael (*Legiunea Arhanghelului Mihail*), a messianic ultra-nationalist movement founded in 1927 by Codreanu. Some Anglophone scholars use 'the Legion', 'Legionary Movement' and 'legionary' when referring to the movement and its members; others prefer the looser terms 'Iron Guard' and 'Guardists'. This author is amongst the latter.
10. Nicholas Nagy-Talavera (1970), *The Green Shirts and Others: A History of Fascism in Hungary and Rumania* (Stanford: Hoover Institution Press), p. 247.
11. *Liga Apărării Naţional-Creştine.*
12. I am grateful to Maurice Pearton for this assessment.
13. Eugen Weber (1965), 'Romania', in H. Rogger and E. Weber (eds), *The European Right: A Historical Profile* (London: Weidenfeld and Nicholson), p. 541.
14. Two basic studies on the Iron Guard are Francisco Veiga's (1989), *La Mistica del Ultranacionalismo: Historia de la Guardia de Hierro* (Barcelona: Universitat Autonoma de Barcelona, Bellaterra), translated into Romanian as *Istoria Gărzii de Fier, 1919–1941: Mistica Ultranaţionalismului* [*The History of the Iron Guard,*

1919–1941: The Mystique of Ultranationalism] (Bucharest: Humanitas, 1993); and Armin Heinen's (1986), *Die Legion 'Erzengel Michael' in Rumänien Soziale Bewegung und Politische Organisation* (Munich: R. Oldenbourg Verlag); see also Armin Heinen and Oliver J. Schmitt (2013) (eds), *Inszenierte Gegenmacht von rechts. Die 'Legion Erzengel Michael' in Rumänien 1918–1938* (Munich: R. Oldenbourg Verlag).

15. See Biographies of Key Figures.
16. *Totul Pentru Ţară* is often translated by Anglophone scholars as 'All for the Fatherland', but a preferred term for 'fatherland' in Romanian is *patrie.*
17. Weber (1965), 'Romania', p. 549.
18. Corneliu Zelea Codreanu (1936), *Pentru legionari* [*For the Legionaries*] (Sibiu: Totul pentru Ţară), p. 413.
19. *Universul*, 11 February 1937, p. 10 and 15 February 1937, p. 9.
20. *Din Luptele Tineretului Român, 1919–1939* (1993) [*From Amongst the Struggles of Romanian Youth, 1919–1939*] (no place of publication: Editura Fundaţiei Bunavestire), p. 120.
21. The pact was invoked by the Communist prosecutors during Maniu's trial in autumn 1947 as evidence of his complicity with the extreme right.
22. I am indebted here to Keith Hitchins (1994), *Rumania 1866–1947* (Oxford: Oxford University Press), p. 419.
23. Roberts (1951), p. 191.
24. Ibid.
25. *Universul*, 1 January 1938.
26. Carol Iancu (2000), *Evreii din România de la emancipare la marginalizare, 1919–1938* [*The Jews in Romania from Emancipation to Marginalization, 1919–1938*] (Bucharest: Editura Hasefer), p. 257.
27. These anti-Semitic measures are discussed by Paul Shapiro (1974), 'Prelude to Dictatorship in Romania: The National Christian Party in Power, December 1937–February 1938', *Canadian-American Slavic Studies*, Vol. 8(1): 45–88. The situation under Goga was described in a report of January 1938 from the Board of Directors of British Jewry and the Anglo-Jewish Association to the British Foreign Secretary: 'You will be aware that year by year the position of the Jews of Roumania has worsened from every aspect – political, economic, moral. Conspicuous and distressing examples of this trend have been the Law for the Protection of National Labour of July 1934; the decrees of September and October 1937 issued by the former Ministry of Industry and Commerce, Monsieur Pop, to all individual and community establishments, strongly recommending that 50 per cent of the administrative personnel and 75 per cent of unskilled labourers employed in all undertakings should be of Romanian ethnic origin; and the decree issued by the Ministry of Justice, dated October 3rd 1936, to all public prosecutors, in accordance with which the citizenship of Jews and all other minorities in certain provinces will be reviewed' (Larry Watts (1993), *Romanian Cassandra: Ion Antonescu and the Struggle for Reform, 1916–1941* (Boulder, CO: East European Monographs), p. 160).
28. Dov B. Lungu (1988), 'The French and British Attitudes towards the Goga-Cuza Government in Romania: December 1937–February 1938', *Canadian Slavonic Papers*, Vol. 30(3): 323–41 (335).
29. Iancu (2000), p. 263.
30. 'It cannot be denied that there is a strong anti-Semitic feeling in the country. That is an old question in our history. The measures to be taken to deal with

it are on the principle of revision of Rumanian citizenship for those Jews who entered the country after the war. What happened was something in the nature of an invasion of Galician and Russian Jews who came in illegally. Their number has been exaggerated; some say as many as 800,000, but the maximum was about 250,000 who invaded villages and are not a good element... Those Jews who have lived in Rumania before the war will remain untouched. But those who came after the war are without legal rights, except as refugees. About them we shall consider what we must do' (Watts (1993), p. 161).

31. Bela Vago (1975), *The Shadow of the Swastika: The Rise of Fascism and Anti-Semitism in the Danube Basin, 1936–1939* (London: Saxon House), p. 267.
32. Watts (1993), p. 162.
33. Sima was born on 6 July 1906 in Bucharest. As a secondary school teacher in Lugoj and Caransebeş, he joined the Iron Guard and became its local leader in 1933.
34. Watts (1993), p. 176.
35. Hitchins (1994), p. 422.
36. Sima returned secretly to Romania on 2 September 1939 – according to police reports, to plot a coup against Carol – but returned to Berlin at the end of the month (ANIC, Ministerul Afacerilor Interne (Ministry of Internal Affairs), trial of Ion Antonescu, File 40010, Vol. 22, p. 2).
37. Watts (1993), p. 177.
38. TNA, FO 371/24988, Document 59107. 'Memorandum: Mission to Roumania in May 1940'. Hall was the author of a sensitive travelogue of Romania entitled *Romanian Furrow* (London: Harrap, 1939).
39. Hitchins (1994), pp. 424–5.
40. For the figures see Roberts (1951), p. 214, note 13. Romanian oil exports to Germany in the mid-1930s represented some 25 per cent of total exports to that country (Călin-Radu Ancuţa (2004), 'Die deutsch- rumänischen Wirtschaftsbeziehungen während der Kriegsjahre 1940–1944', in Krista Zach and Cornelius R. Zach (eds), *Modernisierung auf Raten in Rumänien. Anspruch, Umsetzung, Wirkung* (Munich: IKGS Verlag), p. 335).
41. Roberts (1951), pp. 214–15.
42. Mark Axworthy, Cornel Scafeş and Cristian Craciunoiu (1995), *Third Axis, Fourth Ally: Romanian Armed Forces in the European War, 1941–1945* (London: Arms and Armour), p. 21.
43. Ibid. According to Andreas Hillgruber (1965), *Hitler, König Carol und Marschall Antonescu: Die Deutsch-Rumänischen Beziehungen, 1938–1944* (Wiesbaden: Franz Steiner Verlag), p. 161, 1.27 million tons of petroleum products were exported by Romania to Germany in 1939, and 1.17 million tons in 1940. Axworthy et al. (1995), p. 190 gives higher figures: 1.56 million tons for 1939, 1.30 million for 1940, and 3.14 million for 1941.
44. By contrast, Hungary's population grew from about 9 million in 1939 to an estimated 14.7 million in 1941, including almost one million Romanians (Axworthy et al. (1995), p. 17).
45. Roberts (1951), pp. 219–20.
46. *Documents on German Foreign Policy* (henceforth *DGFP*), Vol. XI (Washington, DC: Government Printing Office, 1960), Doc. No. 17, p. 22. For a biography of Ion Antonescu, see Deletant (2006).
47. Rebecca Haynes (1999), 'Germany and the Establishment of the Romanian National Legionary State, September 1940', *The Slavonic and East European Review*, Vol. 77(4) (October): 700–72 (711).

48. Hitchins (1994), p. 476.
49. Rebecca Haynes makes these points in her *Romanian Policy towards Germany, 1936–40* (Basingstoke: Macmillan Press Ltd, in association with SSEES, 2000), p. 159.
50. The Iron Guard was the paramilitary successor to the anti-Semitic 'Legion of the Archangel Michael', hence the adjective 'legionary'.
51. Paul Schmidt (1949), *Statist auf diplomatischer Bühne, 1923–45; Erlebnisse des Chefdolmetschers im Auswärtigen Amt mit den Staatsmännern Europas* (Bonn: Athenäum-Verlag), pp. 511–12. One must bear in mind that Antonescu spoke through the interpreter, which drew out the length of his tirade.
52. Quoted from Axworthy et al. (1995), p. 26.
53. Paul D. Quinlan, *Clash over Romania: British and American Policies towards Romania, 1938–1947* (Los Angeles, CA: American Romanian Academy), p. 71.
54. Andreas Hillgruber (1969), *Les Entretiens Secrets de Hitler, septembre 1939–decembre 1940* (Paris: A. Fayard), pp. 432–41.
55. Matatias Carp (1946–8), *Cartea Neagră. Suferinţele Evreilor din România, 1940–1944*, Vol. 1 (Bucharest: Socec & Co.), pp. 219–323.
56. The Special Commissioner for Economic Questions, sent by the German Foreign Ministry to Bucharest in January 1940.

3 The Drift into Germany's Orbit: Romania, 1938–1941

1. Maurice Pearton (1998a), 'British Policy Towards Romania: 1939–1941', in Dennis Deletant and Maurice Pearton (eds), *Romania Observed* (Bucharest: Editura Enciclopedică), p. 95.
2. For this chapter I draw in part on my own study of the Antonescu regime published (2006) as *Hitler's Forgotten Ally: Ion Antonescu and his Regime, Romania 1940–1944* (Basingstoke: Palgrave Macmillan).
3. Although Romanians represented less than 30 per cent of the inhabitants in the province.
4. See Biographies of Key Figures.
5. This point is made by Axworthy et al. (1995), p. 38.
6. Carol's discussions with the British and Germans are analysed in Haynes (2000), pp. 57–8; see also Dov B. Lungu (1989), *Romania and the Great Powers, 1933–1940* (Durham and London: Duke University Press), pp. 142–4.
7. Haynes (2000), p. 68.
8. For a discussion of this so-called 'ultimatum', see ibid., pp. 77–8.
9. A. Chanady and J. Jensen (1970), 'Germany, Rumania and the British Guarantees of March–April 1939', *Australian Journal of Politics and History*, Vol. 6(2) (August): 201–17.
10. Haynes (2000), pp. 78–9. The guarantee was also the result of French pressure on Britain to guarantee Romania as the price of France's willingness to help guarantee Greece: D. Cameron Watt (1983), 'Misinformation, Misconception, Mistrust: Episodes in British Policy and the Approach of War, 1938–1939', in Michael Bentley and John Stevenson (eds), *High and Low Politics in Modern Britain: Ten Studies* (Oxford: Oxford University Press), pp. 247–9 (I am grateful to Rebecca Haynes for this reference).
11. See Roberts (1951), pp. 215–16 where he analyses the terms.
12. Grigore Gafencu (1945), *Prelude to the Russian Campaign* (London: Frederick Muller), p. 237.
13. See Robert Westerby and Robert M. Low (1940), *The Polish Gold* (London: Methuen).

14. On 14 October 1939, Smigły-Ridz was moved to a village called Dragoslavele. He eventually escaped from his place of internment, at the third attempt, during the night of 15–16 December 1940 and crossed into Hungary, before making his way back clandestinely to Poland. Details from Stanley S. Seidner (1977), 'Reflections from Rumania and Beyond: Marshal Smigły-Rydz in Exile', *The Polish Review*, Vol. 22(2): 29–51.
15. *Refugiații polonezi în România 1939–1947. Documente din Arhivele Naționale ale României. Polscy uchodżcy w Rumunii 1939–1947. Dokumenty z Narodowych archiwów Rumunii* (2013) (2 Vols.) (Warsaw-Bucharest: Arhivele Naționale ale României, Institutul Memoriei Naționale – Comisia pentru Condamnarea Crimelor Împotriva Națiunii Poloneze).
16. These were later to provide the model and precedent advanced by the Soviets for the establishment of the joint Soviet-Romanian companies provided for in the Soviet-Romanian Armistice of September 1944.
17. Gafencu (1945), p. 222.
18. Pearton (1998a), pp. 539–47.
19. Lungu (1989), p. 223.
20. Haynes (2000), p. 130.
21. Killinger recounted this meeting with Moruzov to Gheorghe Barbul, a Romanian diplomat, on 22 March 1943; see Arhivele Naționale Istorice Centrale [The Central Historical National Archives, Bucharest], henceforth ANIC, Ministerul Afacerilor Interne [Ministry of Internal Affairs], Trial of Ion Antonescu, File 40010, Vol. 28, p. 293.
22. Ibid., pp. 293–7.
23. Valeriu Pop (1992), *Bătălia pentru Ardeal* [*The Battle for Transylvania*] (Bucharest: Editura Enciclopedică), p. 253.
24. Ibid.
25. Ibid., p. 255; see also Lungu (1989), pp. 229–30.
26. *DGFP*, Vol. VII (Washington, DC: Government Printing Office, 1956), Doc. No. 229, p. 247.
27. Marilynn G. Hitchens (1983), *Germany, Russia and the Balkans: Prelude to the Nazi-Soviet Non-Aggression Pact* (Boulder, CO: East European Monographs), p. 221.
28. Unpublished MS of Archibald Gibson, *The Times* correspondent in Romania 1928–40, notes in possession of this author.
29. Alesandru Duțu and Constantin Botoran (1994) (eds), *Al doilea război mondial: Situația evreilor din România* [*The Second World War: The Situation of the Jews in Romania*], Vol. 1 (1939–1941), Part 1 (Cluj-Napoca: Centrul de Studii Transilvane, Fundația Culturală Română), No. 8, pp. 64 and 67.
30. Ibid., No. 8, p. 70.
31. Ibid., No. 8, p. 55.
32. Ibid., pp. 101–2.
33. Alex Mihai Stoenescu (1998), *Armata, Mareşalul şi Evreii* [*The Army, the Marshal and the Jews*] (Bucharest: RAO), p. 114.
34. Ibid., p. 115.
35. Ibid.
36. See Watts (1993), p. 234.
37. Ibid., p. 235.
38. Ion Şerbănescu (1997) (ed.), *Evreii din România între anii 1940–1944* [*The Jews in Romania between the Years 1940–1944*], Vol. III, Part 1, 1940–1942: *Perioada unei mari restrişti* [*The Period of a Great Sadness*] (Bucharest: Hasefer), Doc. 22, p. 36.

39. These incidents were reported to the Ministry of Justice on 3 July by the local prosecutor; see *Martiriul Evreilor din România, 1940–1944. Documente şi Mărturii* [*The Martyrdom of the Jews in Romania, 1940-1944. Documents and other evidence*] (Bucharest: Editura Hasefer, 1991), No. 10, pp. 33–4.
40. Duţu and Botoran (1994), No. 26, p. 96.
41. *Curierul israelit*, No. 22 (10 July 1940), p. 1, quoted from Stoenescu (1998), p. 106.
42. *Curierul israelit*, No. 22 (10 July 1940), p. 1, quoted from ibid., p. 107.
43. Stoenescu (1998), p. 107.
44. Wladyslaw W. Kulski (1951), 'Soviet Comments on International Law and International Relations', *The American Journal of International Law*, Vol. 45(3) (July): 556–64 (558–9).
45. Malbone W. Graham, 'The Legal Status of the Bukovina and Bessarabia', *The American Journal of International Law*, Vol. 38(4) (1944): 667–73 (671).
46. Based on language affiliation, the figures gave the numbers of Romanians as 920,919 (47.6%); of Ukrainians as 382,169 (19.7%); and of Russians as 155,774 (8.05%) (*Pervaia vseobshchaia perepis' naseleniia Rossiskoi Imperii 1897g.*, Vol. 3 (St Petersburg, 1905). By 1930 the population breakdown, according to the Romanian census, was as follows: Romanians 1,610,752 (56.2%); Russians 351,912 (12.3%); Ukrainians 314,211 (11%); Jews 204,858 (7.2%); and Bulgarians 163,726 (5.7%) (*Anuarul statistic al României 1939 şi 1940* [*The Statistical Yearbook of Romania 1939 and 1940*] (Bucharest: Institutul Central de Statistică, 1940), p. 60).
47. 853,009 of whom 379,691 (44.5%) were Romanians; 236,130 (27.6%) were Ukrainians; 92,492 Jews (10.8%); 75,533 Germans (8.8%); and 30,580 Poles (3.5%). In his analysis of the population of the areas annexed by the Soviet Union in June 1940 Anton Golopenţia shows that in eight districts of the counties of Rădăuţi, Storojineţ, Cernăuţi and Hotin, which constituted most of the area of Northern Bukovina and the northern part of Bessarabia lost by Romania, Ukrainians represented an absolute majority of 67% of the population. The population by nationality of the eight districts, based on the 1930 census, is given as Ukrainians 301,271; Romanians 53,115; Russians 37,635; Jews 31,595 (Anton Golopenţia (1941), 'Populaţia teritoriilor româneşti desprinse în 1940' ['The Population of the Romanian Territories Amputated in 1940'], *Geopolitica şi geoistoria*, No. 1, 1941 (Bucharest: Societatea Română de Statistică): 10). In the two southern Bessarabian counties of Cetatea Alba and Ismail (the greater part of which were added to the Ukrainian SSR) the Ukrainians, however, represented only 14% compared with 24% for Romanians; 22% for Russians; and 20% for Bulgarians. If the figures for the other two southern Bessarabian counties of Tighina and Cahul are entered into the calculation (and parts of them were incorporated into the Ukrainian SSR) the Ukrainian percentage drops to a mere 8% compared with the figure for Romanians of 37%; for Russians of 17%; for Bulgarians of 15%; for Gagauz of 9%; and for Jews of 3% (the figures are: Cetatea Albă 341,000 (Romanians 63,000; Ukrainians 70,000; Bulgarians 71,000; Russians 59,000; Jews 11,000; Gagauz 8,000): Cahul 197,000 (Romanians 101,000; Ukrainians 619; Bulgarians 29,000; Russians 15,000; Jews 4,000; Gagauz 35,000): Ismail 225,000 (Romanians 72,000; Ukrainians 11,000; Bulgarians 43,000; Russians 67,000; Jews 6,000; Gagauz 16,000): Tighina 307,000 (Romanians 164,000; Ukrainians 9,000; Bulgarians 20,000; Russians 45,000; Jews 17,000; Gagauz 39,000) (*Anuarul statistic al României 1939 şi 1940* (Bucharest: Institutul Central de Statistică, 1940), p. 60).

48. The breakdown of county population figures for Bukovina, based on the 1930 Romanian census, was: Câmpulung 94,816; Cernăuţi 306,194; Rădăuţi 160,778; Storojineţ 169,894; Suceava 121,327 (*Anuarul statistic al României 1939 şi 1940* (Bucharest: Institutul Central de Statistică, 1940), p. 60).
49. Golopenţia (1941): 37–8.
50. TNA, War Office 208/1745, 'Balkan Invasion: Russian Invasion of Roumania', 30 July 1940. 'Of 7 Infantry and 3 Cavalry Divisions located on territory now occupied by Russians, 3 Infantry and 1 Cavalry Division lost everything; 2 Infantry and 1 Cavalry Division [lost] 50 to 70 per cent of all war materiel, remainder no loss. These losses include literally everything since units concerned were composed of Bessarabian troops who made off home leaving weapons behind and taking horses and carts with them. Casualties: Officers (?) 16 dead, 23 missing; Warrant Officers 49 dead, 416 missing; Other Ranks unknown, but since in addition to deserters all men of Bessarabian origin are allowed to return home, I estimate loss to army at least 150,000 men' (I am grateful to the late Brigadier-General Geoffrey Macnab for these details); see also Watts (1993), p. 233.
51. Dorel Bancoş (2000), *Social şi naţional în politica guvernului Ion Antonescu* [*The Social and National in the Politics of the Ion Antonescu Government*] (Bucharest: Editura Eminescu), p. 322.
52. Ibid.
53. Haynes (1999): 700–25 (702).
54. Ibid.
55. *DGFP*, Vol. IX, Doc. No. 67, p. 69.
56. Carlile A. Macartney (1956), *October Fifteenth: A History of Modern Hungary, 1929–1945*, Vol. 1 (Edinburgh: Edinburgh University Press), pp. 336–87.
57. Ottmar Traşcă (2000), 'URSS şi diferendul româno-maghiar din vara anului 1940', in Liviu Ţîrău and Virgiliu Ţârău (eds), *România şi relaţiile internaţionale în secolul XX in honorem Profesorului Universitar Doctor Vasile Vesa* ['The USSR and the Romanian-Hungarian Dispute in Summer 1940', *Romania and International Relations in the 20th Century in Honour of Professor Vasile Vesa*] (Cluj-Napoca: Biblioteca Centrală Universitară), p. 192.
58. Arhiva Ministerului Afacerilor Externe [Archive for the Ministry of Foreign Affairs], Bucharest, Fond 71/Germania, Vol. 80, pp. 129–34. I am grateful to Rebecca Haynes for providing this citation and reference.
59. Haynes (1999), p. 158.
60. Gibson (1946), p. 289.
61. One Romanian source gave the area ceded as 43,591 square kilometres and the breakdown of population in northern Transylvania at the time of the award as 1,305,000 Romanians; 968,000 Hungarians; 149,000 Jews; and 72,000 Germans (Silviu Dragomir, *La Transylvanie avant et après l'Arbitrage de Vienne* (Sibiu, 1943), p. 43). Another put the area at 42,610 square kilometres in which there were 1,315,500 Romanians and 969,000 Hungarians as well as other nationalities (Golopenţia (1941): 39–40). Compare this with the Hungarian census of 1941, taken after an exodus of Romanians to southern Transylvania, which put the population of northern Transylvania *by language* at 2,577,000, of whom 1,347,000 were listed as Hungarians; 1,066,000 as Romanians; 47,500 as German speakers; and 45,600 as Yiddish speakers. Of the total Jewish population of about 200,000 in the province before the partition, 164,000 lived in the area ceded

to Hungary (Randolph L. Braham (1983) (ed.), *Genocide and Retribution: The Holocaust in Hungarian-ruled Transylvania* (Boston, The Hague: Nijhoff), p. 10).
62. Bancoş (2000), p. 329.
63. Figures prepared by the Romanian General Staff in spring 1944 for the German-Italian Commission that monitored the situation in northern Transylvania gave the following breakdown of population by county:

County	Total Population	Romanians	Hungarians	Others (including Jews)	Refugees (to 31.1.1944)
Bihor	332,917	150,083	138,102	44,732	35,876
Ciuc	158,918	23,520	128,215	7,183	5,609
Cluj	274,401	154,968	91,179	28,254	55,659
Maramureş	176,147	103,816	11,871	60,460	6,709
Mureş	294,471	129,492	128,832	36,147	22,693
Năsăud	157,150	114,936	7,942	34,272	10,610
Odorhei	131,852	6,200	119,446	6,206	2,193
Sălaj	375,245	215,104	114,451	45,690	29,734
Satu-Mare	321,393	198,516	78,865	44,012	18,170
Someş	239,152	188,390	35,887	14,875	25,456
Trei Scaune	138,250	19,442	111,393	7,415	7,335
Târnava Mare	1,149	322	63	764	322
Târnava Mică	2,623	188	2,125	310	188

(Arhivele Naţionale. Direcţia judeţeană Bistriţa-Năsăud, Fond 'Dumitru Nacu', dosar 2). I am grateful to Ion Bolovan at Cluj University for this reference.

64. Bancoş (2000), p. 330.
65. The area represented almost 7% of the total area of Romania and had a population of 378,000 according to the 1930 census. Of these 143,000 (37.5%) were Bulgarian; 129,000 (34.1%) were Turkish-speaking Tatars; and 78,000 (20.5%) Romanian. However, under the terms of the Romanian-Turkish Convention of 4 September 1936, some 14,500 Romanians and almost 7,000 Macedo-Romanians were settled from Turkey on the land of 70,000 Turks in Dobrogea who opted to go to Turkey. This settlement brought the number of persons registered as Romanian in 1940 to 98,619. To this figure must be added the natural growth in population over the decade since 1930 (Golopenţia (1941): 39). The transfer of population began on 5 November 1940 and was largely completed by 14 December.
66. Bancoş (2000), pp. 93–5. In a selfish act, which provided eloquent testimony to his priorities, Carol, in the knowledge that Romania would cede southern Dobrudja to Bulgaria, was reported to have 'sold the Balcic Castle [located there] to the Bucharest City Council in order to avoid a personal loss' (quoted from Watts (1993), p. 228).
67. 'Minute of the Meeting between General Ion Antonescu and the German Chancellor Adolf Hitler on 12 June 1941', in Andreas Hillgruber (1969), *Staatsmänner und Diplomaten bei Hitler. Vertrauliche Aufzeichnungen über die Unterredunger mit Vertreten des Auslandes 1939–1941* (Munich: Deutscher Taschenbuchverlag), pp. 276–91.

68. Axworthy et al. (1995), p. 47. Antonescu was promoted to the rank of Marshal by the King on 22 August 1941 for the recovery of Bessarabia and Northern Bukovina.
69. Constantin (Dinu) Brătianu (1866–1953), second son of Ion C. Brătianu (1821–1891), appointed leader of the National Liberal Party in 1934. Constantin (Dinu) Brătianu was arrested by the Communist authorities on – according to one source – 3 May 1950, and imprisoned without trial at Sighet, where he died on 23 August 1953 (see Florian Tănăsescu and Nicolae Tănăsescu (2005), *Constantin (Bebe) I. C. Brătianu – Istoria P.N.L. la interogatoriu* (Bucharest: Editura Paralela 45), p. 179.)
70. Aurel Simion (1979), *Preliminarii politico-diplomatice ale insurecției române din august 1944* (Cluj-Napoca: Editura Dacia), p. 208.
71. Radu Ioanid, *The Holocaust in Romania: The Destruction of Jews and Gypsies under Antonescu Regime, 1940–1944* (Chicago: Ivan Dee. Published in association with the United States Holocaust Memorial Museum), p. 289.
72. Axworthy et al. (1995), p. 216. After Italy signed an armistice with the Allies on 8 September 1943, Romania became the second Axis power in Europe.

4 The Prelude to Hostilities: Projecting Britain in Romania

1. Ioannis Stefanidis (2012), *Substitute for Power: Wartime British Propaganda to the Balkans, 1939–44* (Farnham: Ashgate), p. 132.
2. I would like to express my thanks to Helen Meixner, Christopher Rennie, and Tamara Read at the British Council for facilitating access to most of the primary materials upon which this chapter draws, and to Maurice Pearton for identifying certain documents in The National Archives (TNA) in Kew.
3. Arthur John Stanley White (1965), *The British Council: The First 25 Years, 1934–1959* (London: The British Council), p. 19.
4. It was housed at Strada Boteanu 3. Tilea's memoirs were edited and published by his daughter, Ileana Tilea under the title *Envoy Extraordinary: Memoirs of a Romanian Diplomat* (London: Haggerston Press, 1998).
5. TNA, British Council, BW 53/1.
6. Ibid.
7. Ibid.
8. Ibid.
9. Among those who lectured were Robert Bruce Lockhart (4 March); Harold Nicolson (18 and 19 April with lectures entitled 'Are the English Hypocrites?' and 'The British Empire Today'); and Sir Ronald Storss (24 October on 'T. E. Lawrence'). From Lockhart's talks in Romania and elsewhere in South-Eastern Europe came *Guns or Butter* (London: Putnam, 1938), an optimistic assessment of the Balkan nations tempered by fears of German aggression.
10. TNA, BW 53/1.
11. Burbank was joined by an assistant, also sponsored by the Council, in March 1939. His name was Ivor Porter and he recounted his experiences of the time in *Operation Autonomous* (1989). Miss E. J. Cumming was appointed as a teacher at the Institute by Amery in November 1939.
12. TNA, BW 53/1 [in the original the emphasis is in underlined text]. Manning's view of Romania is the subject of a revealing analysis by Ernest Latham (1995), 'Watching from the Window: Olivia Manning in Romania 1939–1940', *Journal of the American Romanian Academy of Arts and Sciences*, No. 20: 92–112. It was while

he was on summer leave in London in 1939 that Smith met Olivia Manning, who was working at the time at the Medici Society, and they married shortly afterwards. The newly-wed couple arrived in Bucharest on 3 September 1939, the day Britain declared war on Germany, and stayed there until early October 1940, shortly after the Romanian government ordered all British civilians out of the country on 30 September 1940.

13. TNA, BW 53/6, 22 May 1940; Latham (1995), p. 96. A seasoned observer of Romanian society at the time might well have argued that the 'more serious sections of Romanian life' would have given ample material to Joyce and Lawrence!
14. TNA, BW 53/1.
15. See the correspondence between Sir John Simon and Lord Halifax, March 1940, TNA, FO 371/24995; I have taken this reference from Maurice Pearton (1998), 'British Policy Towards Romania 1939–1941', *Occasional Papers in Romanian Studies*, No. 2, Rebecca Haynes (ed.) (London: School of Slavonic and East European Studies, University of London), p. 73, note 33.
16. TNA, BW 53/4.
17. Amery went to Sarajevo to work with the Yugoslav-British Society, while Smith and Manning were evacuated to Athens where Reggie worked as a British Council lecturer until the spring of 1941 when once again a German advance forced them to leave, this time for Cairo. The British Council lecturers in Cernăuţi, Iaşi and Timişoara, also left. According to a statement of proposed British Council expenditure in Romania for the year 1940–1, the Council teacher in Cernăuţi was a Mr Balister; in Timişoara a Mr Kingdon; and in Iaşi a Mr Ennals. The Council was also contributing to the rent of Anglo-Romanian Society premises in Cernăuţi, Cluj, Constanţa, Galaţi and Iaşi, as well as making small payments to locally-engaged teachers in Cluj and Constanţa. Ennals was an enterprising figure and sent the British legation a memorandum in July 1940 giving an eyewitness account of the treatment meted out to some of the peasants and Jews from Bukovina by the Romanian authorities as they returned to the province after its cession to the Soviet Union: 'I entered Bukovina on July 3rd [1940] with a group of Bukovinan peasants, workers and Jews who were returning from other parts of Roumania, particularly from Bucharest. Many of the Jews amongst them had been attacked on the train and several had severe head injuries. The Roumanian authorities would do nothing towards giving them medical treatment. I managed to obtain some bandages, cotton wool and antiseptics and did what I could. We waited three hours in a waiting room at Dorneşti and eleven hours at the local gendarmerie. During this time the people were not allowed to go out and look for anything to eat. Everyone's name was entered on a list and then we were told that we were to walk with our baggage to Adancata on the other side of the frontier. It is a distance of about 30 kilometres. We were forced to walk along the railway and as we did not start till seven in the evening, most of the distance was covered in the dark. We were accompanied by Roumanian soldiers with fixed bayonets who did not allow us to stop until we had walked for four hours at a very swift pace. Many of the travellers were not fit to walk, being old and ill. They were all carrying with them all their possessions. At one point all the Jews were separated from the remainder of the party and they were forced to hand over money at the point of a bayonet. Soon after this, the Roumanian soldiers began firing and using their bayonets and as it was very dark there was a complete panic, almost everybody dropped their luggage and ran desperately in the direction of the Russian

frontier. Many of them arrived in the early hours of the morning when they were picked up by Russian army lorries. Others did not arrive, of them we could find out nothing' (TNA, FO 371/24856/192).

5 Challenging German Ambitions: Clandestine British Military Operations in Romania, 1939–1941

1. An earlier version of this chapter appeared as 'British Plans and Attempts at Subversion in Romania, 1939–40', in Dennis Deletant (ed.), *In and Out of Focus: Romania and Britain. Relations and Perspectives from 1930 to the Present* (Bucharest: British Council, 2005), pp. 71–86.
2. Pearton (1998a), pp. 65–102 (66).
3. Its charter read, 'So to influence opinion in any part of the world as to be favourable to the policy of His Majesty's Government' (TNA, 'MIR', HS 8/214).
4. Nigel West (1983), *MI6: British Secret Intelligence Operations, 1909–45* (London: Weidenfeld and Nicolson), p. 60.
5. Peter Wilkinson and Joan Bright Astley (1997), *Gubbins and SOE* (London: Pen and Sword), p. 34.
6. A. Chanady and J. Jensen, 'Germany, Rumania and the British Guarantees of March–April 1939', *Australian Journal of Politics and History*, Vol. 6(2) (August): 201–7.
7. Pearton (1998a), p. 87.
8. A condition not dissimilar to that placed by Marshal Antonescu and Iuliu Maniu in their peace feelers towards Britain and the United States during 1943 and 1944; the difference being that the Soviet Union had replaced Nazi Germany as the potential enemy.
9. Lt. Col. Geoffrey Alex Colin Macnab (1899–1995), British military attaché to Romania, 1938–40.
10. Pearton (1998a), p. 87.
11. Maurice Pearton (2000), 'British Intelligence in Romania, 1938–1941', in George Cipăianu and Virgiliu Ţârău (eds), *Romanian and British Historians on the Contemporary History of Romania* (Cluj-Napoca: Cluj-Napoca University Press), p. 190.
12. Ibid., pp. 192–3.
13. The MI(R) missions to Romania and Poland left together from London in August 1939 for Marseilles by train. They then embarked on the cruiser *Shropshire* to Alexandria. From Alexandria they flew to Piraeus in a flying-boat, travelled to Athens, and then in a Polish LOT aircraft to Bucharest. The Polish mission continued by LOT to Cernăuţi in Bukovina on 1 September but could go no further as the Germans were bombing airfields in Poland. The group took a taxi across the frontier to Lvov and from there a coach to Lublin. When they heard of Britain's declaration of war on Germany on 3 September they changed from civilian to military dress and went on to Warsaw which they reached on the same day. The mission left the Polish capital on 17 September and returned to Bucharest. They were then ordered to Cairo, with the exception of Harris-Burland who managed to persuade MI(R) to let him stay because of his previous experience of working in Bucharest as an accountant for various foreign companies (author's interview with William Harris-Burland, 10 August 1984).
14. Ottmar Traşca and Dennis Deletant (2013), 'The German Secret Services in Romania: "Kriegsorganisation Rumänien"/"Abwehrstelle Rumänien" and

Intelligence Cooperation between Romania and Germany over the Defence of the Romanian Oil-Fields, 1939–1944', in Daniel Dumitran and Valer Moga (eds), *Economy and Society in Central and Eastern Europe: Territory, Population, Consumption. Papers of the International Conference held in Alba Iulia, April 25th–27th, 2013* (Vienna-Zurich-Munich: Lit Verlag), pp. 343–62 (347).

15. Pearton (2000), pp. 194–5.
16. 'Report on MIR mission to Roumania, 19.12.40', communicated by the SOE adviser to this author on 3 August 1988.
17. For a presentation of the *Abwehr*'s activity in Romania in this period, see Traşca and Deletant (2013).
18. Ibid., p. 349.
19. Canaris (1887–1945) was found guilty of conspiring against Hitler and executed on 9 April 1945 in Flossenberg concentration camp.
20. I have taken these details from Pearton (2000), p. 194.
21. Traşca and Deletant (2013), p. 355.
22. The Iron Gates is the term used in English to cover a series of gorges on the Danube, the largest of which is known as the Kazan gorge. The Greben rock near the Kazan gorge was a notorious obstacle in the passage of the Danube.
23. Traşca and Deletant (2013), pp. 355–6.
24. Ibid.
25. Pearton (2000), p. 197.
26. See Biographies of Key Figures.
27. See Biographies of Key Figures.
28. Pearton (2000), p. 199.
29. In a secret report prepared by *Havas*, the French news agency, for the Headquarters of the French General Staff and dated 10 April 1940, the weapons found were listed and other vessels in the flotilla named. They were the tugs *Britannia, Elizabeth, Danubia Shell, King George, Scotland, Albion* and *Lord Byron*; a chartered Greek freighter *Dionysia*; and several barges (*Polnische Dokumente zur Vorgeschichte des Kriege*, erste folge (Berlin: Zentralverlag der NSDAP, Franz Eher Nachf, 1940), No. 36, pp. 82–3). Despite its title 'Polish documents on the Early History of the War', the volume contains several secret documents of the French General Staff, captured by the Germans on 19 June 1940 in a train at Charité-sur-Loire, and translated for publication into German.
30. A report of Section D provides 'sabotage results' in Romania: '6.12.1939: Ploieşti Orion Oil Refinery. Explosion – fire destroyed plant and 200 wagons of oil. Roumania July 1940: Regular axle box sabotage continued on a large scale. July 1940: Breakdown of 5 wagons in two days as a result of interference with axle boxes' (TNA, HS 8/214).
31. A Romanian government controller was put in charge of Astra Română on 24 July (I am grateful to Maurice Pearton for this information).
32. A copy of the plan, dated 1 October 1939, drawn up by the French engineer Léon Wenger, who had participated in the sabotage of the Romanian oil wells in 1916, was passed on by the German authorities to the Romanian Intelligence Service (SSI). Wenger visited Bucharest on 16 September 1939, accompanied by Captain Pierre Angot of French Intelligence. Discussion of the plan was held with the French and British ministers, and with Colonel Gubbins, Commander Watson and Colonel Tom Masterson. The plan was highly optimistic. It proposed the rapid destruction by French and British agents with explosives of the oil wells, all the refineries and pumping stations within 24 hours. It took little account of

the heavy German and Romanian security around these facilities. On 18 October General Maurice Gamelin (1872–1958), Chief of the French General Staff, recommended to his Minister of Defence that Wenger be entrusted with 'the possible destruction of the Romanian oil fields' (CNSAS, Fond P, 10644, Vol. 12, p. 269; see also Traşca and Deletant (2013), p. 358, footnote 52.

33. Ibid., p. 359.
34. See Biographies of Key Figures.
35. TNA, 'History SOE Romania', HS 7/186, p. 2. In the foreword to the 'History' it is stated, 'Many files on the activities of the section in the years 1939–1941, previously held by the Istanbul office, which had been sent to Cairo for safe keeping, were burnt during the panic created in 1942 by the advance of German forces under Field-Marshal Erwin Rommel to El Alamein. Many unique documents were destroyed, including detailed reports prepared by W. R. Young, H. G. Watts, J. E. Treacy, R. Hazell, John Toyne, de Chastelain himself, and other of SOE's original collaborators.' In a 1941 report of the Romanian Security Police (*Siguranța*), Toyne's date of birth is given as 15 September 1891. His cover at the time was as a representative of Hall and Pickles Engineering Company based in Manchester. He left Romania on 15 February 1941 (CNSAS, Ministerul Afacerilor Interne, File 308, Vol. 461, f.453). Even these details are missing from Toyne's autobiography *Win Time For Us* (Toronto: Longmans, 1962) which tantalizes the reader with an amusing narrative of his experiences in Russia and South-Eastern Europe. Toyne was born in Lincolnshire and sent in 1911 to Odessa as the representative of a Lincoln engineering firm. In the following year he married the daughter of German pastor from Odessa. He tells us that he was recuited by a visiting friend into the 'Intelligence Department' (British Secret Service) – a process of deduction points the reader to the year 1915. His duties required gathering information about the state of the Russian army. He remained in Russia throughout the revolution and civil war until 1921 when he visited Bucharest 'to sell tractors and ploughs' (p. 137). After two years travelling in South-Eastern Europe he emigrated to Canada in May 1924. Ten years later he returned to Britain and resumed work for MI6 in Germany, being sent on to Romania in May 1940.
36. 'Report on MIR mission to Roumania, 19.12.40', communicated by SOE adviser to this author on 3 August 1988.
37. Pearton (1998a), p. 90. In October 1940 several of those engineers who had remained were kidnapped and beaten. Not surprisingly they were withdrawn from Romania and with their departure went the last hope of executing any sabotage.
38. Pearton (2000), p. 201.
39. Their names were Alfred Crawford Anderson, John Edward Treacy and his wife Esther, Reginald Young, Charles Brasier, Alexander Miller and Percy Clark. Anderson was arrested on 24 September; Mr and Mrs Treacy, Young and Brasier on the following day; Miller on 1 October; and Clark on 3 October (see the report on the arrests dated 23 October 1940 from Heydrich, head of the *Sicherheitspolizei* and the SD, to Ribbentrop, German Foreign Minister referred to in Traşca and Deletant (2013), p. 360, footnote 58).
40. Traşca and Deletant (2013), p. 360.
41. A subsidiary of the Standard Oil Company of America. The principal British oil companies with interests in Romania at this time were Phoenix Oil and Transport Company Ltd, Steaua Română (British) Ltd, and the Shell Group. Phoenix

was a holding company and owned all the shares in the Unirea Societate Anonimă de Petrol. Steaua Română (British) Ltd was also a holding company with about 25% of the shares of Steaua Română. The Shell Group controlled the Astra Română Societate Anonimă through its ownership of the majority of the company's shares. Concordia and Columbia were French-controlled (TNA, FO 371/24984. For the activity of these companies in Romania see Maurice Pearton (1971), *Oil and the Romanian State* (Oxford: Clarendon Press).

42. TNA, 'History SOE Romania', HS 7/186, p. 2.
43. Ibid.
44. Ion Popovici was born in Bucharest on 20 May 1898 and was a chemical engineer by profession. He worked for the British-owned Unirea Oil Company and became a close friend of the director of the company, Alfred George Gardyne de Chastelain (1906–1974). Popovici joined Unirea as head of sales on 5 Oct. 1924 (CNSAS, Fond I, 937873, f.79). In early 1940 de Chastelain became head of SO(2) operations in Romania, working under SO(2)'s Balkan representative in Istanbul, Colonel Bill Bailey. Popovici headed a group of pro-British activists until his arrest in August 1941; see Direcţia Justiţiei Militare, dosar nr 2218, p. 21.) He died in Bucharest in 1946.
45. The sum involved was £5,000; see TNA, HS 5/830. On 7 January 1941 Hoare drew the attention of the Romanian Foreign Minister, Mihail Sturdza, to his previous notes to him of 9 October and 9 November 1940 in which he enquired as to whether those responsible for the ill-treatment of the British subjects had been identified and measures taken against them. Hoare informed him of the result of the enquiries made on behalf of the British legation which established that 'the ringleader in brutality' was a Victor Enechescu (or Enachescu) from Ploieşti. Another person involved was Gheorghe Cârciumaru who was 'almost certainly connected with the Legionary Police at Ploieşti'. Other legionaries thought to have been implicated in the maltreatment were a certain Gabriel Popescu, a Ianacescu, and a Professor Grigorescu (TNA, HS 5/830).
46. Valeriu Florin Dobrinescu and Ion Pătroiu (1992), *Anglia şi România între anii 1939–1947* (Bucharest: Editura Didactică şi Pedagogică), p. 96.
47. TNA, 'History SOE Romania', HS 7/186, p. 1.
48. Leader of the Armenian community in Romania. His SOE code number was DH/25 (TNA, HS 5/821).
49. TNA, 'History SOE Romania', HS 7/186, p. 1.
50. 'Early in 1940 at the request of the London office, Ion Popovici well-known under the pseudonym of Procopius, was engaged on a voluntary basis as postbox and cut-out for Jean Kurciusz, one of the leading members of the Polish Secret Service', ibid.
51. Ibid.
52. The files prepared for Antonescu's trial containing letters of protest addressed to him and seen by this author run to only a handful of volumes; whether the letters, which were filed by the Romanian Intelligence Service (SSI), ever reached Antonescu's desk is unclear; see ANIC, Fond Ministerul de Interne, Trial of Ion Antonescu, File No. 40010, Vols. 35 and 37.
53. TNA, 'History of SOE Romania', HS 7/186, p. 5. See also Biographies of Key Figures.
54. Virgil Madgeanu, (1887–1940), Professor of Economics at Bucharest University and Finance Minister in the National Peasant Party governments of 1929–30 and 1932–3.

55. Ion Mihalache (1882–1963), a teacher who became a leading figure in the Peasant Party and, after its union with the National Party in 1926, in the National Peasant Party; Minister of Agriculture in the governments of Alexandru Vaida-Voevod and Iuliu Maniu (1919–20 and 1928–30); Minister of Internal Affairs (1930–1 and 1932–3); President of the National Peasant Party (1933–7). He was arrested with other leading members of the party in 1947, tried for espionage in favour of the United States and Britain, and sentenced to hard labour for life. He died in Râmnicul Sărat prison on 6 March 1963.
56. TNA, 'History SOE Romania', HS 7/186, p. 5.
57. Ibid.
58. Ibid.
59. Ibid.
60. The British propaganda campaign in Romania is admirably analysed in Stefanidis (2012), pp. 127–59, for which reason I do not propose to discuss it in detail here.
61. See Biographies of Key Figures.
62. Viorel Tilea (born 6 April 1896; died 20 September 1972), Romanian Minister to London, 1938–40. He was granted political asylum in London in September 1940 after being recalled to Bucharest following Ion Antonescu's accession to power.
63. Dimitrie Demetrios Dimancescu (born 7 July 1896; died 8 December 1984). A graduate of the University of Bucharest, he received the British Military Cross for sabotaging Rumanian oil wells during World War I to hamper the German war effort. After the First World War he studied engineering at the Carnegie Institute of Technology in Pittsburgh. He was counsellor at the Romanian legation in London in 1940 when German troops entered Rumania, and he then resigned his position. After the Second World War he lived in Morocco for eight years and then settled in Hartford Connecticut in 1956 (see Ernest H. Latham, Jr. (2012c), 'Useful Service Rendered: The Romanian Life of Dimitri Demetrius Dimancescu', in Ernest Latham, Jr., *Timeless and Transitory: 20th Century Relations between Romania and the English-Speaking World* (Bucharest: Vremea), pp. 397–445.
64. Stefanidis (2012), p. 151.
65. AMAN, Fond 5465, Direcţia Justiţiei Militare, File No. 2218, p. 24.
66. Păsătoiu received 10 million *lei* (ibid.).
67. Pearton (2000), p. 202.
68. TNA, 'Statement of policy for S.O.2 work in Romania', HS 5/783 [in the original document the italicized text was underlined].
69. TNA, 'Roumania', HS 5/783.
70. TNA, 'History SOE Romania', HS 7/186, p. 6.
71. 'Interference with German Oil Supplies'. Memorandum by the Special Operations Executive, 8 January 1941', in David Stafford (1983), *Britain and European Resistance, 1940–1945* (Toronto and Buffalo: University of Toronto Press), pp. 225–33.
72. Ibid., p. 228.
73. Ibid., pp. 230–1.
74. Ibid., p. 232.
75. Pearton (1998a), p. 94 quoting from TNA, FO 371/29992. Among the British who left on 12 February 1941 were the lecturer Ivor Porter and the journalists Clare Hollingworth and David Walker.
76. Porter (1989), p. 66.

77. The other members were Ion Beza, Iuliu Bălan, Ştefan Cosmovici, Ion Deleanu, Ion Dragu, Mihai Iaroslavici, Iosif Păsătoiu, Ion Popovici, Corneliu Radocea, and Augustin Vişa (author's interview with Corneliu Coposu, 13 August 1986). Bălan, a nephew of Maniu, was head of the Bucharest repair shop at AEG, the German electrical manufacturer and actually transmitted the messages which were brought to him by Vişa. Popovici, de Chastelain's assistant at Unirea, recruited Beza, a wireless operator at the Romanian airline Lares (ibid., p. 72).
78. Barker (1976), p. 77.
79. To avoid confusion I shall henceforth refer to SO(2) as SOE.
80. Barker (1976), p. 77.
81. Stefanidis (2012), p. 156.
82. Ibid.
83. Ibid., p. 157, footnote 195. This view was confirmed by Lord Glennconner (Christopher Grey Tennant, 2nd Baron Glenconner, 1899–1983), head of the Cairo Headquarters Directorate of SOE, in a minute on Romania dated 9 February 1942: 'We have obtained a copy from New York of a letter from Pangal, ex-Roumanian Minister at Lisbon, to King Carol. This letter, which was intercepted at Bermuda, shows that Pangal is scheming for the return of King Carol, and is in communication with Tilea. The Poles have a W/T set in Bucharest and are (presumably) passing messages into Roumania for Tilea. It is therefore probable that there is an intrigue going on between the Poles, Tilea and King Carol, who are opposed to Maniu' (TNA, 'Minute on Roumania', HS 5/765).
84. Ibid.
85. The Romanian losses in the Third and Fourth Armies in the period from 19 November 1942 to 7 January 1943 were put at 155,010 dead, wounded and missing, most of the latter being taken prisoner (*România în anii celui de-al doilea război mondial*, Vol. 1 (Bucharest: Editura Militară, 1989), p. 489.
86. Stefanidis (2012), p. 152. Antonescu's own senior commanders expressed serious misgivings about the wisdom of committing so many Romanian troops to the Russian campaign. In a series of memoranda Antonescu's Chief of Staff, General Iosif Iacobici, fearing a surprise Hungarian attack from the West against southern Transylvania which was considered at risk because of the withdrawal of forces from there to support the campaign in the Soviet Union, urged the Marshal to limit his involvement east of the Dniester (*România în anii celui de-al doilea război mondial*, Vol. 1 (Bucharest: Editura Militară, 1989), p. 556. Iacobici was dismissed in January 1942 and replaced by General Ilie Şteflea, who endorsed his predecessor's views.
87. TNA, 'History SOE Romania', HS 7/186, p. 7. Ivor Porter, in an email sent to this author on 23 May 2008, gives a slightly earlier date: 'It is quite clear from my material that the first radio contact between Maniu and SOE Istanbul was made on 4 April 1941 with Balan's transmitter. This was hand-made by Balan from components he normally had on his bench. Balan's operation, which lasted until 15 August 1941, was associated with no other transmitter. When I joined SOE in March 1941 I was based in Cairo. Early in 1943 when I visited Istanbul, de Chastelain who was then head of the SOE office told me of his attempts to keep in touch with Maniu after the arrests of August 1941. He talked at length of how he had finally succeeded in sending Maniu an SOE set "to replace Balan's" via a buccaneering Turk called Lufti Bey. He made no mention of the suitcase set he had left with Georgescu in Romania in 1940 and I probably knew nothing about it. There is no evidence that the 1940 suitcase transmitter was ever used and it

was almost certainly the one referred to in SOE papers. Balan's home-made stationary set proved to be a successful stand-by. I agree with your conclusion [i.e. that de Chastelain's transmitter was never used. DD].'

88. TNA, 'History SOE Romania', HS 7/186, p. 7.
89. Ibid. A note on this page in TNA, HS 7/186 adds: 'The attack took place on 22 June, being delayed a week on account of the signing of the German/Turkish Pact of Friendship'.
90. TNA, 'History SOE Romania', HS 7/186, p. 7.
91. Under questioning during his trial with Ion Antonescu and their associates, Mihai Antonescu stated that the Germans wanted Georgescu to be put on trial but he 'did not consider it to be in the Romanians' interest... because that interest did not require that publicity should be given to a matter of espionage involving Britain at that time... I intervened [to ensure] that there should never be a trial' (Ciucă (1995–8), Vol. 1, pp. 289–90).
92. Ioan Beza (b. 15 February 1909 in Bucharest). Released from prison on 23 August 1944 only to be re-arrested by the NKVD on 17 June 1947 and sentenced to 25 years in jail. He was taken to the Soviet Union and returned to Romania in December 1958 to serve the remainder of his jail term at Gherla. He died in January 1958 (I am grateful to Ioan Ciupea of the National Musem of History in Cluj-Napoca for these details).
93. Iosif Păsătoiu was arrested in 1946 for membership of an anti-Communist group. He was later interned for 24 months on 20 September 1951.
94. For further information about Archibald Gibson and MI6 activity in Romania, see Chapter 8.
95. Politisches Archiv des Auswärtigen Amtes Berlin [The Political Archives of the Foreign Office, Berlin] (henceforth PAAAB), R 100114, Inland II Geheim, Bd. 423, Berichte und Meldungen zur Lage in Rumänien-1941. E 267273–267275. D II 119 g.Rs. Schnellbrief des Chefs der Sicherheitspolizei und des SD vom 11.09.1941, gez. Heydrich (I am grateful to Dr Ottmar Traşcă of the George Bariţiu Institute of History in Cluj-Napoca for identifying the report and providing me with a copy).
96. Vişa was born in the commune of Şeica Mare, county of Târnava Mare in Transylvania on 5 June 1904, and worked at the Casa de Economii şi Consemnaţiuni (CEC, Post Office Savings Bank) in Bucharest. He joined the National Peasant Party in 1927 and became a leading figure and head of its student wing in 1936. He was a lawyer by profession.
97. Augustin Vişa (1997), *Din închisorile fasciste în cele comuniste din URSS şi România* (Bucharest: Institutul pentru Analiză şi Strategie Politică), p. 47.
98. Bălan was born on 16 February 1908 in the village of Valea Vinului in the county of Satu Mare (AMAN, Fond 5465, Direcţia Justiţiei Militare, File No. 2218, p. 40).
99. In a declaration given after his arrest in August 1941 to the military prosecutor Captain Camil Bărbulescu, Vişa alleged that it was he that had asked Bălan to construct the radio and that Bălan had offered to build it free of charge since it was 'a work of national importance'. Vişa did not mention Maniu's involvement (AMAN, Fond 5465, Direcţia Justiţiei Militare, File No. 2218, p. 37). Popovici had used some of the money left by de Chastelain to finance the construction of a radio transmitter.
100. Vişa (1997), p. 77; see also Vişa's declaration to Bărbulescu (AMAN, Fond 5465, Direcţia Justiţiei Militare, File No. 2218, p. 38.) Vişa suspected that Maniu had other channels of contact with SOE because of the content of messages that

he deciphered and passed on to Popovici for Maniu (Vişa (1997), p. 49). These channels were through couriers. There is no evidence to support the claim that the suitcase transmitter left by de Chastelain with Rică Georgescu in October 1940 was used for transmissions at this time. Vişa was released on 24 August 1944. He was re-arrested on 28 February 1948 by order of the Soviet authorities on a charge of 'war crimes against the Soviet army', tried in Constanţa by a Soviet tribunal in the Soviet tank garrison, sentenced to twenty years hard labour on 4 October 1948, and taken to the Potima camp in the autonomous republic of Mordovia in the Soviet Union. He was released from Soviet imprisonment in November 1958 – other sources say that he was allowed to serve the remainder of his sentence in Romania until his release from Râmnicu-Sărat prison on 5 November 1957 – and died in September 1989 in Bucharest (*La voix de l'effroi: La Roumanie sous le communisme. Récits et témoignages*, ed. E. Cosmovici, M. Cosmovici and Marie-Joelle Desserre (Bucharest: Association Europe Chrétienne, 2000), pp. 93–9).

101. Bărbulescu – the son of Constantin and Victoria – was born on 20 March 1907 in Bucharest and studied law at Bucharest University. He was arrested on 29 July 1949 on the charge of 'crimes against humanity', tried and sentenced to seven years in prison for 'applying inhuman treatment as an interrogating magistrate'. He served his time in Craiova jail (I am grateful to Ioan Ciupea of the Museum of National History in Cluj-Napoca for this information).
102. Vişa (1997), p. 81.
103. AMAN, Fond 5465, Direcţia Justiţiei Militare, File No. 2218.
104. In the parlance of the Romanian *Siguranţa* (Security Service) and of the *Serviciul Secret de Informaţii* (Intelligence Service) no distinction is made between the various British security and intelligence agencies, a practice which continued in the Communist period.
105. Maria Gibson, née Theodoru, was said by Bărbulescu to have described her husband Archibald as 'vice-ridden, a frequenter of Bucharest bars, capable of anything' (AMAN, Fond 5465, Direcţia Justiţiei Militare, File No. 2218, p. 13).
106. Ibid., p. 3. In Mircea's statement to Bărbulescu he claimed, among other things, that de Chastelain asked him for an introduction to Maria Tănase, the celebrated Romanian folk-singer, who was visiting Istanbul at the time. Tănase allegedly used the opportunity to ask for de Chastelain's help in improving the lot of her friend, Maurice Negre, who was being held in Bucharest on suspicion of spying for the British (ibid., p. 16).
107. Ibid., p. 5.
108. Born in Bucharest on 10 April 1900. After completing his studies in London he took a law degree in Bucharest and found a position as a representative of the Phoenix factory in Baia Mare (ibid., p. 13).
109. Ibid., p. 6.
110. Ibid., p. 38
111. Ibid., p. 7.
112. Ibid., p. 8.
113. From this sum Popovici paid Andrei Ion Deleanu 134,000 *lei* to print anti-German manifestoes as part of the *Ardealul* programme (ibid., p. 22).
114. Ibid., pp. 10–11. Those listed by Bărbulescu as being held under arrest were, alongside Rică Georgescu and Ion Popovici (Aurelian Rădulescu had disappeared), Ilarie Bălan, Augustin Vişa, Corneliu Radocea (a friend of Vişa), Ion Beza, Plesnilă, Ecaterina Levasz, Sandu Klamer, Adolf Regenstreif, Adela

Abramovici, Iosif Păsătoiu, Amedeu Bădescu, Andrei Ion Deleanu, Mihai Iaroslavici-Bădică and Ştefan Cosmovici.
115. Ibid., p. 32.
116. TNA, 'History SOE Romania', HS 7/186, p. 8.
117. Commander V. Wolfson directed the Naval Intelligence Division in Istanbul which was part of an inter-service Balkan Intelligence Centre (a cover name for MI6). Brigadier Allan Arnold OBE MC, was given the task of heading the Centre in Istanbul in December 1939. Its existence, which was supposed to be highly secret, was announced in a German news broadcast within a week of its inception. By summer 1940 it encompassed the activities of SOE, MI6 and the Naval Intelligence Division (which monitored enemy shipping movements (West (1983), p. 86). Colonel Traian Teodorescu was appointed Romanian military attaché to Ankara in June 1940. In reply to a question from Mihai Antonescu about Teodorescu's position, Marshal Antonescu wrote on 20 December 1941: 'Colonel Teodorescu, by virtue of his knowledge and outstanding qualities, has won such confidence and favour of the Turkish General Staff and the Axis military attachés that Turkish military circles reveal to him matters which they do not convey to any other foreign military attaché, while the Axis military attachés have such faith in him that they do nothing without consulting him' (Arhiva MAE, Archive of the Romanian Foreign Ministry, Fondul Constantinopol, 35/79).
118. Ibid., p. 10.

6 Clandestine British Operations in Romania, 1942–1943

1. Quinlan (1977), p. 71.
2. *Universul*, 9 December 1941.
3. This seizure of Romanian territory had been followed by other acts of provocation which signalled a continuation of the Soviet policy of expansion and conquest. These acts were listed as follows:

   (1) The occupation of four islands at the mouth of the Danube in the autumn of 1940.
   (2) Daily frontier incidents involving attempts to move the frontier.
   (3) Attempts by Soviet vessels to enter Romanian waters by force in January 1941.
   (4) Incessant incursions, despite Romanian protests, into Romanian airspace amounting during April, May and June to up to seven daily overflights.
   (5) A massive concentration of Soviet military forces on the Romanian frontier made up of 30 infantry divisions, 8 cavalry divisions, and 14 motorized brigades.
   (6) The imposition of a regime of systematic repression in Bessarabia and Northern Bukovina involving the deportation of hundreds of thousands of Romanians to Siberia. (*Universul*, 9 December 1941)

4. Ibid.
5. Gunther (1885–1941) was appointed Envoy Extraordinary and Minister Plenipotentiary to Bucharest on 31 July 1937. His mission ended when Romania declared war on the United States on 12 December 1941. He died just ten days later in Bucharest of leukemia and was buried there.
6. ANIC, Ministerul Afacerilor Interne, Trial of Ion Antonescu, File 40010, Vol. 8, p. 100.

7. Mircea Agapie and Jipa Rotaru (1993), *Ion Antonescu: Cariera militară. Scrisori inedite* (Bucharest: Editura Academiei de Înalte Studii Militare), p. 177.
8. ANIC, Ministerul Afacerilor Interne, Trial of Ion Antonescu, File 40010, Vol. 8, p. 101. See also Ernest H. Latham Jr. (2012a), 'All Thankful: Reports by Neutral Observers of American Prisoners of War Held in Romania', *in Timeless and Transitory: 20th Century Relations between Romania and the English-Speaking World* (Bucharest: Vremea), p. 274.
9. Vlad Georgescu (1991), *The Romanians: A History* (Columbus, OH: Ohio State University Press), p. 217.
10. The United States remained neutral until the declaration of war on Japan following the attack on Pearl Harbor on 7 December 1941. Germany declared war on the United States on 11 December, and in response the United States Congress declared war upon Germany a few hours later. Romania declared war on the United States on 12 December 1941. It was only on 5 June 1942 that the United States declared war on Romania, Hungary and Bulgaria. An order was issued on that date by the Secretary of State to all American Missions: 'You are instructed to notify the Government to which you are accredited that the Government of the United States, by unanimous resolutions of Congress signed today by the President, has declared that a state of war exists between the United States and Bulgaria, and Hungary and Rumania.' (*Foreign Relations of the United States* [*FRUS*] (1962), *1942*, Vol. II, *Europe* (Washington, DC: US Department of State), p. 841)). This was apparently to establish belligerency status and to ensure that the prisoners of war conventions were operative seven days later when thirteen B-24s under Colonel A. Halverson made the first American bombing raid of the war on the oilfields at Ploieşti (Latham (2012a), p. 274).
11. Graham Ross (1984) (ed.), *The Foreign Office and the Kremlin: British Documents on Anglo-Soviet Relations, 1941–45* (Cambridge: Cambridge University Press), p. 82.
12. Ibid.
13. Ibid., pp. 18–25.
14. Churchill to Roosevelt, 2 March 1942, in Winston S. Churchill (1950), *The Second World War.* Volume IV: *The Hinge of Fate* (London: Cassell and Co.), p. 293.
15. Quoted from Gibson's personal unpublished memoir, courtesy of Mrs Kyra Gibson.
16. TNA, HS 7/186, p. 10.
17. Barker (1976), p. 224.
18. Ibid and TNA, HS 5/760, 'Tom [code name of Maniu] departure from Romania', telegram from Cairo to SOE in London, 19 January 1942.
19. TNA, HS 5/763.
20. TNA, HS 5/765, incomplete pagination.
21. Ibid., p. 12.
22. Author's interview with William Harris-Burland, 10 August 1984; see Biographies of Key Figures.
23. The SSI (*Serviciul Secret de Informaţii al Armatei Române*, the Secret Intelligence Service of the Romanian Army), acquired a distinct status within the army in 1922, one which was consolidated by the appointment of Mihail Moruzov as its head in 1924 (or in 1925 according to some sources). Known as Diviziunea II, then Secţia II, it was reorganized and expanded in 1928 under Moruzov's supervision and formally christened the SSI (Cristian Troncotă (1997), *Mihai Moruzov şi Serviciul Secret de Informaţii al Armatei Române* (Bucharest: Editura Evenimentul Românesc), pp. 44–7). On 13 November 1940 it was renamed *Serviciul Special de Informaţii,*

relabelled simply *Serviciul de Informații* on 15 September 1944, and reverted to *Serviciul Special de Informații* on 27 April 1945.

24. Unpublished memoir (courtesy of Mrs Kyra Gibson) of Archibald McEvoy Gibson (born 3 March 1904; died 6 October 1982), a correspondent for *The Times* in Bucharest in the interwar years. Gibson left Romania on 22 October 1940 and joined his elder brother Harold, head of the South-East European station of the Secret Intelligence Service, in Istanbul. He liaised there with exiled anti-German Romanians. For further details of Archibald Gibson, see Deletant (1985), pp. 135–48 and Deletant (2011), pp. 662–89 (666–8).
25. Barker (1976), p. 225.
26. Ibid.
27. Born on 19 March 1907 in Dobrici in Bulgarian Dobrogea, Gheorghe joined the Bulgarian Revolutionary Organization in 1927, part of the wider Communist movement in the Balkans. In 1940 he became a member of the Dobrogea committee of the Communist Party in Romania and in 1941 secretary of the Ilfov district just north of Bucharest. He was arrested on 19 May 1942. The charge levelled against him at his trial was 'crime against the security of the state' which police reports show to have been based on evidence that he had received instructions from the Soviet consulate in Varna through the intermediary of Soviet agents to carry out industrial sabotage at sites in Bucharest (see Mihai Burcea (2014), 'Judecarea comuniştilor în timpul războiului. Procesul lui Petre Gheorghe', in Adrian Cioroianu (ed.), *Comuniştii înainte de Comunism. Procese şi Condamnări* (Bucharest: Editura Universităţii din Bucureşti), p. 370).
28. Ibid., pp. 307–88 and ANIC, Ministerul Afacerilor Interne, Trial of Ion Antonescu, File 40010, Vol. 8, pp. 33–4.
29. Ibid., p. 103.
30. Stefanidis (2012), p. 154.
31. Edward Masterson, younger brother of Tom Masterson. He spent his childhood and youth in Romania and studied in the United States. He returned to Romania as an oil engineer and was appointed a director of the Unirea (Phoenix Oil and Transport Company). In 1940 he assisted in drawing up plans for the sabotage of the Romanian oilfields. He joined SO(2) in Cairo in autumn 1940.
32. Stefanidis (2012), p. 154.
33. George Beza (born 1907 in Constanţa) had formed a small organization in Romania in 1936–7 consisting largely of peasants whose chief object was to break up Iron Guard meetings and to assist the National Peasant Party at the elections. He and Vulpescu offered their services to SOE representatives in Bucharest and they were eventually sent to Jerusalem to work at the radio station. George settled in France at the end of the Second World War. He was a brother of Ion Beza who was also an NPP activist. A third brother, Constantin (born 5 December 1910), occasionally assisted the other two in their activities. He was arrested by the Communist authorities and interned between 17 January and 25 July 1952 and then given obligatory domicile for a period of five years. Constantin died on 9 August 1975.
34. See Biographies of Key Figures.
35. Stefanidis (2012), p. 155.
36. TNA, HS 7/186, p. 11.
37. Stefanidis (2012), p. 155.
38. Ibid., p. 156.
39. Ibid.

40. Patrick Macdonald (1990), *Through Darkness to Light: The Night Bomber Offensive against Romanian Oil, 1944* (Edinburgh: The Pentland Press), p. 33.
41. Gheorghe Buzatu (2003), *România şi Marile Puteri, 1939–1947* (Bucharest: Editura Enciclopedică), p. 548.
42. Vlădescu-Olt (born 1 June 1912 in Bucharest; died ?) joined the Romanian Foreign Ministry in 1938 after completing a law doctorate. On 15 March 1942 he was posted to Istanbul as vice-consul. In the following year he married Beatrice Schmidlin, a colleague, and both were transferred to the embassy in Ankara. He was recalled on 1 August 1945 to Istanbul and then to Bucharest but did not return, arguing that he was undergoing treatment for a skin disease. The Ministry approved sick leave for him. On 2 September 1946 the Romanian embassy in Ankara informed Bucharest that Vlădescu-Olt and his wife had left Turkey two weeks earlier and that their whereabouts were unknown. In May 1947 the Ministry reported that the Vlădescu-Olts were in Paris. On 27 June 1947 Foreign Minister Gheorghe Tătărescu issued an order dismissing Vlădescu-Olt from the ministry on grounds of financial stringency (MAE, Problema 77, dosar V 51, Personnel Files (1920–44)).
43. Ion Christu (born 31 October 1895, Craiova; died 2 June 1953, Sighet jail); see Dorin Dobrincu (2008) (ed.), *Listele Morţii. Deţinuţii Politici Decedaţi în Sistemul Carceral din România Potrivit Documentelor Securitaţii, 1945–1958* (Iaşi: Polirom). Minister of Foreign Trade, February–June 1940; Minister at Sofia, May 1943–July 1944; member of delegation sent to Moscow for the signature of the Armistice, 12 September 1944. He was appointed head of the economic section of the Romanian peace treaty delegation in July 1946.
44. TNA, HS 7/186, p. 14.
45. Ibid., pp. 14–15.
46. See Biographies of Key Figures.
47. Gheorghe Brătianu (1898–1953), nephew of Dinu Brătianu and son of Prime Minister Ion C. Brătianu (1864–1927), Professor of History at the universities of Iaşi and Bucharest. In 1930 he led a dissident Liberal faction which supported the return to Romania of King Carol. His ardent Germanophile sentiment compromised him in his uncle Dinu's eyes. Gheorghe was arrested on 6 May 1950 and imprisoned at Sighet where he committed suicide on 27 April 1953 (Tănăsescu and Tănăsescu (2005), p. 241).
48. Ion Lugoşianu (1890–1957), advisor to the Romanian delegation at the Paris Peace Conference in 1919–20, and *chef de cabinet* in the Vaida Voievod government in the same period. A member of the National Peasant Party and a close associate of its leader Iuliu Maniu, Lugoşianu was Minister of Industry and Commerce from 1932 to 1933. A frequent contributor to the daily *Universul*, he became Director of the newspaper before the war and retained this position until the paper's suppression in June 1945. He was arrested in 1949 and sentenced to a long jail term which he spent in prisons at Aiud, Piteşti and Gherla. He died in custody on 7 November 1957 (see Cicerone Ioniţoiu (2003), *Victimele Terorii Comuniste. Arestaţi, torturaţi, întemniţaţi, ucişi. Dicţionar H, I, J, K, L* (Bucharest: Editura Maşina de scris), pp. 387–8).
49. Nicolae Caranfil, an engineer by training, was appointed Under-Secretary of the Air in the Ministry of National Defence in April 1935 and Minister of Air and Naval Forces from November 1936 to January 1937 in the government of Gheorghe Tătărescu. Major Walter Ross of the US Office of Strategic Services, in a letter from Bucharest to his commanding office Lieutenant Commander Edward

Green dated 2 September 1944, gives the following appreciation of Caranfil: 'At noon we went to a luncheon given by a person who is acknowledged by the ones who know to be the leader of the underground movement in Roumania. He is a very powerful person financially and politically. If certain plans for the crowd he has in mind should work out, he might conceivably run the government some day, either from behind the scenes or in the open. His name is Nicky Caranfil... He is a sort of utilities tycoon, has been in the telephone company, the water company and the light company and still in one or more. He is as sharp as the devil, very intelligent and a very high grade cultured person... Stircea [Marshal of the Palace], Buzeşti, the Foreign Minister and aligned with them is [Rica] Georgescu... they all check into Caranfil, who is the money, power, suaveness etc' (see Ernest H. Latham Jr. (2012b), 'Efficient and Rapid: The Letters of Major Walter Ross of OSS to his Commanding Officer, Lieutenant Commander Edward Green, during the Evacuation of Allied Airmen from Romania, 30 August–2 September 1944', in *Timeless and Transitory: 20th Century Relations between Romania and the English-Speaking World* (Bucharest: Vremea), pp. 334–5).

50. Romanian ambassador to Bulgaria (1941–3) and Finland (1943–5).
51. See Biographies of Key Figures.
52. Savel Rădulescu (1895– ?) studied law at Bucharest University and completed a doctorate in Paris. Between 1925 and 1928 he served as financial counsellor at the Romanian legation in London. Appointed Under-Secretary of State in the Foreign Ministry in 1928 and held the same positions in the National Liberal governments of the 1930s. President of the Romanian Armistice Commission (November 1944–April 1945).
53. TNA, HS 7/186, p. 15.
54. Ibid.
55. Barker (1976), p. 225.
56. Ibid.
57. Ibid., p. 226.
58. Hambro had replaced Sir Frank Nelson as head of SOE in April 1942. Nelson withdrew as head on the grounds of ill health.
59. January 1938–February 1946.
60. TNA, HS 8/957.
61. Barker (1976), p. 226; Porter (1989), p. 93.
62. Nicolae Ţurcanu (born 2 March 1911 in Bălţi; died ?) aka Nikola Vella, code name 'Reginald'.
63. An SOE report, reference DH 109 [Major E. C. Boxshall] /RO/169/3 dated 29 July 1943 from D/HV [Lt. Col. J. S. A. Pearson] stated: 'We have received a reply from Cairo to the following effect. Russell was educated at Eton and Cambridge where he took his BA in Agriculture. He was later at Heidelberg and Bonn universities and speaks fluent German. In September 1942 he took part in the raid on Tobruk and, dressed as a German officer, was later responsible for arranging the escape of two officers and eight other ranks from Tobruk for which he was awarded the Military Cross. Russell was parachuted into Yugoslavia on 15 June with instructions to endeavour to cross into Romania and to establish himself in the Godeanu mountains where he is to arrange a reception area for further British Liaison Officers' (TNA, HS 5/798).
64. Rootham gave an account of Russell's time with him in Yugoslavia in his wartime memoir *Miss Fire* (London: Chatto and Windus, 1946), Chapters 4 and 5.
65. Ibid., p. 64.

66. Ogden (2010), p. 242.
67. Rootham (1946), p. 68.
68. Letter to this author dated 6 July 1984 from Christopher Woods, SOE adviser to the Foreign and Commonwealth Office. Ţurcanu, or Vella as he was known when he worked clandestinely in Romania, gave an outline of his wartime experience in the Bucharest daily *Timpul* on 1 October 1944. He told his interviewer that he was a Bessarabian, bilingual in Romanian and Russian, and had served in the Romanian merchant navy. His ship was in a British port when Britain and Germany declared war, so he transferred to the British merchant navy. He was recruited by SOE, given parachute and wireless training, and the rank of Lieutenant. After making his way to Bucharest in autumn 1943, he was given shelter by friends and began transmissions for Maniu. Contacts in the police warned him whenever German trackers got on his scent but on 10 July 1944 they located him and had him arrested by the Romanian police. He managed to hide his radio and recovered it after 23 August, using it, he said, to communicate with the Americans who sent bombers to attack German positions at Otopeni airfield on 26 August.
69. Among those willing to act were Virgil Tabacu, a police inspector in Bucharest, and Sandu Ioan, an airforce captain (details taken from Porter (1989), pp. 99–100).
70. Ogden (2010), pp. 242–9. I am grateful to the author for allowing me to quote extensively from it in respect of Russell's mission; see also Alan Ogden (2007), 'Romanian Riddle: The Unsolved Murder of Capt. David Russell MC, Scots Guards', *The Scots Guards Magazine*: 124–9.
71. Ogden (2010), p. 243.
72. Ibid.
73. Ibid. and Turcanu's report on the 'Reginald' mission (TNA, HS 9/1293/3).
74. Their first radio messages reached Cairo on 12 and 13 August (Ogden (2010), p. 243).
75. Russell wore his personal Longines watch as well as an Army issue model; see Ţurcanu's report on the 'Reginald' mission (TNA, HS 9/1293/3). This fact made it easy for the Germans to track the team according to a member of the *Abwehr* based in Bucharest, Oberleutnant Rudolf Pander: 'The British dropped three agents along the Rumanian bank of the Danube. Equipped with W/T sets and large quantities of gold, they were to observe activities along the Danube and observe political trends. The man in charge, a Major Thomas (?), was easily tracked down in the mountains of the Rumanian Banat because he wore wrist watches or similar instruments on both wrists. But the Germans bungled the job of capturing the agents, according to Pander. German reconnaissance planes scoured the region, and radio monitoring trucks drove around conspicuously, thus giving the agents sufficient warning' (National Archives and Records Administration – henceforth NARA: Rudolf Pander – interrogation report 7 December 1945, Military Intelligence Center USFET, CI–IIR/35, RG 165, Entry (P) 179C, Box 738 (Location: 390: 35/15/01), p. 7). See also Appendix 3.
76. Ogden (2010), pp. 243–4. Ivor Porter, who was a member of the following SOE mission into Romania, code-named 'Autonomous', wrote, 'he [Russell] is generally thought to have been murdered by the Serb guide for the gold sovereigns we always carried on these operations (Porter (1989), p. 84).
77. Translation by this author of a report by 'Reginald'. Original written in Romanian in Cairo, 31 October 1944 (TNA, HS 5/831). Ţurcanu came to be known by the 'Ranji' mission's call sign 'Reginald' in post-1943 documents.

78. SOE report by Captain S. G. Metianu, 23 March 1945 (TNA, HS 9/1293/3); see also Ogden (2010), p. 245.
79. Ibid. As Ogden writes: 'No murder weapon was found. Police reports state that the body was recovered after some days and that the bullet was a 12 mm or .455. But whose gun? When the Mission had stayed with Madgearu, they had allowed him to cache two out of their three .455 revolvers. This is made clear by Russell when he signalled Cairo on 24 August: "only weapon is one pistol. Please send colt automatic and magazines".' (ibid.).
80. TNA, HS 9/1293/3.
81. On 1 June 1944, Russell was posthumously mentioned in despatches, somewhat ungenerous recognition given the importance of his mission. His father, Captain E. Russell, corresponded with the War Office about his grave. His other son, George, had been killed at El Alamein with the 7th Battalion Rifle Brigade, but at least in his case his father had managed to visit his grave with its view over the Mediterranean. Russell's grave, a wooden cross at Vârciorova, had been left unmarked – 'here lies an unknown' – since neither the Germans nor the Romanians would have countenanced detailed recognition. Now that the area was under the control of the Allied Commission, a headstone was organized to replace the simple anonymous cross with the inscription 'Captain David Russell, a gallant gentleman who died in the battle for the liberty of Europe'. His father wondered whether the MC could be added and offered to pay for the cost and upkeep of the grave. The advice of the British Commission was sanguine – 'best not as we cannot guarantee that the mayor will use the funds for the purposes you intend' (TNA, HS9/1293/3).
82. TNA, HS 7/183, p. 22.
83. James Dugan and Carroll Stewart (1962), *Ploieşti: The Great Ground-Air Battle of 1 August 1943* (New York: Randon House); see also John Sweetman (1974), *Ploieşti: Oil Strike*, Ballantine's Illustrated History of the Violent Century, Battle Book No. 30 (New York: Ballantine).
84. Macdonald (1990), p. 36.

7 The 'Autonomous' Mission

1. I rely in this paragraph on the phrasing of Maurice Pearton in his stimulating article 'Puzzles about the Percentages', *Occasional Papers in Romanian Studies*, No. 1 (London: SSEES, 1995): 9.
2. Porter (1989), p. 78.
3. Ibid., p. 102.
4. See Biographies of Key Figures.
5. Silviu Meţianu (born 23 June 1893 in Făgăraş, resident in Barford, England).
6. See Biographies of Key Figures.
7. Porter (1989), pp. 111–18.
8. TNA, HS 7/183, pp. 19–20. Livia Stella (Pussy) Nasta (born 18 August 1916; died 2006), aka Olga Procmozka, aka Mary Anne Wilson, daughter of a prominent pro-British Bucharest journalist Liviu Nasta, left Bucharest in December 1940 and travelled via Hungary and Greece to the Middle East where she was engaged by the Ministry of Information as speaker for the Romanian news broadcasts from Cairo. With the development of SOE work in the Cairo office, she was engaged by Lt. Col. E. C. (Ted) Masterson and proved – according to the SOE report on Romania – 'a valuable assistant'. She helped in the preparation of propaganda

leaflets, translations of cipher messages to and from Romania, the preparation of special Romanian ciphers, and at the same time continued to broadcast to Romania. She was 'of great assistance' on the arrival in Cairo of Barbu Stirbey and Constantin Vişoianu (TNA, HS 7/186/306085). In 1943 she married Bill Deakin, a Fellow of Wadham College, Oxford, who had assisted Churchill with his literary research before the war and who had led the British mission to Tito in May. Liviu Nasta (born 1 April 1891) became correspondent of the *New York Times* in Romania after 1945. He was arrested on 25 July 1949 on a charge of spying for the US, tried and sentenced, together with Constantin Mugur, Eleonora Bunea de Wied, and Annie and Nora Samuelli on 25 April 1950 to twenty years hard labour. He died in Văcăreşti prison hospital on 6 December 1956 (I am grateful to Ioan Ciupea of the National Museum of History in Cluj-Napoca for this information).

9. Eugen Cristescu (born 3 April 1895 at Grozeşti in the county of Bacău; died 13 June 1950 in the prison hospital at Văcăreşti), one of nine children of a school teacher. Cristescu studied theology at the 'Veniamin Costachi' seminary in Iaşi and then completed a doctorate in law at the Faculty of Law in Iaşi in 1926. In the same year he joined the *Siguranţa*, the Security Police. On 15 November 1940 he was appointed head of the *Serviciului Secret de Informaţii al Armatei* (SSI), the Intelligence Service, and became a close confidant and servant of Ion Antonescu. He was arrested on 24 August 1944 and handed over to the Soviet authorities who took him to the Soviet Union. On 17 May 1946 he was sentenced to death for his part in the war, a sentence commuted to hard labour for life. He died in Văcăreşti prison hospital on 12 June 1950.
10. General Constantin 'Piki' Z. Vasiliu was appointed Under-Secretary of State in the Ministry of the Interior on 3 January 1942. Arrested on 23 August 1944, he was tried for war crimes in May 1946, found guilty and executed on 1 June 1946, alongside the two Antonescus and Gheorghe Alexianu, Governor of Transnistria.
11. Part of de Chastelain's official report on the 'Autonomous' mission has been reproduced in Ardeleanu, Arimia and Muşat (1984), Vol. II, pp. 796–825.
12. ANIC, Ministerul Afacerilor Interne. Trial of Ion Antonescu, File 40010, Vol. 34, p. 162.
13. Notes on an unpublished manuscript of A. Gibson, in the possession of this author (courtesy of Mrs Kyra Gibson).
14. De Chastelain sent a telegram to the FO from Istanbul on 20 October 1943 informing them of the 'Black' plan. Its gist – the word used in the official record – was, 'On 8 October a Romanian colonel, herinafter referred to as Colonel Black, approached the Romanian Vice-Consul of Istanbul, who happened to be on leave in Bucharest. He disclosed a scheme for the overthrow of Marshal Antonescu' (TNA, HS 5/782).
15. The memorandum was based on a telegram from Colonel Talbot Rice of MI3 in the War Office to the embassy in Washington dated 3 February 1944 which was repeated to the embassy in Moscow (TNA, HS 5/782).
16. Ardeleanu, Arimia and Muşat (1984), Vol. II, pp. 114–15.
17. Ibid., p. 116.
18. Notes on an unpublished manuscript of A. Gibson, in the possession of this author (courtesy of Mrs Kyra Gibson).
19. Porter (1989), p. 92.
20. 'Reginald' was the radio set used by Nicolae Ţurcanu on the 'Ranji' mission.
21. Porter (1989), p. 142.
22. Ibid., pp. 143–4.

23. Petermann was a translator in the *Abwehr*, based in Bucharest. He was born in Dresden on 29 January 1899; see PAAAB, Deutsche Gesandtschaft Bukarest, Einzaelfalle Band 2872 (I am grateful to Dr Ottmar Traşcă of the George Bariţiu Institute of History in Cluj-Napoca for this reference).
24. It was later discovered that Eugen Cristescu and General Tobescu were responsible and that both acted without the knowledge of Marshal Antonescu (TNA, HS 7/183, p. 20).
25. Ibid; see also Ardeleanu, Arimia and Muşat (1984), Vol. II, p. 804.
26. TNA, HS 7/183, pp. 20–1.
27. *Foreign Relations of the United States* [*FRUS*] (1966), p. 170. The terms were also passed to the Romanian minister in Stockholm by the Soviet chargé who transmitted them on the same day (13 April) to Bucharest; see Buzatu (1990), Vol. 1, pp. 418–20 and Porter (2005), p. 94.
28. TNA, HS 7/183, p. 21.
29. Alexandru Ştefănescu, born 1 November in Ploieşti, representative of British cotton companies in Romania. A frequent visitor to Ion Antonescu whilst he was held in detention at Bistriţa monastery in 1938, he put Maniu in contact with the general. He was arrested and accused of espionage in favour of Britain as part of the Lucreţiu Pătrăşcanu group on 25 August 1948, tried and sentenced to life imprisonment on 14 April 1954 for high treason. He died in Aiud jail of heart failure on 15 February 1956 (I thank Ioan Ciupea of the National Museum of History in Cluj-Napoca for these details).
30. Grigore Niculescu-Buzeşti (born 1 August 1908; died 12 October 1949), brother-in-law of Edwin Boxshall of SOE. He was appointed head of the cipher section on 20 May 1941 and was Minister of Foreign Affairs 23 August 1944–3 November 1944. He fled Romania for Switzerland in December 1946 and settled in New York where he died at the age of 41.
31. TNA, HS 7/183, p. 22.
32. David M. Glantz (2007), *Red Storm over the Balkans* (Lawrence, KS: University Press of Kansas), pp. 373–4.
33. Ibid., pp. 375–6.
34. TNA, FO 371/44001.
35. Macdonald (1990), p. 44.
36. Romanian Second World War fighter ace (born 11 November 1905; died 26 May 1958) (TNA, HS 5/835).
37. Racotta had the SOE code name 'Lilo'; Hurmuzescu that of 'Silkworm'; Auşnit 'Cocoon'; and Cantacuzino 'Crysalis'.
38. An agency of MI6.
39. TNA, HS 5/835/SC/2(1)1. According to the study *Intelligence Cooperation between Poland and Great Britain during World War II: The Report of the Anglo-Polish Historical Committee Volume I*, Tessa Stirling, Daria Nałęcz and Tadeusz Dubicki (eds) (London and Portland, OR: Vallentine Mitchell, 2006), p. 318, the purpose of 'Yardarm' was to safely evacuate British agents from Romania but I could find no mention of this particular aim in the Foreign Office papers relating to the mission.
40. TNA, HS 5/835/SC/2(1)1.
41. See Biographies of Key Figures.
42. TNA, HS 9/1453/5.
43. He returned to Romania where he continued to be active in spiriting anti-Communists out of the country, among them the National Liberal Party politician

and editor Mihai Fărcăşanu and his wife. Ghica also fled the country and eventually settled in Caracas; see Ivor Porter (1989), pp. 239 and 249.

44. TNA, HS 5/835, 'Instructions dated 21 September 1944'. Frank Gardiner Wisner (born 23 June 1909, Laurel, Mississippi; died 29 October 1965, Locust Hill Farm, Maryland). Wisner's experience in Romania alerted him to the insidious nature of Communist practice and with the support of George Kennan he was instrumental in the creation in 1948 of the Office of Special Projects. Wisner was appointed Director. Shortly afterwards it was renamed the Office of Policy Coordination (OPC) and became the espionage and counter-intelligence branch of the CIA. Wisner became a legend in his own time for his work in covert operations during the Cold War but the stress associated with this work was the likely cause of his suicide, with his son's shotgun. In the opinion of Ernest Latham, the most complete account of Wisner's career is probably that given by Evan Thomas in *The Very Best Men. Four Who Dared: The Early Years of the CIA* (New York: Simon and Shuster, 1995) (see Latham (2012), p. 330, footnote 58).
45. Military Intelligence Section 9 (MI9), was a department of the British Directorate of Military Intelligence tasked with recovering Allied troops who found themselves behind enemy lines (for example, aircrew who had been shot down). MI9 was set up in December 1939 on the recommendation of the Joint Intelligence Committee of the British government. Major John Holland of MI(R) was asked by Major-General Beaumont-Nesbitt, the head of military intelligence, to advise on the feasibility of setting up an inter-service department to help prisoners of war to escape by providing them with maps, compasses and money. Holland submitted a paper which was approved by the JIC and was asked to suggest an officer to head the new department. Holland had a suitable person working with him in MI(R) and proposed to Beaumont-Nesbitt the name of an ex-infantry major, Norman Crockatt, and he was duly appointed. At first the department, christened MI9, was placed in Room 424 of the Metropole Hotel in Northumberland Avenue in London. In summer 1941 a Middle East section was established in Cairo under Lieutenant-Colonel Dudley Clarke. In September Clarke summoned Lieutenant-Colonel Anthony Simonds, head of SOE's Greek country section, to Cairo to head MI9's activities in South-Eastern Europe (Michael Richard Daniell Foot and James Maydon Langley (1979), *MI9* (London: The Bodley Head), pp. 32–3 and 89).
46. All the American and British aircrews captured by the Romanians were transferred by Allied aircraft to Italy on 2 and 3 September. According to Romanian sources they numbered 1,114 men. Four US airmen, shot down during the raid on Ploieşti on 1 August 1943, were hidden by Princess Ecaterina Caragea on her estate north of Bucharest until the overthrow of Antonescu; see Pelin (1986): 297.
47. Foot and Langley, p. 231. According to another source a different team, composed of Gideon Jakobson and Josef Hanany, was dropped on the same day with the same result (Şlomo Leibovici-Laiş (1997), '1944. În misiune pentru libertate: Paraşutişti evrei în România', *Magazin Istoric* (October): 52–3). Thousands of propaganda leaflets were scattered over southern Romania from the 'Mantilla' aircraft. One of them showed London's St Paul's Cathedral in flames; on the back was a photograph of the US raid on Ploieşti of 1 August 1943. The caption under St Paul's read ‚This is St Paul's Cathedral. The bombs responsible for this sacrilege were filled with oil from Ploieşti.' A second leaflet issued the warning: 'The attack on Ploieşti shows that Romania is within range of the allies... We want to spare Romanian lives. Therefore we say to you, flee from military and industrial

areas!' (Mihai Pelin (1986), 'Misiune în România'['Mission to Romania'], *Almanah Flacăra*: 298) (I am grateful to Claudiu Secaşiu for drawing my attention to this article).

48. Other Jews parachuted into Romania to help gather details about Allied prisoners of war and who also helped to organize immigration to Palestine were Rico Lupescu and Arye Măcărescu (alias Joseph Marcus) (2–3 May 1944, code name 'Anti-Climax Goulash'). Two more teams were dropped under the code names 'Anti-Climax Ravioli' (30–1 July over Arad) and 'Anti-Climax Donier' (late summer 1944). I wish to thank Alan Ogden for his help in gathering this information. The names of Dov Harari, Baruch Kamin, Uriel Kaner and Yeshayahu Dan are also recorded as parachutists (see Yoav Gelber (1990), 'Parachutists', *Encylcopedia of the Holocaust*, Volume 3, ed. Israel Gutman (New York: Macmillan), pp. 1104–7; and Leibovici-Laiş (1997): 52–3).
49. M. Rudich (1987), 'Nu-i aşa, dragă Şaike?' ['Isn't that so, my dear Shaike?'], *Minimum*, Tel Aviv, No. 3 (June): 5 (I am grateful to Claudiu Secaşiu for drawing my attention to this article).
50. TNA, HS 7/186, p. 22.
51. King Michael was in possession of three W/T sets, two of which he kept in the attic of the palace, and one in the woods outside Bucharest. Damage to the latter, and the breakdown of the palace sets, prompted de Chastelain to fly to Istanbul on 24 August to obtain military support for Michael's coup. According to Ivor Porter the set used was the 'Reginald' set which was retrieved by Georgescu from the Malmaison prison on Calea Plevnei (information received from Katerina Porter). Information about the wireless sets sent into Romania clandestinely by SOE was given by Colonel David Talbot Rice in a letter to A. Dew of the Foreign Office dated 1 June 1944: 'I did not mention two of the sets which had not been in operation for a very long time. These are both in the possession of Maniu, one having been sent in November 1941 and the other in March 1942. To the best of our belief neither of these is in working order. The other sets . . . are as follows: (1) The set known as REGINALD which has worked on and off until 4.5.44 but which then went off the air and has not come up since; (2) The set taken in by De Chastelain which was captured by the Romanians with him and in March was believed to be in the possession of Marshal Antonescu; (3) The set in possession of Maniu which has so far never worked; (4) The set sent in by a Romanian agent, which has never operated; (5) The set sent in on 27 May of this year addressed to Buzeşti [Grigore Niculescu-Buzeşti, head of the cipher section in the Romanian Foreign Ministry, who was in close contact with King Michael] in the Romanian Foreign Office' (TNA, FO 371/44000). I am grateful to Katerina Porter for this detail.
52. Ardeleanu, Arimia and Muşat (1984), Vol. II, p. 801.
53. Haralamb Zincă (1971), *Şi a fost ora 'H'* (Bucharest: Editura Militară), p. 311.
54. Refused permission by the Foreign Office to return to Romania, de Chastelain settled ultimately in Canada where he died in 1974. The Foreign Office was anxious not to upset the Russians who believed that the purpose of the 'Autonomous' mission had been to conclude a separate peace with Antonescu behind their backs. Molotov had made such a complaint to Churchill on 30 April 1944 (Barker (1976), p. 234). A Soviet study claimed that de Chastelain arrived secretly in Bucharest from Ankara in the second half of February 1945 'to pass on instructions to Prime Minister Nicolae Rădescu. Having received these instructions Rădescu began to implement the plan for the suppression of the [Communist]

revolution [in Romania]' (A. A. Shevyakov (1985), *Otnosheniya mezhdu Sovetskim Soyuzom I Rumyniey 1944–1949* (Moscow: Nauka), p. 79).

55. Eduard Mark (1994), 'The OSS in Romania, 1944–45: An Intelligence Operation of the Early Cold War', *Intelligence and National Security*, Vol. 9(2): 320–44 (321); see also Ernest H. Latham Jr. (1998–9), 'Efficient and Rapid: The Letters of Major Walter Ross of OSS on the Evacuation of Allied Airmen from Romania, 30 August–2 September 1944', *Romanian Civilization: A Journal of Romanian and East Central European Studies*, Vol. 7(3) (Winter): 3–36, reprinted in Latham (2012b), pp. 299–345.
56. Ernest H. Latham Jr. (1996), 'All Thankful: Reports by Neutral Observers of American Prisoners of War Held in Romania, 1943–1944', *Romanian Civilization: A Journal of Romanian and East Central European Studies*, Vol. 5(1) (Spring): 5–28, reprinted in Latham (2012a), pp. 270–98.

8 MI6 and Romania, 1940–1945

1. This chapter is based in part on my article 'Researching MI6 and Romania, 1940–49', *Slavonic and East European Review*, Vol. 89(4) (October 2011): 662–88.
2. In a declaration, made after his arrest, at Odobeşti on 21 June 1944 at the insistence of Lt. Col. Nicolau of Romanian military intelligence, Eck disclosed the task assigned to him in Slovakia by General Destrémeau of organizing an intelligence bureau composed of Czech and Slovak officers. In the furtherance of his duties Eck provided valuable information to the Romanian army operating in Hungary in 1919 against Bela Kun (CNSAS, Fond I, 203732, Vol. 1, f.148; transcribed by Raluca Tomi (2009), 'Institutul de Istorie Universală "Nicolae Iorga" în anii directoratelor Gheorghe Brătianu (martie 1941–septembrie 1947) şi Andrei Oţetea (octombrie 1947–iulie 1948)', in Ana Maria Ciobanu (ed.), *Institutul de Istorie 'Nicolae Iorga' 1937–1948* (Bucharest: Editura Oscar Print), pp. 105–63 (128, footnote 112).
3. Amongst his major publications are *Le Moyen Âge Russe* (Paris: Maison du Livre Étranger, 1933) and *L'Histoire de Russie* (Paris: Librairie du Recueil Sirey, 1934). A bibliography of his works can be found in *Annuaire de l'Institut de Philologie et d'Histoire Orientale et Slaves de l'Université Libre de Bruxelles*, IV, 1936, pp. 1004–5, and in XI, 1951, pp. 533–4. See also the obituary notice by Boris Unbegaun (1953) in *Revue des Études Slaves*, Vol. 30(1–4): 326–8.
4. See the *Siguranţa* file on Eck in CNSAS, Fond I, 203732, Vol. 1, f.5.
5. Tomi (2009), p. 129.
6. This institute had been given a seat in Bucharest by Nicolae Iorga and opened in May 1938.
7. A *Siguranţa* report dated 21 April 1943 states that Laurent and Eck were suspected of being delegates of the Gaullist group in Syria and that 'Professor Laurent will seek to establish links with the French cultural institutes in the Balkans, and especially that in Istanbul where all orders which have to be given to the heads of the French cultural institutes in this part of Europe will be received' (Tomi (2009), p. 133).
8. Haller was born in Iaşi on 27 December 1910 (CNSAS, Fond I, 203732, Vol. 1, f.121).
9. See the obituary of Eck by Marc Szeftel in *Jahrbucher für Geschichte Osteuropas*, Vol. 3 (Munich, 1955): 351–4 (I am grateful to Professor Andrei Pippidi for drawing my attention to this).

10. For the policy of Romanianization, see Ştefan Cristian Ionescu (2015), *Jewish Resistance to 'Romanianization', 1940–44*, Palgrave Studies in the History of Genocide (Basingstoke: Palgrave Macmillan).
11. Stopoziński was attached to the British legation and left with it. He and the radio operators were amongst the thousands of Polish soldiers who had taken refuge in Romania after the invasion of Poland by German and Soviet armies in September 1939 (see Chapter 3). The radio operators were detected by the Germans, arrested on 8 January 1944 by the Romanian police, and interned (CNSAS, Fond I, 203732, Vol. 1, f.129). They were part of a Polish intelligence group led by Zdzisław Gałaczyński, whose members were Mieczsław Wieraszko, Lt. Włodzimierz Czupryk, Maria Wilczyńska and Maria Gałaczyńska (Stirling, Nałęcz and Dubicki (2006), p. 317) (I am grateful to Keith Jeffrey for this reference). Post-war interrogation by US counter-intelligence of Oberleutnant Rudolf Pander, an officer of the *Abwehr* station in Bucharest between 1942 and 1943, revealed that the Polish intelligence network in Romania was held in high regard by the Germans (see Appendix 3).
12. Louis Philippe Olivier Laurent, known under the name he took as a monk of Vitalien Laurent, was born in Séné, Brittany, in 1896. He grew up in Belgium, studied theology at the Jesuit College in Antwerp, and was admitted to the Order of the Augustinians of the Assumptionists at their centre at Kadiköy, a district of Istanbul. The Order had founded a centre for Eastern studies at Kadiköy on 7 October 1895 which was to become an Institute for Byzantine Studies. The Institute flourished until 1937 when the Turkish authorities, suspicious of what they deemed to be its proselytizing activities, threatened to close it. Laurent, who had become Director of the Institute in 1930, sought unsuccessfully a new home for it in Athens, Jerusalem and Strasbourg. On learning of Laurent's predicament, Nicolae Iorga, the eminent Romanian historian, offered the Institute a home in Bucharest and it opened in its new location on 8 May 1938. The Institute's renowned journal, *Échos d'Orient*, resumed publication in 1944 as *Études Byzantines* and in 1946 changed its title to *Revue des Études Byzantines*. Laurent was a close friend of Eck and of several prominent members of the National Peasant Party and made no secret of his distaste for the Communist regime. In summer 1947 he gave refuge in the Institute to Camil Demetrescu, a leading figure in the National Peasant Party, whose colleagues were being rounded up in preparation for a show trial as 'spies'. Demetrescu was eventually traced to the Institute and arrested in October, as were Laurent and two other monks of the Order. Laurent was held for more than forty days but on the insistence of the French government he was released and expelled from the country together with his two colleagues on 22 November 1947. He continued his academic career as Professor at Munich and Harvard universities and published an impressive number of studies (for a bibliography of his academic work see *Revue des Études Byzantines*, Vol. 32 (Paris, 1974): 343–67 (details taken from Petre Ş. Năsturel, 'Amintiri la telefon despre Părintele Vitalien Laurent', in Ana Maria Ciobanu (ed.), *Institutul de Istorie 'Nicolae Iorga' 1937–1948*, pp. 164–8 (esp. 164) and doc. 144, pp. 284–6.
13. In his declarations to the *Securitate* after his arrest in 1950 Tomaziu used the form 'Gheorghe' for his first name.
14. CNSAS, Ministerul Afacerilor Interne, File 308, Vol. 461, f.453.
15. Enescu's letters to his godson, as well as the numerous family photographs, were confiscated in 1949 after Tomaziu's arrest by the *Securitate*.

16. Mihnea Gheorghiu (1919–2011). His Communist sympathies led him to be appointed the editor of *Scânteia Tineretului* in September 1944, a position he held for two years. A writer and accomplished translator of Shakespeare, Gheorghiu became a senior figure in the Communist Party in the 1980s, being appointed President of the Academy of Social and Political Sciences by Nicolae Ceauşescu.
17. Declaration of Gheorghe Tomaziu, 22 March 1950, CNSAS, Fond Penal 1076, Vol. 3, f.208. Irina's sister Tania was also a member of Eck's network.
18. George Tomaziu (1995), *Jurnalul unui figurant* [*The Diary of a Stand-In*] (Bucharest: Editura Univers), p. 42.
19. CNSAS, Fond Penal 1076, Vol. 3, f.209.
20. Another member of the network was Iorgu Tunis. Grigorescu in his turn recruited Mircea Munteanu, Gheorghe Bujor and Constantin Polzer, all of whom were serving in the Romanian army; see Tomaziu (1995), pp. 39–40 and CNSAS, Fond Penal 1076, Vol. 3, f.209, Vol. 4, f.5. A Romanian account dates the arrest of Eck and Haller to April 1944 and claims that it took place in Odobeşti following an unsuccessful attempt by Eck to persuade a Romanian NCO (Polzer) to pass on information to him; see Florin Pintilie (2003), *Serviciul Special de Informaţii din România, 1939–1947* (Bucharest: Editura ANI), p. 231.
21. CNSAS, Fond Penal 1076, Vol. 3, f.210. In gathering intelligence about German troops movements Tomaziu drew on junior officers in the Romanian army with Anglophile sentiments. Amongst their number were Mihnea Gheorghiu, Constantin Grigorescu, Mircea Munteanu and Gheorghe Bujor.
22. Dennis Deletant (2002), 'Transnistria 1942: A Memoir of George Tomaziu. An Eyewitness Account of the Shooting of a Column of Jews near the Rov River in 1942', in Kurt Treptow (ed.), *Romania: A Crossroads of Europe* (Iaşi: The Centre for Romanian Studies), pp. 231–44.
23. Declaration given by Tomaziu to the *Securitate* on 4 May 1955 whilst serving his sentence for espionage (ASRI, Fond Penal, File 25374, f.158v). I was given a copy of this file by a Romanian colleague before it was transferred to the CNSAS; see also Pintilie (2003), p. 230.
24. See note 36 below.
25. A Romanian Army captain who passed on details of German troop movements in the area of Bacău (Report on the interrogation of Gheorghe Tomaziu, no date, CNSAS, Fond Penal 1076, Vol. 4, f.5).
26. ASRI, Fond Penal, File 25374, Vol. 2, f.142v. The Statistical Office came under the authority of the Second Bureau (Military Intelligence) of the Romanian General Staff.
27. Declaration given by Tomaziu to the *Securitate* on 8 August 1950 whilst under arrest (CNSAS, Fond Penal 1076, Vol. 1, f.4).
28. Author's interview with Traian Borcescu, head of Romanian counter-intelligence under Antonescu, 8 March 1995, and Declaration of Viacislav Hâncu, once of the officers who interrogated the group at Odobeşti, given on 1 November 1954 (ASRI, Fond Penal, File 25374, f.148r).
29. The Institute was given Iorga's name in 1941 after the historian's murder at the hands of the Iron Guard in November 1940.
30. The armistice between France and Germany was in fact signed on 22 June.
31. Lt. Col. Geoffrey Macnab.
32. MI6.
33. The British Embassy in Turkey was in the capital Ankara; the Consulate-General was located in Istanbul.

34. In Transnistria.
35. Eck was probably unaware that SOE used Satvet Lutfi Tozan, a Turkish financier who acted as honorary Finnish consul in Istanbul, to carry in a radio to Bucharest in spring 1942 (author's interview with William Harris-Burland, 10 August 1984).
36. Declaration in French of Alexander Eck, given at the request of the military prosecutor Captain Ion Săvulescu on 8 July 1944 in CNSAS, Fond I, 203732 (Arhiva Operativă, File 203, 732/1), 1, ff.140r–146v, translated by this author. A misprint in a (partial) transcription of this declaration in French, published by Raluca Tomi, gives the date as 8 August (in fact Eck had been moved to Malmaison jail by this date) (Tomi (2009), p. 129, footnote 116). Mihnea Gheorghiu, in his declarations to his interrogators between 26–9 June 1944, stated that he received a monthly sum of 15,000 *lei* from Tomaziu which rose incrementally to 70,000 *lei* (Alesandru Duţu, Ioana Negreanu, Elena Istrăţescu, Vasile Popa, Maria Ignat, Alexandru Oşca and Nevian Tunăreanu (2002), *România: Viaţa Politică în Documente* [*Romania: Political Life in Documents*] (Bucharest: Arhivele Naţionale Ale României), pp. 166–7).
37. Author's interview with Traian Borcescu, 8 March 1995. According to the declarations of two of the officers involved in the interrogation of Eck and his colleagues at Odobeşti, great care was taken to prevent the Germans finding out about the capture of the network (Declaration given by Major Mircea Smeu to the *Securitate* on 30 October 1954 and that of Major Viaceslav Hâncu (1 November 1954), ASRI, Fond P, dosar 25374, Vol. 2, ff.142–9).
38. Pintilie (2003), p. 231.
39. As far as Smeu could remember the order for the transfer came either from Marshal Antonescu's office, or from the Ministry of National Defence (Declaration given by Major Mircea Smeu to the *Securitate* on 30 October 1954, ASRI, Fond P, dosar 25374, Vol. 2, f.144v).
40. Chrisoghelos' wife Lucia was a close friend of King Michael and according to Borcescu in his interview with me, was passing information at the time to the NKVD (interview with T. Borcescu, 8 March 1995).
41. This is the date given by Brătianu in his memoir; Pintilie (2003), p. 232 dates the departure as 29 August.
42. The nephew of Dinu Brătianu, the leader of the National Liberal Party, Dan (1908–1991) had helped Traian Borcescu during the Iron Guard uprising in January 1941 when, at the latter's request, he had provided the Romanian Secret Service with a list of telephone numbers of Iron Guard members (Dan M. Brătianu (1996), *Martor dintr-o ţară încătuşată* [*Witness from a Country in Chains*] (Bucharest: Fundaţia Academia Civică), p. 19).
43. *Cartea Albă a Securităţii* [*The White Book of the Securitate*] (1994–5), Vol. 1 (Bucharest: SRI), doc. 4, p. 125. During Borcescu's trial in 1949 for serving the Antonescu regime, Eck's declaration was mentioned in Borcescu's defence in the following terms: 'Eck declared that Colonel Borcescu and Lieutenant in the reserve Florin Begnescu cannot be held responsible in any way for the activity of Eugen Cristescu [head of the SSI]. It is obvious since even in the Allied camp Colonel Borcescu's efforts to extract Romania from the war and his democratic sentiments were known. That is why Professor George Durant [*sic*] asked Colonel Borcescu in the name of Britain and her Allies to release the entire group held by the Germans who were facing execution' (*Tribunalul militar al Regiunii II Bucureşti* [*Military Tribunal of the Second Region, Bucharest*], File 297, 1957). This

information was contained in a typewritten note which Borcescu's daughter gave to me (Borcescu was in his nineties when he received me, yet quite lucid with a remarkable memory). I could not locate the details which it contains in the military archives (not surprising in cases where intelligence officers were tried in Romania).

44. Eck returned to the University of Brussels where he resumed teaching until 1947 when he retired. He died in March 1953 (this date was communicated to me by Professor Keith Jeffrey to whom I express my thanks).
45. Alice Bejan. Major Arthur Naylor Ellerington was commissioned as a Second Lieutenant on 6 January 1940, promoted to Captain in April 1940, and Major in January 1943. He was assigned to MI6 and served in France and Romania until the British legation withdrew most of its staff in October 1940 (George Beza (1977), *Mission de Guerre au Service de la Cause Alliée* (Paris: Laumond), p. 148). From there he was posted to Istanbul where he ran the Romanian section of the MI6 station, headed by Colonel Harold Gibson.
46. Brătianu (1996), pp. 38–9.
47. Declaration of Gheorghe Tomaziu, 8 August 1950, CNSAS, Fond P, 1076, Vol. 1, f.4.
48. See Chapter 7. Porter was transferred to the British legation in Bucharest in May 1946 to give him firmer diplomatic immunity. He left Bucharest in 1948.
49. Annie Samuelli (1910–*c.*2003) was arrested in July 1949 on a charge of 'high treason'. She was found guilty on 28 April 1950 and sentenced to twenty years' hard labour which she served at Mislea and Miercurea-Ciuc jails (with periods of interrogation at Jilava and Malmaison prisons in Bucharest). She was ransomed out with her sister Nora in 1961 by friends in Canada and the United States (letter to this author from Annie Samuelli dated 8 September 1984). See also note 53 below and Chapter 10.
50. Report on the interrogation of Gheorghe Tomaziu, no date, CNSAS, Fond Penal 1076, Vol. 4, f.4. For his missions for Boullen Tomaziu received 'nine gold coins' (Declaration of Gheorghe Tomaziu, 8 August 1950, CNSAS, Fond Penal 1076, Vol. 1, f.9).
51. Declaration of Annie Samuelli to the *Securitate*, 25 September 1949, CNSAS, Fond P, 17016, 22, f.248. According to the *Securitate* report on the interrogation of Tomaziu, Guiraud left Romania in April 1945 (CNSAS, Fond P, 1076, Vol. 4, f.4).
52. Declaration of Gheorghe Tomaziu, 8 August 1950, CNSAS, Fond Penal 1076, Vol. 1, ff.4–10.
53. The members of the group, sentenced on 28 April 1950 (ASRI, Fond Penal 17016, Vol. 9, f.1) were Constantin (Costica Mugur), a cashier at the British Information Office, sentenced to hard labour for life; Annie Samuelli, a secretary at the BIO, sentenced to twenty years' hard labour; her sister Nora, an employee at the American Information Service, sentenced to fifteen years' hard labour; Eleonora Bunea de Wied, also an employee of the BIO and a cousin of King Michael, sentenced to fifteen years' hard labour, who died in Miercurea Ciuc prison in 1956 from an overdue operation (letter to this author from Annie Samuelli dated 8 September 1984); and Liviu Nasta, correspondent of the *New York Times* in Romania after 1945. Arrested on 25 July 1949 on a charge of spying for the US, tried and sentenced to twenty years' hard labour, he died in Văcăreşti prison hospital on 6 December 1956 at the age of 65 (I am grateful to Ioan Ciupea of the National Museum of History in Cluj-Napoca for this information about Liviu Nasta).

54. For the trial documents see CNSAS, Fond Penal 1076, Vol. 1. The sentence handed down is recorded on f.95. Tomaziu was amongst 127 prisoners amnestied by the State Council on 9 September 1963; see ANIC, Fond 'Consiliul de Stat. Decrete', dosar 551/1963. His original sentence of 15 years' hard labour was registered as No. 1075/1950 and confirmed by the Military Court of Cassation and Justice, sentence No. 2646/1951 (I am grateful to Ioan Ciupea of the Museum of National History in Cluj-Napoca for this information).
55. The artist Jules Perahim blocked his admittance to the Union of Artists and it was only in 1965 that, with the help of the art critic Pompiliu Macovei, he was permitted to have an exhibition. From the time of his release from prison in 1963 until his departure into exile in 1969, he was closely watched by the *Securitate* and a certain Mr Munteanu visited him regularly. He was eventually allowed to leave Romania later that year, following the repeated interventions of the British government, the last made during the visit of Prime Minister Ion Gheorghe Maurer to London.

9 The Eradication of Opposition to Communist Rule

1. The inspiration for this view is Hugh Seton-Watson's *The East European Revolution* (London: Methuen, 1950); see especially Chapter 8.
2. See, for example Norman Naimark and Leonid Gibianskii (1997), 'Introduction', in N. Naimark and L. Gibianskii (eds), *The Establishment of Communist Regimes, 1944–1949* (Boulder, CO: Westview Press) and Liesbeth van der Grift (2012), *Securing the Communist State: The Reconstructions of Coercive Institutions in the Soviet Zone of Germany and Romania (1944–1948)* (Lanham, MD: Lexington Books).
3. *Conditions of an Armistice with Roumania*, Miscellaneous No. 1 (1945) (London: HMSO) (Cmd. 6585).
4. Maurice Pearton and Dennis Deletant (1998b), 'The Soviet Takeover in Romania, 1944–1948', in Dennis Deletant and Maurice Pearton, *Romania Observed* (Bucharest: Editura Enciclopedică), p. 145.
5. Pearton (1971), pp. 265–7.
6. Pearton and Deletant (1998b), p. 145.
7. TNA, HS 7/186, p. 24.
8. Molotov had made such a complaint to Churchill on 30 April 1944 (Barker (1976), p. 234). A Soviet study claimed that de Chastelain arrived secretly in Bucharest from Ankara in the second half of February 1945 'to pass on instructions to Prime Minister Nicolae Rădescu. Having received these instructions Rădescu began to implement the plan for the suppression of the [Communist] revolution [in Romania]' (Shevyakov (1985), p. 79).
9. TNA, HS 7/186.
10. Quinlan (1977), p. 109.
11. Hansard, 5th series, Vol. 403, col. 488, http://hansard.millbanksystems.com/commons/1944/sep/28/war-and-international-situation#column_488.
12. Winston. S. Churchill (1985), *The Second World War*. Volume VI: *Triumph and Tragedy* (London: Penguin), p. 202. See also Barker (1976), p. 145.
13. Pearton (1971), p. 265. For the wider pressures on Churchill at the time see Maurice Pearton (1998), 'Puzzles about Percentages', in Dennis Deletant and Maurice Pearton (eds), *Romania Observed* (Bucharest: Editura Enciclopedică), pp. 119–28.

14. *Cartea Albă a Securităţii* (1994–5), Vol. 1 (Bucharest: SRI), p. 92. The officers arrested were Eugen Cristescu, the head of the Intelligence Service (SSI); Gheorghe Cristescu and Nicolae Trohani, both department heads; Florin Begnescu, an officer in the counter-espionage section; and Eugen Haralamb.
15. The policing and public order duties were carried out by the Directorate General of the Police (to which the *Siguranţa* was subordinated), the Corps of Detectives, and the General Inspectorate of the Gendarmes. The latter were responsible for public order in rural districts. All three bodies came under the aegis of the Ministry of the Interior.
16. Alesandru Duţu (1992), 'Comisia Aliată de Control Destructurează Armata Română (3)', *Revista de Istorie Militară*, No. 5: 221.
17. One of the advantages of a class theory of politics is that it legitimates casual murder. The Guards' victims, who were killed or later died of their injuries, have yet to be counted. Apart from their role as 'shock troops', the Guards (known in Romanian as *Formaţiunile de Luptă Patriotice*) also played an intelligence role and infiltrated the SSI and Romanian Military Intelligence (Section II of the Romanian General Staff). These FLP agents went on to occupy senior positions in the Communist *Securitate* and militia: see Claudiu Secaşiu (1995), 'Serviciul de Informaţii al PCR; Secţia a II-a Informaţii şi Contrainformaţii din cadrul Comandamentului Formaţiunilor de Luptă Patriotice (FLP) – Penetrarea Serviciilor Oficiale de Informaţii (23 August 1944–6 Martie 1945)', *6 martie 1945. Inceputurile Comunizării României* (Bucharest: Editura Enciclopedică), pp. 146–57.
18. See the digest of OSS reports in TNA, FO to Minister Resident, Cairo, No. 3251, 16.09.1944 (FO 371).
19. Pearton and Deletant (1998b), pp. 142–63 (147–8). The fate of *Viitorul* – the old National Liberal organ – is instructive. Between the Armistice and February 1945, publication was frequently suspended by order of the Control Commission, in consequence of its exposure of official communiqués claiming the liberation by Russian troops of towns already freed by Romanian units, and of its editorials attacking Communist leaders. Within the enterprise, from November a self-appointed Communist committee prevented printing of articles critical of the NDF. The workers capitulated, on the threatened withdrawal of their ration cards, and of possible deportation. The editor received death threats. Finally, the Control Commission ordered the paper's suppression, on 15 February, when all non-Communist journals were closed down. One of the charges was that the paper was printing suspicious abbreviations. They turned out to be the distinctions of Air Vice Marshal Stevenson, head of the British Military Mission, his 'CBE, DSO, MC' being interpreted as a coded message.
20. The same argument was invoked forty-five years later by former Communists in Romania in defending the retention of the Ceauşescu bureaucracy after the revolution of 1989.
21. Quinlan (1977), p. 116, note 58.
22. James Marjoribanks, assistant to the British political representative on the Allied Control Commission, sent a minute to the Foreign Office on 2 December 1944 describing a conversation with Penescu: 'Penescu said that he had taken office with two aims: a) to ensure order in the country; b) to hold communal elections. The Communists had agreed to his appointment because they considered him an agrarian member of the National Peasant Party's left wing. Mr Penescu had positive evidence: a) that the shooting incident which was being used to discredit his Ministry involved a man who was not a simple workman but a wealthy

ex-legionary who had been shot because he was having an affair with someone else's wife; b) that ex-legionaries were encouraged to join the Communist party (he said that he would send me a photostatic copy of the order to this effect); c) that a considerable quantity of arms – machine guns, rifles, grenades etc. of which he had the exact location and particulars – had been supplied to the Communist Guards by the Soviet Army' (TNA, FO 371/48547, R/95/28/37).

23. Rădescu (1874–1953) won the Order of Michael the Brave, the highest Romanian military decoration, during the First World War. From April 1926 to July 1928 he served as Romanian military attaché in London. Upon his return to Romania, he became a member of the military household of the royal palace. In 1930 he was discharged from the army on grounds of age. In November 1941 he was interned on Antonescu's orders for writing a defiant letter to Baron Killinger, Hitler's envoy, in reply to disparaging remarks made by the Baron about Romania. On 15 October 1944 he was appointed Chief of the General Staff and held this position until the beginning of December. On 6 December he was appointed Prime Minister and Minister of the Interior.
24. 'In Bucureşti acum 50 ani', *Magazin Istoric*, Vol. 28(12) (December 1994): 49–50 [author name not printed with article].
25. Dinu C. Giurescu (1994), *Romania's Communist Takeover: The Rădescu Government* (Boulder, CO: East European Monographs), p. 135. Pătrăşcanu, in conversation with the *Tass* Russian news agency correspondent in late December 1944, considered that the Communist Party had made a mistake in provoking the fall of the Sănătescu government since the more energetic Rădescu had replaced him: 'If before we had a prime minister whom the NDF had in its pocket, now we have a prime minister who is in someone else's pocket.' When asked to explain what he meant by this, Pătrăşcanu declared that hostile internal and external forces were behind Rădescu: 'He meant the British', the *Tass* correspondent told Moscow (Florin Constantiniu, Alesandru Duţu and Mihai Retegan (1995), *România în război, 1941–1945* (Bucharest: Editura Militară), p. 285).
26. Giurescu (1994), p. 137.
27. TNA, HS 7/186, p. 26.
28. Gheorghi Dimitrov (1997), *Dnevnik (9 marta 1933–6 februari 1949)* (Sofia: Universitetsko izdatelstvo 'Sv. Kliment Ohridski'), p. 458 quoted from Dan Cătănuş and Vasile Buga (2012) (eds), *Gh. Gheorghiu-Dej la Stalin. Stenograme, Note de Convorbire, Memorii, 1944–1952* (Bucharest: Institutul Naţional pentru Studiul Totalitarismului), pp. 27–9. Doubts about Dej meeting Stalin during his visit to Moscow are conveyed in a telegram from the Earl of Halifax, British ambassador in Washington, to the Foreign Office, dated 3 February 1945. Burton Berry, the senior American political representative on the Allied Control Commission in Romania, had reported on 30 January a conversation with the Marshal of the Court in which the latter stated that King Michael 'had talked with Gheorghiu-Dej who confessed that he had not (repeat not) had interviews with Soviet leaders but had "gained the general impression" that the Romanians' position vis-à-vis the Russians would be improved if a Communist government were installed'. Commenting on the telegram, a Foreign Office hand notes, 'Dej's confession suggests that he and Pauker have claimed Russian support for their programme without having really received it' (TNA, FO 371/48547, R2516/28/37).
29. 'Programul de Guvernare al Frontului National Democrat', in Ion Scurtu and Constantin Aioanei (1994) (eds), *Viaţa politică în Documente* (Bucharest: Arhivele Statului), pp. 93–6.

30. 'Stenograma Şedinţei Consiliului FND', in Scurtu and Aioanei (1994), pp. 97–119.
31. *Cartea Albă a Securităţii* (1994–5), Vol. 1 (Bucharest: SRI), pp. 12 and 92. The number of police officers remained virtually the same until the reorganization of the police according to the Soviet model in August 1948.
32. Text in the private papers of Ivor Porter, to whom I owe a sight of this document. A similar disregard for Rădescu had been shown one month earlier by Georgescu and Bodnăraş.
33. N. Tampa (1995), 'Starea de spirit din România la începutul anului 1945' ['The Atmosphere in Romania at the Beginning of 1945'], *6 martie 1945. Începuturile Comunizării României* (Bucharest: Editura Enciclopedică), pp. 312–18.
34. A broadsheet issued by the workers at the Malaxa factory on 23 February read: 'We protest most strongly at the terror tactics which irresponsible persons from outside the factory are employing at the Malaxa works in support of the committee of dishonourable agitators which has been kept in place against the workers' will. We protest at the violence of the armed mercenaries who were brought in by lorries under the direction of Gheorghiu-Dej, who has come to impose the will of a disparate minority which has even shot its own supporters. We denounce the hooligans who wish to halt with gunfire the free expression of the workers' will. We demand the arrest of the armed bands of NDF supporters, who have been brought in from outside and have no place amongst us. We demand the arrest of Gheorghiu-Dej and the other Trotskyist agitators. We want free elections and a secret ballot. We want trade unions based on professions and not politically-manipulated hordes. We demand that the government ensure freedom and the secret ballot, and prevent the terror practised against us by irresponsible criminals. We want work and order. We want peace. Down with the terror in the trade unions!'
35. *Cartea Albă a Securităţii* (1995), Vol. 1 (Bucharest: SRI), p. 122.
36. Roberts (1951), p. 263, note 29. Rear-Admiral L. Bogdenko, Vice-Chairman of the Allied Control Commission, wrote in a report sent to Moscow that 'Romanian troops who were guarding the Ministry of the Interior opened fire. Some of the demonstrators responded with fire. Simultaneously, shooting started from the building of the prefecture in Bucharest.' At 1700 hours Bogdenko demanded that Prime Minister Rădescu order all troops, gendarmes and police to cease firing from their side. The same ultimatum was given to the Romanian military commander as well as to the head of the gendarmerie. It was accepted (see Tatiana Andreevna Pokivailova (1995), 'A. Y. Vyshinski, first deputy Commissar for Foreign Affairs of the USSR and the Establishment of the Groza Government', in *6 martie 1945. Începuturile Comunizării României* (Bucharest: Editura Enciclopedică), pp. 53–4.
37. The text of the speech can be found in Scurtu and Aioanei (1994), pp. 149–50.
38. Photocopies Russia, packet XIII, document 5, p. 21. Quoted in M. Ignat, 'The Implications of the Armistice Convention for Romanian Politics', in *6 martie 1945. Începuturile Comunizării României* (Bucharest: Editura Enciclopedică), p. 33.
39. The nominal Chairman, Marshal Rodion Malinovsky, as Commander of the Second Ukrainian Front, was preoccupied with hostilities in Hungary and Czechoslovakia.
40. Quinlan (1977), p. 128.
41. Following his dismissal Rădescu was taken under British protection and lived in the legation building for nine weeks until an agreement was reached between the British and Soviet governments assuring the former that Rădescu would not be harmed on returning home. On 11 November he received orders from the

Ministry of the Interior to stay at home, from which he did not move until the spring of 1946 when the police provided him with a car, a driver and a detective. An incident on 13 May 1946 persuaded him to leave Romania as soon as possible. That day, while attending a function at the Athenaeum in Bucharest, he was attacked by a group of men armed with clubs, and he and his detective were injured. His escape was arranged by his secretary, Barbu Niculescu. On 15 June Rădescu, together with his secretary and four other persons, including a Romanian airman, took off from Cotroceni airfield and flew to Cyprus. He settled in New York in 1947 where he helped to found the anti-Communist Romanian National Committee under the patronage of King Michael. Its work was financed by several million dollars secreted out of Romania between 1945 and 1946. In February 1950 Rădescu requested that this money be publicly accountable but other committee members disagreed and he resigned. He died in New York on 16 May 1953. The Committee, whose chairmanship was taken over by Constantin Vişoianu, remained active until 1975 (*Free Romanian Press*, Vol. 29(3) (March 1984)).

42. Susaikov gave this explanation at the end of October 1945, asking Stevenson and Schuyler whether they would have done otherwise. They agreed that they would not, but thought that it was a pity that this had not been explained before (Harry Hanak (1998), 'The Politics of Impotence: The British Observe Romania, 6 March 1945 to 30 December 1947', in Ion Agrigoroaie, Ghrorghe Buzatu and Vasile Cristian (eds), *Românii în istoria universală*, Vol. III/1 (Iaşi: Institutul de Istorie 'A. D. Xenopol'), p. 433). Soviet sensitivity to disorder behind their lines had been conveyed to Schuyler at the time by A. Pavlov, the Soviet Political Representative. At a meeting of the Allied Control Commission on 14 February 1945, Pavlov had told Schuyler that 'no disorder can be permitted to occur in the rear of the Soviet armies... nor can any Fascist activities within the state of Romania be permitted' (Giurescu (1994), p. 67). Soviet unease about the possibility of a Romanian uprising had been fuelled by the infiltration of German agents and German-held Romanian prisoners of war into Romanian units in order to instigate mutinies. Roland Gunne, an SD officer from Transylvania, had wormed his way onto the staff of the Romanian Fourth Army which was fighting in Hungary. The commander of the Fourth Army was General Gheorghe Avramescu who, before the 23 August coup, had fought against the Russians in the Crimea and whose son-in-law, Ilie Vlad Sturdza, was the son of the foreign minister of the Iron Guard government in exile set up in Vienna on 10 December 1944. Avramescu's anti-Russian sentiments made him a prime candidate for German manipulation and Gunne and Iron Guard sympathisers persuaded the General to defect with his forces to the German side in the event of a successful German counter-offensive (Perry Biddiscombe (1993), 'Prodding the Russian Bear: Pro-German Resistance in Romania, 1944–5', *European History Quarterly*, Vol. 23(2) (April): 205–12, and Gunter Klein (1995), 'Începuturile rezistenţei antisovietice în România (23 august 1944–6 martie 1945)', in *6 martie 1945. Începuturile Comunizării României* (Bucharest: Editura Enciclopedică), pp. 295–311. On 3 March 1945 Avramescu and his chief-of-staff, General Nicolae Dragomir, were arrested at the command post of the Second Ukrainian Front at Divin in Czechoslovakia, on the orders of Marshal Malinovski, by Soviet counter-espionage officers. Avramescu's fate is unclear. According to a report presented to Stalin by Beria and his deputy Abamukov, he was killed in a German air attack on Budapest (Klein (1995), p. 309). This is confirmed by a reply sent in summer 1963 by the USSR Supreme Court to a

request from the Romanian Ministry of Justice for information about Avramescu's fate. The letter stated that the General had died on 3 March 1945 near the town of Iasbereni following a German air attack and was buried in Soshalom, a district of Budapest (Alesandru Duţu and Florica Dobre (1997), 'S-a mai dezlegat o enigmă în cazul Avramescu?', *Magazin Istoric*, Vol. 31(5) (May): 7–8). No mention was ever made by the Soviet authorities of his arrest. His wife and daughter were arrested on the same day. The daughter committed suicide three days later, and Avramescu's wife spent eleven years in Soviet labour camps before being allowed to return to Romania (Johann Urwich-Ferry (1997), *Fără Paşaport prin URSS* [*In the USSR without a Passport*], Vol. II (Munich: Iskra), pp. 51–7). Dragomir was taken straight to the Soviet Union where he was tried and sentenced to eight years' hard labour. After completing his sentence, he was sent on 4 April 1953 to work as a veterinary assistant on a state farm in the region of Kustanai. He requested repatriation to Romania and was returned on 10 January 1956. On 11 January 1957 he was re-arrested in Bucharest for no apparent reason. He appealed unsuccessfully against his arrest on numerous occasions and was held in various prisons until his release on 27 July 1964. He died in 1981, aged 83 (Alesandru Duţu and Florica Dobre (1996), 'Opt ani muncă silnică pentru un post de felcer veterinar', *Magazin Istoric*, Vol. 30(6) (June): 47–52).

43. Giurescu (1994), p. 67.
44. Pokivailova (1995), p. 52.
45. 'Meeting of the NDF Council, 26 February 1945', MAE, Central Archive of the Institute of Party History of the Central Committee of the Romanian Workers' Party, Fond 80, Inventory 1, File No. 16, pp. 7–8 and 11. Gheorghiu-Dej was to claim later, at a plenary meeting of the Central Committee held on 9–10 June 1958, that 'he alone worked' for a limited coalition with Tătărescu while Pauker, Pătrăşcanu and Soviet officials on the Allied Control Commission argued 'that we should continue with the National Peasants and the National Liberals' (Robert Levy (1995), 'Power Struggles in the Romanian Communist Party Leadership during the Period of the Formation of the Groza Regime', in *6 martie 1945. Începuturile Comunizării României* (Bucharest: Editura Enciclopedică), p. 88). Gheorghiu-Dej's words may have been a retrospective attempt to show that he had acted independently of the Soviet Union and the so-called 'Muscovite faction' of Pauker and Luca, and in doing so omitted any mention of Vyshinski's decisive role.
46. 'Stenograma Şedinţei Consiliului Partidului Naţţional Democrat', in Scurtu and Aioanei (1994), pp. 170–1.
47. 'Piese Noi la "Dosarul Ana Pauker"', *Magazin Istoric*, Vol. 10 (October 1992): 26 [author name not printed with article]; see also Levy (1995), p. 88.
48. Ross (1984), p. 194.
49. Ibid., pp. 196 and 198.
50. Ibid., p. 200.
51. Churchill (1985), pp. 68–9.
52. *Cartea Albă a Securităţii* (1995), Vol. 1 (Bucharest: SRI), p. 92.
53. Ibid. In June 1946 Georgescu reported that the numbers of Ministry of Interior personnel had risen to 8,500, of whom only 4,084 had been employed before 23 August 1944.
54. Ibid., p. 13.
55. The number of officers in the Corps of Detectives was, according to the available documents, halved from 221 in March 1945 to 101 in January 1947. Enrolled in

the Corps after March 1945 were a number of Romanian-speaking Soviet agents, most of whom, like Nicolski, had been captured by the Romanian authorities and subsequently released from jail after 23 August. Among these agents were Andrei Gluvakov, Vladimir Gribici, Mişa Protopopov, Vanea Didenko, Iaşka Alexeev, Mihail Postanski (Posteucă), Mişa Petruc, Alexandru Şişman and Pyotr Gonciaruc (P. Ştefănescu (1994), *Istoria Serviciilor Secrete Româneşti* (Bucharest: Divers Press), p. 163). A serialized biography of Nicolski was published in the Romanian weekly *Cuvântul* (April and May 1992) by Marius Oprea. In October 1944 he joined the police and after the imposition of the Groza government was named head of the Corps of Detectives. On 17 April 1947 he was appointed Inspector General of the security police and when the *Securitate* was established on 30 August 1948, he was named as one of the two deputy directors. For further details see Dennis Deletant (1993), 'The *Securitate* and the Police State in Romania, 1948–64', *Intelligence and National Security*, Vol. 8(4) (October): 13–14.

56. Communist activists were appointed as public prosecutors in the Ministry of Justice in April 1945. They were Stroe Botez, Avram Bunaciu, Alexandru Drăghici, H. Leibovici, M. Mayo, C. Mocanu, M. Popilian, I. Pora, I. Raiciu, Ştefan Ralescu, Dumitru Săracu, Alexandru Sidorovici, V. Stoican, Camil Suciu and C. Vicol. Drăghici, who in 1952 became Minister of the Interior, acted as a public prosecutor in the trial of Ion Antonescu in May 1946.
57. Archibald Gibson, 'Communists are the Real Rulers of Rumania', *The Sunday Times*, 12 July 1945.
58. Deletant (2006), pp. 248–9.
59. *Universul*, 6 June 1945. Macici died in Aiud prison on 15 June 1950 of heart failure.
60. Quinlan (1977), p. 140.
61. Ibid., p. 151.
62. The principal figures were Ion Popovici, Badica Iaroslavici, Ion Beza, Augustin Vişa, Gheorghe Iosif, Franz Wiener and Nicolae Ţurcanu (ibid.).
63. TNA, HS 7/186, p. 24.
64. Ibid.
65. TNA, HS 5/847.
66. Ibid., 'Report on Mission to Bucharest to Liquidate SOE Commitments, 16.12.45–24.01.46', 9 pp.
67. Ibid., p. 9.
68. Ibid., pp. 4–5. This was not the first time that Boxshall had entertained the idea of retrieving SOE gold coins from Romanian hands. On 11 May 1945 he wrote to William Hayter at the Foreign Office, pointing out that one of SOE's W/T sets, left in Romania for maintaining contact with Maniu, was discovered in August 1941 when the Rică Georgescu group was arrested, and along with it SOE's cash reserve of 42 million *lei* (£5000 at the August 1941 exchange rate). SOE had recently instructed Harris-Burland to demand the restitution of this sum from the Romanian government from which it wished to make liquidation payments. It had also instructed him to obtain the refund of 75 gold sovereigns which were confiscated from de Chastelain when he was arrested on the 'Autonomous' mission on 22 December. Boxshall asked Hayter to authorize Le Rougetel to take up the matter with the Romanian Foreign Office. For reasons which are unclear, this request was withdrawn; a note from the Foreign Office dated 21 May and filed with Boxshall's letter, states abruptly: 'SOE have now asked us not to act' (TNA, FO 371, R48565).
69. Quinlan (1977), p. 140.

70. Aldea died in Aiud jail on 17 October 1949 of heart failure. The groups *Haiducii lui Avram Iancu* and *Divizia Sumanelor Negre* took their names from a Transylvanian Romanian, Avram Iancu, and the bands of men (*Cătanele Negre*) who raised a revolt against the Hungarian authorities in the 1848 revolution. Reports on these opposition groups, together with examples of their manifestoes, are preserved in the Archives of the CNSAS, Fond D, File 9046, Vols. 1–4.
71. Mark Percival (1995), 'British Attitudes towards the Romanian Historic Parties and the Monarchy, 1944–47', *Occasional Papers in Romanian Studies*, No. 1, Dennis Deletant (ed.) (London: School of Slavonic and East European Studies, University of London), p. 19.
72. Ibid., p. 20.
73. Quinlan (1977), p. 151.
74. These archives contained 'Confidential reports on the true results of the parliamentary elections'. The results in the counties of Cluj, Someş and Turda show a clear, but not overwhelming, victory for Maniu's National Peasant Party which obtained more than 40 per cent of the votes. In Someş, for example, the Communists were officially credited with 67.9 per cent of the votes, whereas in reality they polled only 22.8 per cent. The National Peasant Party was awarded only 11.1 per cent when it in fact won 51.6 per cent (Virgiliu Ţârău (1994), 'Campania electorală şi rezultatul real al alegerilor din 19 noiembrie 1946 în judeţele Cluj, Someş şi Turda', in Sorin Mitu and Florin Gogâltan (eds), *Studii de Istorie a Transilvaniei* (Cluj-Napoca: Asociaţia Istoricilor din Transilvania şi Banat), pp. 204–12).
75. Copied by this author from a memoir of Archibald Gibson, shown to me by his widow Kyra. No copy of the top-secret order no. 50000 of 1947 under which the arrests were carried out has been found. The reasons for the arrests were manifold and have been reconstituted from local police reports by Dumitru Şandru (1995) in 'Detinuţii politici de la Gherla în 1947', *Anuarul Institutului de Istorie Cluj-Napoca*, Vol. 34: 271–82.
76. The accused, alongside Maniu and Mihalache, were Nicolae Penescu, Ştefan Stoica, Ion de Mocsony-Stârcea, Emil Lăzărescu, Radu Niculescu-Buzeşti, Vasile Serdici, Camil Demetrescu, Victor Rădulescu-Pogoneanu, Dumitru Stătescu, Ilie Lazăr, Nicolae Carandino, Florin Roiu and Emil Oprişan. Tried *in absentia* were Grigore Niculescu-Buzeşti, Grigore Gafencu, Alexandru Creţianu and Constantin Vişoianu.
77. *Trial of the Former National Peasant Party Leaders, Maniu, Mihalache, Penescu, Niculescu-Buzeşti and Others After the Shorthand Notes* (Bucharest, 1947), pp. 10–11.
78. After four years in Galaţi prison (14 November 1947–14 August 1951) Maniu was transferred to Sighet jail where he died on 5 February 1953 (Andrea Dobeş (2006), *Ilie Lazăr* (Cluj-Napoca: Argonaut), p. 176). Mihalache died in Râmnicu Sărat jail on 5 March 1963. All defendants were sentenced to jail in solitary confinement: Penescu to five years; Carandino to six years; Ilie Lazăr to twelve years; Rădulescu-Pogoneanu to twenty-five years; Oprişan to three years; Roiu to five years; Demetrescu to fifteen years; Serdici to ten years; Lăzărescu to two years; Radu Niculescu-Buzeşti to ten years; Mocsony-Styrcea to two years (without solitary); Stoica to eight years (without solitary), and Stătescu to one year (without solitary). Those tried *in absentia* also received long prison terms (ibid., pp. 223–7).
79. Petkov, the leader of the anti-Communist opposition was accused of espionage on behalf of the West. Though he protested his innocence during his stage-managed trial with four other 'co-conspirators', he was found guilty, sentenced to death

on 16 August 1947, and hanged on 23 September 1947. He was buried in an unknown grave.

80. Percival (1995), p. 21.
81. Ghita Ionescu (1964), *Communism in Rumania, 1944–1962* (London: Oxford University Press), p. 142.
82. Quinlan (1977), p. 157.
83. TNA, FO 371/72464.

10 Condemned but not Forgotten: The Fate of Pro-British Activists in Romania, 1945–1964

1. See Biographies of Key Figures.
2. See Biographies of Key Figures.
3. Pearton and Deletant (1998b), p. 145.
4. TNA, BW 53/9. Broad agreement with these views and actions was expressed by W. R. Wickham when he wrote in reply to Le Rougetel on behalf of the Council on 16 April 1945, ibid.
5. Ibid.
6. A Note of the *Securitate* dated 12 February 1948, gave the following list of employees at the 'British Press Office on Bulevardul Republicii 34'. The date of arrest has been added by this author:

    (1) John Bennett (head).
    (2) Francis Bennett (deputy head).
    (3) Annie Samuelly (assistant to the heads). Arrested in 1949.
    (4) Roger Woodham (secretary).
    (5) Chipperfield (secretary's typist).
    (6) Costică Mugur, formerly Emil Brenner (cashier). Arrested in 1949.
    (7) Angela Rădulescu (administration clerk). Arrested in 1949.
    (8) Princess Eleanora Bunea de Wied (Mugur's assistant). Arrested in 1949 and died in prison.
    (9) Mrs Wiedeman (typist).
    (10) Ion Vorvoreanu (Romanian translator and Romanian press reviewer). Arrested in 1949.
    (11) Mrs Cremniter (translator who made a daily digest of the Romanian press). Arrested in 1949 and died shortly afterwards.
    (12) Dumitru Fijer (telephone operator).
    (13) Gheorghe Ratz (handled British promotional material). Ratz had Czech citizenship but was resident in Romania. Using his Czech passport he and his wife managed to leave Romania for Czechoslovakia and then to Britain. He was employed by the Romanian service of the BBC for a while.
    (14) Andrei Bolgar Tizesy (press distribution).
    (15) Mircea Iacob (information distribution).
    (16) Octav Alexandrescu (cinema projectionist).
    (17) Deszy Spann (telephone operator).
    (18) Puiu Staudt (press distribution).
    (19) Johan Hass (reprographics), a former sailor, interned during the war in a British camp in Palestine.
    (20) Paul Precup (driver).
    (21) Lazăr Pârnoaga (John Bennet's chauffeur).

(22) Barbu (driver).
(23) Alexandru Stănicel (Francis Bennett's chauffeur).
(24) Cartargi (librarian).
(25) Mrs Donici (librarian).
(26) Maria Golescu (librarian). Arrested in 1949.
(27) Maria (cleaning lady).
(28) Paraschiva (cleaning lady).
(29) Vasile (odd-job man).
(30) Gheorghe Spegalschi (doorman).
(31) Murin (probably a misspelling of T. W. Morray who was appointed the representative of The British Council in summer 1947 (CNSAS, Fond P, 17016, Vol. 20, f.21 and personal communication from Roger Woodham, 29 November 2006). Since the Romanian government refused to permit the opening of a British Council centre in Bucharest, Morray's presence proved futile and he was recalled to London at the end of February 1948; see Dennis Deletant, 'Good Wine needs a Bush: The British Council and Romania, 1937 to 1990', in Deletant (2005) (ed.), pp. 31–2).

7. The Press Office was established in Bucharest after the arrival in September 1944 of the British Military Mission, which formed part of the Allied (Soviet) Control Commission set up to monitor the application of the conditions of the armistice with Romania, signed in Moscow on 12 September 1944. Its head, until he was transferred to the British legation in May 1946, was Ivor Porter. Porter's successor was John Bennett who was succeeded in November 1948 by Herbert Marchant.
8. Mugur was released from Aiud prison in 1962, together with his wife who had also been jailed, and both emigrated to Britain. In reply to an enquiry from Ivor Porter, Charles Thompson of the Northern Department of the Foreign Office wrote that Costica Mugur had left Romania with his wife and that both were living in London (TNA, FO 371/159503, R1016/6A). Mugur died in 1987.
9. Eleonore is the form used by her brother in a memorandum about her plight dated 17 April 1956 and lodged at the British Consulate-General in Munich (TNA, FO 371/122694, R1015/3).
10. CNSAS, Fond P, 17016, Vol. 2, ff.2, pp. 58–60.
11. A Fernanda Friedman (née Ştefănescu), secretary to Nasta, was also arrested at this time. A note received in the Northern Department and dated 19 August 1964, states that 'Colonel [Eddie] Boxshall mentioned Mrs Friedman to Mr Mugur, formerly of the British Information Office in Bucharest and now in London, and the latter said that Mrs Fernanda Friedman (née Ştefănescu) was in fact secretary to Mr Nasta who ran the Britanov News Agency in Bucharest (this agency was controlled by SOE). Mr Nasta also supplied Mr [Ivor] Porter, the Information Officer in Bucharest, with items of intelligence and Mrs Friedman used to type these. Mr Mugur said that Mrs Friedman was arrested with Mr Nasta and used by the Hungarian [*sic*] authorities as a witness for the prosecution in the latter's trial. Having been forced to act for the prosecution she herself was condemned for fourteen years hard labour. There is no record of Mrs Friedman in either our friends' or the SOE archives' (TNA, FO 371/177616, R1015/27). Mrs Friedman had requested financial assistance from the British government after her release from prison in 1964 but her request was rejected on the ground that she did not figure in either SOE's or SIS's records.

12. ASRI, Fond P, 17016, Vol. 9, f.1. Nasta (born 1 April 1891 in Brasov) was arrested on 25 July 1949 on a charge of spying for the US.
13. CNSAS, Fond I, 235577, f.17 and Fond P, 942, Vol. 2, f.102r (I am grateful to Dr Virgiliu Ţârău and Claudiu Secaşiu of CNSAS for identifying these files for me). Maria was born in Bucharest on 28 January 1897.
14. Ştefan Neniţescu had been sent by Maniu to London in November 1940 to act as Cornel Bianu's secretary. Bianu was to act as Maniu's representative. Their journey to Britain took several weeks. Neniţescu returned to Romania after the coup of 23 August 1944.
15. CNSAS Fond P, 942, Vol. 2, ff.103v. Magdalena Cancicov, born 25 June 1904 in Bucharest, had been arrested on 29 September 1949 (ibid., ff.7–8). Cancicov shared Golescu's prison experience, being held in the same prisons. In February 1956 she fell ill with tuberculosis and spent a few weeks, until 10 May, in Văcăreşti prison infirmary. She was sent back to Jilava and on 23 October 1956 was transferred to Miercurea-Ciuc. On 14 April 1964 she was freed under the pardon granted by decree no. 176 of that month (CNSAS Fond P, 942, Vol. 10, f.97) and was able to leave Romania that year with her brother Jean-René, on payment of a ransom by her cousin Helen O'Brien, to take up residence in Britain. Madeleine's memoirs were published posthumously, in France, under the title: *Le cachot des marionnettes: quinze ans de prison en Roumanie, 1949–1964* (Paris: Criterion, 1990). The publication was reviewed by *La Quinzaine Litteraire*, being awarded the Prize of Francophone writers. Madeleine died in London on 6 June 1985.
16. CNSAS Fond P, 942, Vol. 10, f.27.
17. TNA, FO 371/88028, R1022/1, Telegram 96, 4 March 1950, to FO from Bucharest legation.
18. TNA, FO 371/116584, R1017/18, Letter from G. Buchanan Chalmers to E. F. Given, Northern Department, 21 December 1955.
19. Sarry's full name was George Valentin Sarry. He was arrested in autumn 1949 and accused of passing information about port traffic in Constanţa to the British legation. Tried and sentenced in April 1950 to 15 years' hard labour for high treason, he spent several years in the mines of Baia Sprie and Cavnic, and in Aiud and Piteşti prisons. Released on 4 March 1960 he was allowed to join his mother in Britain and arrived in London by air via Brussels on 13 May 1960. In the following year he emigrated to Canada to join one of his brothers. Throughout his period of imprisonment his mother continued to receive his salary from the British authorities; see his interview with George Sava, 'Interviu cu fostul deţinut politic George Sarry', http://paginitv.com/.
20. Ibid.
21. The amnesty was a condition imposed by the United Nations for Romania's admission to that body.
22. TNA, FO 371/116584, R1017/18, Letter from G. Buchanan Chalmers to E. F. Given, Northern Department, 21 December 1955.
23. The legation was also active in ensuring the welfare of British-born wives, some of whom wished to visit the United Kingdom. According to the legation's records in 1955, there were twelve such persons, two of whom were in prison. The other ten included five widows and two divorcées. Three received financial assistance from the British Government and from the legation benevolent fund. Eight lived in Bucharest and were seen regularly by legation staff, except for one who preferred to be left alone. Two lived in the provinces. One of the latter, Mrs Sarry, had three Romanian-born children, one of whom – Valentin – was in prison (see note

19 above). She, Mrs Margit Ghibaldan, née Tester, a daughter of Albert Tester, a British subject through his father (Tester was a German military intelligence officer who was believed to have been killed in western Romania on 24 August 1944) and Mrs Wendy Muston, the divorced wife of the Romanian philosopher Constantin Noica, who had two young children, wished to leave Romania permanently. The legation intervened officially and repeatedly on behalf of these three ladies without success. Unlike the others, Mrs Tester was not a dual national and therefore her case for an exit visa should have been straightforward yet, as the legation reported to London, 'over a period of two years and nine months, 16 written communications and 4 personal appeals to the Minister or the Vice-Minister, have not even elicited a reply' (TNA, FO 371/116591, R1051/8, Telegram from Mr MacDermot, 1 July 1955). The two ladies in prison were Mrs Rose Sussman (see main text above) and Mrs Sylvia Placa who had been tried and found guilty of espionage on behalf of the Vatican (on the matter of Mrs Placa's British nationality, see TNA, FO 371/116591, R1051/8, notes).

24. TNA, FO 371/116626, R1017/11, Letter from Sullivan to H. A. F Hohler, 1 March 1954.
25. TNA, FO 371/116626, R1017/15, Letter from Sullivan to H. A. F Hohler, 15 March 1954.
26. TNA, FO 371/116626, R1017/15, Telegram H. A. F Hohler to Sullivan, 16 March 1954.
27. CNSAS, Fond P, 1321, Vol. 1, f.47v.
28. Hurmuzescu, after serving thirteen years of his sentence, was pardoned under Council of State decree no. 411 of 24 July 1964 and released (CNSAS, Fond P, 1321, Vol. 1, ff.46–60).
29. Deleanu was a member of the *Ardealul* organization, funded by SOE, which collapsed with the arrest of the group led by Rică Georgescu, in August 1941.
30. CNSAS, Fond R, 321416, f.2.
31. See note 65 below.
32. TNA, FO 371/95006, R1073/4, Mason to FO, 30 March 1951.
33. TNA, FO 371/111640, R1151/5, letter from Hohler, 12 March 1954.
34. TNA, FO 371/111640, R1151/6, Minute by Hohler, 8 March 1954. I am grateful to Mark Percival for this reference.
35. TNA, FO 371/122694, R1015.
36. 10 May 1955 (see TNA, FO 371/122694, R1015/1G).
37. TNA, FO 371/122694, R1015/1G, 'Letter from Hohler to MacDermot', 22 March 1956.
38. TNA, FO 371/122694, R1015/3.
39. Ibid.
40. Ibid.
41. Only an unsigned copy is in TNA, FO 371/122694, R1015/3.
42. Ibid., 'Letter to J. S. Somers Cocks from FO', 12 May 1956.
43. Dorin Dobrincu (2008) (ed.), p. 181. Annie Samuelli, in a letter to this author dated 8 September 1984, wrote that Bunea died from an overdue operation.
44. Deakin had married Livia Stella (Pussy) Nasta (1916–2006), aka Olga Procmozka, aka Mary Anne Wilson, daughter of Liviu Nasta, in 1943. Deakin, a Fellow of Wadham College, Oxford, had assisted Churchill with his literary research before the war and had led the British mission to Tito in May 1943. Livia had left Bucharest in December 1940 and travelled via Hungary and Greece to the Middle East where she was engaged by the Ministry of Information as speaker for the

Romanian news broadcasts from Cairo. With the development of SOE work in the Cairo office, she was engaged by Lt. Col. E. C. Masterson and proved – according to the SOE report on Romania – 'a valuable assistant'. She helped in the preparation of propaganda leaflets, translations of cipher messages to and from Romania, the preparation of special Romanian ciphers, and at the same time continued to broadcast to Romania. She was 'of great assistance' on the arrival in Cairo of Barbu Stirbey and Constantin Vişoianu (TNA, HS 7/186, 306085).

45. TNA, FO 371/122694, R1015/6.
46. TNA, FO 371/122694, R1015/24, 'Letter from Dudley to Tom Brimelow in the Northern Department', 22 October 1956 and 'Letter from Dudley to Secretary-General'. There appears to be no copy of Churchill's letter in this file, nor evidence of a reaction from Gheorghiu-Dej.
47. He died in Văcăreşti prison hospital on 6 December 1956 at the age of 65 (Dobrincu (2008), p. 183).
48. TNA, FO 371/177645, R1051/1.
49. TNA, FO 371/177645, R1622/1, 'Letter to C. A. Thompson'.
50. Ibid, 'Letter to M. George Macovescu'.
51. Gheorghe Tomaziu; see Chapter 8.
52. Three former Shell employees, named Capsa, Lingner and Paliuc, were still waiting for exit visas in June 1965, having been released from prison in the amnesties of the early 1960s (TNA, FO 371/182725, R1621/3).
53. Private papers of Eric Tappe, in the possession of this author.
54. Letter from Annie Samuelli to Eric Tappe, dated 19 April 1962, in the possession of this author.
55. Racotta had the SOE code name 'Lilo'; the family estate to the south-west of Bucharest had been the original landing area for the 'Autonomous' mission of December 1943. In an effort to accelerate peace negotiations Maniu despatched Alexandru Racotta, accompanied by Radu Hurmuzescu and the business magnate Max Auşnit, to contact the British directly. Captain Constantin Ghica Cantacuzino stole a Heinkel bomber on 17 June 1944 from an airfield near the Danube port of Brăila and flew the party, code-named 'Yardarm' to Aleppo (see Chapter 7) (TNA, HS 5/835). Tappe had met Racotta in Bari in September 1944 before the former's departure for Bucharest as a member of the British Military Mission.
56. Letter from Eric Tappe to Sandu Racotta, dated 20 August 1962, in the possession of this author.
57. Letter to Eric Tappe from Mr C. A. Thompson at the Foreign Office, dated 7 February 1963, in the possession of this author.
58. Letter in the possession of this author. Tappe wrote to Sandu on 3 October 1962: 'I should like to mention that I have found Mr Jakober very decent. The money had not even been deposited by the time the Golescus reached Paris. He did not receive it till at least a week after' (letter in possession of this author). According to a note of the *Securitate* Maria and her mother left for France on 13 September 1962 (CNSAS, Fond P, 942, Vol. 10, f.76).
59. Maria Golescu was born in Bucharest on 28 January 1897 and died in Eastbourne on 6 November 1987.
60. TNA, FO 371/177616, R1015/4G/R1015/30/Green, 'Letter to C. A. Thompson'. The Westminster Amnesty Group, affiliated to Amnesty International, sent a letter to Murray dated 10 July 1964 signed by Mr M. B. Irvine and Miss S. Shlackman, enquiring after the fate of Modest Grigorcu whom they stated was in Dej prison.

They wished to know whether he was amongst the prisoners reported in the British press to have been 'released in Rumania recently'. I could find no copy of a reply on file in the FO papers (TNA, FO 371/177645).

61. TNA, FO 371/177616, R1015/6G, 'Letter to D. Thomas, Northern Department, 15 October 1964'.
62. TNA, FO 371/177616.
63. i.e. the Secret Intelligence Service.
64. TNA, FO 371/177616, R1015/32(A).
65. CNSAS, Fond R, 321416, ff.18r–18v. Deleanu died on 12 June 1980.
66. CNSAS, Fond R, 321416, f.40.
67. CNSAS, Fond R, 321416, f.20.
68. See Dennis Deletant, 'Tappe, Eric Ditmar (1910–1992)', *Oxford Dictionary of National Biography*, online edn. (Oxford: Oxford University Press, May 2010), http://www.oxforddnb.com/view/article/98435.
69. CNSAS, Fond R, 321416, ff.40–5. Included in this note amongst those of interest to the *Securitate* was this author, 'suspected of being involved with British espionage' (f.44).

Conclusion

1. Barker (1976), p. 40.
2. Ian Le Rougetel (1894–1975) served at missions in Tokyo, Budapest and The Hague. He transferred to Bucharest on 3 January 1939, moved to Moscow on 26 November 1939, and went back to Bucharest on 7 August 1940. He was posted to China on 15 February 1941; promoted to British Political Representative in Romania with the rank of Minister on 13 September 1944; appointed Ambassador to Teheran on 18 April 1946; then Ambassador to Brussels on 18 May 1950; and High Commissioner to South Africa 1951–5.
3. Percival (1995), pp. 16–17. Another FO official noted on 26 December 1944: 'At a time when the Russians are supporting a reasonably representative government, it would be more sensible for Maniu…to try to see some good in them' (TNA, Minute by Pink, FO 371/43989, R21710).
4. TNA, FO 371/44054, Minute dated 3 November 1944, p. 3. I am grateful to Dan Brett for this reference.
5. Copy of a letter in the possession of this author.
6. Barker (1976), p. 242.
7. Porter (1989), p. 238.

Select Bibliography

Primary Sources

Germany

Politisches Archiv des Auswärtigen Amtes Berlin (The Political Archives of the Foreign Office, Berlin) (PAAAB)

Deutsche Gesandtschaft Bukarest, Einzaelfalle Band 2872

E 267273–267275. D II 119 g.Rs. Schnellbrief des Chefs der Sicherheitspolizei und des SD vom 11.09.1941, gez. Heydrich

R 100114, Inland II Geheim, Bd. 423, Berichte und Meldungen zur Lage in Rumänien-1941

Great Britain

The National Archives, Kew, London (TNA)

BW 53/1, BW 53/4, BW 53/6, BW 53/9, HS 5/760, HS 5/763, HS 5/765, HS 5/782, HS 5/783, HS 5/798, HS 5/798, HS 5/821, HS 5/830, HS 5/831, HS 5/835/SC/2(1)1, HS 5/847, HS 7/183, HS 7/186, HS 8/214, HS 8/957, HS 8/971, HS 9/1293/3, HS 9/1453/5, HS 9/653, KV 2/2266, KV 2/617, KV 2/618

FO 371: Political correspondence of the Foreign Office

War Office 208/1745

Romania

Arhiva Ministerului Afacerilor Externe (Archive of the Ministry for Foreign Affairs, Bucharest) (MAE)

Fond 71/Anglia, Volumes 40–2

Fond 71/Germania, Volumes 80 and 97

Fond 80, Inventory 1, File No. 16

Fondul Constantinopol, 35/79

Problema 77, dosar V 51, Personnel Files (1920–44)

Arhiva Ministerului Apărării Naţionale (Archive of the Ministry of National Defence, Piteşti) (AMAN)

Fond 5465, Direcţia Justiţiei Militare, File No. 2218

Arhivele Naţionale Istorice Centrale (The Central Historical National Archives, Bucharest) (ANIC)

Direcţia judeţeană Bistriţa-Năsăud, Fond 'Dumitru Nacu', dosar 2

Fond 'Consiliul de Stat. Decrete', dosar 551/1963 (State Council Decrees File)

Fond Ministerul de Interne (Ministry of the Interior). File No. 40010: Trial of Ion Antonescu, 44 Vols.
Fond Preşedinţia Consiliului de Miniştri (Presidency of the Council of Ministers), Cabinetul Militar Ion Antonescu, Dosar 194/1940

Consiliului Naţional pentru Studierea Arhivelor fostei Securităţii (National Council for the Study of the Archives of the former Securitate) (CNSAS)

Fond D, Fond I, Fond P, Fond R
I 937873
Ministerul Afacerilor Interne, File 308
Arhiva Serviciului Român de Informaţii (ASRI)
Fond Penal

United States of America

The National Archives and Records Administration, College Park, Maryland, USA (NARA)

RG 59, RG 165, RG 226, RG 319

Published collections of documents

Achim, Viorel (2004) (ed.), *Documente privind deportarea Ţiganilor în Transnistria*, 2 Vols. (Bucharest: Editura Enciclopedică).
Ardeleanu, I., V. Arimia and M. Muşat (1984) (eds), *23 August 1944. Documente*, 4 Vols. (Bucharest: Editura Ştiinţifică şi Enciclopedică).
Arimia, V, Ion Ardeleanu and Ştefan Lache (1991) (eds), *Antonescu-Hitler: Corespondenţă şi întîlniri inedite (1940–1944)*, 2 Vols. (Bucharest: Cozia).
Boberach, Heinz (1984) (ed.), *Meldungen aus dem Reich. Die geheimen Lageberichte des Sicherheitsdienstes der SS 1938–1945*, 18 Vols. (Pawlak: Herrshing).
Carp, Matatias (1946–8), *Cartea Neagră. Suferinţele Evreilor din România, 1940–1944*, 3 Vols. (Bucharest: Socec & Co.).
Chanady, A. and J. Jensen (1970), 'Germany, Rumania and the British Guarantees of March–April 1939', *Australian Journal of Politics and History*, Vol. 6(2) (August).
Ciucă, Marcel-Dumitru (1995–8) (ed.), *Procesul Mareşalului Antonescu. Documente*, 3 Vols. (Bucharest: Editura Saeculum, Editura Europa Nova).
——, Aurelian Teodorescu, Bogdan Florin Popovici and Maria Ignat (1997–2004) (eds), *Stenogramele Şedinţelor Consiliului de Miniştri. Guvernarea Ion Antonescu*, 7 Vols. (Bucharest: Arhivele Naţionale ale României).
Conditions of an Armistice with Roumania, Miscellaneous No. 1 (1945) (London: HMSO) (Cmd. 6585).
Documents on British Foreign Policy, 1919–1939 (1949–55), Third Series: 1938–39, 9 Vols. (London: HMSO).
Documents on German Foreign Policy [*DGFP*], Series D: 1937–1945 (1949–76), 14 Vols. (Washington, DC and Arlington, VA: Government Printing Office; and London: HMSO).
Duţu, Alesandru, and Constantin Botoran (1994) (eds), *Al Doilea Război Mondial: Situaţia evreilor din România*, Vol. 1 (1939–1941), Part 1 (Cluj-Napoca: Centrul de Studii Transilvane, Fundaţia Culturală Română).

——, Ioana Negreanu, Elena Istrăţescu, Vasile Popa, Maria Ignat, Alexandru Oşca and Nevian Tunăreanu (2002), *România: Viaţa Politică în Documente* [*Romania: Political Life in Documents*] (Bucharest: Arhivele Naţionale Ale României).

——, and Mihai Retegan (1999) (eds), *Eliberarea Basarabiei şi a Nordului Bucovinei (22 iunie–26 iulie 1941)* (Bucharest: Editura Fundaţiei Culturale Române).

Foreign Relations of the United States [*FRUS*] (1962), 1942, Vol. II, Europe (Washington, DC: US Department of State).

Foreign Relations of the United States [*FRUS*] (1966), 1944, Vol. IV, Europe (Washington, DC: US Department of State).

Michalka, Wolfgang (1985) (ed.), *Das Dritte Reich. Dokumente zur Innen-und Aussenpolitik*, 2 Vols. (Munich: DTV).

Pe Marginea Prăpastiei, 21–23 ianuarie 1941 (1941) (no ed.), 2 Vols. (Bucharest: Preşedenţia Consiliului de Miniştri).

Pelin, Mihai (1993) (ed.), *Mareşalul Ion Antonescu. Epistolarul Infernului* (Bucharest: Viitorul Românesc).

Refugiaţii polonezi în România 1939–1947. Documente din Arhivele Naţionale ale României. Polscy uchodźcy w Rumunii 1939–1947. Dokumenty z Narodowych archiwów Rumunii (2013), 2 Vols. (Warsaw–Bucharest: Arhivele Naţionale ale României, Institutul Memoriei Naţionale - Comisia pentru Condamnarea Crimelor Împotriva Naţiunii Poloneze).

România în anii celui de-al doilea război mondial (1989) 3 Vols. (Bucharest: Editura Militara).

Ross, Graham (1984) (ed.), *The Foreign Office and the Kremlin: British Documents on Anglo-Soviet Relations, 1941–45* (Cambridge: Cambridge University Press).

Scurtu, Ion (1978) (ed.), *Culegere de documente şi materiale privind Istoria României (6 septembrie 1940–23 August 1944)* (Bucharest: University of Bucharest).

——, and Constantin Aioanei (1994) (eds), *Viaţa politică în Documente* (Bucharest: Arhivele Statului).

Traşcă, Ottmar and Dennis Deletant (2007) (eds), *Al III-lea Reich şi Holocaustul din România, 1940–1944. Documente din arhivele germane* [*The Third Reich and the Holocaust in Romania, 1940–1944. Documents from the German Archives*] (Bucharest: Editura Institutului Naţional pentru Studierea Holocaustului din România "Elie Wiesel"), 830 pp.

Secondary Sources

Achim, Viorel (1998), *Ţiganii în istoria României* (Bucharest: Editura Enciclopedică).

Agapie, Mircea and Jipa Rotaru (1993) (eds), *Ion Antonescu. Cariera militară. Scrisori inedite* (Bucharest: Editura Academiei de Înalte Studii Militare).

Ancel, Jean (2011), *The History of the Holocaust in Romania* (Lincoln, NB: University of Nebraska Press, and Jerusalem: Yad Vashem).

Ancuţa, C.-R. (2004), 'Die deutsch-rumänischen Wirtschaftsbeziehungen während der Kriegsjahre 1940–1944', in K. Zach and C. R. Zach (eds), *Modernisierung auf Raten in Rumänien. Anspruch, Umsetzung, Wirkung* (Munich: IKGS Verlag), pp. 333–70.

Angrick, Andrej (1997), 'Die Einsatzgruppe D', in Peter Klein (ed.), *Die Einsatzgruppen in der besetzten Sowjetunion 1941/42* (Gedenk-und Bildungsstatte Haus der Wansee-Konferenz, Berlin: Hentrich), pp. 88–110.

——, (2003), *Besatzungspolitik und Massenmord. Die Einsatzgruppe D in der südlichen Sowjetunion, 1941–1943* (Hamburg: HIS Verlag).

Aparaschivei, Sorin (2013), *Spionajul american în România, 1944–1948* (Bucharest: Editura Militară).

Axworthy, Mark, Cornel Scafeş and Cristian Craciunoiu (1995), *Third Axis, Fourth Ally: Romanian Armed Forces in the European War, 1941–1945* (London: Arms and Armour).

Baciu, Nicholas (1984), *Sell-Out to Stalin: The Tragic Errors of Churchill and Roosevelt* (New York: Vantage Press).

Balta, Sebastian (2005), *Rumänien und die Grossmäche in der Ära Antonescu, 1940–1944* (Stuttgart: Franz Steiner Verlag).

Bancoş, Dorel (2000), *Social şi naţional în politica guvernului Ion Antonescu* [*The Social and National in the Politics of the Ion Antonescu Government*] (Bucharest: Editura Eminescu).

Barbul, Gheorghe (1950), *Memorial Antonescu, Le IIIe Homme de l'Axe* (Paris: Editions de la Couronne).

Barker, Elisabeth (1976), *British Policy in South-East Europe in the Second World War* (London: Macmillan).

Beevor, Antony (1998), *Stalingrad* (London: Penguin).

Beza, George (1977), *Mission de Guerre au Service de la Cause Alliée* (Paris: Laumond).

Beza, Gheorghe (1994), *Misiune de război. Al doilea război mondial* (Bucharest: Niculescu).

Biddiscombe, Perry (1993), 'Prodding the Russian Bear: Pro-German Resistance in Romania, 1944–5', *European History Quarterly*, Vol. 23(2) (April): 205–12.

Bishop, Robert and E. S. Crayfield (1949), *Russia astride the Balkans* (London: Evans).

Blet, Pierre (1999), *Pio XII e la Seconda Guerra mondiale negli Archivi Vaticani* (Milan: Edizioni San Paolo).

Boia, Eugene (1993), *Romania's Diplomatic Relations with Yugoslavia, 1919–1941* (New York: Columbia University Press).

Braham, Randolph L. (1983) (ed.), *Genocide and Retribution: The Holocaust in Hungarian-ruled Transylvania* (Boston, The Hague, Dordrecht-Lancaster: Nijhoff).

——, (1994) (ed.), *The Tragedy of Romanian Jewry*, Social Science Monographs (New York: The Rosenthal Institute for Holocaust Studies, City University of New York, Columbia University Press).

——, (1997) (ed.), *The Destruction of Romanian and Ukrainian Jews during the Antonescu Era* (New York: The Rosenthal Institute for Holocaust Studies, City University of New York, Columbia University Press).

Brătianu, Dan M. (1996), *Martor dintr-o ţară încătuşată* (Bucharest: Fundaţia Academia Civică).

Bucur, Maria (2002), *Eugenics and Modernization in interwar Romania* (Pittsburgh, PA: University of Pittsburgh Press).

Burcea, Mihai (2014), 'Judecarea comuniştilor în timpul războiului. Procesul lui Petre Gheorghe', in Adrian Cioroianu (ed.), *Comuniştii înainte de Comunism. Proceseşi Condamnări* (Bucharest: Editura Universităţii din Bucureşti), pp. 307–88.

Buzatu, Gheorghe (1990), *Mareşalul Antonescu în faţa istoriei*, 2 Vols. (Iaşi: Editura BAI).

——, Gheorghe (2003), *România şi Marile Puteri, 1939-1947* (Bucharest: Editura Enciclopedică, 2003).

Calafeteanu, Ion (1999), *Români la Hitler* (Bucharest: Univers Enciclopedic).

Cameron Watt, D. (1983), 'Misinformation, Misconception, Mistrust: Episodes in British Policy and the Approach of War, 1938–1939', in Michael Bentley and John Stevenson (eds), *High and Low Politics in Modern Britain: Ten Studies* (Oxford: Oxford University Press), pp. 247–9.

Cancicov, M. (1990), *Le cachot des marionnettes: quinze ans de prison en Roumanie, 1949–1964* (Paris: Criterion).

Carmilly-Weinberger, Moshe (1994), *Istoria evreilor din Transilvania (1623–1944)* (Bucharest: Editura Enciclopedică).

Cartea Albă a Securităţii (1994–5), Vol. 1 and Vol. 2 (Bucharest: SRI).

Case, Holly (2009), *Between States: The Transylvanian Question and the European Idea During World War II* (Stanford, CA: Stanford University Press).

Cătănuş, Dan, and Vasile Buga (2012) (eds), *Gh. Gheorghiu-Dej la Stalin. Stenograme, Note de Convorbire, Memorii, 1944–1952* (Bucharest: Institutul Naţional pentru Studiul Totalitarismului).

Churchill, Winston S. (1950), *The Second World War.* Volume IV: *The Hinge of Fate* (London: Cassell and Co.).

——, (1985), *The Second World War.* Volume VI: *Triumph and Tragedy* (London: Penguin).

Ciobanu, Mircea (1991), *Convorbiri cu Mihai I al României* (Bucharest: Humanitas).

Cioroianu, Adrian (2002), 'Antonescu între Hitler şi... Ceauşescu', *Dosarele Istoriei*, No. 6: 55–60.

Cipăianu, George (2014), *Catholicisme et Communisme en Roumanie, 1946–1955. Une Perspective Diplomatique Française* (Cluj-Napoca: Editura Fundaţiei pentru Studii Europene).

Constantiniu, Florin (1997), *O istorie sinceră a poporului român* (Bucharest: Univers Enciclopedic).

Constantiniu, Florin (2002), *1941. Hitler, Stalin şi România* (Bucharest: Univers Enciclopedic).

——, Alesandru Duţu and Mihai Retegan (1995), *România în război, 1941–1945* (Bucharest: Editura Militară).

Coposu, Corneliu (1990), *Armistiţiul din 1944 şi implicaţiile lui* (Bucharest: Editura Gândirea Românească).

Cosmovici, E., M. Cosmovici and Marie-Joelle Desserre (2000) (eds), *La voix de l'effroi: La Roumanie sous le communisme. Récits et témoignages* (Bucharest: Association Europe Chrétienne).

Dan, Ioan (2005), *Procesul Mareşalului Antonescu* (Bucharest: Lucman).

De Weck, René (2000), *Jurnal. Jurnalul unui diplomat elveţian în România: 1939–1945*, ed. Viorel Grecu and Claudia Chinezu (Bucharest: Editura Fundaţiei Culturale Române).

Deakin, Frederick William (2000), *The Brutal Friendship: Mussolini, Hitler and the Fall of Italian Fascism* (London: Phoenix Press).

——, Elisabeth Barker and Jonathan Chadwick (1998) (eds), *British Political and Military Strategy in Central, Eastern and Southern Europe in 1944* (London: Macmillan).

Deletant, Dennis (1985), 'Archie Gibson: *The Times* Correspondent in Romania, 1928–1940', *Anuarul Institutului de istorie şi arheologie 'A. D. Xenopol'*, Vol. XXII: 135–48.

——, (1991), 'The Molotov-Ribbentrop Pact and its Consequences for Bessarabia: Some Considerations on the Human Rights Implications', *Revue Roumaine d'Histoire*, Vol. 30(3–4): 221–2.

——, (1993), 'The *Securitate* and the Police State in Romania, 1948–64', *Intelligence and National Security*, Vol. 8(4) (October): 1–25.

——, (1999), *Communist Terror in Romania: Gheorghiu-Dej and the Police State* (London: Hurst).

——, (2000), *Good Wine needs a Bush: The British Council and Romania, 1937 to the Present* (London and Bucharest: The British Council).
——, (2002), 'Transnistria 1942: A Memoir of George Tomaziu. An Eyewitness Account of the Shooting of a Column of Jews near the Rov River in 1942', in Kurt Treptow (ed.), *Romania: A Crossroads of Europe* (Iaşi: The Centre for Romanian Studies), pp. 231–44.
——, (2004), 'Memoriul unor intelectuali români, înaintat la Palat, în vara 1942', *Sfera Politicii*, No. 107: 49–53.
——, (2005) (ed.), *In and Out of Focus: Romania and Britain. Relations and Perspectives from 1930 to the Present* (Bucharest: British Council).
——, (2006), *Hitler's Forgotten Ally: Ion Antonescu and his Regime, Romania 1940–1944* (Basingstoke: Palgrave Macmillan).
——, (2011), 'Researching MI6 and Romania, 1940–49', *The Slavonic and East European Review*, Vol. 89(4) (October): 662–89.
——, and Maurice Pearton (1998) (eds), *Romania Observed* (Bucharest: Editura Enciclopedică).
Dobrincu, Dorin (2008) (ed.), *Listele Morţii. Deţinuţii Politici Decedaţi îin Sistemul Carceral din România Potrivit Documentelor Securităţii, 1945–1958* (Iaşi: Polirom).
Dobrinescu, Valeriu Florin and Ion Pătroiu (1992), *Anglia şi România între anii 1939–1947* (Bucharest: Editura Didactică şi Pedagogică).
Drăgan, Iosif Constantin (1986–90), *Antonescu. Mareşalul României şi războaiele de reîntregire* (Milan: Nagard).
Dugan, James, and Carroll Stewart (1962), *Ploieşti: The Great Ground-Air Battle of 1 August 1943* (New York: Randon House).
Dumitrache, Ion (1997), *Divizia de cremene. Memorii din campania 1941–1944* (Braşov: Muzeul Judeţean de Istorie).
Duţu, Alesandru (1997) (ed.), *Romania in World War II: 1941–1945* (Bucharest: Sylvi).
——, (2000), *Între Wehrmacht şi Armata Roşie* (Bucharest: Editura Enciclopedică).
——, and Mihai Retegan (1999) (eds), *Pe Ţărmul Nord Pontic (17 iulie 1941–4 iulie 1942)* (Bucharest: Editura Fundaţiei Culturale Române).
Faranga, Dumitru (2001), *Jurnal de soldat, 1942–1944* (Bucharest: Editura Militară).
Foot, Michael Richard Daniell, and James Maydon Langley (1979), *MI9* (London: The Bodley Head).
Gafencu, Grigore (1945), *Prelude to the Russian Campaign* (London: Frederick Muller).
Gelber, Yoav (1990), 'Parachutists', *Encylcopedia of the Holocaust*, Vol. 3, ed. Israel Gutman (New York: Macmillan).
Georgescu, Maria and Mihai Retegan (2007), *SSI-SOE Jurnal Politic, 1941–1946* (Bucharest: RAO).
Georgescu, Vlad (1991), *The Romanians: A History* (Columbus, OH: Ohio State University Press).
Gheorghe, Ion (1952), *RümaniensWeg Zum Satellitenstaat* (Heidelburg: Kurt Wonickel Verlag).
Gibson, Hugh (1946) (ed.), *The Ciano Diaries 1939–1943*, trans. H. Gibson (Garden City, NY: Doubleday).
Giurescu, Dinu C. (1994), *Romania's Communist Takeover: The Rădescu Government* (Boulder, CO: East European Monographs).
——, (1999), *România în al doilea război mondial* (Bucharest: All).
Glantz, David M. (2007), *Red Storm over the Balkans* (Lawrence, KS: University Press of Kansas).

Goerlitz, Walter (1963), *Paulus and Stalingrad* (London: Methuen).

Golopenţia, Anton (1941), 'Populaţia teritoriilor româneşti desprinse în 1940' ['The Population of the Romanian Territories Amputated in 1940'], *Geopolitica şi geoistoria*, No. 1 (Bucharest: Societatea Română de Statistică).

Halder, Franz (1962–4), *Kriegstagebuch*, 3 Vols. (Stuttgart: Kohlhammer Verlag).

Hanak, Harry (1998), 'The Politics of Impotence: The British Observe Romania, 6 March 1945 to 30 December 1947', in Ion Agrigoroaie, Gheorghe Buzatu and Vasile Cristian (eds), *Românii în istoria universala*, Vol. III/1 (Iaşi: Institutul de Istorie 'A. D. Xenopol'), pp. 429–50.

Hausleitner, Mariana (2001), *Die Rumänisierung der Bukowina 1918–1944. Die Durchsetzung des nationalstaatlichen Anspruchs Grossrumäniens* (Munich: Oldenbourg).

Haynes, Rebecca (1999), 'Germany and the Establishment of the Romanian National Legionary State, September 1940', *The Slavonic and East European Review*, Vol. 77(4) (October): 700–25.

——, (2000), *Romanian Policy towards Germany, 1936–40* (London: Macmillan Press Ltd, in association with School of Slavonic and East European Studies, University College, London).

Hazard, Elizabeth W. (1996), *Cold War Crucible: United States Foreign Policy and the Conflict in Romania, 1943–1953* (Boulder, CO: East European Monographs).

Heinen, Armin (1986), *Die Legion, 'Erzengel Michael' in Rumänien Soziale Bewegung unde Politische Organisation* (Munich: R. Oldenbourg Verlag).

——, and Oliver J. Schmitt (2013) (eds), *Inszenierte Gegenmacht von rechts. Die 'Legion Erzengel Michael' in Rumänien 1918–1938* (Munich: R. Oldenbourg Verlag).

Hillgruber, Andreas (1965), *Hitler, König Carol und Marschall Antonescu: Die Deutsch-Rumänischen Beziehungen, 1938–1944* (Wiesbaden: Franz Steiner Verlag).

——, (1969), *Staatsmänner und Diplomaten bei Hitler. Vertrauliche Aufzeichnungen über die Unterredunger mit Vertreten des Auslandes 1939–1941* (Munich: Deutscher Taschenbuchverlag).

Hitchins, Keith (1994), *Rumania 1866–1947* (Oxford: Oxford University Press).

Ioanid, Radu (2000), *The Holocaust in Romania: The Destruction of Jews and Gypsies under Antonescu Regime, 1940–1944* (Chicago: Ivan R. Dee. Published in association with the United States Holocaust Memorial Museum).

Ionescu, Ghita (1964), *Communism in Rumania, 1944–1962* (London: Oxford University Press).

Ionescu, Ştefan Cristian (2015), *Jewish Resistance to 'Romanianization', 1940–44*, Palgrave Studies in the History of Genocide (Basingstoke: Palgrave Macmillan).

Ioniţiu, Cicerone (2003), *Victimele Terorii Comuniste. Arestaţi, torturaţi, întemniţaţi, ucişi. Dicţionar H, I, J, K, L* (Bucharest: Editura Maşina de Scris).

Ionniţiu, Mircea (1991), '23 August 1944. Amintiri şi reflecţiuni', *Revista istorică*, Vol. 2(9–10): 557–75.

Iordachi, Constantin (2004), *Charisma, Politics and Violence: The Legion of the 'Archangel Michael' in Inter-War Romania*, Trondheim Studies on East European Cultures and Societies, No. 15 (Trondheim: Norwegian University of Science and Technology).

Jagendorf, Siegfried (1991), *Jagendorf's Foundry: Memoir of the Romanian Holocaust, 1941–1944*, ed. Aron Hirt-Manheimer (New York: HarperCollins).

Jeffrey, Keith (2010), *MI6: The History of the Secret Intelligence Service 1909–1949* (London: Bloomsbury).

Klein, Gunter (1995), 'Începuturile rezistenţei antisovietice în România (23 august 1944–6 martie 1945)', in *6 martie 1945. Începuturile Comunizării României* (Bucharest: Editura Enciclopedică), pp. 295–311.

Laeuen, Harald (1943), *Marschall Antonescu* (Essen: Essener Verlagsanstalt).

Latham, Ernest (1995), 'Watching from the Window: Olivia Manning in Romania 1939–1940', *Journal of the American Romanian Academy of Arts and Sciences*, No. 20: 92–112.

Latham Jr., Ernest H. (2012a), 'All Thankful: Reports by Neutral Observers of American Prisoner War Held in Romania 1943–1944', in *Timeless and Transitory: 20th Century Relations between Romania and the English-Speaking World* (Bucharest: Vremea), pp. 270–98.

——, (2012b), 'Efficient and Rapid: The Letters of Major Walter Ross of OSS to his Commanding Officer, Lieutenant Commander Edward Green, during the Evacuation of Allied Airmen from Romania, 30 August–2 September 1944', in *Timeless and Transitory: 20th Century Relations between Romania and the English-Speaking World* (Bucharest: Vremea), pp. 299–345.

——, (2012c), 'Useful Service Rendered: The Romanian Life of Dimitri Demetrius Dimancescu', in *Timeless and Transitory: 20th Century Relations between Romania and the English-Speaking World* (Bucharest: Vremea), pp. 397–445.

Lazăr, Traian D. (2006), *Iuliu Maniu Şi Serviciile Secrete* (Bucharest: Editura Mica Valachie).

Lee, Arthur Gould (1950), *Crown against Sickle* (London: Hutchinson).

Leibovici-Laiş, Şlomo (1997), '1944. În misiune pentru libertate: Paraşutişti evrei în România', *Magazin Istoric* (October): 52–3.

Livezeanu, Irina (1995), *Cultural Politics in Greater Romania: Regionalism, Nation Building, and Ethnic Struggle, 1918–1930* (Ithaca, NY: Cornell University Press).

Lockhart, Sir Robert Hamilton Bruce (1938), *Guns or Butter* (London: Putnam).

Lukacs, John (1998), *The Hitler of History* (New York: Alfred A. Knopf).

Lungu, Dov B. (1989), *Romania and the Great Powers, 1933–1940* (Durham and London: Duke University Press).

Macdonald, Patrick (1990), *Through Darkness to Light: The Night Bomber Offensive against Romanian Oil, 1944* (Edinburgh: The Pentland Press).

Mackenzie, William James Millar [1966] (2000), *The Secret History of SOE: The Special Operations Executive, 1940–1945* (London: St Ermin's Press).

Maitland, Patrick (1946), *European Dateline* (London: Quality Press).

Maner, Hans-Christian (1992), 'Zeitgeschichte Rumäniens als Politikum: Eine Studie über die rumänische Literatur zum 23. August 1944', *Südosteuropa*, Vol. 41(6): 388–412.

Marguerat, Philippe (1977), *Le IIIe Reich et le pétrole roumain, 1938–1940: contribution à l'étude de la pénétration économique allemande dans les Balkans à la veille et au début de la Seconde Guerre mondiale* (Leiden and Geneva: A. W. Sijthoff, Institut universitaire de hautes études internationales).

Mark, Eduard (1994), 'The OSS in Romania, 1944–45: An Intelligence Operation of the Early Cold War', *Intelligence and National Security*, Vol. 9(2): 320–44.

Markham, Reuben H. (1949), *Rumania under the Soviet Yoke* (Boston, MA: Meador Publishing).

Michelson, Paul E. (1994), 'In Search of the 20th Century: Marshal Antonescu and Romanian History – A Review Essay', *Romanian Civilization*, Vol. 3(2) (Fall/Winter): 72–103.

Moravec, Frantisek (1975), *Master of Spies: The Memoirs of General Frantisek Moravec* (London: Bodley Head).

Nagy-Talavera, Nicholas (1970), *The Green Shirts and Others: A History of Fascism in Hungary and Rumania* (Stanford, CA: Hoover Institution Press).

Naimark, Norman and Leonard Gibianskii (1999), 'Introduction' in *The Establishment of Communist Regimes, 1944–1949*, ed. Norman Naimark and Leonard Gibianskii (Boulder, CO: Westview Press).

Năsturel, Petre Ş. (2009), 'Amintiri la telefon despre Părintele Vitalien Laurent', in Ana Maria Ciobanu (ed.), *Institutul de Istorie, 'Nicolae Iorga' 1937–1948* (Bucharest: Editura Oscar Print), pp. 164–8.

Neubacher, Hermann (1957), *Sonderauftrag Südost, 1940–1945: Bericht ein fliegenden Diplomaten* (Göttingen: Musterschmidt Verlag).

Ogden, Alan (2007), 'Romanian Riddle: The Unsolved Murder of Capt. David Russell MC, Scots Guards', *The Scots Guards Magazine*: 124–9.

——, (2010), *Through Hitler's Back Door: SOE Operations in Hungary, Slovakia, Romania and Bulgaria, 1939–1945* (Barnsley: Pen and Sword).

Ogorreck, Ralf (1996), *Die Einsatzgruppen und die 'Genesis der Endlösung'* (Berlin: Metropol).

Pantazi, Constantin (1999), *Cu Mareşalul până la moarte* (Bucharest: Publiferom).

Pantazi, Ion (1980–1), 'O mărturie indirectă despre 23 august', *Apoziţia* (Munich): 20–30.

——, (1992), *Am trecut prin iad* (Sibiu: Constant).

Papacostea, Şerban (1996), 'Captive Clio: Romanian Historiography under Communist Rule', *European History Quarterly*, Vol. 26(2): 181–208.

Pătrăşcanu, Lucreţiu (1970), *Sub trei dictaturi* (2nd edn.) (Bucharest: Editura Politică).

Pavlowitch, K. Stevan (1964), 'Yugoslavia and Rumania, 1941', *Journal of Central European Affairs*, Vol. 23(4) (January): 451–72.

Paxton, Robert O. (2004), *The Anatomy of Fascism* (New York: Alfred A. Knopf).

Pearton, Maurice (1971), *Oil and the Romanian State* (Oxford: Clarendon Press).

——, (1986), 'British Policy towards Romania 1931–1941', *Anuarul Institutului de Istorie 'A. D. Xenopol'*, Vol. 23(2): 527–52.

——, (1995), 'Puzzles about the Percentages', *Occasional Papers in Romanian Studies*, No. 1, Dennis Deletant (ed.) (London: School of Slavonic and East European Studies, University of London): 7–13.

——, (1998a), 'British Policy Towards Romania: 1939–1941', in Dennis Deletant and Maurice Pearton (eds), *Romania Observed* (Bucharest: Editura Enciclopedică), pp. 65–102.

——, (1998c), 'Puzzles about Percentages' in Dennis Deletant and Maurice Pearton (eds), *Romania Observed* (Bucharest: Editura Enciclopedică), pp. 119–28.

——, (2000), 'British Intelligence in Romania, 1938–1941', in George Cipăianu and Virgiliu Ţârău (eds), *Romanian and British Historians on the Contemporary History of Romania* (Cluj-Napoca: Cluj-Napoca University Press).

——, (2005), 'British-Romanian Relations during the 20th Century: Some Reflections', in Dennis Deletant (ed.), *In and Out of Focus: Romania and Britain, Relations and Perspectives from 1930 to the Present* (Bucharest: British Council, Cavallioti), pp. 1–10.

——, and Dennis Deletant (1996), 'The Soviet Takeover in Romania, 1944–48', in Gill Bennett (ed), *The End of the War in Europe, 1945* (London: HMSO), pp. 204–20.

——, and Dennis Deletant (1998b), 'The Soviet Takeover in Romania, 1944–48', in Dennis Deletant and Maurice Pearton (eds), *Romania Observed* (Bucharest: Editura Enciclopedică), pp. 142–63.

Pelin, Mihai (1986), 'Misiune în România', *Almanah Flacăra*: 297.

Percival Mark (1995), 'British Attitudes towards the Romanian Historic Parties and the Monarchy, 1944–47', *Occasional Papers in Romanian Studies*, No. 1, Dennis Deletant (ed.) (London: School of Slavonic and East European Studies, University of London).

Pintilie, Florin (2003), *Serviciul Special de Informaţii din România, 1939–1947* (Bucharest: Editura ANI).

Pokivailova, Tatiana Andreevna (1995), 'A. Y. Vyshinski, first deputy Commissar for Foreign Affairs of the USSR and the Establishment of the Groza Government', in *6 martie 1945. Începuturile Comunizării României* (Bucharest: Editura Enciclopedică), pp. 53–4.

Porter, Ivor (1989), *Operation Autonomous: With SOE in Wartime Romania* (London: Chatto and Windus).

——, (2005), *Michael of Romania: The King and the Country* (London: Sutton Publishing).

Quinlan, Paul D. (1977), *Clash over Romania: British and American Policies towards Romania, 1938–1947* (Los Angeles, CA: American Romanian Academy).

Roberts, Henry L. (1951), *Rumania: Political Problems of an Agrarian State* (New Haven, CT: Yale University Press).

România în anii celui de-al doilea război mondial (1989), Vol. 1 (Bucharest: Editura Militară).

Rootham, Jasper (1946), *Miss Fire* (London: Chatto and Windus).

Rotaru, Jipa, Octavian Burcin, Vladimir Zodian and Leonida Moise (1999), *Mareşalul Antonescu la Odessa, Grandoarea şi amărăciunea unei victorii* (Bucharest: Paideia).

——, and Ioan Damaschin (2000), *Glorie şi dramă. Marina Regală Română, 1940–1945* (Bucharest: Editura Ion Cristoiu).

Safran, Alexandre (1987), *Resisting the Storm: Romania, 1940–1947. Memoirs*, ed. Jean Ancel (Jerusalem: Yad Vashem).

Sakmyster, Thomas L. (1994), *Hungary's Admiral on Horseback: Miklos Horthy 1918–1944* (New York: Columbia University Press).

Şandru, Dumitru (1995), 'Detinuţii politici de la Gherla în 1947', *Anuarul Institutului de Istorie Cluj-Napoca*, No. 34: 271–82.

Sebastian, Mihail (2000), *Journal. 1935–1944*, trans. Patrick Camiller, introduction and notes Radu Ioanid (Chicago: Ivan R. Dee in association with the United States Holocaust Memorial Museum).

Schmidt, Paul (1949), *Statist auf diplomatischer Bühne, 1923–45: Erlebnisse des Chefdolmetschers im Auswärtigen Amt mit den Staatsmännern Europas* (Bonn: Athenäum-Verlag).

Screen, John (2000), *Mannerheim: The Finnish Years* (London: Hurst).

Secaşiu, Claudiu (1991), 'Regele Mihai şi executarea Mareşalului Antonescu. Adevăr şi Legendă', *Cotidianul: Supliment Cultural* (8 July): 5.

Seton-Watson, Hugh (1950), *The East European Revolution* (London: Methuen).

——, (1962), *Eastern Europe between the Wars, 1918–1941* (3rd edn.) (New York and London: Harper Row).

Seton-Watson, Robert William (1934), *A History of the Roumanians: From Roman Times to the Completion of Unity* (Cambridge: Cambridge University Press).

Shafir, Michael (1985), *Romania: Politics, Economics and Society* (London: Frances Pinter).

——, (1997), 'Marshal Antonescu's Postcommunist Rehabilitation: *Cui Bono?*', in Randolph L. Braham (ed.), *The Destruction of Romanian and Ukrainian Jews during the Antonescu Era* (New York: Columbia University Press), pp. 349–410.

——, (2004), 'Memory, Memorials, and Membership: Romanian Utilitarian Anti-Semitism and Marshal Antonescu', in Henry F. Carey (ed.), *Romania since 1989: Politics, Economics and Society* (Lanham, MD: Lexington Books), pp. 67–96.

Shapiro, Paul A. (1997), 'The Jews of Chişinău (Kishinev): Romanian Reoccupation, Ghettoization, Deportation', in Randolph L. Braham (ed.), *The Destruction of Romanian and Ukrainian Jews during the Antonescu Era* (New York: Columbia University Press), pp. 135–94.

Shevyakov, A. A. (1985), *Otnosheniya mezhdu Sovetskim Soyuzom I Rumyniey 1944–1949*, (Moscow: Nauka).

Simion, Aurel (1979), *Preliminarii politico-diplomatice ale insurecţiei române din august 1944* (Cluj-Napoca: Editura Dacia).

Şiperco, Andrei (1997), *Crucea Roşie internaţională şi România, 1939–1944* (Bucharest: Editura Enciclopedică).

Stafford, David (1983), *Britain and European Resistance, 1940–1945* (Toronto: University of Toronto Press).

Stefanidis, Ioannis (2012), *Substitute for Power: Wartime British Propaganda to the Balkans, 1939–44* (Farnham: Ashgate).

Stirling, Tessa, Daria Nałęcz and Tadeusz Dubicki (2006) (eds), *Intelligence Cooperation between Poland and Great Britain during World War II: The Report of the Anglo-Polish Historical Committee*, Volume I (London and Portland, OR: Vallentine Mitchell).

Stoenescu, Alex Mihai (1998), *Armata, Mareşalul şi Evreii* [*The Army, the Marshall and the Jews*] (Bucharest: RAO).

Sweet-Escott, Bickham (1965), *Baker Street Irregular* (London: Methuen).

Sweetman, John (1974), *Ploieşti: Oil Strike*, Ballantine's Illustrated History of the Violent Century, Battle Book No. 30 (New York: Ballantine).

Tampa, N. (1995), 'Starea de spirit din România la începutul anului 1945' ['The Atmosphere in Romania at the Beginning of 1945'], *6 martie 1945. Începuturile Comunizării României* (Bucharest: Editura Enciclopedică), pp. 312–18.

Tănăsescu, Florian, and Nicolae Tănăsescu (2005), *Constantin (Bebe) I.C. Brătianu – Istoria P.N.L. la interogatoriu* (Bucharest: Editura Paralela 45).

Ţărău, Virgiliu (1994), 'Campania electorală şi rezultatul real al alegerilor din 19 noiembrie 1946 în judeţele Cluj, Someş şi Turda', in Sorin Mitu and Florin Gogâltan (eds), *Studii de Istorie a Transilvaniei* (Cluj-Napoca: Asociaţia Istoricilor din Transilvania şi Banat), pp. 204–12.

Tilea, Viorel Virgil (1998), *Envoy Extraordinary: Memoirs of a Romanian Diplomat*, ed. Ileana Tilea (London: Haggerston Press).

Tismăneanu, Vladimir (2003), *Stalinism for All Seasons: A Political History of Romanian Communism* (Berkeley, CA: University of California Press).

Tomaziu, George (1995), *Jurnalul unui figurant* (Bucharest: Editura Univers).

Tomi, Raluca (2009), 'Institutul de Istorie Universală "Nicolae Iorga" în anii directoratelor Gheorghe Brătianu (martie 1941–septembrie 1947) şi Andrei Oţetea (octombrie 1947–iulie 1948)', in Ana Maria Ciobanu (ed.), *Institutul de Istorie 'Nicolae Iorga' 1937–1948* (Bucharest, Editura Oscar Print), pp. 105–63.

Toyne, John (1962), *Win Time For Us* (Toronto: Longmans).

Traşcă, Ottmar (2000), 'URSS şi diferendul româno-maghiar din vara anului 1940', *România şi relaţiile internaţionale în secolul XX in honorem Profesorului Universitar*

Doctor Vasile Vesa ['The USSR and the Romanian-Hungarian Dispute in Summer 1940', *Romania and International Relations in the 20th Century in Honour of Professor Vasile Vesa*], Liviu Ţirău and Virgiliu Ţârău (eds) (Cluj-Napoca: Biblioteca Centrală Universitară), pp. 190–200.

——, (2004), 'Relaţiile româno-germane şi chestiunea evreiască: august 1940–iunie 1941', in Viorel Achim and Constantin Iordachi (eds), *România şi Transnistria: Problema Holocaustului* (Bucharest: Curtea Veche), pp. 252–328.

——, and Dennis Deletant (2006) (eds), *Al III-lea Reich şi Holocaustul din România. 1940–1944. Documente din arhivele germane* [*The Third Reich and the Holocaust in Romania. 1940–1944. Documents from the German Archives*] (Cluj-Napoca: Dacia).

——, and Dennis Deletant (2013), 'The German Secret Services in Romania: "Kriegsorganisation Rumänien"/"Abwehrstelle Rumänien" and Intelligence Cooperation between Romania and Germany over the Defence of the Romanian Oil-Fields, 1939–1944', in Daniel Dumitran and Valer Moga (eds), *Economy and Society in Central and Eastern Europe: Territory, Population, Consumption*, Papers of the International Conference held in Alba Iulia, 25–7 April 2013 (Vienna/Zurich/Munich: Lit Verlag), pp. 343–62.

——, and Ana-Maria Stan (2002), *Rebeliunea legionară în documente străine* (Bucharest: Albatros).

Treptow, Kurt (1996) (ed.), *Romania and World War II* (Iaşi: The Centre for Romanian Studies).

Troncotă, Cristian (1997), *Mihai Moruzov şi Serviciul Secret de Informaţii al Armatei Române* (Bucharest: Editura Evenimentul Românesc).

——, (2003), *Glorie şi tragedie: Momente din istoria Serviciilor de informaţii şi contrainformaţii române pe Frontul de Est (1941–1944)* (Bucharest: Nemira).

Udrea, Traian (2004), *23 August 1944. Controverse Istorico-Politice* (Bucharest: Editura Alex-Alex).

Vago, Bela (1975), *The Shadow of the Swastika: The Rise of Fascism and Anti-Semitism in the Danube Basin, 1936–1939* (London: Saxon House for the Institute of Jewish Affairs).

van der Grift, Liesbeth (2012), *Securing the Communist State: The Reconstructions of Coercive Institutions in the Soviet Zone of Germany and Romania (1944–1948)* (Lanham, MD: Lexington Books).

van Meurs, Wim P. (1996), 'Romanian Expansion beyond the Dniester', in Kurt W. Treptow (ed.), *Romania and World War II: România şi cel de-al doilea război mondial* (Iaşi: The Centre for Romanian Studies), pp. 139–52.

Vişa, Augustin (1997), *Din închisorile fasciste în cele comuniste din URSS şi România* (Bucharest: Institutul Pentru Analiză şi Politică Iuliu Maniu).

Völkl, Ekkehard (1996), *Transnistrien und Odessa (1941–1944)*, Schriftenreihe des Osteuropainstituts Regensburg-Passau, Vol. 14 (Regensburg: Verlag Lassleben).

Waldeck, Rosie Goldschmidt (1998), *Athene Palace*, intro. Ernest H. Latham, Jr. (Iaşi; Oxford; Portland, OR: The Centre for Romanian Studies).

Walker, David (1942), *Death at my Heels* (London: Chapman and Hall).

Watts, Larry (1993), *Romanian Cassandra: Ion Antonescu and the Struggle for Reform, 1916–1941* (Boulder, CO: East European Monographs).

West, Nigel (1983), *MI6: British Secret Intelligence Operations, 1909–45* (London: Weidenfeld and Nicolson).

White, Arthur John Stanley (1965), *The British Council: The First 25 Years, 1934–1959* (London: The British Council).

Wilkinson, Peter, and Joan Bright Astley (1997), *Gubbins and SOE* (London: Pen and Sword).

Wylie, Neville (2006) (ed.), *The Politics and Strategy of Clandestine War: Special Operations Executive, 1940–1946* (Abingdon: Routledge).

Zidaru, Marian (2005), *Relaţii politice şi economice româno-britanice, 1939–1947* (Bucharest: Univers Ştiinţific).

Zincă, Haralamb (1971), *Şi a fost ora 'H'* (Bucharest: Editura Militara).

Index

Lightning Source UK Ltd.
Milton Keynes UK
UKOW04n2249100118
315913UK00010B/103/P

9 781137 574510